This book may be kept

FOURTEEN DAYS

A fine of TWO CENTS will be charged for each day
the book is kept over time.

Ap 17 57			
Dec 16 69,			

ACADEMIC PROCESSION

FOUNDING OF DARTMOUTH COLLEGE

In 1770 Dr. Wheelock began the erection of a college in a forest.

ACADEMIC PROCESSION

An Informal History of the American College
1636 to 1953

by

ERNEST EARNEST

THE BOBBS-MERRILL COMPANY, INC.

Publishers

INDIANAPOLIS   NEW YORK

Acknowledgments

It is pleasant to acknowledge the aid of those persons who have helped me obtain material for this study. The reference librarians of Temple, Mr. Elkan Buchhalter and Mrs. Marie Woodard, have spent many hours tracking down elusive items. I wish also to thank Dean Robert G. Crosen of Lafayette College; and President Charles W. Cole, Professor George F. Whicher, and Miss Gladys Kimball of Amherst College for making available to me the faculty minute books of those institutions. At Haverford College Professor Thomas E. Drake and Miss Anna B. Hewitt found useful material for me in the Quaker Collection. Professor Robert Manson Myers of Tulane University, who is editing the letters of Charles Colcock Jones, Jr., and Miss Dorothy Wilson Seago, the owner of the collection, kindly permitted me to examine those letters relating to Princeton and Harvard in the 1850s. My thanks are due also the many people who offered material and suggestions, among them Mr. Archibald L. Chubb, Pittsburgh, Pennsylvania; Mr. Hudson Hawley, Johnstown, New York; Mr. Charles F. Lamkin, Jr., Kansas City, Missouri; and Mrs. Arthur Levy, Westport, Connecticut, all of whom sent me published or unpublished items. Finally, my thanks to Temple University for the grant from the Committee on Research which made possible the necessary travel and secretarial expenses in the preparation of this work.

I wish also to express my gratitude for permission to quote from the following sources:

Trevor Arnett, "Teachers' Salaries," *Occasional Papers, No. 8*, General Education Board, New York, 1928.

Frederick A. P. Barnard, *The Rise of a University*, Vol. I, edited by W. F. Russell, Columbia University Press, 1937.

5

Charles A. Beard, letter to Nicholas Murray Butler, *New York Times,* October 9, 1917.

Stephen Vincent Benét, *The Beginning of Wisdom,* Rinehart & Company, Inc., 1921.

Viva Boothe, "Statistical Summary Given before the O.S.U. Chapter of the A.A.U.P. on the Economic Status of the Profession," Ohio State University Press, 1934.

Arthur H. Cole, *Charleston Goes to Harvard,* Harvard University Press, 1940.

Ellis M. Coulter, *College Life in the Old South,* The Macmillan Company, 1928.

Charles W. Eliot, *The Road Toward Peace,* Houghton Mifflin Company, 1915.

F. Scott Fitzgerald, *This Side of Paradise,* Charles Scribner's Sons, 1920.

Charles M. Flandrau, *The Diary of a Freshman,* D. Appleton & Co., 1931.

———— *Harvard Episodes,* Small, 1897.

Robert S. Fletcher, *A History of Oberlin College,* Oberlin College Press, 1943.

John C. French, *A History of the University Founded by Johns Hopkins,* The Johns Hopkins Press, 1946.

Katharine Fullerton Gerould, "The Land of the Free," *Harper's Magazine,* January 1923.

William G. Hammond, *Remembrances of Amherst; an Undergraduate's Diary, 1846-1848,* edited by George F. Whicher, Columbia University Press, 1946.

Robert Herrick, *Chimes,* The Macmillan Company, 1923.

Owen Johnson, *Stover at Yale,* Little, Brown & Company, 1912.

Publications of The Modern Language Association, March 1943.

George Herbert Palmer, *The Life of Alice Freeman Palmer,* Houghton Mifflin Company, 1908.

William Lyon Phelps, *Autobiography,* Oxford University Press, 1939.

George W. Pierson, *Yale College, 1871-1921*, Vol. I, Yale University Press, 1952.

Charles F. Thwing, *The American College in American Life*, G. P. Putnam's Sons, 1897.

George A. Weller, *Not to Eat, Not for Love*, Random House, 1933.

William Allen White, *Woodrow Wilson*, Houghton Mifflin Company, 1924.

Malcolm M. Willey, *Depression, Recovery, and Higher Education*, McGraw-Hill Book Company, 1937.

Woodrow Wilson, *College and State* (Published Papers of Woodrow Wilson, Vol. II), Harper & Brothers, 1925.

Thomas Woody, *A History of Women's Education in the United States*, The Science Press, 1929.

Yale Alumni Weekly, "Plan for University Development," December 20, 1918.

E. E.

Gladwyne, Pennsylvania
May 1953

Introduction

The history of the American college is an important chapter in the larger chronicle of the nation's cultural history. Reduced to its basic elements, this history is a record of a conflict between inherited tradition and the needs and desires of a restless, dynamic society. The present study is an attempt to describe and evaluate both the tradition and the various forces opposed to it.

The emphasis will be on those men and institutions that have been either typical of a particular period or development or that have been leaders in educational revolutions. They will be used as key points on the graph which shows the curve of our educational evolution. In evaluating these men, institutions and developments this survey will use material from student diaries, college publications and novels of student life by recent graduates to show the impact of the college on its students. For the more formal history it has been necessary to draw on scholarly studies as well as on the painstaking accounts of individual colleges.

This is not an attempt to write a definitive history of every phase of American higher education or to arrive at any final evaluation of our collegiate system. The time span is too great, the forces are too complex to be covered exhaustively in a few hundred pages. Rather, the objective will be to point up the relationships between the work and life in our colleges and those of our society, and also to suggest tentative hypotheses about these relationships.

One method is to point out the college graduates who have become prominent in American life and letters: Jefferson, of William and Mary; Daniel Webster, of Dartmouth ("a little college but there are those who love it"); Hawthorne, of Bowdoin; Emerson, of Harvard; the Roosevelts, T. S. Eliot—the list can be made long and impressive. But it is important to note that a perhaps equally impressive list can be made of those who never sat in college classroom: George Washington, Benjamin Franklin, Abraham Lincoln in public affairs; Whitman, Melville, Emily Dickinson, Ernest Hemingway in letters. That Emily Dickinson's father was treasurer of Amherst hardly makes her a coed. Stephen Crane dropped out of Lafayette; James Fenimore Cooper was dropped from Yale, reputedly for setting off a keg of gunpowder in his room.

One of our most intellectually sterile Presidents was a graduate of Amherst at a time when that college was turning out men who became eminent scholars; whereas Andrew Jackson, the central figure of his age according to an eminent Harvard professor, had little formal education. What influence on politics or literature can be predicated on such instances? Rather, these scattered examples will suggest how difficult and dangerous it is to base any theory of the influence of American colleges on citations of prominent graduates or even prominent flunk-outs.

Furthermore, the mere fact of graduation from a particular college does not prove the decisive influence of that college on the alumnus. The influence of a Jefferson on William and Mary was probably greater than that of the college on the man. The roots of his liberal philosophy are in sources not included in the curriculum of the first half of the eighteenth century. But the modernization of that curriculum in 1779 grew from his suggestions.

On the other hand it seems pretty generally agreed that the political philosophy of Franklin Roosevelt owed a debt to the teaching of Josiah Royce, of Harvard. This suggests that at some periods the college courses have had a more direct bearing on their times than in others. This is one of the problems to be considered in the present study.

In the main this is an account of collegiate rather than of graduate and professional education. At times, as at Harvard under Eliot, the two have a close relationship. Always, the type of educational training afforded the teacher is closely linked with the kind of teaching he will do. Generations of American faculty members had no formal education beyond that of a Bachelor of Arts in colleges offering little more than a prep-school course of instruction. Therefore the post-Civil War development of graduate study had a profound influence on undergraduate education and properly becomes a part of this history. So too does the growth of universities, for an undergraduate in a university is exposed to different sorts of influences from his contemporary taking a theoretically similar course at a small college. As will appear, the college environment, methods of discipline and instruction, as well as the mores of the community as a whole, all have an impact on the student. Here again completeness is impossible, but some attention will be given to all of these elements as they affect the college.

In so far as the study is governed by an educational philosophy, it is the one stated by John Milton:

I call therefore a compleat and generous Education that which fits a man to perform justly, skilfully and magnanimously all the offices both private and publick of Peace and War.

This will not be interpreted, nor was it intended to mean, a narrowly vocational training. It seems obvious that the usual engineering, business or premedical course falls far short of fitting its graduates either for a cultured private life or public service. On the other hand, college education in America has had from the beginning a vocational function. Harvard College was founded specifically to provide ministers of the gospel. From earliest times the American college has attracted the student of limited means who sought an education primarily as training for a profession. The self-supporting ambitious young man has been one of the most characteristic American student types.

In addition to training for a vocation, the early college was expected to perform two other principal functions: to give a sound training in morals and religion and, especially since the

Revolution, to educate future citizens and leaders of the Republic. Along with these primary aims the college was believed to be useful in developing some of the social graces and the ability to get along with one's fellows. The more recent objectives of training for self-understanding and family living are in the American tradition.

In many respects, therefore, those "traditionalists" who at various times have deplored vocational aims and social studies are in a real sense reformers who would substitute for the traditional functions of the American college the Platonic ideal of an education for a Brahmin caste. They would make a sharp distinction between "liberal" and useful studies. Opposed to this view is the equally radical notion that the only useful subjects are those with an immediate *ad hoc* (and frequently transitory) application. Neither of these views will be sympathetically treated here.

Often, of course, educational controversies have not been over objectives but rather the means to obtain them. Should the future citizen study Plato or Jefferson? What is more useful in training the student to write acceptably—Latin, grammar or English literature, or working for the college paper? Is a knowledge of Greek history more important than one of American history?

This account cannot hope to answer the more specific questions. Often the answer lies in the way something is taught. As will appear, the so-called cultural subjects have often been transformed into stultifying memory exercises or professional specialties. The present study will attempt to determine the extent to which various major disciplines have served their intended functions.

But the curriculum is by no means all there is to college education. The undergraduate's way of life, his activities, interests and enthusiasms are always vital parts of his experience. As such they form a large part of the story of *Academic Procession*. This will not be a useful source for those seeking chauvinistic propaganda in the form of dates and "firsts." Few things are so unreliable and misleading as the alleged founding dates of colleges. For instance, Rutgers received a charter as Queens College in 1766, a second in 1770, and actually began classes in 1771. It suspended as a college in 1794 to run as a grammar school until 1810. It again suspended in 1816, and reopened in 1825 under the name of Rutgers College. Which date is to be used? Other college histories show similar vicissitudes. The date, 1817, given in *Webster's Collegiate Dictionary* for the University of Michigan represents only a gleam in the eye; the first students were admitted in 1841.

Nor are such dates very significant except for purposes of determining the order of academic processions. Thus in 1899 the trustees of the University of Pennsylvania decided that it had been founded in 1740 instead of 1749 when its ancestor, the Academy of Philadelphia, was chartered, instead of 1751 when classes first began, or 1753 when it was first given the right to grant collegiate degrees. The evidence was that the Academy had taken over a building which had been constructed in 1740 as a school for Whitefield, but which had never held classes. If the evidence was shaky, the reasoning was sound: Pennsylvania wanted to march in academic processions ahead of Princeton which had selected 1746 as its date of founding. The logic of this has, however, never convinced Princeton.

The futility of this sort of thing is even clearer when one considers the very small beginnings of many a college. During its first sixty-five years Harvard graduated an average of eight men a year. At one point (1804) the University of Pennsylvania had just fourteen students. Granting that the early college graduates exercised an influence out of proportion to their numbers, it is proper to keep such figures in mind. Even in 1838, 200-year-old Harvard had a total enrollment of only 216 —thirty-one fewer than there were at the thirteen-year-old University of Virginia. As late as 1870 Columbia's enrollment was a mere 122. The influence of Harvard or a somewhat larger Yale was, moreover, undoubtedly greater than that of other equally small institutions. Therefore the mere fact of the existence of a college or the introduction of this or that pioneering experiment in a curriculum is not necessarily synonymous with an important development.

The purpose of this book, therefore, is to examine the major forces which have operated in American higher education and to evaluate the colleges of each period on the pragmatic basis of the extent to which they educated men and women to live and earn a living in the world of their times. This obviously is a rejection of the T. S. Eliot-Robert Maynard Hutchins concept of an unchanging, universal order. Perhaps there are universal values, but each age must reach them by a different road. This book will be a story of some of the roads, and of some of the blind alleys. It is also the story of a vital past of our history: the story of the formative period in the lives of the young men and women of America.

ERNEST EARNEST

Contents

CHAPTER   PAGE

1. Classicism and Calvinism   19

2. False Dawn   48

3. The Myth of Cloistered Halls   81

4. Student Life   102

5. Death and Transfiguration   133

6. High Seriousness in Bloomers   169

7. The Golden Age and the Gilded Cage   204

8. The Age of Conflict and Coonskin Coats   245

9. Question Period   295

10. The Wide Wide World   317

    Notes   343

    Index   361

Illustrations

Founding of Dartmouth College   *Frontispiece*

Yale College in 1807   30

Columbia Seniors, 1857   31

The Annual Cane Fight, Columbia, 1877   64

Physical Education—Then and Now   65

An Unequal Match   96

Three Educational Pioneers: Matthew Vassar, Andrew D. White, William Watts Folwell   97

Commencement Women's Medical College, 1873   160

Maria Mitchell and Mary Whitney in Vassar Observatory   161

Wells College Crews, 1878   192

High Seriousness in Bloomers   193

Yale Football Team, 1888   256

Princeton–Yale Game, 1889   257

Princeton–Yale Football Crowd, 1915   288

Registration: Temple University, 1950   289

1

Classicism and Calvinism

The first college curriculum introduced in British America was already obsolescent. Yet it became the standard one in American colleges for nearly two hundred and fifty years. During most of that period the work was not on a college level; it was mainly secondary-school education. The students were not of college age; they were chiefly boys between fourteen and eighteen. The emphasis in teaching and discipline was on conduct and religion; the behavior pattern of the students was one of riot and anarchy. In almost all its official aspects the system was a failure, yet it produced a high proportion of the intellectual and political leaders of the nation. The how and why of these paradoxes will be the subject of the following chapters.

To a large degree the failures have been the result of academic traditionalism; the successes due to native forces in American life. In the beginning both the curriculum and the system of discipline were as a matter of course patterned on those of English schools and universities. By 1640 there were seventy men from Cambridge and thirty from Oxford in America. It is not surprising therefore that the Reverend Nathaniel Eaton, the first master of Harvard, introduced the British method of inculcating the classics by means of a stick applied to the buttocks.

Eaton, however, laid on the rod with such a puritan fervor that his assisting usher, Nathaniel Briscoe, hailed him into court. It came out that Eaton had discharged Briscoe for "talking back" and, on the usher's return to the college, had beaten him for two hours with a walnut club while servants held the victim down. Many of the freshmen testified that Eaton had also beaten them unmercifully. Yet this was a man described by Cotton Mather as a "rare scholar." Apparently his appointment had been due largely to his publication of a Latin paper on the nature of the Sabbath.

Although subsequent officials did not go in for beatings, the mixture of harsh discipline and public piety was to become the standard pattern of the early colleges. The first commons are also symbolic. The master's wife, Mrs. Eaton, was the pioneer in the long line of harpies and incompetents to undertake the feeding of students. In 1639 the Harvard boys protested that she served thin beer and hard crusts, hasty pudding containing goats' dung, and mackerel "with their guts in them."

The tenure of the Eatons was brief. Even in a profession so notorious for quick turnover as the headship of a college, Nathaniel Eaton set some sort of a record if not a precedent by skipping town after his first year. To avoid a church trial for embezzlement of Harvard funds, Eaton embarked for Virginia. When three constables sent by Governor Winthrop took him off the ship, the "rare scholar" politely allowed two to debark first, pushed the third overboard and rowed himself back to the ship. Some years later when he was about to be extradited from Virginia, he deserted a second wife to flee to England where he married a third and ended his days in a debtors' prison.

After its inauspicious beginning under Eaton, Harvard suspended for a year to resume in 1640 under its first real president, Henry Dunster. A graduate of Magdalene College, Dunster introduced at Harvard essentially the Cambridge curriculum, one which was to set the pattern in American colleges for over two hundred years. In a terse summary he described it as follows:

*Primus annus Rhetoricam docebit, secundus et tertius Dialecticam, quartus adiungat Philosophiam.**

In *A History of Higher Education in America,* Charles F. Thwing estimates the relative amount of emphasis given to the various subjects as follows:

* The first year will teach rhetoric; the second and third, dialectic; the fourth will add philosophy.

Philosophy, including physics, logic, ethics, politics, occupied about one third of the course; Greek, especially the New Testament, was next in importance; then rhetoric, with perhaps more speaking than writing; then Oriental languages, including Hebrew, Chaldaic and Syriac—perhaps one sixth of the course. Mathematics, which occupied about one fifteenth of the time, consisted of arithmetic, geometry and some astronomy. Algebra was unknown. In addition there were the catechism, history, botany and other subordinate studies. Latin at first received little attention because the student had studied it in his preparatory work. President Josiah Quincy stated that the principles of education established by Dunster were not materially changed during the seventeenth century.

As Thwing points out, this curriculum failed to represent adequately the knowledge which the world had secured by the first half of the seventeenth century. Copernicus died in 1543; Galileo in 1642; it was the age of Kepler, Napier, and Harvey. Chaucer, Spenser, Shakespeare, Cervantes, Montesquieu were of course no part of a college curriculum. It is as if a modern student heard no reference to Darwin, Freud, Shaw or Einstein.

Yet this curriculum with minor changes was followed in most American colleges at least until the Civil War. Experiments with revised curriculums at William and Mary, Virginia and Pennsylvania tended to lose their momentum under the pressure of orthodox classicism. Many of the changes, like the introduction of lectures on mineralogy and electricity, were little more than gestures in the direction of modern knowledge; they did not alter the prevailing emphasis on Greek, Latin, mathematics, logic, and moral philosophy. Many of the subjects were pursued only an hour or so a week for a term, one third of a college year. And those places offering a modern language usually made it an optional additional study requiring a special fee.

Through an irony in semantics the traditional curriculum has often been described as a liberal education. Yet its original purpose was vocational. As stated by its founders, Harvard was first of all intended to provide the colony with educated ministers of the gospel. As late as 1753 the General Assembly of Connecticut resolved in reference to Yale: "That one principal end proposed in erecting the college was to supply the churches in this Colony with a learned, pious and orthodox ministry."

Certainly the instruction provided by the early colleges was not liberal in the larger connotations of that term. It was not designed to free the mind, but to discipline and channel it. The emphasis was never on free inquiry, but always on orthodoxy. The Connecticut Assembly ordered the teaching of the Assembly's Catechism, Ames's *Medulla* and *Cases of Conscience*, and urged the president and fellows of Yale "that special care should be taken in the education of students, not to suffer them to be instructed in any different principles or doctrines; and that all proper measures should be taken to promote the powers and purity of religion and the best edification and peace of the churches." In 1743, because of "the intolerant spirit of the present governors of Yale," some of the senior class reprinted Locke's *Essay on Toleration*. Although Harvard was less insistent on orthodoxy, the Harvard Corporation in 1722 secured from Professor Edward Wigglesworth a statement guaranteeing his orthodoxy before it appointed him Professor of Divinity.

By the first quarter of the nineteenth century the curriculum had been pretty much standardized into four divisions: 1. the classics, 2. rhetoric and belles-lettres, 3. mathematics and natural philosophy and 4. mental and moral philosophy. Greek and Latin, the backbone of the course, were given during the first three years, usually four hours each a week; rhetoric, one or two hours, and mathematics, about three hours, were given during the first two years; natural philosophy, which meant the rudiments of physics and chemistry, usually came in the third; and logic, metaphysics, ethics and the evidences of Christianity occupied the fourth. Hebrew was often included, especially by students preparing for the ministry.

To those who venerate the terms *Classics, Latin, Greek, Philosophy,* this might seem a rich, if not broad, educational program. However, an examination of the course content and methods of teaching indicates something far different. The classic authors were carefully selected and pruned of anything which might taint morals or orthodoxy. Cotton Mather, the son of a Harvard president, warned against "conversation with muses that are no better than harlots," and wished there were some way of studying Greek and Latin without reading the heathen writers.

Even in the works studied the student was given no insight into literary values or the classic way of life and thought. For three years he prepared each day an assigned number of lines on which he was required to recite. Benjamin Lord, Yale 1714, writing to President Ezra Stiles says that Tully and Vergil were recited, as well as Ramus' *Logic* and Herrebord's *Set Logic*. "We recited the Greek Testament; knew not Homer; received the Psalms in Hebrew."

Andrew White, later the first president of Cornell, entered Yale in 1850. He complained of the system of recitation by rote, and said that in Greek students merely rattled off translations. They were drilled in the synopses of verbs. In Latin, *De Senectute* was used merely as "a series of pegs on which to hang Zumpt's rules for the subjunctive mood." During his whole course there was not a single lecture on literature, ancient or modern.

Yale, "the mother of colleges," exported this system to the new colleges in the South and West. In the seventy-five colleges operating before 1840, thirty-six presidents came from Yale, twenty-two from Princeton, and only eight from Harvard. Josiah Meigs, who rebelled against the Federalism of Yale, introduced the Yale curriculum and methods into the frontier Franklin College (later the University of Georgia) during the 1830s. True, Meigs did introduce an atmosphere somewhat more scientific than the clerical climate of Yale. Jefferson wrote him a letter of congratulation, saying the hope of science lay in the South, unshackled by the clerical chains of New England. But so strong was the tradition that Meigs used his mathematics to calculate, according to the law of falling bodies, that in nine days the rebel angels plunged 1,832,303,363 miles deep into hell.

So powerful was the hold of the traditional education that when Allegheny College was founded in 1817 in a frontier Pennsylvania town of 700 people, the cornerstone enclosed a chip from Plymouth Rock, a bit of plaster from the tomb of Vergil, and a fragment of marble from Dido's temple. At the first commencement there were an address in Latin by a citizen of the town, a response in Latin by the president, followed by another Latin oration, one in Hebrew, and a Latin dialogue.

There were, as we shall see, attacks on the system and attempts to modify it. Because of these attacks the trustees at Yale in 1827 requested faculty opinion on the "dead languages" as absolute requirements. The result was the famous Yale report of 1828, a sweeping denunciation of the critics and of all attempts at even mild change. This defense of the existing curriculum became the bible of the educational conservatives. All over the country official pronouncements and inaugural addresses echoed and re-echoed the sentiments of the Yale faculty. The classics were a vested interest and faculties had no intention of relinquishing a fragment of a province so ancient and so hallowed. These men were products of the system; therefore it seemed to them the only possible system.

The fundamental argument of the Yale faculty was the one always advanced in favor of subjects of little demonstrable value—that is, mental discipline. It is based on the now discredited psychological principle of transfer of training. "The two great points to be gained in intellectual culture," wrote President Jeremiah Day, "are discipline and the furniture of the mind. The former is, perhaps, the most important of the two." (He disdained the correct comparative form for the more sweeping superlative.)

Professor James L. Kingsley in his part of the same report argued that the classical writers in form and style constituted a standard for determining literary merit—a theory Alexander Pope had preached a century before. Modern languages were a mere accomplishment; those who would substitute them were "visionaries in education, ignorant of its true design and objects and unfit for their places."

The extreme traditionalism of college faculties in the rapidly changing America of the nineteenth century is an indication of the stultifying effect of the type of education in vogue. As Andrew White says of the Yale faculty of his student days (1850-1853), there were distinguished men like James Hadley, who "would have drawn throngs" at Berlin or Leipzig, but they "were fettered by a system which made everything of gerund-grinding and nothing of literature." Even the study of history was merely requiring the student to repeat from memory the dates from Putz's *Ancient History*.

W. T. Harris, later United States Commissioner of Education (1889-1906), who entered Yale in 1854, withdrew after a year, dissatisfied with the course of study "and impatient for the three moderns—modern science, modern literature, and modern history." That this was symptomatic is indicated by the figures on college enrollment. Francis Wayland, then president of Brown, compiled figures in 1850 to indicate that despite the increasing wealth of New England, there was a decreasing proportion of students going to college. Thus, in 1830, according to his figures, one in 1,365 was in college; whereas, in 1850 the figure was only one in 1,408. At a later period President Frederick A. P. Barnard, of Columbia, presented statistics showing the same tendency throughout the nation, a tendency which continued until at least 1870. His figures show a proportion among the white population of one college student to 1,549 people in 1840; one to 2,012 in 1860; one to 2,546 in 1869. It is significant that both Wayland and Barnard found in such figures the same meaning: traditional curriculum was not meeting the needs of the United States. The Amherst faculty in 1827 told the trustees just that. At the time the warning was not heeded.

There is evidence that the classical studies did not even turn out good classical scholars. Dr. Samuel Johnson, who in 1753 became the first president of Columbia, said of the Yale of his undergraduate days:

The utmost in classical learning that was now generally aimed at, and indeed twenty or thirty years after, was no more than to construe five or six of Tully's orations, and as many books of Vergil poorly, and most of the Greek Testament, with some chapters of the Hebrew Psalter. Common arithmetic and a little surveying were the *ne plus ultra* of mathematical requirements.

Almost a century later Wayland pointed to the 120 colleges of 1850, all of which taught Latin and Greek, and asked: "Where are our classical scholars? All teach mathematics, but where are our mathematicians?" Of the student under the traditional system he said:

He can read nothing but his textbooks, and he turns mechanically from one to the other. He learns to cram for a recitation or for an examination; and when the cast is over, his work is done, and he is willing to forget all that he has studied. It gave him no pleasure, it has yielded him no fruit.

As late as 1871 President Barnard, discussing the traditional curriculum still required at Columbia, wrote:

The majority of our students do not become so proficient even in the classical tongues, as to be able to read with facility the works of the classic authors which they have not read before; and yet these are the subjects in which they are required to be tolerably versed before they enter the college.

It would seem probable that the college student studying the classics for three years became no more proficient in Greek and Latin than does the American student in three years of French or German today. After all, at a great many institutions, modern language is still taught in the gerund-grinding fashion of a century or two ago. And just as the older teachers justified their subjects by arguing the value of a knowledge of the classical heritage, so the modern teacher argues the need for a knowledge of the culture of Europe. Certainly the student of old got little real insight into classical culture. And the modern student usually reads French or German literature in courses offered by the English department.

Contrary to those who long for the mythical good old days

in education when students "really studied and knew how to spell," the evidence is that the student before 1860 had a pretty easy time of it. In the 1840s William Gardiner Hammond, a student at Amherst, attended classes three hours a day five days a week with an additional two hours on Saturday. He noted in his diary: "I find that one can get along without much study." Of course then as now if one wanted to rank high he had to work hard. Charles W. Eliot estimated that between 1817 and 1867 a young man of any ability at all could accomplish all the prescribed tasks, including attendance at recitations, in a small number of hours a day. Four hours were ample for a bright student, and three of these would be spent in class. And ancient diaries kept by undergraduates show little evidence of mastery of spelling or syntax.

Increasingly during the last of the eighteenth and first half of the nineteenth centuries the academies became rivals of the colleges. In the 1770s in Timothy Dwight's private academy at Greenfield Hill, he carried some boys through the college course. In fact, because of the reputation of Dwight as a teacher, some students moved from Yale to finish their college work at the academy. Later, when he was president of Yale, he is reported to have told a prospective student to enter the junior class if his circumstances were easy, if not to enter the senior class. In the smaller colleges it was not unusual for the president to do most of the teaching, assisted by perhaps one or two tutors. Some presidents taught every subject listed in the college catalogue. This was true of Samuel Johnson of Columbia (1753), Jacob R. Hardenbergh of Rutgers (1786), and Daniel C. Sanders of Vermont (1791). Often the senior class had the president as its only teacher. It must be remembered that most of the college presidents and teachers before 1850 had engaged in no graduate study except in a theological seminary. Most of the early presidents continued as active clergymen after their appointment to college posts.

It is small wonder that a family in moderate circumstances often chose to send a boy to a near-by academy taught by a local Yale or Harvard graduate instead of to a distant college.

The neighboring clergyman was perhaps fully as competent as the college professor to hear the student recite his twenty or thirty lines a day of Vergil or the Greek Testament. And the student shenanigans at college were not likely to give parents a feeling of confidence about "wholesome Christian influences."

Dean Andrew West, of the Princeton Graduate College, was probably correct when, in 1900, he summed up the early American college thus: "Up to the close of the Civil War it was mainly an institution of secondary education with some antici- pations of university studies toward the end of the course."

This anticipation of university study took the form of a course usually taught by the president and labeled variously moral philosophy, moral science, intellectual philosophy, sci- ence of mind and morals, metaphysics and ethics. Students looked forward to it eagerly as a change from the stultifying routine of recitations in Greek, Latin and mathematics. In an excellent chapter in *The Old Time College President,* George P. Schmidt describes the course as containing material from biology, psychology, religion and ethics. As the title "moral philosophy" suggests, the emphasis was on religion and ethics. An early American textbook for the course defines it as that science which gives rules for the direction of the will of man in his moral state, such rules to serve for the guidance of the individual, the community and the nation. Coming as it did in the senior year, taught not by a tutor but by the presi- dent—usually the ablest and most dominating person the stu- dent had met in college—being presented in the form of lectures and dealing for the first time with the problems of actual life, the course had a powerful impact on the minds of boys between seventeen and twenty. It was the first course in college which asked them to think.

In form and in much of its content, moral philosophy went back to Aristotle. It came to America from English and Scottish universities as early as 1640 when President Dunster mentioned it as an important part of the course at Harvard. The other colonial colleges—William and Mary, Pennsylvania, Yale and Kings—also carried it. During the eighteenth century the course was modified by the Enlightenment to add more material from politics, sociology, and economics. Much of the political theorizing goes back to Locke, whose writings were often used as a text. But it leaned especially on the works of a group of Scottish philosophers and theologians: Francis Hutchinson, Thomas Reed, James Geattie, Adam Ferguson, Dugald Stewart, Thomas Brown; and on two Englishmen, Dr. William Paley, the Christian apologist, and Bishop Butler, famous for his *Analogy of Religion*. It is significant that in his rejection of rationalistic philosophy Emerson specifically mentioned Locke, Paley and Stewart as opposed to Spinoza, Kant and Coleridge. In effect Emerson was rejecting the reigning academic philosophy of his time.

There was some infusion of Kantian ideas after 1840 but in the main the course in moral philosophy relied on the Scottish school with its assumption that man is capable of evolving standards of right and wrong and even of discovering the nature of God by the use of his reason. John Daniel Gros, professor at Columbia in the 1790s, defined moral philosophy as "the science which gives rules for the direction of the will of man." Samuel Stanhope Smith of Princeton said its object was to "propose principles to enable a rational and reflecting mind to deduce the point of duty for itself," and Samuel Johnson of Columbia stated: "It must be our business in this essay, to search out all the truths that relate both to ourselves, to God, and our fellow-creatures, and thence to deduce the several duties that do necessarily result from them."

All this is far removed from the ideal of knowledge for its own sake preached by such men as Cardinal Newman, Matthew Arnold and the followers of Robert Maynard Hutchins. Americans take more naturally to utilitarian ideals. Even today pure research is justified on the ground of its eventual usefulness. The modern courses grouped under the phrase of "teaching how to live" have as their function almost exactly that of the once universal course in moral philosophy.

The real difference between the methods of our ancestors and ours is their dependence on syllogistic logic and a priori assumptions. The college teacher of a century or two ago simply did not have the tools to handle the materials of the course; his education did not provide them. The failure of formal logic in affording valid scientific concepts is notorious. Witness such classic examples as the "proof" that a moving body could not reach its destination because it must always first traverse half the distance, and then half of what remained, etc., or the theorem that parallel lines could meet only in infinity—in fact, most of the theorems of Euclidian geometry. Mathematicians now recognize that these give us not a picture of the universe, but only propositions true within an artificial, closed system.

Even more misleading were the a priori assumptions, the most misleading of all being those that man was primarily a rational being, that in this he differed from all other animals, and that truth and virtue were the same in all places and all times. It would be absurd to imply that our ancestors should have been aware of Darwinian and Freudian concepts or that they should have known cultural anthropology. The point is not that the college teachers were often wrong; it is that they took so little trouble to be right. They had developed almost no tools for the verification of reported fact. Thus, in 1829, we find President Eliphalet Nott of Union telling his classes of a boy in Connecticut who because of prenatal influence had mud-turtle flappers for arms. And in preaching total abstinence he gave a lurid description of the habitual drinker who died from spontaneous combustion. He insisted that such deaths had become "so numerous and so incontrovertible, that I presume no person of information will now be found who will venture to call the reality of their existence in question." After 1660 many pioneer scientists in England and America had gathered material and developed hypotheses which were little known in the colleges. On both sides of the Atlantic science developed almost entirely outside the colleges until well after the middle of the nineteenth century.

Because of the need to arrive at orthodox conclusions, the teachers did not even use the tools they had. In the latter part

YALE COLLEGE IN 1807

President Dwight stands at the far right watching students play football.

COLUMBIA SENIORS, 1857

of the eighteenth century such men as John Witherspoon and Samuel Stanhope Smith of Princeton, Timothy Dwight of Yale, and Reverend John D. Gros of Columbia were able to "prove" by the use of reason the beliefs of revealed religion. Benjamin Silliman of Yale prepared a geology text in the 1830s which was prefaced by an orthodox account of the creation and the deluge. Francis Wayland of Brown, an original thinker in educational matters, nevertheless preached the dependence of science on revealed religion. In the nineteenth century there was a swing away from the emphasis on reason and the "light of nature" toward a revised orthodoxy.

In the political field the teachers of moral philosophy tended to find universal truth very much the same as the reigning ideas of their place and time. The United States with its written Constitution and principle of the separation of powers was held up as the ideal form. In the early days of the Republic the teaching, except in a few Southern colleges under the influence of Jefferson, was mainly Federalist. Timothy Dwight may be regarded as the leader of the Federalist school of teaching. Later on when the country divided over slavery, the Northern presidents tended to find Biblical authority for emancipation; the Southern presidents Biblical authority for slavery. Witherspoon and Smith of Princeton, and Wayland of Brown, preached gradual emancipation. Princeton and Brown had large numbers of Southern students.

It would be a mistake to argue that because of some manifest absurdities or even because of faulty premises or methods the course in moral philosophy had no value. Taught as it often was by able men with a lifetime of experience behind them it could furnish much in the way of practical guidance for life. Dubious theoretical foundations do not necessarily lead to faulty applications. And increasingly, as Schmidt demonstrates, a philosophy of common sense came to be substituted for or superimposed on the more speculative systems. Late in the nineteenth century President James McCosh of Princeton argued that this was a new philosophy—the American philosophy. He wrote, "The change from the speculative to this thoroughly realistic philosophy could not be unlike that from the European Monarchies to the American Republics." At a number of colleges such practical topics as marriage, the duties of parents and children, co-operation in community enterprises, property rights and, of course, slavery were part of the discussions. It may well be that such discussions were as valuable for their time as those based on the essays read in English composition are today. Many of the topics are the same.

The great limitation of the course in philosophy is perhaps best revealed in the work of one of the few original philosophers who emerged from it. In his famous essay *Nature*, Ralph Waldo Emerson shows the same tendency to organize ideas in abstract categories such as "beauty," "commodity," "discipline," "idealism," "spirit"; the same dependence on very sketchy scientific knowledge as a basis for deriving moralizing general principles; the same hortatory tone. Whatever its philosophical backgrounds, it was essentially a system of thinking growing out of the Protestant ministry, and in turn furnishing the basis for the training of clergymen.

In judging the effect on the students of this traditional classical, mathematical, philosophical system it is impossible to separate the teaching from the system of discipline which accompanied it. The manner in which a student lives, his relations with faculty and other students have at least as much influence on him as does formal instruction. Cardinal Newman argued that if he had to choose, he would select the association of students with one another in a university as having more educational value than a mere system of lectures and examinations. Certainly a large part of the education of the American student grew out of his associations with his fellows.

However, in so far as the college officials had anything to do with it, the system was designed to present the development of mature students. The elaborate rules of the early colleges were organized on the pattern of a strict prep school, and more than a little tinged with the Calvinistic doctrine of the total depravity of man.

These rules operated in a physical environment little calculated to promote culture or gracious living. Except for boys from the farm the conditions of life must have been considerably cruder than those to which most of the students had been accustomed at home.

As a rule the college first occupied a single barrack building with classrooms on the first floor and student rooms on the two or three floors above. When the college began to grow, other buildings like it would be added. Andrew White described the Yale of his day (the 1850s) as "a long line of brick barracks, the cheapest which could be built." So poor was the construction of a number of the early buildings that, like the first Harvard Hall, they had to be abandoned as unsafe after a few years. Holworthy Hall (1812) at Harvard was the first college dormitory to have a study between bedrooms, a design which eventually became more or less standard. But the great majority of early students shared a small room with a roommate.

The campus was likely to be an unfenced barren plot of ground overrun with livestock. John T. Kirkland in the 1830s was the first Harvard president to clear the yard of privies, pigpens, brewhouse and wood lot, and to plant elms.

Privies were a constant source of trouble. At Amherst students were always complaining of them and from time to time forced renovation by setting them on fire. Faculty minutes resort to various euphemisms in referring to the perennial problem. Thus, in 1800, the Prudential Committee of Yale authorized the building of three "Necessary Houses," each eight feet square and divided into four separate apartments. They were to be at a considerable distance from one another. Three years later three more were needed—those to be of brick. Apparently the others had been burned. However the sophomores tried to blow up the brick ones.

The usual practice was for students to purchase their own firewood, which they cut themselves and lugged up to their rooms. All water had to be carried from the college well. In view of such arrangements and the custom of holding chapel in an unheated building at 5:30 to 6:00 in the winter, it is unlikely that there was extensive bathing or even washing. The

Amherst boys of the 1840s did rig up a shower bath in the grove. It was operated by pouring buckets of water into a system of sluices—obviously not an arrangement practical for cold weather. At Harvard in the 1850s all water was carried by students to their rooms from two college pumps, and there was no hot water unless a student heated it himself. Jacob Rhett Motte, a student in the 1830s, notes the purchase of a spirit lamp to heat shaving water. But President Charles Eliot remarks that in his college days there was a limited amount of bathing. The first two bathtubs were introduced during the early years of his administration and placed in the cellar of Matthews Hall. At pioneer Oberlin, however, daily bathing was in vogue because of its supposed benefit to health.

It is not surprising that boys caged up by rigid rules in primitive barracks took no pains to protect college property. Smashing of doors and windows was a favorite sport. It was a rare college bill which did not carry charges for damages. At the Yale commencement of 1847 a visitor was shocked to see the graduates smashing the windows in their rooms—presumably after the college could send them no more bills. At the University of North Carolina students rode horses through the dormitories and shot up the place. After the Revolution, Harvard students broke into the arsenals on Cambridge Common to steal cannon balls, which they rolled down the halls—an activity widely copied at other colleges. When tutors at Hobart began to catch and impound the cannon balls, students heated them nearly red hot before sending them down the corridors. At the University of Georgia it was found that cannon balls rolled down stairs effectively interrupted classes. Even as late as the 1920s colleges still using antiquated dormitories were plagued with window smashing and major property damage. And students were still breaking up unsanitary toilet facilities as the only means of getting new ones.

In pre-Civil War colleges there were of course no such things as student lounge rooms, study halls, or even library reading rooms. The usual small library was housed in some locked room, opened perhaps once a week for an hour or so for the withdrawal and return of books. At Yale in Dwight's administration only juniors and seniors were permitted to borrow books, with rental fees depending on the size of the volume. The early colleges did not encourage nonsense like comfort, athletics, or reading. As a result they got riot and disorder.

The only places with some attempt at comfort and attractiveness were the rooms of the literary societies. Each college had at least two, stimulated by an intense rivalry. At some places members were elected; at others like Amherst each student was assigned to one as soon as he entered college. Members of the societies, even at poor, pioneer colleges like Oberlin, raised money for rugs, draperies and comfortable, even luxurious, furniture.

Members of one society were rigidly excluded from the rooms of the other. Like the fraternities, which to some degree supplanted them, there was a good bit of secret hocus-pocus. There seems, however, to have been some exchange of books. Very often the literary societies had libraries almost as large as that owned by the college. When Timothy Dwight became president of Yale in 1795 there were only 2,700 books in the library, a third of them the gift of Dean Berkley sixty-two years before. Harvard's library, after being destroyed by fire, was replaced by the General Assembly and private donors. It numbered 13,000 volumes around the turn of the century. Under Dwight the Yale library increased to 7,000 volumes. By 1809 each literary society possessed 700 volumes. As late as 1845 the Rutgers College library numbered only 5,000 volumes. Yet a few years later, the literary societies at the University of Georgia each had libraries of about 2,600 books—this at a time when the enrollment was down to about 100. At Oberlin in 1862 the college library had 6,000 volumes; the literary societies, 3,000; in 1863 the figures were 6,500 and 4,000. Students were not encouraged to waste time in the college library, and had to pay fees for the use of books. These literary societies, as we shall see, were perhaps the most vital educative forces in the early colleges.

They were also schools for manners. At the University of

Georgia, then close to the frontier, the literary societies set up a system of fines for fifty varying offenses such as sitting with crossed legs or with feet on the rungs of a chair. Smoking was prohibited during meetings. Similar rules were put in effect by the societies at Oberlin.

If the literary society was a civilizing force, the college commons was not. Twenty-seven years after the filthy regime of Mrs. Eaton there was the "Butter Rebellion" when students wrote a *Book of Harvard* in biblical style, containing such texts as:

Behold! Bad and unwholesome butter is served unto us daily; now therefore let us depute Asa the Scribe, to go unto our Rulers, and seek redress. Then arose Asa, the Scribe, and went unto Belcher, the Ruler, and said behold our butter stinketh, and we cannot eat thereof; now give us, we pray, the butter that stinketh not.

The result was similar to that of similar protests ever since:

And Belcher the Ruler, said, trouble me not, but begone unto thine own place, but Asa obeyed him not.

A "Bread and Butter Rebellion" in 1805 led to the suspension of half the students.

The dining hall which Yale used until 1763 doubled as a chapel, with the library in a room upstairs. As morning prayers came before breakfast, it is likely that on cold mornings students paid more attention to odors from the kitchen than to the familiar exhortations. Cider, the table drink, was served in pewter mugs. Glass tumblers did not come into use until 1815, and for good reason. As at Harvard, disorder was common, especially when students became dissatisfied with poor food or service. A future senator, of the class of 1802, once chastised the head cook because the pewter platters were not clean. A student of a few years later mentions that while he was in college 600 tumblers and 30 coffeepots were destroyed or stolen in a single term. There were three terms in a college year. To keep order the tutors sat on a raised platform, trying to eat and watch 200 boys. When peas were served, the students were required to shell them. If anyone was absent the pods were collected and thrown in the shirker's room. A contemporary of James Fenimore Cooper at Yale says that salt beef and dry cod were the principal dishes, with stewed oysters on Sunday mornings.

The natural result of poor and monotonous food was that students bought snacks between meals. Often the butler had a little racket of his own in supplying "sizings." At Yale in the late eighteenth century this official made about $1,000 extra a year—about half the salary of the president—selling 500 pies a week at sixpence each. Later, the butler was usually a resident graduate student of two or three years' standing. One of these, Lyman Beecher, paid off $300 he had borrowed to buy stock and $100 for other debts, bought a suit of clothes, cleared commencement expenses and ended up with $100 in his pockets. Not all of this was profit on food; the butler furnished other supplies, such as candles and stationery.

Other sources of food were taverns in college towns—forbidden but patronized—and peddlers. Jacob Rhett Motte mentions in his diary "an old peripatetic gentleman who goes from room to room, and from building to building, with peaches, cherries, strawberries, black-berries and every other kind of fruit." The students rounded up some tumblers, spoons, and the diarist ate his fruit from the top of a tin bucket—saucers being unobtainable.

Then, as now, ice cream and soda pop were student favorites. In the 1830s Harvard boys made carbonated drinks by mixing sugar and tartaric acid. Motte also frequently mentions ice cream. In fact, one Sunday he drank some mead and ate two ice creams, undoubtedly the generous portions of earlier days. Ice cream and soda water were advertised for University of Georgia students by the local merchants in the forties and even in poor and pious Oberlin in the sixties.

The college adolescent's longing for good food gave rise to a Yale song beginning:

When streams roll down in aureal flood,
    On Australasian shores,
When every swamp has golden mud,
    And every stone its ores;
A youth from fair New England's clime,
    Was often heard to sigh,
I'd give my pile of golden dust,
    For one good pumpkin pie.

And of course one of the most famous poems by a Yale graduate is Joel Barlow's "Hasty Pudding."

Students in the South, with its tradition of good living, fared
better in commons. In the 1830s breakfast at the college commons at the University of Georgia consisted of coffee, tea, corn
and wheat bread, butter, bacon or beef. At noon dinner there
was corn bread, bacon, vegetables, beef, lamb, mutton, shoat
or poultry. If there was no fresh meat, milk or molasses was
served with the second course of "confectionary." For supper
there was corn and wheat bread, with butter, coffee and tea,
or coffee with milk.

In the 1840s Yale tried to insure wholesome and adequate
food by requiring the butler to serve the following:

Breakfast for four: 1 loaf of bread, the dough to weigh 1
                      pound.
Dinner for four: 1 loaf of bread, 2½ pounds of beef, veal,
                      or mutton, 1 quart beer, 2 pennyworth
                      of sauce.
Supper for four: 2 quarts milk, 1 loaf bread. When milk
                      not available, then an apple pie made
                      of 1¾ pounds dough, ¼ pound hog's fat,
                      2 ounces sugar, and 1 peck apples.

At Oberlin, where the ideas of the diet faddist, Graham, held
sway, tea, coffee, condiments, and meat became moral issues.
Professor George Whipple told a convention in New York of
a young lady who died in convulsions as a result of drinking
strong tea. However, after eleven months of student protests,
those who wanted meat were permitted to have it at an additional charge. An unmarried professor who brought a pepper

shaker to the table was ordered by the trustees to remove it. Partly because of the incident he was soon dropped. As butter was frowned upon by Graham, one group of students lived on bread and water.

As a rule the authorities gave more attention to the chapel than to the commons. Daily chapel was an invariable requirement of the early colleges—a requirement which persisted longer than almost any other. With the characteristic puritan desire to make people uncomfortable, chapel was then set at 5:30 in the morning during the winter, 5:00 in the summer. Until the nineteenth century the service was usually held in an unheated room. A second prayer service came in the late afternoon or evening. Two long services on Sunday were the rule; additional short services were common.

No amount of experience seems to have suggested to the faculty that a surfeit of religion produced irreverence and riot. Professor "Elephant" Pearson, who kept a diary of student disorders at Harvard in the 1780s, noted:

> Disorders coming out of chapel . . .
> Bisket, tea cups, saucers, and
> a KNIFE thrown at the tutors.
> At evening prayers, the lights were
> all extinguished by powder and lead.

A week later he recorded disorders worse than he had ever before known.

> The Bible, cloth, candles and
> branches I found laid in confusion
> upon the seat of the desk. During
> lectures several pebbles were snapped.

Student diaries mention similar events. Jonathan Fisher, in the 1790s, noted that a stink bomb of some sort had been set off in chapel. Jacob Motte, in the 1830s, jotted down an account of a student demonstration against a tutor. They scraped their feet at prayers to drown out the speaker. In the 1840s at Amherst, William Hammond was given "a blowing" for plaguing Professor Hatch at prayers. Hammond was a good student and one who noted an occasional good sermon with approval. His comment is: "I really think these public prayers do more harm than good to the religious feeling of a majority of the students; they are regarded as an idle bore." A Haverford student of the 1830s, William Canby, recorded that the superintendent seemed to have lost all control over the boys: "At our collections boys throw *shot* and *corn* about the room."

In his history of the University of Georgia, E. Merton Coulter sums up the situation there by saying that there is ample evidence that students "hated all the exercises connected with prayers and even the building in which devotions were held." Even in pious Oberlin a coed recorded going to a sermon, "but my own thoughts did me good. I listened little to the former, but much to the latter." Another coed of 1860 reported laughing and the passing of notes at a Thursday service. The kind of strong-arm piety enforced by college authorities is perhaps best illustrated by Robert Bishop, president of Miami, 1824-1840, who prayed with one eye open. When he saw a disturbance, he would take a flying leap from the platform, quell the offender, and then return to the rostrum to finish the prayer.

All through the 1880s and 1890s the Amherst faculty were regularly assigned police duty in chapel: two to the desk, one at the north door, one at the side door, one at the mid door, and two in the gallery. Students were going to worship God if they had to be dragooned into it. And dragooned they were. For a century the minutes of the faculties of such colleges as Amherst and Lafayette are filled with disciplinary action over chapel cuts. The problem was one of the chief items of faculty business.

It was the daily chapel which caused most of the trouble. Students as a rule seem to have made no objection to services on Sunday; they had been brought up in the tradition of the Puritan Sabbath. A good sermon was received with approval. President Dwight, who preached a sensible, practical form of Christianity, had immense influence on the students. He came to Yale at a time when eighteenth-century agnosticism was the rule among students: only one member of the entering class in the fall of 1796 was a professing Christian. In the spring of 1802 there was a sweeping religious revival which converted one third of the students. Other revivals followed in 1807 and 1814. Dartmouth and Princeton—but not Harvard—went through similar revivals. It all was part of a nation-wide return to orthodoxy, but there is considerable evidence of Dwight's leadership in the movement. Students testified to the effectiveness of his preaching. In his history of *The Old Time College President,* Schmidt credits Dwight with doing more than any other person in turning back the rising tide of deism and materialism and bringing about a revival of old-fashioned religion.

Other able preacher-presidents had great influence on their students, from the liberal Horace Holley of Transylvania, to the hypnotic, hell-fire evangelist Charles Finney of Oberlin. When Dr. John McLean of Princeton made a trip to Europe in 1850, students swarmed to his home to say good-by, and a hundred of them escorted him to the station. Except for a period at the end of the eighteenth century the American student had even a certain enthusiasm for sermons. William Hammond noted in his diary the points made in those he liked, and the fun-loving Charles Motte once attended four Sunday services in Cambridge. True he did add: "There were two very pretty girls in the pew just in front of me, and I'm afraid I attended more to them than to the sermon."

But Calvinistic presidents and faculties could be satisfied only with an all-out religious program premised on the doctrine of the total depravity of man. In the 1850s a Princeton student's Sabbath consisted of prayers at 6:30, prayer meeting at 9:00, church at 11:00, Bible class at 3:00, church in town at 4:00, prayer meeting at 5:00, and church at 7:30. Fourteen or more compulsory religious services a week did much to encourage student depravity as a relief from boredom.

The system of rules governing the student were as doctrinaire and unrealistic as the curriculum and the system of multitudinous religious services. His whole life was regimented from the time he arose at 4:30 or 5:00 until the compulsory bedtime at 9:00 or 10:00. The usual schedule provided for morning and evening prayers; two or three recitation periods, one or two in the morning, the other in the afternoon; a morning and afternoon study period (not always used for that purpose), at least one being two hours long; breakfast, dinner and supper. This left three free periods, one in the morning, one from noon to two, and the third from evening prayers to 7:00 in winter, 9:00 in the summer. As late as 1841 almost the same schedule was decreed by the Regents of the new University of Michigan. In Northern colleges the student often used his free morning period to cut firewood and lug it up to his room. Even his leisure time was hedged about with multiple restrictions. The earliest Harvard students were commanded to pray in secret and read scriptures twice a day. Not only was swearing forbidden, but also all idle, foolish, bitter, scoffing, frothy and wanton words—rather a blanket coverage of normal student conversation. Students were forbidden to sell or exchange articles above the value of 6d, and could not go to town without permission from a college official. This last was a rule almost universal in colleges for 200 years, and one which filled faculty minutes with disciplinary actions. As the years went on, college rule books became even longer and more detailed. In 1802 the Laws of Union College, for instance, contained eleven chapters of from seven to twenty-three sections each. Every student was required to own a copy and know its contents. The University of Georgia, founded on the Yale pattern, had sixteen pages of rules.

To enforce the rules an elaborate system of fines was in vogue. At Harvard about the middle of the eighteenth century, lying, drunkenness, tumultuous noises, and skating each carried a shilling penalty. Firing a gun or pistol in the yard cost two shillings. By President John T. Kirkland's time (1810-1828), going to a theater carried a penalty of $10. At Yale also, amusement, athletics, and high spirits were regarded as reprehensible. There was a fine of 6d for "hollowing," singing, or loud talking in the yard; 8d for handball or football near windows—a law with some reason—but also 34d for leaving to go fishing, sailing or swimming, and 50 cents for firing gunpowder in the yard. There were fines for playing billiards, calling for a drink at a tavern within two miles of the college, and for countless other offenses. When Timothy Dwight became president, he substituted moral suasion for fines, with excellent results. As Dwight's biographer puts it, President Thomas Clap "had imposed fines and enforced police power with a strict Calvinistic fervor that was rewarded with riot and disorder."

However, it was a long time before all presidents and faculties recognized the merits of Dwight's system. Among the exceptions were Jeremiah Day, Dwight's successor at Yale; Eliphalet Nott of Union, and Kirkland and Quincy at Harvard. Perhaps more typical were Joseph Caldwell of North Carolina, who is said to have taken nightly walks to catch offenders, and John McLean of Princeton, who did the same, sometimes chasing them to their rooms or up trees. It was, of course, a universal custom to have faculty proctors live in dormitories—a provocation for student pranks at least as late as the 1920s.

One of the pioneers in changing the system, President Nott, described the methods he found in vogue at Union:

Fines, suspensions, and expulsions were the principal instruments of college government. The Faculty sat in their robes as a court; caused offenders to be brought before them; examined witnesses, and pronounced sentences with the solemnity of other courts of justice.

Nott determined never again to convene the faculty on questions of discipline, but to deal with offenders individually. However, the minutes of other institutions show that a major part of faculty business was the hearing and disposition of cases of discipline.

The puritanical system of discipline was particularly unsuited to the South. The sons of planter aristocrats revolted against the restrictions and surveillance imposed by the petty autocrats trained at Northern colleges. Gentlemen were not to be ordered around; that was for slaves. Even some of the faculty refused to do police duty. Professors were snowballed and hanged in effigy at the University of Georgia. Cursing the faculty was a common pastime. At Mercer a student dangerously wounded a professor; at the University of Georgia, in 1840, six drunken students painfully wounded the president and bruised a professor with missiles. A favorite greeting to a patrolling tutor was a shower of sticks and stones. At the University of Virginia students horsewhipped members of the faculty. In a riot in 1842 Professor John H. G. Davis was shot dead by an exuberant undergraduate, and at Oakland College in Mississippi a student stabbed President Jeremiah Chamberlin to death.

The elaborate system of rules set by the authorities was copied, especially at Yale, by the undergraduates in dealing with new students. Thus such faculty rules as one at Princeton requiring students to raise their hats to the president at a distance of ten rods, to tutors at five (at Yale the student was required to remain uncovered) had their counterparts in those published for Yale freshmen. These regulated the type of clothes to be worn and the side of the stairs permitted for use. It was the duty of the upper class to inspect the manners of the lower. Before passing a gate a freshman was to survey all approaches, and if he saw a superior within three rods he was to wait for a signal to proceed. He was not to run in the yard or on stairways, or call through a window. A system of fagging was in vogue. When, in 1795, Dwight, after consultation with the Corporation, tried to revise some of these laws, Professor Josiah Meigs and three tutors submitted a written protest. More humane rules would, they said, result in insubordination, throw "an unreasonable burden" on the faculty and bring "degradation" on the school. Yale would degenerate into a "Court of Dissipation." That the militantly Jeffersonian Meigs joined in such a conservative statement can best be explained by his predilection for violent controversy, first at Yale and later as president of the University of Georgia.

Disorder in the early colleges was not mere good-humored roistering. At the close of Dwight's own freshman year, the three lower classes were suspended for two months, charged with ill-treating the president, breaking tutors' windows, and threatening their lives. At about the same time some Harvard students on the way home from dinner at three in the morning "grossly insulted the President" by yells, challenges, curses, threats of burning his house, and by throwing clubs and stones. As has been noted, students in the South were often even more violent.

Following the French Revolution there was some inclination to blame this sort of thing on radical political views abroad in the land. Thus President Samuel Stanhope Smith believed the burning of Nassau Hall in 1802 was the work of incendiaries demoralized by antireligious principles. Whatever the cause of the trouble, President Smith was faced five years later with a riot of such proportions that he expelled 125 of a student body of 200.

Nor did things quiet down after the Napoleonic Wars. In the mid-nineteenth century Andrew White saw a clerical professor buried under a heap of mattresses, another driven through a broken door panel under a shower of books, boots, brushes, etc., and the president himself forced to leave a lecture room by a ladder from a window. On another occasion this worthy was kept at bay by a shower of beer bottles. This was at Hobart, which boasted that owing to the small number of students and its church connections, it was "able to exercise a direct Christian influence upon every young man committed to its care." At Lafayette where, in the 1860s, the faculty minutes state, "it is designed to make the Bible the central object of study in the whole college course," the same minutes record a more or less serious disturbance almost annually for that and the next two decades.

White sums up the reason for so much uproar at Hobart, a statement which applies to most colleges before 1860:

There was no other outlet for animal spirits of these youth. Athletics were unknown; there was no gymnasium, no ball playing and though the college was on a lake, no boating.

Town-and-gown rows were another problem. In New Haven sailors on leave would join town bullies to jeer at students— often the prelude to a fight. Even tutors were not safe: a town mob once sent a shower of clubs and stones through Professor Benjamin Silliman's windows. Animosity ran so high that all one summer he never left his house without carrying two loaded pistols. At Williams students dared not leave their rooms after dark for fear of attack by townspeople. In town-and-gown riots, especially around 1800, it is probable that radical political sentiments may have helped to inflame the underprivileged against the colleges. After all, only one person in about 1,500 ever became a college student.

Most riots, however, were not politically motivated. Competition with collegians for a limited number of girls has always been a source of resentment on the part of town boys. Then, too, the early-nineteenth-century student with his high hat and long-tailed coat offered a tempting target. In 1825 the Amherst faculty meted out very light penalties to students who had thrown stones and used profane language in a row with the local fire company. At the hearing it developed that the engine company had come out to drill about sundown on a spring evening. Seeing some students standing near by, the captain of the company turned the nozzle toward them and doused several. The faculty apparently felt that the students had some provocation for throwing stones.

One December evening in 1837 some Quaker students were returning to Haverford from an afternoon party. One of them, William Canby, noted: "We had a splendid time, but like to have had a row with the village loafers. John (Bull) Fuller knocked half a dozen of them down." Thus a Quaker peace prevailed. Such incidents are amusing bright spots in a picture that was more somber than a portrait of youth should be. Too often the student disorders of an earlier day are symptomatic less of high spirits than of a desperate, even brutal, attempt to break out of an intolerable system.

Considering all the evidence, it is hard not to conclude that in its official aspects the American college before the Civil War was a failure. The curriculum failed to meet the needs of an expanding modern nation; the religious training produced either revolt or, especially after 1800, a narrow orthodoxy which fought educational progress; and the system of rules and methods of instruction failed to develop mature, responsible adults.

Yet the American college as a whole was not a failure. The story of the successful features of the early colleges is the story of too often unheeded educational pioneers, but perhaps even more of an American people who developed a vital system of education despite the hidebound bigotry of college faculties. A few brilliant educational thinkers, various community pressures, and the American students themselves saved the colleges from their own folly.

2

False Dawn

The first attempt to develop a college curriculum to meet the needs of Americans came in 1756 at the College of Philadelphia, later the University of Pennsylvania. The philosophy of the course was developed in two pamphlets: Franklin's *Proposals Relating to the Education of Youth in Pennsylvania* (1749) and William Smith's *General Idea of the College of Mirania* (1753). Both of these proposed an education with four basic elements which a century or a century and a half later became characteristic of American college education: 1. preparation for varied professions and vocations, 2. the use of English rather than Latin, 3. emphasis on citizenship rather than religion, 4. education for the many rather than the few.

Franklin's *Proposals* led to his founding of an academy which eventually became the University of Pennsylvania. Smith's utopian *College of Mirania* was originally prepared for some gentlemen in New York who were planning a college there. However, Franklin, recognizing in Smith's plan the sort of educational system he was seeking, was influential in bringing Smith to Philadelphia. So it was Pennsylvania rather than Columbia which became the first modern college.

Philadelphia in the mid-eighteenth century was the logical place for a truly modern educational institution. Not only was it larger than New York and Boston; it was rapidly becoming next to London the largest city in the British commonwealth. Boston had been the port of entry for seventeenth-century Protestantism; Philadelphia was the port of entry for the eighteenth-century Enlightenment. Before the Revolution the Pennsylvania city was a center of trade with the West and South, with the West Indies, and with Europe. Hundreds of ships a year entered its port, bringing not only goods but scholars,

48

books, and ideas. Franklin's Philosophical Society, the leading scientific body in the country, drew together men like John Bartram, Benjamin Rush, and David Rittenhouse—all scientists who, like Franklin, became internationally known. Philadelphia had libraries, bookstores, and publishing houses. Increasingly the Quakers were being absorbed or pushed aside by a wealthy, sophisticated society living in handsome Georgian brick mansions and cultivating a taste for art, literature, and especially for good food and wines. By comparison Paul Revere's Boston was a hick town.

Philadelphia, if anywhere in the colonies, was the place for a new start in American college education. As with so much else in that city, Franklin began it, and as with so much else there, it declined after his death. But Franklin did not think specifically in terms of college training; it was the Reverend William Smith who organized basic ideas into a curriculum. Rarely, if ever, has a new educational program been so quickly given form and substance. To an amazing degree the actual college course followed the seemingly utopian plan of the College of Mirania.

Smith's plan was for a college with two main divisions: one for students preparing for the learned professions—divinity, law, physics, and the chief offices of state; the other for students destined for "the mechanic professions and all the remaining people of the country." This second division was not realized in Smith's lifetime, nor for over a century. And his ideal of some form of higher education for a whole people is still to come. It was the first part of his plan which formed the basis of the course adopted by the trustees in 1756. Two items are especially noteworthy: Smith's inclusion of medicine in the learned professions, and the emphasis on the training for government office.

The plan as outlined provided for a five-year course, based on a five-year prep school. The preparatory training was much along traditional lines, with a thorough grounding in Latin and Greek. The first year of college was also relatively traditional, except that the classical authors were Theocritus, Hesiod,

Homer, Xenophon, rather than the Greek Testament. Students were to study arithmetic and begin algebra and geometry.

But in the second year the course became original. Students were to devote "but a small space of time" to mathematics, logic, metaphysics, and were to be exercised in practical geometry, surveying of land and waters, making maps. There was to be provision for further improvement in Greek and Latin.

In the third year students were to study ethics, physics, natural history, "mechanic and experimental philosophy," and history. They were to read Plato, Cicero, Locke, Hutchinson, and Pufendorf.

The first three years were to give what today is called general education; the last two were to be devoted to practical training. In the fourth year the emphasis was to be on training in writing and speech. The means to this end were analytical criticism and practice in composition.

The fifth year was to include the study of agriculture and history—but not on a mere utilitarian level. Physics was part of the one, philosophy of the other. But the history was not, as was the custom elsewhere, chiefly ancient history; it was to come down to the present and conclude "with a view of our colonies in this hemisphere; their state, produce, interests, government, etc., taking some notice as they go along of the French and Spanish settlements that we are chiefly concerned with in trade." The exercises were to be chiefly in English. The Miranians "greatly condemn the practice of neglecting the mother tongue, and embarrassing a student by obliging him to speak or compose in a dead language."

And in contrast to the Calvinistic emphasis on religion, Smith proposed that "every Sunday night about an hour is spent in the study of Bible history." His emphasis was on citizenship:

What can we figure to ourselves more noble than the whole wisdom of a community thus using every human effort to train up and secure to the state a succession of good citizens to the last generations?

As actually adopted the curriculum was compressed into three years of ten months each. Instead of the usual three dreary years of drill upon Latin and Greek, this was confined to the first year. A third of the freshman course was devoted to mathematics. Logic was begun. In the second, or junior, year the study of the classics became a course not in grammar and syntax but in rhetoric and literary criticism: Longinus, Horace's *Art of Poetry*, Aristotle's *Poetics*, selections from Quintilian— all studied critically. Mathematics was continued, with work also in surveying, dialing, and navigation. In the third term the course was split into three main divisions: moral philosophy, natural philosophy and composition, written and oral.

In the third, or senior, year these three divisions continued. Lest the old terms *moral philosophy* and *natural philosophy* obscure the nature of the subject matter, it should be noted that moral philosophy was broken down into ethics, political science, history, trade and commerce; natural philosophy included mechanics, hydrostatics, pneumatics, light, etc.—in other words, physics, botany, zoology, chemistry, including the chemistry of agriculture. It was an education focused on the world in which the student would live and earn a living.

In contrast with the textbook education then in vogue, the published outline of the course carried a list of collateral readings for the student's "private hours." This included philosophy, English literature, literary criticism, history, science, and the Bible—the last to be read daily.

Following the outline of the plan came a statement beginning with a paragraph which could well be incorporated in every college catalogue:

Concerning the foregoing plan, it is to be remarked that life itself being too short to attain a perfect acquaintance with the whole circle of the sciences, nothing can be proposed in any scheme of collegiate education, but to lay such a general foundation in all the branches of literature, as may enable the youth to perfect themselves in those particular parts, to which their business or genius, may afterwards lead them, and scarce anything has more obstructed the advancement of sound learning, than a vain imagination, that a few years, spent at college, can render youth such absolute masters of science, as to absolve them from all future study.

The whole influence of the faculty was to "propagate a contrary doctrine" in the hope "that the youth committed to their care, will neither at college, nor afterwards, rest satisfied with a general knowledge, as is to be derived from the public lectures and exercises." Had the whole influence of faculties been more often thrown in this direction, contemporary college graduates might less often feel smug about "keeping up with the world" by reading *The Saturday Evening Post* and *Reader's Digest*.

During Provost Smith's regime literature was not something which had existed only in the remote past; it was even encouraged in college. Four years after he became head of the college, he helped to launch *The American Magazine, or Monthly Chronicle for The British Colonies*, a literary magazine whose chief contributors were young men from the college. This was no mere local student publication; it had 850 subscribers, from New England to the West Indies. Although it endured for only a year, it published the work of two students who made some mark in American literature: Thomas Godfrey, the first American playwright, and Francis Hopkinson, essayist, poet, and signer of the Declaration of Independence. In its brief career it became the most distinguished college publication of its century.

Smith's encouragement of creative writing, his emphasis on collateral reading, and the suggestion for later specialization according to the special bents or needs of individuals are all far different from the regimentation of minds under the traditional system. Unlike the Yale faculty of seventy-five years later or Robert Maynard Hutchins two centuries later, Smith had no notion of an educational program engraved on tablets of stone.

In contrast to a curriculum based on the ideals of the Enlightenment, Samuel Johnson stated in 1754 as the aim of King's College (Columbia):

The chief thing that is aimed at in this College is to teach and engage the Children to *know God in Jesus Christ,* and to love and serve him in all *Sobriety, Godliness, and Righteousness* of Life. . . .

However there is a note of modernity in his "lastly," which included surveying, navigation, geography, history, husbandry, commerce and government—"and of everything *useful* for the Comfort, the Convenience and Elegance of Life, in the chief *Manufactures* relating to any of these Things. . . ."

Thus as the curriculums of the seventeenth century were designed to train ministers of the gospel, those at Philadelphia and King's were to meet the needs of men going into business, government, and the law. It is significant that the attempt to justify the traditional curriculum on other grounds than vocational usefulness came at a time when it was no longer vocationally useful to most students. As we have seen, the Yale faculty report of 1827 came the same year that the Amherst faculty bluntly stated that the old curriculum was "not sufficiently modern and comprehensive, to meet the exigencies of the age and country in which we live."

The frequently held notion that a cultural college education became gradually perverted into vocationalism seems to be almost the reverse of the truth. What happened was that educational programs designed to meet the intellectual and professional needs of their periods were later defended on cultural grounds when they ceased to be useful.

It would seem that the Philadelphia curriculum was sufficiently flexible to be adapted to changing conditions. At first it did have some influence on other institutions, or it might be more accurate to say that the eighteenth-century ideas and needs which produced it produced others somewhat like it. It cannot be said with certainty that the reforms at William and Mary were or were not influenced by William Smith. These reforms are due chiefly to Thomas Jefferson, who had of course spent considerable time in Philadelphia. Furthermore, Smith's ideas had been published both in the original pamphlet and in *The Pennsylvania Gazette.* When Smith went to Washington College in Maryland in 1782, he carried the curriculum with him. Thus even though Jefferson did not specifically mention Smith's curriculum, there is a real possibility that he knew of it.

Jefferson stated that when in 1779 he became one of the Visitors of William and Mary, he brought about a change in the organization of the college. This resulted in abolishing the grammar school and the professorships of Divinity and Oriental Languages. For these were substituted a professorship of Law and Police, one of Anatomy, Medicine and Chemistry, and one of Modern Languages. As the charter limited the number of professorships to six, Fine Arts and the Law of Nature and of Nations were added to the chair of Moral Philosophy; Natural History to the chair of Mathematics and Natural Philosophy. The substitutions clearly indicate a shift from the seventeenth-century curriculum to one emphasizing law, politics, and science. The teaching of Fine Arts was new in America. Most revolutionary of all were the three provisions: 1. that a knowledge of the ancient languages was not required for admission; 2. that students might attend what courses they pleased and in what order they chose, and 3. that the time required for a degree depended on the qualifications of the candidate. Thus in one jump the College of William and Mary had abolished entrance requirements in Greek and Latin, had adopted an elective system, and had broken the lock step of the traditional four-year course.

However the new dawn was by no means at hand. Both Pennsylvania and William and Mary went into a period of decline as a result of the Revolution. The troubles at Pennsylvania were aggravated by the political activity of Provost Smith —a situation not unknown to colleges since.

First of all Smith intrigued mightily to bring the college completely under Anglican control although it had been founded "on a coalition of all religious Societies." This naturally brought opposition from the Presbyterians. Next, Smith took the side of the Penns in their controversy with Franklin and the Assembly. Only three years after Smith's appointment

Franklin was writing in exasperation that he wished Smith would "learn to mind Party-writing and Party-Politicks less, and his proper Business more"—a wish which has been repeated at Pennsylvania about a more recent president. At one point Smith managed to get himself jailed for publishing "a most virulent and slanderous address" against the Assembly. With the coming of the Revolution he was accused, with considerable reason, of Tory sympathies. The Assembly took a hand in the matter and Smith resigned in 1791. William and Mary also had political troubles. Because of its connection with the Church of England, it too was an anathema to ardent Whigs. The college barely kept alive during the Revolution.

After Smith's resignation the resources of the rechristened University of Pennsylvania were at a low ebb and there were controversies about its operation. During the first decade of the nineteenth century, the course was reduced to two years, and at one point, 1807, there were only seventeen students in the institution. Geography, history, and chronology disappeared from the curriculum, and English translations of the classics were banned. The history of the next thirty years shows a nominal adherence to some of Smith's curriculum, but with the loss of flexibility and liberty of private study. Instead of leading the way for other colleges, Pennsylvania increasingly fell into the traditional pattern. Post-Revolutionary Philadelphia was a wealthy city, but after the death of Franklin it was no longer the cultural center of the nation. Harvard, Yale, and Princeton—all in smaller and less wealthy communities— were eventually richly endowed by friends and alumni. The University of Pennsylvania never received comparable gifts and endowments. Philadelphia's taste for good food and wines has been more constant and enduring than its interest in college education.

It was the South and West that led educational evolution during the first part of the nineteenth century. Horace Holley, a graduate of Dwight's Yale, tried to make Transylvania University in Kentucky a liberal nonsectarian institution. When he was called to the presidency in 1817, the majority sentiment in

Kentucky was Jeffersonian in politics, liberal or agnostic in religion, and nonpuritanical in social views and mores. Holley's appointment was made possible when the legislature replaced a board of trustees dominated by Presbyterians with one composed of men of affairs: judges, legislators, businessmen.

Holley's influence is less noteworthy for curricular reform than for the liberal, undogmatic approach he introduced into the classroom. In his course in Moral Philosophy he encouraged students to examine conflicting views. He, the faculty and trustees drew up a plan to invite as chapel speakers representatives of the leading religious denominations. The Catholics, Baptists, Episcopalians, and Methodists agreed to support the plan, but the Presbyterians refused and tried to get the trustees to repudiate Holley's religious instruction and opinions.

A traveler in 1819 noted that Holley had selected his faculty not for their unanimity of religious views but for their ability —a radical departure from custom. Equally unusual for a college president of the time was Holley's social life. He attended the theater and entertained extensively. Among his guests were notables such as President Monroe, General Jackson, Lafayette and frequently Henry Clay. Even more unusual in a day when faculty and students rarely mingled outside the classroom, he invited students to his parties. He even offered a course in manners to such students as wished to attend.

All this led to a prolonged and bitter attack by the Presbyterians, who accused him of being a Socinian—the theologian's word for deist—an infidel, a corrupter of youth. In sermons and letters to the press, preachers ranted about the theater, the card and billiard table, the ballroom. Horrendous tales were spread concerning students who found his parties too ungodly to endure. Apparently pious students were sometimes sent as spies to his social gatherings. The sectarian attack, using, often unscrupulously, the weapons of theology and puritanical mores, was a pattern which was often to be repeated in holy wars against state universities. At the University of Georgia, President Meigs had been forced to resign in 1803 under an early fundamentalist onset. In Kentucky the Presbyterians numbered only about 3,000 in a population of half a million, but so savage and unremitting was their attack that Holley resigned in 1827. As Sonne puts it in his history of the university: "Calvinism denied was indeed a ferocious force."

Meigs and Holley were the first of a long line of distinguished college presidents, including such men as Thomas Cooper of South Carolina, Horace Mann of Antioch, Henry Philip Tappan of Michigan, and William Watts Folwell of Minnesota, to be crucified by crusading sectarians.

After Holley's resignation Transylvania struggled along for fifteen years under a rapid succession of presidents and then expired. In pronouncing its elegy Sonne concludes:

The ideal of a great central state university, open to all religious denominations, and conducted on liberal principles, had been effectively quashed. . . . Collegiate education in Kentucky now became the function of the small denominational college.

Other state colleges in the South were more successful in resisting sectarian attacks. Georgia, North Carolina and South Carolina all chartered state colleges or universities before 1802, and Jefferson's University of Virginia opened its doors in 1825. Alabama followed in 1831. Only Vermont (1791) in the North, and Indiana (1820) in the West had founded public institutions by that time. Despite their public character, religion was still an important force in the curriculum, and required chapel was the rule. Coulter, in his history of the University of Georgia, deplores the fact that the Yale curriculum was introduced there with little change. Even so there was a greater emphasis on science than at Yale, and President Thomas Cooper of South Carolina was a freethinking scientist of the Jeffersonian school.

Of all these early quasi-state institutions Virginia is the most noteworthy for educational pioneering. To a considerable extent it took up where William and Mary left off. Because of the sectarian character of the older college Jefferson urged the founding of a nonsectarian state-controlled institution. He had in mind a real university whose students were to be college graduates. No genuine university then existed in America despite the brave assumption of that term by a number of institutions. However, because the country was not ripe for a real university, the plan was modified to create an essentially undergraduate institution.

The unique feature of the school was that the student might choose any one of eight departments: Ancient Languages, Modern Languages, Mathematics, Natural Philosophy, Natural History, Anatomy and Medicine, Moral Philosophy, or Law. Not all departments went into immediate operation. As at William and Mary there were flexible entrance requirements and the length of the course depended on the student's performance. Another novel feature in a period of patriarchal presidents was a system of rotating chairmen of the faculty in place of a permanent head of the university.

Jefferson put much more emphasis on the library than was customary. He himself drew up a detailed plan of classification including such subdivisions as Law—Nature and Nations, Law —Common, Law—Equity, Law—Merchant, Law—Maritime, Law—Foreign, Law—Civil Polity; and for Fine Arts: Architecture, Gardening, Painting, Sculpture, Music, Epic Poetry, Romantic Poetry, Pastoral Poetry, Didactic Poetry. Unlike most modern makers of library systems, Jefferson had some knowledge of the fields he was classifying. However, there were two characteristic exclusions: books designed only for amusement, and religious books of a sectarian nature. The first appropriation was $10,000. When the first wagonload of books arrived, the aged man rode over to inspect them and at once discovered a misprint in the title of Gibbon's *Decline and Fall*. In his will he had provided that most of his library should go to the university; however, it had to be sold by his grandson to pay creditors. Even so, the library selected for the college by Jefferson had 6,860 volumes—about the same number that Yale had accumulated in well over a century.

At first the Virginia library was, according to the usual custom, open only one day a week for about an hour, but by 1826 it was accessible to students daily except Sunday. By the following year the library was subscribing to all the principal American and English reviews, although soon after it was necessary to ask the faculty to help defray the cost.

Another idea of Jefferson's, student self-government, with a jury of students to try cases, had to be abandoned almost at once. American students of the era were not a well-behaved lot, and the sons of planters were especially impatient of rules and regulations. To them the system of student enforcement smacked of spying and talebearing. After a brief period of such anarchy that all the professors tendered their resignations, Jefferson himself reluctantly agreed "that coercion must be resorted to, where confidence has been disappointed."

Nor was the elective system at first a complete success. This too was something for which the immature, raw boys of the time were not ready. In the absence of clearly defined classes— freshman, sophomore, etc.—students failed to develop group loyalties which fostered a desire to graduate with the class. And the lack of well-defined prerequisites led students to elect courses for which they were not ready. The result was that in the early day two out of three students dropped out at the end of the first year.

On the whole, however, Virginia managed to retain the Jeffersonian ideals of democracy and freedom of thought. The elective system remained, and eventually student self-government came back. In a period of growing orthodoxy in religion and triumphant traditionalism in college education, Virginia remained perhaps the one liberal college in America before 1850. By 1838 it was larger than Harvard; in 1856 there were 645 students—more than at either Yale or Harvard; even four years after the Civil War it had more students than Dartmouth or Amherst, and only 171 fewer than Yale. Virginia long remained one of the largest and most influential of American colleges.

Quite a different type of educational pioneering was under-taken at Oberlin. Its origin and special character was the result of the converging of a number of early-nineteenth-century forces: religious revivalism, popular democracy, utopian ideal-ism. It absorbed into itself at one time or another almost every reformist enthusiasm of an expanding nation, a nation passion-ately engaged in an attempt to form a new and better social order. Thus at Oberlin brilliant educational pioneering was combined with health fads; ideals of racial and sex equality developed side by side with religious bigotry. It is not sur-prising that foreign travelers interested in American education headed for Oberlin. The story of Oberlin College is one of the most interesting in our educational history.

The impetus for Oberlin came from New England. As Robert S. Fletcher states in his history of the college:

The early annals of Oberlin College are a part of the history of the mighty outpouring of New Englanders over the nation and the world which took place in the late eighteenth and early nineteenth centuries.

Christian workers, especially in Connecticut, saw the West as a place to make a new nation and a new world "purified of evil in order that from it might be spread to all the rest of the Earth the millennial order foretold in Scripture."

These Christian soldiers marching as to war organized them-selves into countless battalions: missionary societies, Bible societies, Sabbath reformers, religious education and Sunday-school societies, tract societies, the Yale Band—a missionary group dedicated to setting up schools and colleges in the South and West. Allied to these were antislavery societies, peace societies, temperance societies, physiological reform and moral reform societies.

As Fletcher says of Oberlin:

Nowhere else was the vision quite so clearly seen; nowhere else was consecration to the great Cause quite so complete and fer-vent. . . . In Oberlin the story of Christian reform is com-plete; Oberlin was the embodiment of the movement.

The two men most responsible for the founding of the college were Reverend Charles Grandison Finney and Reverend John Jay Shipherd. Finney had been a lawyer, but gave up his practice to become a revival preacher of tremendous power. Even his photographs show the hypnotic quality of his eyes. Shipherd, a friend of Finney's, was one of the "new measures" men, a group which preached a doctrine of "human ability" to accept Christ and live a good life. The logic of revivalism seemed to demand this idea that men could choose salvation. Dwight's modified Calvinism at Yale had pointed in this direction. On the other hand, Princeton and the colleges under its influence represented the orthodox doctrines of divine sufficiency, predestination, and total depravity.

The first activity of the "new measures" men nearly wrecked Hamilton College. One of them, Reverend George W. Gale, organized the Oneida Institute to educate young men preparing for the ministry. This was one of the early "manual-labor" schools where students worked on a farm to help pay expenses. Another of the organizers of the school, Reverend John Monteith, was a professor at Hamilton College and a believer in a more practical education. It soon became clear that the new academy was a rival to the older college. At a revival in Utica, Professor Monteith prayed:

Thou knowest, O Lord, that the faculty of Hamilton College have sinned in high places; and we pray thee, O Lord, if they are obstacles to thy work, that thou wouldst remove them out of thy way.

In the course of the uproar over religion and education many Hamilton students went elsewhere, leaving the college tottering.

Gale and Monteith went on to preach the manual-labor idea and found other manual-labor schools. The theory was that moral truth was linked with manual labor, an idea Ruskin was later to preach. Gale and others founded a Society for Promoting Manual Labor in Literary Institutions and apparently sold the idea to Finney.

In the meantime Shipherd, then a "new measures" pastor in Elyria in the Western Reserve, planned a school "to educate school teachers for our desolate valley, and many ministers for our dying world." He selected Oberlin, then an uncleared wilderness, for the site. With great dreams but no money Shipherd went east in search of funds. He and his followers collected tiny sums, for instance, $14.50 in Geneva, N. Y., but they prayed daily "that the barley loaf be baked at that institution which shall make the camp of Midian tremble." Shipherd did manage to get a gift of 500 acres of land, and an agreement with the owners to sell 5,000 additional acres to colonists at $1.50 per acre. Thus developed a unique feature of the Oberlin plan: the simultaneous development of a college and a community devoted to the same ideals and having the same apocalyptic vision.

The school opened its doors in 1833 in a frame boarding-house while the land was still being cleared with the help of a steam sawmill. (There had been a long argument over the desirable size of the steam engine, conducted with all the fervor of theological debate.) The collegiate department opened the following year, and Shipherd was already projecting the addition of a theological school. "The system of education in this Institution will provide for the body and heart as well as the intellect; for it aims at the best education for the *whole man*," wrote Shipherd. Therefore, the manual-labor department was to be regarded not as an appendage but as an integral part of the literary department. Thus in an uncleared wilderness and obscured by the fog of theological debate, Oberlin College introduced into American education the Greek ideal of a sound mind in a sound body. Two hundred years of "classical" education had failed to grasp this fundamental classical ideal.

During all this time Finney had been in the background, the chief figure in the "new measures" group, but not in the founding of Oberlin. He was brought into the picture after an upheaval at near-by Lane Institute, an upheaval which was prophetic of things to come. Lane, a manual-labor institution in Cincinnati, had developed an active antislavery movement among students and faculty. Conservative businessmen on the board of trustees had tried to forbid antislavery societies there and even discussion of the topic. After all, much of the business in Cincinnati was with the South. The result was that a group of Lane rebels offered to set up a theological school at Oberlin if Oberlin would accept Negroes. Oberlin students voted 36 to 26 against this—a majority of the men voting yes, the women overwhelmingly no. But Oberlin had been offered $10,000, plus $600 a year for eight professors, if Finney was brought in as Professor of Theology. He accepted on condition that the faculty should control the admission of students and the internal affairs of the institution. The trustees accepted the conditions—which implied the admission of Negroes.

Oberlin was not the first college to admit Negroes: one had graduated from Bowdoin in 1827 and possibly another from Dartmouth in 1836. However it became the first college to have them as a sizable proportion of the student body—probably about five per cent. Most of these were in the preparatory and ladies' courses, but in 1862 Mary Jane Patterson graduated to become probably the first Negro woman in the world to receive a bachelor's degree.

From the start Oberlin had been coeducational. Some of the older academies had been open to both men and women, but no colleges had been. It was commonly believed that women had neither the mental capacity nor physical stamina for higher education. A more immediate reason for the all-male college was that the colleges were designed to educate for the ministry, law, medicine, and public office—all occupations closed to women. But from the first Oberlin had been concerned with the education of teachers.

After two years the faculty met with the trustees to discuss the results of the experiment of having men and women together in classes. The faculty reported that the plan was working excellently in the cultivation of mind and manners for both sexes. Ten years later a special committee on the subject complained of men and women spending too much time together—in the evening taking walks and buggy rides—

and of too early matrimonial engagements. The committee recommended stricter rules rather than abolition of coeducation. One of these which still remains in effect is the one forbidding students to marry while in college. Whatever its effect at first, it later led to liaisons between engaged couples or to secret marriages.

Because of poor preparation and more limited occupational objectives, women tended to be enrolled in the Female Department, a noncollegiate course. However, in 1837 four were admitted to the Collegiate Course, and four years later three of them became the first women in the world to receive bona fide A.B. degrees.

The influence of Asa Mahon, the first president, on the educational program is somewhat hard to assess. For one thing the curriculum was far less original than other phases of the institution. Oberlin did not, as did some Western colleges, banish the classics, but Hebrew was often substituted. In 1839 the requirement in the college course was 800 pages of Latin as compared to 1,300 at Yale. Instead of Horace, Plautus, Seneca, and Livy, the students read Hugo Grotius' *De Veritate Religionis Christianae,* a manual of apologetics. Some Greek classics were read and 300 pages from the Greek Testament. In 1845 the trustees resolved that no student should fail to graduate because "of any want of knowledge in the heathen classics." Cowper, Milton, the English Bible, and sacred music were part of the course. However between 1840 and 1860 the curriculum gradually came into conformity with those elsewhere. Cowper and Milton were casualties and the classic authors came in.

As educators Mahon and Finney were not notable for curricular reform but for the superheated revivalistic atmosphere which they fostered. It started off with a bang. Finney and the new faculty were inaugurated in a huge tent holding 3,000 people, over which flew a banner proclaiming "Holiness to the Lord." For hours the speakers held forth to an audience which, according to Shipherd, hung on the speakers' lips without a sign of weariness. For the next fifteen years there were con-

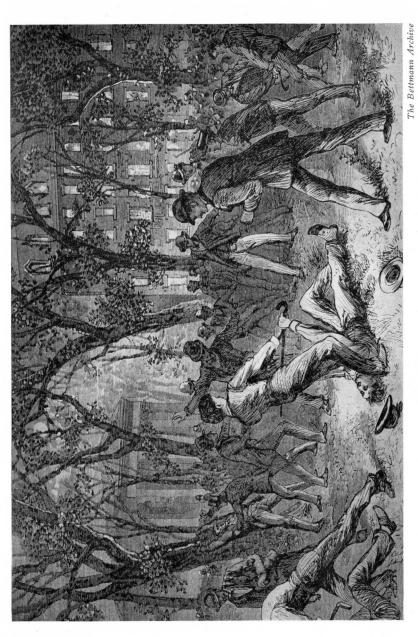

THE ANNUAL CANE FIGHT BETWEEN FRESHMEN AND SOPHOMORES, COLUMBIA, 1877

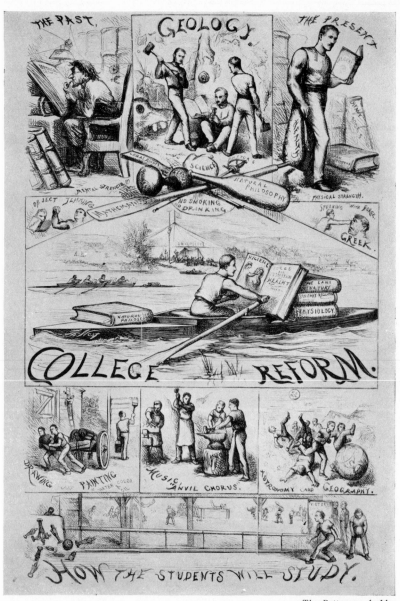

PHYSICAL EDUCATION—THEN AND NOW

Thomas Nast's satire on overemphasis on physical education, 1869.

stant revivals at the college, some lasting several weeks and one, celebrating Finney's return from England in 1860, going on for two months. One meeting whipped up such emotion that a student fell prostrate and the rest clapped and shouted, "Glory to God!" In the early years professors visited students in their rooms to hold religious conversations with each one. Official reports noted the prevalence or the scarcity of conversions.

In the 1840s students rose as early as four o'clock to pray aloud in their rooms. There was chapel before breakfast and evening prayers at six. Classes were opened with a prayer or a hymn, and after supper students would read a chapter from the Bible and pray once more. There were of course two services on Sunday.

It is not surprising that in this superheated religious atmosphere students were attracted to all sorts of cults. One became a Mormon and married nine wives—after he left college of course; there was a rule against student marriages. There was interest in Millerite and millennial theories. Oberlin's own "heresy," which led to many attacks by orthodox Calvinists, was "perfectionism" or "sanctification"—an extension of the doctrine of human ability to find salvation. President Mahon argued that Christ could give a person complete victory over sin, and that he could attain to Christian perfection before death. This doctrine, preached more or less by most Oberlin leaders, helps to explain the multitudinous prayers and frequent revivals.

It helps too to explain the reformist zeal which led to the formation of a peace society, moral-reform societies, and anti-slavery agitation. In these Oberlin was unique only in emphasis. In the 1830s there were moral-reform or moral-purification societies at Brown, Williams, Oneida Institute, and Amherst. At Western Reserve there was a standing committee on lewdness. Oberlin of course went them one better and had two such societies, one for men and one for women. The women's group, which included married women from the faculty and the community, was the more active. Three "reformed ladies" from

New York were brought in and enrolled as students. The society adopted a resolution providing that members should report all cases of immorality at the next meeting, and if a delinquency occurred among students, members should report it to the Female Principal. They listened to such things as a student's account of her perils on a journey from Oberlin to Boston and her warning to beware of gentlemen too ready to proffer assistance. One of the married women told the girls to engrave on their hearts "as with the point of a diamond" the maxim: *Never allow yourself to be caressed or fondled over by the other sex till after marriage.*

However, the activity which most distinguished Oberlin was antislavery agitation. In the South the name Oberlin became a byword for fanatical abolitionism; in New England it was a shining symbol of a heroic struggle. From the mid-thirties until the Civil War, Oberlin was an important station on the Underground Railway. In 1837, when a former student brought a slave in a wagon, the fugitive was taken to supper in the dining hall, then to the sitting room where crowds of students flocked around. A bodyguard of students armed with dirks and butcher knives went along on the northward journey. Townsmen, students, faculty and officials were all involved in illegal activity. Students looked on the arrival of a band of Negroes as a chance for a lark. The pent-up youthful drives which in other colleges led to purposeless riots found outlet in an exciting game of cops and robbers. Students crossed into Dixie to guide slaves to freedom. One was jailed for nearly five years, another for four. A woman graduate, Delia Webster, was found guilty but pardoned.

On one occasion, as a visiting speaker was finishing a commencement address, the firebell rang to call out townsmen and students to rescue some Negroes threatened with abduction. On another, students, faculty and citizens rescued a Negro from the slave catchers, drove him to Oberlin in a buckboard and lodged him in the home of James Harris Fairchild, professor of Moral Philosophy. The slave got to Canada but the rescuers were jailed. Before the trial was concluded, four slave catchers were indicted for kidnaping in Lorain County. An exchange of prisoners was effected, and the Oberlin men were escorted to the station in Cleveland with a brass band and salutes fired from cannon. At Oberlin the senior class held a special reception for Professor Peck, one of the released prisoners, and presented him with a seventeen-volume set of the *Works of W. H. Prescott* bound in sheepskin. Rarely has a professor been so well received.

On the day John Brown was hanged, the college bell was tolled for one hour and there was a mass meeting in the chapel.

It was of course fanaticism such as this on both sides which made civil war inevitable. And to a large degree the fanaticism of Oberlin was a natural product of a crusading Protestantism which sought short cuts to the millennium. The frantic revivals, the moral-reform societies, the prohibitionists, the intransigent abolitionists were all part of the same cultural pattern. Oberlin was a microcosm of a large part of nineteenth-century America.

On the positive side it must be recognized that to a degree unknown elsewhere in the colleges of the time Oberlin students were participants in the larger world outside the classroom. Students gave time to teach freed Negroes; they participated in the activities of the community; they went out as teachers and missionaries—later as soldiers. They were too often fanatical, yes, but slavery was the great national problem. The fanaticism of the abolitionists should not obscure the fact that these men and women living near the border of slave states recognized a social and economic system as alien to a free, moral America. Exhausted soil, ignorant, brutalized poor whites were also products of the system. And in the Western states people knew firsthand the immense pressures for the extension of slavery. Oberlin graduates went to Kansas; Oberlin students sat in classrooms with illegitimate mulatto children sent there by their planter fathers. Oberlin students saw at firsthand fugitive slaves illiterate and ill taught in religion; they heard Negroes tell of separated families, of savage punishments—exaggerated no doubt, but with a core of fact. The slave catchers who pursued them were a notoriously unscrupulous, brutal class of men. For Oberlin students slavery was not a remote evil, not the sentimentalized abstraction it so often became in New England.

If too often Oberlinites went to extremes, so too did those who opposed abolition. Free speech, the freedom to preach the truth as opponents of slavery saw it seemed threatened. Mobs broke up meetings, threw rotten eggs, thrashed students with bullwhips, tarred and feathered them. The victims became heroes at the college. Abolition was not popular in Ohio, or in the North, until the slaveholders' greed for new territories proved insatiable. Oberlin provided students with something too often lacking in the American college: a sense of dedication to a great cause. They could say with Justice Holmes, "Our hearts were touched with fire."

This extended account of Oberlin is not due merely to the unusual features of the college but to its importance. It must not be thought that this was a tiny, local institution. In the early years a majority of the students came from New York and New England. They took the Erie Canal, sleeping twenty-six to thirty in a ten by twelve-foot cabin, crossed Lake Erie on small steamboats, and then took a coach over the worst roads in the world from Cleveland to Oberlin. By 1852 the railroad had reached the town. The first generation of faculty had men from Yale, Andover, Dartmouth, Williams, and Hamilton. By 1841 Oberlin had over 500 students as compared with a few over 200 at Harvard and 400 at Yale. Pennsylvania had a handful over 100. Eleven years later the enrollment exceeded 1,000, making Oberlin probably the largest educational institution in the nation. Many of these, of course, were in the Preparatory Department, but Fletcher estimates that 99 out of 100 Oberlinites went out as missionaries for Oberlinism.

Because of its unique features Oberlin became a subject of violent controversy. Even its scandals increased its fame. Professor John P. Cowles, a Yale graduate, and therefore a champion of the classics and foe of coeducation, also ridiculed the

dietetic reforms and publicly attacked the doctrine of sanctification. In fact he wrote sixteen letters to the newspapers, attacking Oberlin. The trustees, feeling that he did not quite fit
in, fired him. Professor Cowles charged that their action was
due to his having once brought a pepper shaker to the table.

A freethinking student, Delazon Smith, was expelled from
the literary societies and, on charges of certain Oberlinites,
jailed. In 1837 he engaged in the sport of kicking Alma Mater
in the teeth by publishing *Oberlin Unmasked.* He attacked
the neglect of the classics, the manual-labor system, the Graham
diet, coeducation, revivalism, and abolitionism. What gave his
book considerable circulation were his charges of immorality
among students and the teaching of miscegenation. (There
were no interracial marriages at Oberlin.) Smith's book went
into erotic detail.

Then a preparatory student who wrote obscene letters to a
coed was beaten up in the woods. Some of the townsmen and
students were tried and found guilty of assault. An Elyria
paper called them "lynchers." Shortly after this, Horace Taylor,
one of the confessed lynchers and editor of the *Oberlin
Evangelist,* was proved guilty of embezzling *Evangelist* funds,
of stealing from the post office, of seducing a young servant
and procuring an abortion. Taylor had also been active in
the Seventh Commandment Cause, a moral-reform society.

To a large number of Americans, Oberlin was a name for
dangerous radicalism and immorality. But it was that very radicalism which brought throngs of students even before the first
building was completed and while President Mahon was still
living in a log cabin. The ultraconservatism of almost every
other college except Virginia, which was expensive and Southern, left the Northern liberal or radical student nowhere else
to go. Low fees and the manual-labor system made college
education possible for hundreds of men and women who could
not have obtained one otherwise. Students at other colleges,
notably Dartmouth, had worked for their own expenses, but
Oberlin made this part of its system. To be a pioneer in coeducation, in educating the self-supporting student, in racial

equality, and in developing practical education—this was no small achievement.

A very different sort of educational pioneering developed at the University of Michigan. William and Mary, Pennsylvania, Transylvania, and Virginia had their sources in the Enlightenment, with some influence of French education; Oberlin was a child of militant nineteenth-century Protestantism; Michigan showed the impact of the German university system.

In the 1830s two men sitting on a log in a clearing in the forest in the Northwest Territory discussed a grandiose plan for a state-supported system of schools culminating in a great university. The men were the Reverend John D. Pierce, an alumnus of Brown, and Isaac E. Carey, a lawyer and a graduate of Trinity. Carey had got hold of an English translation of an American edition of *Rapport sur l'état de l'instruction publique en Prusse.* Pierce had read it and conceived the plan for the system of education which he outlined to Carey that day in the forest. The plan had three main features: a State Superintendent of Public Instruction to administer the whole school system; a Board of Regents appointed by the governor to have charge of the university; and a provision that land grants would not be released under political pressure.

After some discussion the two men became missionaries for the plan. Carey went to see the twenty-four-year-old governor, Stephen D. Mason. Mason, a Jackson appointee, had briefly attended Transylvania. In the plan Carey described, the governor saw the implement for his ideal of a free education which he was trying to incorporate in the new state constitution. Mason sent Pierce east to study colleges and academies.

When Michigan was admitted to the Union in 1837, Carey had managed to get Congress to provide that the usual grant of 48,000 acres should belong to the state rather than to individual townships. Thus Michigan was able immediately to organize a university. A Board of Regents was appointed that same year to assume control of America's first real state university. Others like North Carolina and Georgia were essentially state-aided colleges.

The projected university immediately experienced that bane of publicly controlled institutions—political pressure and finagling. The public lands were sold to squatters at low cost; the next governor began to undermine the educational structure by getting the Superintendent of Public Instruction to quit and by firing Professor Asa Gray, the famous botanist and the first faculty member appointed for the university. But building had begun, and when another governor came in he looked over the four faculty residences and the one classroom building connected by plank sidewalks across a sea of mud. "Well," he said, "we've got the buildings. . . . I don't think they're good for anything else, so we might as well declare the University open." Thus in 1841 began the institution which within twenty-five years was to be the largest college in America.

It was the coming of Henry Philip Tappan as president in 1851 which began the transformation of a frontier college into a great university. Tappan, suggested for the position by George Bancroft, was a graduate of Union College, a minister, and professor of philosophy at New York University. He had traveled in Europe, where he had come to admire the German university system. Even before he came to Michigan he had written:

In our country we have no Universities. . . . They have neither libraries and material of learning, generally, nor the number of professors and courses of lectures, nor the large and free organization which go to make up Universities.

Basically a conservative, he argued that the multiplication of colleges "to place them at everyone's door" had cheapened education by attempting to put it within reach of everyone.

He at once set about building Michigan on the German pattern. Arguing that it was not the function of a university to provide board and lodging, he abolished dormitories and used the space for a library, museum of natural history, and art gallery. The change was vastly more radical than a mere shift of students to town boardinghouses; it ran counter to the whole *in loco parentis* philosophy of American colleges. For two hundred years faculties had used a great part of their time and energy trying to act as policemen. At Tappan's urging departments of physics and civil engineering were established and in 1858 an M.A. program was begun. He brought in such faculty members as Dr. Francis Brunnow from the Royal Observatory of Prussia; Henry Simmons Frieze, who had studied at the University of Berlin and who later became president of Michigan; Andrew White, who became the first president of Cornell.

Such men soon gave Michigan a vitality often lacking in the older colleges. White, who had turned down a job at Yale because of the fetters of old-fashioned orthodoxy, introduced the kind of teaching he had experienced at Berlin and Paris. He discarded the Yale system of rote recitation from textbooks and introduced the lecture system with collateral reading. Students were encouraged to think on national problems. Instead of holding aloof from students as was then customary, he invited his classes to his home once a fortnight. Here they had an opportunity to browse in his huge personal library, to see firsthand a medieval missal or psalter and to read directly from the works of Luther, Erasmus, Robespierre, and Marat. White tried to make history "less a matter of annals, and more and more a record of the unfolding of humanity."

He found in his classes energetic young men, often poorly prepared, but eager to discuss historical questions. In order to keep up with his students White found he had to study as never before. In his classes were some of the ablest minds he ever encountered. From among them came senators, congressmen, judges, professors, lawyers, heads of business enterprises and foreign ministers. One of them, Moses Coit Tyler, became a famous historian of American literature. At Michigan, White found the student discussions "of a higher range than any [he] had known at Yale."

President Tappan himself taught a course in English literature which included readings in Scott, Wordsworth, Byron, Shelley, and Tennyson—in other words, recent and contemporary literature. Even a century later some of the English department at Princeton regarded such writers as too modern to be worth serious study by graduate students.

The whole atmosphere was different from puritanical Oberlin. White, remembering the elm-shaded campuses of New England, got students interested in helping him to plant trees on the unkempt, muddy campus at Ann Arbor. In the library building Tappan built up an art gallery with copies of famous paintings and sculpture. Professor Frieze, a superb pianist and a collector of Bohemian folk songs, used to come over to White's house, where there was the only piano in town, to enjoy musical evenings. He, Mrs. White and Professor Brunnow would play Beethoven, Handel, Mozart, Haydn and Weber. President Tappan scandalized the prohibitionists by serving wine at his table and by telling students that if they wanted a glass of beer to stop and get it at a German saloon.

At a banquet in 1902 White said of Tappan:

To him more than to any other is due the fact that about the year 1850, out of the old system of sectarian instruction mainly in petty colleges obedient to deteriorated traditions of English methods, there began to be developed universities drawing their ideals and methods from Germany.

Such radical innovations naturally stirred up controversy. Part of it was due to Tappan's personality: he tended to be condescending in manner, to get fixed aversions to various faculty members, and to rebuke them publicly. But his most bitter opposition came from the church people and demagogic newspapers. Presidents of denominational colleges wanted state funds appropriated to them instead of to a "godless" university. There was criticism of Tappan's discontinuance of faculty appointments on a quota system for various sects. And when a student died as a result of a drinking party, the church people went after Tappan's scalp. His use of wine at the table and his remark to students about beer were cited as evidence that he condoned and fostered riotous living. The Methodist conferences passed resolutions deploring the moral condition of the university.

The newspaper attack was led by W. F. Storey, the rabble-rousing editor of the *Detroit Free Press*. Storey raised a hulla-baloo over Tappan's use of the term "Chancellor" and referred to him as a "Prussianized professor." When Tappan brought in Brunnow, the attack became indecent, hinting at homosexuality. Tappan was accused of being too Eastern, too European, of lacking an appreciation for and understanding of Western character. "It is not to be expected," wrote Storey, "that a man can escape from an atmosphere of codfish aristocracy." Other papers took up the cry, and within two years of his appointment he was being hounded by a baying pack. The he-men of the West feared culture and education as effeminizing agencies—a phobia not yet entirely absent in America. And Mrs. Tappan, exhibiting an attitude not even now completely unknown in the East, was quoted as saying that she and her husband regarded themselves as missionaries to the West.

A series of anonymous letters to the *Free Press* attacking Tappan were apparently written by Eli Bishop, one of the Regents. Tappan himself made some blunders in talking with the legislators. The upshot was that in 1863 a retiring Board of Regents fired him in an action of dubious legality. Citizens, students, and alumni held mass meetings of protest, but the church people rallied their forces against Tappan. James Burrill Angell, a later president of the university, summed it up: "Tappan was the largest figure of a man that ever appeared on the Michigan campus. And he was stung to death by gnats."

Other state universities in the West tended to copy important features of the Michigan pattern. Both Wisconsin and Minnesota started universities before the Civil War, but their important period of development began with the Morrill Act of 1862 granting lands and federal aid to state colleges.

In the East during the 1830s, Lafayette College, under its first president, George Junkin, introduced a course in teacher training with a model school, an experiment which had only a brief life. It was the conservative East which also furnished another important development in college education during the 1850s—the new curriculum introduced at Brown by Francis Wayland. Moderate changes had taken place before this at Harvard under Josiah Quincy and at Vermont under James Marsh. In his inaugural address in 1829 President Quincy had stated it to be the duty of literary seminaries to keep pace with the spirit of the age and supply its needs. By 1841 he proposed making Latin and Greek elective after the first year. At Vermont Marsh had made more extensive changes by establishing four departments from which a student might choose one or two as a field of concentration. As at Virginia no time limit was set for graduation, and a student might take various courses in succession. However, to receive the A.B. he still had to complete the traditional amount of languages, sciences and philosophy.

The program of Francis Wayland was much more revolutionary. In the 1840s he wrote and spoke on the need for changes in the collegiate system. During a visit to the University of Virginia he was impressed by the curriculum and the freedom from the shackles of academic tradition. His conviction of the need for a complete overhauling of the old system culminated in the famous *Report to the Corporation of Brown University*. Just as the report of the Yale faculty in 1827 became the bible of the traditionalists, the Brown report of 1850 became the gospel for reformers. Officially it was the work of a committee; actually it was in the main an expression of Wayland's ideas.

The *Report* reviews the history of American colleges, pointing out their original purpose of training clergymen, and then goes on to show how the original pattern had become crystallized in a standard four-year course for all students. It then points out the unsuitability of this course to Americans:

That such a people should be satisfied with the teaching of Greek, Latin and the elements of mathematics, was plainly impossible. Lands were to be surveyed, roads to be constructed, ships to be built and navigated, soils of every kind, under every variety of climate, were to be cultivated, manufactures were to be established . . . all the means which science has provided to aid the progress of civilization, must be employed, if this youthful republic would place itself abreast of the empires of Europe.

For the colleges there were now two alternatives: 1. to keep the old curriculum and add new subjects, thus increasing the length of the course, or 2. to leave each student free to select his own studies. The *Report* goes on to show the absurdity of the usual attempt to solve the problem by adding additional subjects to the old curriculum while keeping the four-year course. At Harvard, for instance, the student took Latin, Greek, mathematics (including geometry, algebra, plane and spherical trigonometry, analytical geometry), ancient and modern history, natural history, chemistry, rhetoric, French, psychology, ethics, physics, logic, botany, political economy, the evidences of religion, the Constitution of the United States, mineralogy, geology, German or Spanish, and elocution. As about seven eighths of the first year and half of the second were devoted to Latin, Greek, and mathematics, this left about six weeks or less to each of the other studies.

After thus revealing the dilution of the traditional curriculum the *Report* goes on to argue that ". . . our colleges are not filled because we do not furnish the education desired by our people." This proposition is supported by figures showing that, despite the growing wealth of America, there had been a decline of the proportion of people going to college. Nor were the colleges well supported financially. In a pattern all too familiar to faculties past and present, Brown had built a library, chapel, classrooms and museum, and a house for the president, but had not in twenty-two years increased faculty salaries. The scale of 1827—$1,500 for the president, $1,000 for professors, and $400 for tutors—was now totally inadequate. The trustees had recently voted a $200 increase but student fees with which to pay it were declining.

The *Report* therefore proposed to seek an increase in endowment and "carefully survey the wants of the various classes of the community in our own vicinity, and adopt our courses of instruction, not for the benefit of one class, but for the benefit of all classes."

It outlined what today would be called "a seven-point program":

1. The abandonment of a fixed four-year course for everyone.
2. The length of each course to be determined by its nature.
3. The right of the student to study what he chose unless parents or guardians insisted on prescribed courses.
4. That a course once begun should continue without interruption. [This was in contrast to the method of sandwiching such things as science into the work of various semesters.]
5. New courses should be established whenever community needs required.
6. Students in any course should have the liberty of attending others.
7. No student should be required to proceed to a degree unless he chose.

The committee proposed the working out of a system of equivalents among studies as a basis of determining the requirements for a degree—essentially the system of semester hours now in vogue. Of the classics they said:

If by placing Latin and Greek upon their own merits, they are unable to retain their present place in the education of civilized and Christianized man, then let them give place to something better.

The situation at Brown must have been desperate, for the trustees accepted the recommendations and raised $125,000 to put the plan into effect. But like so many other attempts at a modern educational program before the Civil War, this too gradually gave way to the pressures for traditionalism.

The account of these pioneering experiments can fittingly conclude with the tragedy of Antioch. It was founded by the Christian Denomination as a nonsectarian, coeducational college. When Horace Mann was invited as president, Harriet Beecher Stowe tried to dissuade him. Mann, who had largely won the crusade in the North for the right of every child to an education, saw in Antioch an opportunity for "redressing the long-inflicted wrongs of woman by giving her equal advantages of education." Other factors which led to his acceptance of the presidency were his aversion to sectarianism and his desire to bring up his children in the less conventional society of the West.

When Mann arrived at Yellow Springs, he found the unfinished buildings standing amid the stumps of recently felled trees. There was not a book in the library nor a shelf for one. The whole property was deep in debt and with the added liability of perpetual, transferable scholarships which had been sold for $100 each. This means of raising funds had already caused much trouble at Oberlin. Nevertheless, Antioch opened its doors in 1853.

Mann was not an original educational thinker but an able, sincere educational statesman. Even his limitations should have endeared him to his fellow workers. Very much a man of his period, he was part of the reformist crusade which had founded Oberlin and other schools in the West. At an early faculty meeting he noted with satisfaction:

. . . A most remarkable coincidence of opinion and sentiment among the persons present. . . . We were all teetotalers; all anti-tobacco men; all anti-slavery men; a majority of us believers in phrenology; all anti-emulation men—that is, all against any system of rewards and prizes. . . .

On the positive side Antioch, like Oberlin, was coeducational, accepted Negroes, and introduced a course in the theory and practice of teaching. Scientific and historical studies constituted a larger proportion of the work than in the traditional curriculum, and there was an alternative course without Greek and Latin but leading to an A.B. Electives were offered in each of the first three years. Standards for entrance and graduation were designed to be equal to those of the best colleges in the East, so much so that of the 200 applicants the first year, only six were found to be properly prepared to enter the freshman class. (As at Oberlin there was a preparatory department.)

In his classes Mann used the modern method of assigning topics for investigation and report—this at a time when the old textbook-recitation method still held sway in the older colleges. His classes discussed such topics as soil fertilization, canals, population, schools, churches and public charities in their economic relations; also the relationship of art and science to rising civilizations.

Thus Antioch began as a relatively modern college with high standards and a famous, able president. Mann's optimistic ideal appears in his statement in a letter of 1856: "In all this Great West ours is the only institution of first class character which is not directly or indirectly under the influence of the old school of theology. . . ."

He spoke too soon. For although the Articles of Incorporation of the college defined the Christian Connection to be a denomination professing no creed but the Bible and having no test of fellowship but Christian character, the label was inaccurate. Almost at once there were charges that Mann was trying to "Unitarianize our sons and daughters." When he joined the Christian Denomination and became a minister, one group charged that he had sacrificed his real convictions; another that he did not observe the ordinances of the sect. When Mann refused to permit a revival, there was much uproar.

The attack was led by the Reverend Ira W. Allen, Professor of Mathematics, but was joined by the sectarian press. Allen's book, *History of the Rise, Difficulties and Suspension of Antioch College,* is a classic of sectarian vituperation. Insisting that he has always maintained a Christian spirit, Allen uses such phrases as "dark plot," "clique which had mainly controlled the college," "fault finding busybodies" (people on Mann's side of course; Allen always addressed his own supporters as "Dear Brother in Christ"), "despicable injustice," "Mrs. Mann's sullen and overbearing manner." He charged:

. . . It is evident, we think, that Mr. Mann's intention was to take Antioch College from *its denominational basis,* and place it on *"a thoroughly liberal basis"* in the hands of "new friends," so that himself, his relatives, and particular favorites might have full control of the institution.

The *Gospel Herald* took up the cry in an editorial entitled "Antioch College—A Warning" which said:

Some powerful influence has been at work among the students ever since its opening, preventing all religious power from operating on them, and turning them away from vital piety and every spiritual motive, so that no revival season has ever been enjoyed in this College—no conversions made during the whole period of its existence. What a melancholy thought.

This of a college which had daily chapel services. Allen quotes many similar editorials demanding denominational control, such as the wail, "Antioch being now dead to us, beyond the possibility of a resurrection. . . ."

Tortured beyond endurance, Mann wrote to a clergyman who had questioned his religious views that he had never been among more sectarian people in his life than among the supposedly liberal Christian Connection and added that there were some souls so small that if a million were sprinkled on the surface of a diamond, they would not make it dusty.

In June 1859 the college was sold to clear its debts. In his baccalaureate address Mann closed with the words: "Be ashamed to die until you have won some victory for humanity." During the commencement exercises he was fatally stricken and died at the age of sixty-three. At Antioch he had won no victory for humanity. It is a symbolic close for the era.

Only at Thomas Jefferson's nonsectarian Virginia did the ideal of a modern college endure. That too is perhaps symbolic.

3

The Myth of Cloistered Halls

The American student has often been wiser than his teachers. One reason for this is that students have represented a wider cross section of the population than have college faculties. During the first two centuries college presidents—who in those days knew enough to teach—and other faculty were overwhelmingly drawn from the clergy. More recently, as the churches failed to attract the abler intellects, the teaching staff, especially in the humanities and social sciences, has included many of the type of people who in an earlier generation would have gone into the church. Sociology departments in particular have contained a high proportion of "sprung" clergymen and Y.M.C.A. secretaries. Technical and business faculties have of course attracted somewhat different types.

The kind of person who becomes a college teacher is likely to be a special breed. He has many estimable qualities: intellectual interests, sometimes high intelligence, integrity and a genuine desire to help his fellow man. Few college professors have been indicted for rape, swindling, theft or assault and battery. Only one, a professor of chemistry at Harvard, has been hanged for murder. On the other hand, the college teacher is likely to be introverted, conservative, overconscientious and sexually inhibited. Dr. Kinsey has discovered that it is the less sexually active part of the male population which goes to college; it is likely that this applies especially to those men who go on to graduate work and teaching.

As a result of his special qualities the college teacher tends to develop a type of education suited to the psychological needs of his own kind. It is quite probable that the traditional emphasis on Greek, Latin, and mathematics was due much more to subconscious drives for stability and to escape from the com-

81

plexities of human problems than to a reasoned evaluation of the worth of these subjects or, as the teacher significantly calls them, "disciplines."

Much of the failure to deal realistically with students, especially in the past, grew out of the professional failure to make acceptable provision for the social and biological drives of normal human beings. Healthy young men needed good food, exercise, and fun. As human beings preparing for a life in human society they needed knowledge of and experience with the social life, politics, and business of that society. The system of rules, the regimented life, the curriculum—all failed to provide adequately for these needs. Therefore the students developed their own solutions for meeting their requirements.

Subjected to a curriculum and methods of instruction which had little relation to the world outside the classroom, students turned to the literary society as a means of training themselves to think, write, and speak. In the history of almost every college, even the most poverty-stricken and primitive, two rival literary societies sprang up almost as soon as the first classes began. The first coeducational college, Oberlin, had societies for both men and women.

The heart of the literary society was public debate. Just as the dueling club is a characteristic expression of German student life, so public speaking on public questions was a natural development in America. It was in the debating society that students prepared themselves for the ministry, law and public life.

Very early they seemed to have combined discussions of the abstractions of the formal ethics and philosophy of the classroom with those of a practical and contemporary nature. Thus in 1721 the Spy Club at Harvard debated not only "Whether there be any standard of truth," but also "Whether it be fornication to lye with one's sweetheart before marriage"—the latter a college argument still going strong, though in different phraseology.

The University of Georgia was scarcely two years old when

the juniors organized a society "for the promotion of extempo-
rizing, or extemporary speaking." As Coulter puts it:

Exactly two weeks later they turned on a flow of oratory that
was to resound and reverborate for a century—that was to set
up a custom and institute a method of popular control long to
dominate the whole South.

The students debated topics from history, literature, philosophy, logic, religion, plus a large number of current topics. In
1829 the Demosthenians debated "Which is to be the most
feared, religious or political fanaticism?" The vote was nineteen
to twelve that religious fanaticism was the more dangerous.
In 1836 the Demosthenians met the Phi Kappas on the topic:
"Laying aside all scriptural authority, could we reasonably conclude that all men were descended from the same pair?" The
negative won fourteen to two. On a more practical level a
debate in the 1830s led to a vote approving the admission of
Catholics to America and their right to hold office. Twenty
years later, however, another discussion led to a vote against
the toleration of Catholics. At Delaware College in the 1850s
the Athenaean Literary Society was also debating the question of admitting Catholics to America. Amherst students in
the 1840s were arguing the evils and benefits of immigration.
  Delaware students debated too on "Should bonds and mortgages be taxed?" They argued whether England and France
would remain at peace and whether modern warfare indicated
any progress of civilization. The affirmative won on this last.
Like Georgia students they debated prohibition, always a lively
topic in a period when college temperance societies flourished,
even at the University of Virginia. A subject with a strangely
modern ring comes from Amherst of the 1840s: "Do military
qualifications of the highest order fit a man for the Presidency?"
  All over the country there was a great similarity in the subjects chosen; they reflected the current issues being debated by
the nation. It is difficult to determine the extent to which victories for one side or another were determined by student

sentiment or by the skill of the speakers. The indications are that on the whole the decisions reflect student opinion in various periods. Thus, Georgia students sided with Nicholas Biddle against Jackson on the question of the Bank, favored the purchase of Texas, opposed prohibition, favored the establishment of free schools and universal suffrage.

Like the Harvard students of a century earlier they debated questions of sexual morals: "Does a change of mind justify a violation of a marriage engagement?" (seventeen to nine, yes); "Should a man be compelled by law to marry the victim of his seduction?" (One club said yes; the other no.) They argued the question of parental rights in regulating their children's marriages; also the problem of divorce.

From the beginning of the nineteenth century, slavery was one of the most universal topics for student discussion. It appears often in the minutes of the Philological Society (1807-1812) at Pennsylvania along with debates on the best location for a college and the relative advantages of law or the ministry as professions. At Georgia in 1827 the Phi Kappas upheld Calhoun's argument that slavery was beneficial, but the next year voted that it was unjustifiable and should be abolished. The Demosthenians in 1833 approved it by the narrow margin of six to five. The debate on nullification seesawed back and forth over the years. Even as late as 1857 a Georgia society decided against the right of a state to secede from the Union. As might be expected, Oberlin discussions were heavily weighted against slavery. In 1850 one society took up the topic: "Ought Webster to be hung?" The decision is not recorded.

Not all colleges permitted such free discussion. One of them, oddly enough, was theoretically liberal Virginia. In 1832 the Jefferson Society obtained faculty permission to have one of their members make a public address on Jefferson's birthday. With the approval of the society's chairman the student orator spoke in favor of emancipation, citing the opinions of Washington, Jefferson, and other founders of the Republic. Although there was at the time in Virginia a very considerable public demand for abolition, the faculty was upset by the address.

Following an all-too-familiar pattern, they said that because the university was supported by all parties, it was unwise to bring up such a controversial topic. Hereafter, they ruled, there should be no oration on any distracting question of state or national policy nor on any point of theological dispute. In this latter they were being forehanded: Virginia students had showed no disposition to discuss theology. At about the same time there was an uproar at Lane Institute in Cincinnati over the same issue. Professor Theodore Weld had got up a discussion of slavery, and on one occasion a Negro ex-slave debated the question with students who were the sons of slaveholders. Some students went out to lecture on abolition. The trustees, largely Cincinnati businessmen, alarmed about the effects of this on their customers in the South, ruled that:

. . . education must be completed before the young are fitted to engage in the collisions of active life [and] that no associations or Societies among the students ought to be allowed in [the] Seminary except such as have for their immediate object improvement in the prescribed course of studies.

Thus, early in our collegiate history, we have the perennial problem of student debate spreading into the larger area of public controversy. The right of free speech becomes entangled with the obligation of a college to maintain a nonpartisan position. Once an institution is identified with any cause, it increasingly becomes, as did Oberlin, the agency of a group or party. It attracts sympathizers of that group and repels others to a point where freedom of speech and inquiry become free only to the controlling party. On the other hand, the refusal to permit students and faculty to discuss controversial issues leads to intellectual sterility or revolt. On the whole the colleges have probably listened too often to the counsels of timidity. As happened at Lane Institute, these counsels originate more often from the trustees than from faculty.

By the time slavery became the great national issue neither students nor faculty were content to confine the discussion to the literary society and the classroom. At Lane the trustees dismissed Professor John Morgan for siding with the students in their contention that freedom of discussion was a *right* the institution "could neither give nor take away." Within a period of two days thirty-nine students requested dismission. All over the country the conservative interests suppressed or disciplined antislavery organizations and abolitionist teachers and faculty in the academies and colleges. There was a purge at Western Reserve; fifty students left Phillips-Andover Academy because they were forbidden to form an antislavery society; at Amherst, President Herman Humphrey asked the abolition society to disband; and at Hamilton the faculty dissolved the one there. Students at Hanover College in Indiana organized a society despite the opposition of the faculty.

Even issues less charged with emotional dynamite than slavery aroused student interest. Every public question from the admission of Utah as a state to the expediency of maintaining West Point as a military academy became a topic for the literary societies. As student diaries show, the preparation of the speeches took up a considerable amount of time. The very fact that the diarists so frequently mention the preparation for debates and the composition of essays for the societies' meetings indicates how important they were in the students' lives.

Before fraternities became general, the literary societies commanded the same sort of loyalty. Students raised considerable sums to furnish the clubrooms and buy books. As has been noted, the libraries thus accumulated rivaled those of the colleges. In the South it was the custom to elect prominent men as honorary members. At Virginia, Jefferson declined an honorary membership on the ground that as one of the Board of Visitors he could not properly identify himself with any one group. However, both Presidents Madison and Monroe accepted such memberships. At the University of Georgia, where Whig sentiment was strong, Jackson was first voted down and had to wait nine years for election. Societies scoured the earth for honorary members: even Napoleon III was elected at Georgia. Not only did a roster of prominent names lend prestige, it also had a practical value: honorary members were expected to contribute books and money for buildings. The Philo Society at Pennsylvania once elected the whole Board of Trustees as honorary members in gratitude for grants of money for the library or annual exercises. Eventually of course the colleges took over this little racket from the students by using the honorary degree for the same purposes.

Offices in the literary societies were sought after and connived for with the intensity which characterized the campus politics of a later era when athletic managerships became the prizes. Rivalry between the societies was so intense that the members had secret rituals and tried to spy on one another. At Georgia it was considered a *casus belli* for members of one society to walk under the windows of the hall of the other during a meeting. Some of the animosities developed there between rivals persisted into the old age of the participants. More usual, however, was the kind of suspicious reciprocity which later characterized fraternities. Societies lent books to each other and, for special occasions such as Exhibition Day, lamps and furniture.

The significance of all this enthusiasm and rivalry is that they rested on an intellectual foundation. The honors went not to the organization with the biggest tackle but to the one with the ablest debater or the most polished essayist. As we shall see, essays and literary discussion were important features of the programs. Frequently literary publications originated in these organizations. The college literary societies were probably more effective than the curriculum in fitting a man "to perform justly, skilfully and magnanimously all the offices both private and publick of Peace and War."

The account of this phase of student activity indicates how fallacious is the commonly held notion that American colleges were, until recently, ivy-covered retreats from the world. The ivory tower may have existed for some professors of Latin and Greek, but the students didn't live there. Nor did a large proportion of the faculty. Whatever the limitations of the early college president, he was seldom an unworldly recluse. Not all took such direct action as ex-President Naphtali Dagget of Yale, who, carrying a long fowling piece and mounted on an old black mare, went out to meet the British invasion of New Haven. He was captured and prodded with bayonets, an experience which probably caused his death soon after. President Hardenbergh of Rutgers, wanted by the British, slept with a musket beside his bed. Fifteen-year-old Ashbel Green, a future president of Princeton, worried all his life over having taken a pot shot at the British during the Battle of Princeton.

In view of the conservative and clerical traditions of the colleges, an astounding proportion of college presidents, teachers, students and alumni took an active part in the Revolution. Thwing estimates that of about 2,500 living college graduates in 1775, about one fourth entered the service. Such men as John and Samuel Adams, John Hancock, James Otis, Francis Hopkinson, Thomas Jefferson, John Trumbull, John Jay, Philip Freneau, Alexander Hamilton and the Lees of Virginia were graduates of American colleges. John Hancock was treasurer of Harvard; Charles Thomson, a member of the faculty at Pennsylvania, became secretary of the Continental Congress; another delegate, Frederick Frelinghuysen, and John Taylor, both tutors at Rutgers, rose to colonelcies in the army. President Hardenbergh several times had to flee his home and was so active in the American cause that the British set a price of £100 on his head; President Witherspoon of Princeton signed the Declaration of Independence; future college presidents Dwight, of Yale, and Brown, of Georgia, saw service in the army. Of the college presidents only Nyles Cooper of King's, and Smith of the College of Philadelphia, were Royalists.

Before the Revolution, as before the Civil War, students took much interest in public affairs. The Harvard class of 1768 voted unanimously to take their degrees in gowns made of American cloth. Six Harvard students joined the minutemen. Student diaries there and at Yale are more concerned with war news than with college affairs. Paul Litchfield, a senior at Harvard, noted the engagement at Concord, following which his company was called up for guard duty. He and his fellows captured six Tories. Soon after he was chosen captain of a militia company, the Royal Americans.

Of course not all college men were Whigs: of the 310 Massachusetts Tories who were banished in 1778, sixty were Harvard graduates. But among college students and faculties Whig sentiments seem to have predominated.

After the Revolution several presidents engaged in political controversy. President Ezra Stiles of Yale, an ardent believer in civil and religious liberty, noted in his diary of 1789 his enthusiasm for the French Revolution: "I am a Democrat, yea I am a Jacobin—I glory in the name." His successor, Timothy Dwight, became the champion of New England Federalism. Other presidents tended to divide on sectional lines: those in New England warned against atheism, French ideas, and Jefferson; whereas the ardent Federalist President Chapman of North Carolina had his gate tarred and feathered, his home damaged, and he received threatening letters. Professor Josiah Meigs of Yale proclaimed his republican sentiments so vigorously that the authorities threatened to discharge him. His wife charged that Timothy Dwight had persecuted him; in any case Meigs went to the more congenial Jeffersonian atmosphere of Georgia to become the first president of the new Franklin College (the University of Georgia). Another ardent anti-Federalist was Thomas Cooper, president of the University of South Carolina.

As has been mentioned, presidents in the North and South again divided on sectional lines over the question of slavery. When it is realized that of the 300 pre-Civil War college presidents studied by Schmidt every one was a teacher, it becomes clear that the students had an opportunity to hear political discussion as well as to participate in it through their literary societies. Politics and modern history might be minor parts of the curriculum, but they were discussed by their teachers on the public platform. As Schmidt remarks of the old-time president: "Next to the sermon, itself frequently of a political nature, the patriotic oration was his specialty."

The nineteenth-century American public had an immense appetite for sermons and spread-eagle oratory. Often the college president owed his position to his mastery of these art forms, and a public address was an excellent form of public relations work for the college. Even late in the nineteenth century Russell Conwell, the founder and president of Temple University, supported it largely through his famous lecture, "Acres of Diamonds."

Another aspect of the speeches of college presidents is that they were an early form of adult education. It was not only the presidents who engaged in this activity. Members of college faculties gave evening lectures of a popular nature to which the community was invited. Chemistry, with moderately spectacular demonstrations, was a favorite topic. Such lectures served another function: boys could escort the young ladies of the community to enjoy an elevating and inexpensive evening.

The debates, orations, recitations, and occasional dramatic skits staged by the literary societies were another means of combining edification with feminine society. Although many of the meetings were for members only, most of such organizations arranged programs where the students could demonstrate their skill in public.

Just as the student met his needs for information about contemporary affairs by debating in the literary society and listening to public orations, so too he supplemented the curriculum in two other areas: English, including American, literature, and creative writing. Before the Civil War few colleges except Pennsylvania under Smith gave much attention to English. In the mid-eighteenth century Harvard had no work at all in this field. In the 1770s three young tutors at Yale—Joseph Howe, John Trumbull and Timothy Dwight—agreed that the greatest weakness in the educational system was a contempt for belles-lettres. These men still in their teens advocated a modification of the hallowed curriculum to include not only belles-lettres but also oratory, English grammar, and the cultivation of an effective style.

The energetic Dwight set about remedying the situation by delivering after hours a series of lectures on style and composition. That students felt a need for such work is shown by the fact that they came in large numbers to listen eagerly to Dwight's literary discussions. He got them to practice elocution, heard them read their compositions, and offered a "valuable book" as a prize for the best one.

So popular was this instruction that the seniors petitioned the Yale Corporation for permission to "hire" Mr. Dwight to instruct them that year in rhetoric, history, and belles-lettres in addition to the usual subjects. It isn't often that college students ask for extra work and are willing to pay for it. The Corporation, "being willing to encourage the improvement of the youth in those branches of polite literature," granted the request, provided the students had permission of a parent or guardian. Among the puritans literature was always looked on as a dangerous subject to be handled with gloves.

It often happens that the teaching of writing and literature is closely allied with attempt at creative work. Philology and gerund-grinding produce no creative writing. It is no accident then that Dwight tried his hand at an epic poem, "The Conquest of Canaan"; then a montage of Goldsmith, Thomson, Denham, Milton and Pope in his *Greenfield Hill*. His fellow tutor, Trumbull, was more successful with such satiric poems as *The Progress of Dulness* and *M'Fingal*. The point is not that the poems were imitative; it is that Yale men tried to write poetry.

Even in the 1840s at Amherst, lectures on Chaucer, the ballads, "Milton's obligation to Caedmon" were extracurricular evening affairs to which the public was invited. Tappan's introduction of a course in English literature at Michigan in the 1850s was an innovation.

College libraries were likely to be weak in this field. Though the Virginia library was large for its time, Jefferson's austere taste led to the omission of *Paradise Lost,* all English comedy and most English poetry. Shakespeare got in under the heading of tragedy; Pope with his translation of the *Iliad.* Jefferson's selection was made largely on intellectual grounds; at more puritanical institutions fiction, drama, and a good bit of poetry were excluded for moral reasons. Until 1864 Oberlin forbade the study of Shakespeare in mixed classes. Although these colleges may represent extremes, the forces of classicism and puritanism which they exemplified were powerful elsewhere. President Waddel of Georgia objected to novel reading by students. In the absence of formal work in English literature it is unlikely that college libraries devoted much space to it and that only to the more ancient and hallowed authors.

However student demand for living literature had some effect. Despite the fact that Oberlin students were not encouraged to use the library, were required to pay a special fee, and could draw only one book at a time, Goldsmith, Irving, and Scott's *Napoleon* were frequently taken out. Novels were officially disapproved, but the library had works of Milton, Dryden, Cowper, Burns and Southey.

The students filled this vacuum in the curriculum and library for themselves. The books collected by the literary societies of course included many which related to or were useful for the college courses, but there were also many not on the official lists. At Oberlin the male students hotly debated the propriety of the Ladies' Literary Society Library Association owning a copy of Byron. This had been a present; the first books purchased by the Association had been Motley's *Dutch Republic,* Tennyson's works in two volumes, and Irving's *Washington.*

Everywhere Byron was a favorite. Motte of Harvard decided that he should be in perfect health because his diet was Byron, crackers and soda water, his exercise riding a velocipede to Boston and back.

At the University of Virginia where students usually had considerable spending money, the ledgers of local bookstores show that many young men bought books not on college reading lists of the time. Next to Byron in popularity came Thomas Campbell and Tom Moore. *Don Quixote, Gil Blas,* and *Tom Jones* were the favorite novels; next came *Tristram Shandy* and *A Sentimental Journey.* Students also bought *Rasselas, Thomson's Seasons,* Maria Edgeworth's novels, Gibbon's *Decline and Fall,* and the *Spectator.* By the 1840s Bulwer-Lytton became a favorite as he was at Amherst, Delaware, and even Oberlin.

The extent to which some students did extracurricular reading is revealed in the diary of William Hammond of Amherst covering his sophomore and junior years, including vacations (1846-48). Undoubtedly Hammond was more of a reader than most students, but certainly he was no bookworm; he was extremely active in college politics, a prankster and an indefatigable ladies' man, sometimes managing as many as three dates a day. He had not been at college long before he noted that he could get along with little study. Thus within less than two years he noted the following things he had read either for pleasure or occasionally in preparation for essays to be read before the literary society:

> *The Gesta Romanorum*
> More, *Utopia*
> Sidney, *Defence of Poesie*
> Shakespeare, *Love's Labor's Lost*
> *Much Ado about Nothing*
> *As You Like It*
> *The Merchant of Venice*
> *Hamlet*
> *The Tempest*
> Suckling's poems
> Some of Swift
> Chesterfield's letters
> Cowper, *Conversation*
> Byron, *Cain*
> *Childe Harold*
> Shelley, *The Sensitive Plant*
> Keats, *The Eve of St. Agnes*
> *Hyperion*
> Hunt, *The Indicator*
> Southey, *The Doctor*
> Hazlitt, *Table Talk*
> Carlyle, *Heroes and Hero Worship*
> Goethe, *Wilhelm Meister*
> Macaulay, *Lays of Ancient Rome*
> Charlotte Brontë, *Jane Eyre*
> Bulwer-Lytton, *Eugene Aram*
> Martin Tupper (probably *Proverbial Philosophy*)

Thackeray, "Titmarsh"
(Probably *Comic Tales and Sketches*)
Dickens, *Dombey and Son*
The Battle of Life

And in American Literature:

Some of Jefferson's letters
Irving, *The Sketch Book* (twice)
Cooper, *The Crater*
Drake, *The Culprit Fay*
Emerson's poems
Longfellow, *Outre Mer*
          Evangeline
Lowell's poems
Ingraham, *Arthur Dentwood* (a dime novel)
A life of Aaron Burr

In addition, Hammond read *Punch, Harvardiana, The North American Review, The Democratic Review,* and *The Living Age.* In discussing his reading he shows familiarity with *Don Quixote* and *Gil Blas,* and has read some of Molière in French. Thus outside the classroom a student in the 1840s was doing an amount of reading comparable to that covered in a modern survey course in literature. That this was not an eccentric lonely occupation is shown by a bull session over some "grand coffee" during which he and some companions read and discussed Cowper, Coxe and Longfellow. Then they went on to Shakespeare and Homer, who kept them up till long past midnight.

Oberlin students of the same period were indoctrinated with a belief that novels were evil.

PUT DOWN THAT NOVEL, repeated five times, appeared in the *Advocate of Moral Reform* and again in *The Oberlin Evangelist.* The warning ended: "It will ruin your soul." Inspired by such teaching, a student (male) wrote:

I loved her for her mild blue eye
And her sweet quiet air,

But I'm very sure that I didn't see
The novel on the chair.

Thus beguiled, the victim told the sequel in which, as so often happened at Oberlin, morality became confused with diet:

The live-long day does Laura read
In a cushioned easy-chair,
In slip-shod shoes and dirty gown,
And tangled, uncombed hair.
For oh! the meals! I'm very sure
You ne'er did see such "feeding"
For the beef is burnt, and the veal is raw,
And all from novel reading.

Another Oberlin young man gave his fiancée Bulwer-Lytton's *Eugene Aram*—apparently very popular among college students, for both Amherst and Delaware students noted it in their diaries. However she laid it aside, telling herself, "It cannot be wrong not to read it—and I like to be on the safe side." It was *Uncle Tom's Cabin* which changed Oberlin's opinion about the immorality of fiction.

Closely allied to the desire of students to read modern literature was their urge to write. Probably there has never been a college which at some time—usually very early—failed to spawn one or more literary magazines. Often these were begun by one of the literary societies.* The complete story of college journalism is much too long and complex for inclusion here. Literary magazines sprang up and died every few years. Harvard's first one, the *Lyceum* (1810), perished within a year despite a board of editors including Edward Everett and Samuel Gilman, whose song, "Fair Harvard," is still very much alive. Next came the *Register* in 1827, and as quickly faded; then the *Collegian* in 1830, which carried several poems by Oliver Wen-

---

* For instance, the Zelosophic Society at Penn started one in 1834. At Virginia the literary societies teamed up in 1849 and again in 1856 to start literary magazines. In 1858 the Phi Beta Society at Oberlin proposed that all four literary societies join in producing a magazine "of 40 pgs. same size and style as the Atlantic." Thus began the *Oberlin Students' Monthly.*

dell Holmes, could not survive the year. *Harvardiana* managed to keep going from 1836 to 1839 largely through the efforts of an undergraduate named James Russell Lowell.

Even when a periodical survived for a longer period, it varied greatly in quality with the inevitable changes in staff and contributors. The *Yale Literary Magazine,* better known as the *Yale Lit,* is not only the longest-lived of its kind; it is the oldest magazine in America, having been founded in 1836 at a time when Yale was the largest college in America. It therefore may not unfairly be used as the leading example of its genre. Both the prestige of Yale and the practice of exchanging college periodicals undoubtedly caused the *Yale Lit* to have a wide influence. By the 1850s the Yale editors listed exchanges from seventeen magazines and asked for others. It is significant that many of those listed came from distant and sometimes relatively new colleges: institutions in Georgia, North and South Carolina, Illinois, Wisconsin, as well as from the older colleges in the East.

However, the *Yale Lit* did not create the pattern of the college magazine; that had begun to take form as early as the mid-eighteenth century with Provost Smith's *American Magazine and Monthly Chronicle* at Pennsylvania. In it we find the Addisonian essay, the philosophic essay, the neoclassic poem, the somewhat self-conscious literary manner. A more typical undergraduate publication was that of a Pennsylvania literary society, *The Zelosophic Magazine,* started two years before the *Yale Lit.* Here we find, in addition to the earlier types of writing, short stories, discussions of college matters, such as a demand for the teaching of science, and of practical problems such as overcrowding or opportunities in various professions. As in the *Yale Lit* there are essays suggesting the assigned class exercise: essays on history, constitutional law, Greek Studies, Mythology, "Reflections on the Beautiful," "Reflections on the Sublime." The academic antiquarianism of the faculty is reflected in the attitude toward American literature. Anticipating Henry James, a student writer complained:

AN UNEQUAL MATCH

Practical Business Man to College Graduate: "Young man, you'll have to get stouter gloves than those, and train in a harder school before you compete with me."

Matthew Vassar
1792-1868

Andrew D. White
1832-1918

William Watts Folwell
1833-1929

THREE EDUCATIONAL PIONEERS

[Americans] have no tombs of their ancestors; no monuments of the skill of their forefathers; no time-honored remnants to which memory clings when all else is lost in the sea of oblivion; no majestic heaped-up riches of successive ages. . . . Above all they have no splendor of kingly government, no pride of hereditary rank, no gorgeous ecclesiastical domination, no beauty of chivalry, no glittering pageantry of war. Their existence seems to have been but for a day. . . . They have no romantic tradition of a former era, no tender legends. . . . They have none of the elements of poetry.

It was this sort of academic antiquarianism that Emerson attacked three years later in *The American Scholar*.

Only rarely were there bits which give a glimpse of student life or interests, such as a satirical essay on gentlemen's wigs and ladies' rouge—and even this had an Addisonian echo.

The *Yale Lit* followed some of the same pattern but added to it the characteristically undergraduate items of news of and editorials on college affairs. In fact, the pattern of the *Yale Lit* is much that of college magazines ever since.

The style of the early years was the rather pedantic prose of nineteenth-century periodicals generally. Only rarely did a writer become colloquial, although student slang sometimes appeared incongruously in formal writing. Attempts at humor were afflicted with the ponderous mock-heroic style in which Victorian writers captured the worst features of Addison. Thus, fraternity meetings were "interspersed with various gastronomic, potatory and fumigatory processes." Or there was the characteristic student mixture of styles as:

These seasons of refreshment yclep "convivial entertainments" —ranging from a 3 cent "bust" on pea-nuts to a full-grown champagne supper with every man under the table—enter more or less into the habits of all these associations.

The literary essays, although ponderous, often showed considerable thoughtfulness, such as one on the desirable qualities in a teacher or another on "Discipline of College Life." This latter made such points as that a Yale student's standing is determined not by what he was before he entered college but by what he *does* and *is* in college; and that college teaches "liberality of opinion" through association with students from all sections. At times, as at Penn, the essays showed marks of having been prepared first as class exercises; for example, a rather pompous dissertation on the relation of national ideals and manners to American literature or another on "Poetry, Originally a Sacred Principle, as Indicated by its Early History."

It was when the students were being themselves that they were most interesting, as when the editors gathered statistics on whiskers (1857):

The number of the faculty blessed in this respect	18
Of the Editorial Board (the entire board)	5
Of Seniors	59
Of Juniors	37
Of Sophomores	45
Of Freshmen	7
Total	171

The "matrimonial statistics" of the senior class "carefully collated from the most reliable sources" revealed:

23 Engaged
7 In love, but not engaged
21 Deep in a flirtation
39 Wholly heart free
11 Confirmed old bachelors

So too there was a liveliness in discussions of New Haven politics, of foolish customs like the annual "Burial of Euclid," and on the official misrepresentation of the cost of board. It would seem that the further college writing was removed from the classroom the better it became.

Although the short stories were clearly apprentice work, they compare favorably with those in student publications in this day of courses in the short story. There is the usual undergraduate emphasis on plot rather than character, but this was also true of the then contemporary work of Poe. Of course there is the inevitable attempt at humor with the suspense story ending in a surprise anticlimax, a device O. Henry later patented. But there is also a skillfully worked-out thriller of some medical students disinterring the corpse of a Negro. Unknown to them the deceased was a friend of the Negro servant from whom they had borrowed rope and tools. He in turn tricked the students to rescue and bury his friend's body.

Here again we find students developing a form of writing not taught in the classroom. What they knew of the short story came from their private reading. That this reading was often done perceptively is shown by the generally high quality of the occasional reviews. The *Lit* editors devoted space to such things as a lecture by Orestes Brownson, Margaret Fuller's *At Home and Abroad,* Mrs. Gaskell's *Life of Charlotte Brontë,* and Tennyson's *Maud.* Among the poets quoted are Milton, Thomas Moore, James Thomson, and Longfellow ("A Psalm of Life"). However there is little indication of an enthusiasm for reading at Yale in the three decades before the Civil War.

In the *Lit,* as in *The Zelosophic Magazine* at Pennsylvania, the student verse is almost invariably pale, hackneyed, and sentimental—the "I love the moonlight hours" sort of thing. This kind of mandolin music echoes throughout student publications for nearly a hundred years. It was not until the 1930s that college poets managed to get away from it.

Only the humorous verse was alive, as this in 1857:

I saw a youth careering down busy Chapel rue,
Following the wake of a silken skirt that flashed before his view.
He heard the "countless laughter" of the "many-twinkling feet,"
The music of the bronze-tipped heel—the patter all complete;
He neared and peered most carefully to spy those "things" divine
But couldn't—so he heaved a sigh and cursed the crinoline.

It was, however, a Harvard professor, George Martin Lane, who wrote the most famous humorous poem of the period. According to a Harvard historian, Charles A. Wagner, the "Lay of the One Fishball" originated in Cambridge, growing out of Professor Lane's experience when, short of change, he tried to order a half portion of macaroni. As told in the song:

> The waiter brings one fishball on,
>   The guest he looks abashed down.
> The scantiness of fare he sees:
>   "A piece of bread now, if you please."
> The waiter roars it through the hall,
>   "We don't give bread with one fishball!"

Wagner says it was first published in 1857. That Professor Lane's opus may have been a reworking of an earlier student song is suggested by an advertisement in the *Yale Lit* of 1856 for a song, "Lone Fish Ball." Apparently further scholarly research is needed on this problem.

Whatever the origin of the song, it not only became a student favorite, but also the basis of an opera, *Il Pesceballo*. "Opera Seria: In Un Atto. Musica del Maestro Rossibelli-Donimozarto, Cambridge, 1862." The writer of the score was Lane's colleague, the eminent Professor Francis J. Child, and the English translation of the lyrics was supplied by James Russell Lowell. During the Civil War the Child-Lowell opus was produced several times for soldier benefits.

It is significant that in the academic world both Child and Lowell were pioneers in the study of literature: Lowell with his lectures and critical writing, Child with his study of folklore and the ballads. Both men moved a step away from the stuffy academic traditionalism of their time. Lowell, of course, was interested in writing, even colloquial writing, as his *Bigelow Papers* show. Child, however, was more typical of the early professors of rhetoric—colleges did not yet dare to have a professor of English—in that he turned over the work in rhetoric to an assistant while he taught Anglo-Saxon and philology. At Amherst also, the earliest formal work in English was the study of Anglo-Saxon.

Therefore Tappan's introduction at Michigan in the 1850s of

a class in English literature, including recent and contemporary writing, was a real innovation. Despite the exceptions, pre-Civil War-period students had, by means of their literary societies and publications, provided most of their own education in writing and in the literature of their own language.

4

Student Life

Although students devised means for their intellectual development, they were less successful in finding proper outlets for their physical energies. The history of every college before the Civil War is filled with accounts of riot, violence and disorder. The incidents mentioned in Chapter I are only a tiny fraction of the total. A historian of the University of Virginia devotes six chapters to student offenses between 1825 and 1842, and several more to the problems of discipline—but only one to athletics during that era.

The earliest colleges not only made little or no attempt to provide physical exercise for their students; they had a detailed list of prohibitions and fines for playing football near buildings (which meant on the campus), for going boating or fishing, even for running up and down stairs. In the early nineteenth century there were some halfhearted attempts at providing gymnasiums. Jefferson's plan provided for two gymnasiums although he declared himself in favor of military drill in preference to athletics. However, the long low rooms provided in 1824 at Virginia were so unsuited to gymnastic exercise that they were used chiefly for banquets. Within four years the Visitors were considering their conversion into lecture halls. Boxing, fencing, and singlestick were taught almost from the start, but it was not until 1851 that instruction was offered in gymnastics. In the 1850s the *Yale Lit* pictures a typical grind as practicing "Langdonics," a system of gymnastic exercises taught by Professor Langdon. The tone of the account indicates that this was something only a grind would do, the sort of thing ladies' seminaries went in for.

At Amherst, William Hammond occasionally went to the gym, but his favorite sport was pitching "loggerheads," a form of quoits. Where there were ponds or rivers, students all over the country skated in winter and went swimming as soon as the weather got warm enough, which at both Harvard and Delaware College meant the end of May. Both Jacob Motte and Joseph Cleaver swam even on Sunday, the latter noting: "If swimming on the Sabbath is a sin I am damned. T. says, 'Go and swim no more.' " Motte, who braved the Charles in May, tried the "mill dam" in July with the pleasant experience of meeting "some pretty girls coming out—looking quite pretty with their faces washed."

In addition to frequent swims Motte got a lot of exercise on his "wooden Horse," a velocipede he impulsively bought at an auction where he had gone to bid for a desk. His first experience was not too happy:

Made an exhibition of myself riding my horse home through the streets at a time when all the ladies were sitting at their windows.—However I came the back way and consoled myself with the reflection that nobody knew who I was.

Soon he was going back and forth to Boston on it. Coming home across the bridge, he raced the hourly stage: "Morse was compelled to put his horses to the gallop, to save the honor of his establishment."

Motte, who had the thing painted light blue, managed to attract a good bit of attention. In Cambridge a crowd of boys chased him; at the Port he met a fellow who was "a great connoisseur of velocipedes, having been on one for about five seconds once."

Such detailed accounts of their activities by the students make it quite clear that whatever sports they engaged in were seldom organized into team play until perhaps the 1840s when each of the four classes at Harvard had competing boat clubs. The first regatta against Yale took place in 1852, with Andrew White on the Yale team. Another future college president, Charles W. Eliot, rowed for Harvard a few years later. Football "rushes" appeared as early as 1826, but as the name suggests these were more in the nature of mass combat between classes than an organized sport. By 1856 the *Yale Lit* was bemoaning the passing of the game, which, it was claimed, "cultivated a spirit of class unity."

Some commentators on the early colleges, such as Andrew White, attribute the riots and disorder chiefly to this lack of organized athletics. This was no doubt a factor. However, as is shown by these examples, students could get a considerable amount of exercise if they wanted to. In Northern colleges they also had to do a great deal of physical labor: cutting wood, lugging fuel and water to their rooms, keeping their rooms habitable, etc. A few Harvard students employed their less well-to-do fellows to do chores, but apparently only at Virginia was it customary to have servants haul wood and water and build fires. At all colleges students did a great amount of walking: to see girls, to go into town, to attend fairs and revival meetings, to pick berries or gather nuts, or just to be on the move.

Another hypothesis is that the violence and uproar at early colleges was due less to lack of exercise than to two other causes: excessive piety and a college curriculum which bored the students beyond endurance. This undisciplined behavior of our more respectable ancestors may at first glance seem strange. In the frontier colleges one might expect violent behavior, but it was equally common in puritan New England. Gunplay was usually confined to the South, but physical violence to property and college officials characterized the most pious institutions. What appears is the two sides of the same coin. The overemphasis on religion and the repressive morality in colleges both North and South—and in American life generally—bore a direct relationship to the explosive outbreaks of revolt. It is no accident that the most puritanical of nineteenth-century colleges, Oberlin, produced the most lawless form of abolitionism. Of the early colleges, Harvard seems to have quieted down before its more puritanical rivals, Yale and Princeton.

Andrew White, who had experience in half a dozen colleges at home and abroad, stated that "in all of these together I have not seen so much carousing and wild dissipation" as he saw in a little "church college" [Hobart]. As has been mentioned in Chapter I, White also saw there outrageous violence against college officials. He experienced nothing like it at frontier Michigan. There was brutality in interclass fights—black eyes and bloody noses; drinking parties sometimes led to riots; but there was not the constant uproar nor revolt and disrespect to authorities like that in the older schools. The early University of Wisconsin presents a similar picture, but at the University of Iowa the faculty had to prohibit students from carrying pistols and knives. Yet at these same colleges students attended daily chapel, held prayers in their rooms, often attended Sabbath afternoon services held in college buildings, and again went to church in the evening.

Whatever mistakes in disciplinary methods or overpiety were made, it becomes evident that the pattern of student misbehavior and disorder was too universal to blame entirely on the colleges themselves. Rather it was part of the whole social fabric. The ultrareligious America of the nineteenth century was also a land of heavy drinking, rough horseplay, and brutal fights. A small-town Fourth-of-July celebration usually ended with most of the males drunk; many a city fire burned on while rival fire companies fought with fists and brickbats; children were thrashed with straps in the woodshed or beaten with sticks in school; even late in the century a President of the United States was reputed to have chastised his young wife.

Violence was not merely a product of the frontier. In long-settled Philadelphia, the 1830s and 1840s brought a series of riots so severe that the militia often had to be called out. It was a rare election day which did not produce riots and fires. In a series of race riots anti-Negro mobs burned Negro homes, an orphanage, and a large new public hall built by abolitionists; the "Native American" riots led to bloodshed, the burning of whole rows of Irish homes, several Catholic churches, a library, and a school. Usually the mobs fought off any fireman rash enough to appear on the scene.

Granting that college students usually came from a more

sedate social class than did the perpetrators of such acts, one cannot help noting a similarity of pattern: hysterical revolts against order and discipline. The Saturday-night spree with fist fights, the election-day shootings, the race riots, the destruction of property—all had their counterparts in student life. No doubt the exuberance of a young nation explains some of this, but much of it happened in communities and colleges vastly older than many relatively well-behaved cities and colleges in present-day America. And whereas economic forces contributed to violent social conflict, these had no part in student riots. It becomes tempting therefore to seek some of the causes for uproar in the early colleges not only in the social order but in Freudian psychology.

Certainly the early student lived under a system of rules which repressed normal fun as rigidly as it forbade sin. A student had to get official permission for the most innocent excursion, such as going fishing. Attending a theater was a more heinous offense than getting drunk. And the available evidence suggests that he observed a sex code equally repressive. Even the physical conditions of the early colleges contributed to this: small towns in which they were situated simply did not provide enough girls for even the most innocent feminine companionship. The enduring legend that mothers lock up their daughters when Dartmouth men come to town symbolizes the deeply rooted knowledge that young men long caged up together have bottled up a lot of libido.

The extent to which anything relating to sex was bottled up appears in both student diaries and faculty minutes, not by what is said, but by what is not said. So strong was the puritan tradition that student diarists who speak frankly of drinking or gambling usually vanish into the bushes as far as sex is concerned—not only in relation to themselves but for their fellows. A Haverford diarist in 1851 recorded the suspension of some students for running off to Philadelphia to play billiards and to engage in other activities "from which it is to be feared drinking and visiting disreputable haunts were not excluded." Elsewhere a diarist mentions hearing dirty stories; Cleaver, of

Delaware, records two incidents of girls in the dormitory, but adds, ". . . no doubt it has happened but is oftener told of than it happens." Much more common at the same college was the forbidden pastime of standing near a stile to watch the girls cross. And the embarrassed laughter at lantern slides of nude statues in a lecture on ancient art is more indicative of naïveté than experience. These, however, are rare glimpses.

Even more rare is a faculty minute referring to sexual irregularity. An examination of the records of two nineteenth-century colleges failed to reveal a clear reference to faculty action in a single case of this kind, a lacuna also apparent in the histories of individual colleges. In a detailed history of the University of Wisconsin, the authors, often referring to faculty records on drinking and gambling, add: "Of wenching there is no record." Philip A. Bruce, in his account of the University of Virginia, devotes four chapters to "Major Offenses": Dissipation, Tavern Haunts, Assaults, Riots. Here, too, wenching is absent although it is doubtful that it was equally absent from the university.

Weir Mitchell, a student at Pennsylvania in the late forties, attributed his purity of life at the time to an innate modesty— a rather clear implication that some of his fellow students were less squeamish. The point of all this is that whatever sexual activity existed was so carefully concealed from the record that no accurate information is available. It was not until the twentieth century that the publication of the diary of President Stiles of Yale revealed that Harvard President Locke's resignation in 1773 was due to his getting a servant girl "great with child."

But unless human nature during the eighteenth and nineteenth centuries was vastly different from that of any other period in history, it must be supposed that some students visited prostitutes in the larger towns or found complaisant factory girls, just as boys in rural areas discovered willing farmers' daughters. Jonathan Fisher, a pious Harvard student (1788-1792), had an experience with a servant girl whose "impure and unadvised conversation" and "wanton behavior" put thoughts in his mind that troubled him for years. On the other hand, at least three factors operated to limit sexual activity: well-enforced rules about being in dormitories early; the extreme youth of a large number of students; and, during the nineteenth century, the extreme social disapproval of illicit sex. The limited available evidence points to a high degree of student chastity. This may well have bearing on student misbehavior in other particulars.

If illicit sexual activity was the exception, dating was not. American mores have long sanctioned a considerable amount of unchaperoned association between boys and girls. In small college communities this led to the development of such behavior patterns as the communal call on a girl or girls, the inviting of girls to student debates, musicales and exhibitions, the keen competition for dates with the resulting impermanency of relationships. The "fusser" and the "college widow" were natural products of the system.

The pattern began early. In the 1770s twenty or thirty Yale students would gather at the home of President Stiles, where, after the formal entertainment and conversation, they could spend the rest of the evening with his three daughters. Jonathan Fisher spent one year calling on Miss Betty Heath, shifted his affections to Miss Dolly Battle, and scarcely a month later laid plans to marry her. He began seeing her in November; by February he had proposed and been accepted.

Student diaries of the early nineteenth century show that boys took girls sleigh riding, escorted them to debates and exhibitions, gathered at the young ladies' homes to chat, sing, eat apples and cakes—the dating pattern of America until the introduction of movies and the motorcar. A girl with a piano was especially popular. The diaries also indicate that there was a great increase in the amount of student social life after 1800. Students were a little older than heretofore, college rules were a little less strict, and getting about was easier.

The informal, unself-conscious relationship of boys and girls comes out in incident after incident. Motte of Harvard, going over to Boston one morning, took a girl for a walk through the

Mall and to the frog pond, bought her some ice cream, and then went with her on a shopping errand. At President Quincy's he met "an uncommonly fine girl" with whom he "spent such delicious moments in conversation" that he let everyone else go home first. He spent a pleasant evening listening to still another girl play the piano and soon after met one even more charming. "Oh ye gods! she was irresistible. . . . Oh, such eyes! she had teeth too, and such teeth! ye gods, was the like ever seen?" He walked this vision home, but apparently forgot her for Byron and his velocipede.

William Hammond of Amherst, despite his extensive reading and student politicking, managed to conduct one of the most complicated series of flirtations on record. In nineteenth-century America boys and girls drifted from house to house in couples or groups to chat, eat, and sing. Thus one October day young Hammond walked home with Mary Warner, called on Jennie Gridley but declined to make calls with her, saw Sabra Howe at a window and dropped in. Jennie turned up and, finding him "very much at home on the arm of a sofa . . . looked most unutterable things." Later that day he ran into Mary Adams in the bookstore and walked her home, where he spent an hour or two. He cut prayers to call with her on Miss Henry. It should be noted that despite a consistent application to such diversions, Hammond was able to make a good college record. Obviously college work in the 1840s was not too onerous.

There were more exciting adventures than paying calls. Going over to Mount Holyoke for a blind date with Ellen Holman, he feared he might meet Miss Lyon and "the assistant dragoness." Instead, he was ushered into a parlor: "a huge apartment furnished with a rusty stove, cherry table, and multitudinous cane-bottomed chairs." Within a half hour he and the young lady were *Willy* and *Nelly*. He was duly taken for a tour of the seminary where he met "any number of plain young ladies" and caught "sly peeps into their little boxes of sleeping rooms," and said "beautiful" at every eligible window, and did all other things right and proper in *"viewing the building."*

It could all have happened a hundred years later—at least at Holyoke.

He played backgammon with his landlady's daughter, Miss Ferry; learned through Miss Gridley that Mrs. Ferry had too many boarders; moved to Mrs. Dwight's, where he taught chess to Fannie Dwight. Then he called on Jennie Gridley, who was a bit cool because he had not appeared earlier. Jennie, just back from boarding school, he found "rather *improved* for the worse with new *airs,* etc." However, before long he and Jennie were kissing good-by in the hall.

It was not the voluptuous kiss of love, or the *lip*-touching, *tip touching* of a prude, but the pure kiss of friendship, the *beau ideal* of kissing without alloy.

The F. Scott Fitzgerald note is even more marked in Hammond's comment, ". . . much as I like her, I am not fool enough to believe that Tom and Frank have not received as much or more."

Hammond's association with Miss Mary Warner began on more utilitarian grounds: her father was on the faculty.

Mrs. Warner gave me a particularly and pressing invitation to call—a privilege I shall gladly make use of. . . . I want to cultivate the Prof. for his rhetoric, Mrs. Prof. for her elegant manners and *lead* among the ladies of the village, and Miss Prof. for the same reason that one desires the acquaintance of any pretty, intelligent girl.

A few months later he took the young lady on a sleigh ride. "Oh ye gods, what a glorious time!" Looking at Mary, he failed to see a snowbank, upset the sleigh and "down I came . . . with a mingled mass of red cloak and disheveled curls." The horse ran away, jumped into an old man's sleigh and smashed it. Someone else took Mary home, and Hammond had to pay for the broken sleigh.

Even at puritanical Oberlin boys and girls went sleighing and buggy riding. A girl telling of a drive to Elyria reported that the boys had raced carriages, the crowd had had a big sup-

per, played blindman's buff, and on the way home a boy had
let the writer drive so that he could sit close to her. Her considered opinion was "I do not wish *truly* and honestly to have
another *kiss* from Perkins K. Clarke to the longest day I live."

At Yale, a student meeting a girl who claimed to have read
Shakespeare and the *Essays of Elia* jotted down his reactions:

Heighho! to-morrow I must leave her. What a humbug it is—
this going to college! But, on the whole, I wouldn't do anything
else; though it sadly interrupts the chief business of a man's
life, which undoubtedly is to mirror the changes in that Heaven
called woman.

As this particularly literate heavenly being kissed him
good-by, she slipped into his hand a note with her name on it
(apparently this was a blind date) and a quotation from the
Psalm of Life. As might be expected, the gentleman met dis-
illusion: the young lady's comment at seeing Niagara Falls was
"I declare, it beats the bugs."

The pattern was universal. In the South the *Georgia University Magazine* of the 1850s described a college type:

. . . the Lady's man courting his glass and the ladies much
more than his books, whispering soft notes of love into each
one's ears, declaring to her that she is the little *angel,* sings
charmingly, and performs, admirably on the piano. . . .

The custom of going out serenading was almost universal.
It is not surprising then to find the *Yale Lit* of the same period
computing that over half of the senior class was engaged, in
love, or "deep in flirtation." And it is quite clear that the
lounge lizard, the flapper, and petting did not have to wait for
F. Scott Fitzgerald to invent them. Only slang was different.

The church, parents, and college faculties all preached the
strictest chastity, especially of the kiss-not, touch-not-before-
marriage variety. Yet the kissing game is one of the most ancient and universal American pastimes, as also were the sleigh
ride, the walk in the woods, the good-night kiss. Probably

illicit sexual relationships were rare, but an immense amount of limited sexual experimentation was the rule. Most modern sociologists and psychologists would probably agree that the young people had developed a sounder ethic than the one which the church and the college authorities tried to enforce. Despite the dour puritanism of nineteenth-century preachers and teachers, young people had a lot of fun and developed a wholesome give-and-take relationship between the sexes.

Just as the student's dating behavior reflected American mores, so too did his drinking habits. In both there was a considerable dichotomy between official doctrine and accepted practice.

In the eighteenth century when it was still customary for the most respectable clergyman to accept a glass of wine from a parishioner, Yale students could obtain beer, mead and cider from the college butler. But as hard liquor was common in most homes of the period, it is not surprising to find relatively young students using it. Elijah Backus, a Yale senior not quite eighteen, noted in his diary in 1777: "Today we began the third volume of Locke and I got a quart of rum at Atwaters at 2s. per quart." After studying he made a mug of flip at night. On the way home for vacation he and two friends stopped at a tavern for flip and a big dinner followed by "a large quantity of childish conversation, a warm fire, a bowl of egg punch, and an excellent supper, a good bed to lie on, and your petitioner farther saith not." The three got up a resolution in Congressional style stating their reasons for staying another day— the real reason being that they were hugely enjoying themselves. Yet only a month later this same young man was writing:

This day have I completed my eighteenth year, and what am I?—an awkward, foolish boy—who has done nothing in service of "my master."

It must be remembered that in the early nineteenth century at Harvard the fine for getting drunk was fifty cents, but for going to a theater, ten dollars. Fisher noted the two chief sins at Harvard in 1790 as drunkenness and profanity. Exhibitions by the Speaking Club were often followed by drunkenness in the Yard and at taverns.

In the South, where students were accustomed to seeing liquor served at home, drinking was common. At the University of Georgia, despite fines of five and ten dollars, drunkenness was the second most common offense to bring official punishment. From the very beginning, students at the University of Virginia established the tradition of drinking, for which that institution has been somewhat famous ever since. Any assembling of the military company was likely to be the excuse for "a treat" involving large quantities of apple toddy. One member somehow remembered that at such a meeting he had consumed about five glasses of brandy julep. Yet like all colleges, Virginia had rigid rules against drinking. An assistant proctor who was especially diligent in sniffing suspicious glasses in student rooms nevertheless followed local custom in providing a bountiful supply of toddy, brandy and wine to guests at his own parties. In the period when Christmas vacations were not granted, holiday drinking was more or less officially winked at as long as it did not become too boisterous. "It was the general custom of the country," argued a hotelkeeper (steward) in defending students before the faculty.

At Virginia and elsewhere the faculty were especially concerned with the problem of student drinking at taverns. Even worse were the confectioneries with backrooms where drinks were served, and drunkenness was common. Although the problem seems to have been less acute in more restrained New England, it was by no means absent. Hawthorne, who graduated from Bowdoin in 1825, has a scene in *Fanshawe* wherein the president of the college, hearing singing at an inn, enters to look for students. Finding some, he tries to look angry, but has a smothered gleam in his eye.

At Amherst in the forties students were disciplined for holding "convivials" in their rooms and for getting drunk in taverns. Hammond spent a hectic afternoon helping fellow students deal with two others who had got roaring drunk in Northampton and driven to Amherst in a sleigh, which they had upset. One of the roisterers tried to horsewhip a freshman —one of the few recorded hazing incidents in the diary. After a council of war the sober students calmed down one of the drunks and locked up the other. Apparently these two got away with their exploit, but soon after, another student was expelled for drunkenness—although it seems to have happened during a vacation. His friend Hammond commented sourly:

But here as everywhere also, men are punished, not for sinning, but for being found out. . . . With all his faults he [the culprit] is a noble man and when he leaves I shall lose my best friend in college.

This was at least the second case of the expulsion of an essentially decent student within two years at a very small college (a graduating class might number eighteen). Hammond's disillusioned comment represents a fairly universal student attitude. All over the country student-drinking and occasional drunkenness were extremely common, yet disciplinary authorities, especially after the eighteenth century, treated these as if they were examples of exceptional depravity. Not until the 1930s and 1940s did college authorities begin to recognize and permit such things as the sale of beer on the campus and fraternity cocktail parties.

Accounts of student drinking appear in every college history and student diary. In the 1830s Quaker students smuggled sherry into the dormitory at Haverford. At frontier Michigan drinking parties often ended in riots. In the fifties a Delaware student frequently noted liquor parties in the dormitory. One of them across the hall from the diarist "sounded like a fire scare but we tried to hold our patience and our curiosity, but reading went badly." As has been noted, Andrew White witnessed scenes of wild dissipation in a small church college in Geneva, New York. All the evidence points to the conclusion that considerable student drinking was universal whether in the skeptic eighteenth century or the pious nineteenth, at

Southern colleges filled with the sons of planter aristocrats, or at Northern institutions populated by the descendants of the Puritans. As in the 1920s, prohibition sentiment flourished among the more pious students and was official faculty doctrine at the same time that the community and many of the students consumed large quantities of liquor. Most colleges, including Georgia and Virginia, had temperance societies and lectures against the use of alcohol. But the more usual student attitude is probably reflected in Hammond's account of Junius Hatch's illustrated lecture on the evils of drunkenness: "Went on purpose to have fun; and succeeded most emphatically." Drunken Georgia students broke up a temperance meeting with shots and brickbats. Yet two years later two thirds of the students joined the Sons of Temperance. Perhaps only in pre-Civil War days could a student have had Hammond's experience of dropping in at Professor Warner's where he found "nice beer, and family prayers; both of course, homemade." Yet, except for the prayers, that too could have happened in the 1920s. The American college, like the American public, talked dry and drank wet.

Another universal drive on the part of the American student is his desire to get out of town. Before the days of the mass hegira to football games, any public event served as an excuse: a camp meeting, a revival, a political rally, a county fair, a circus, even an auction. From New England to Georgia students petitioned the faculty, sometimes successfully, to be permitted to make such excursions. The year after Dartmouth opened, a party of students got permission to camp out on a winter night. More often excursions were forbidden, especially to circuses. As a result students took impromptu holidays on such occasions as May Day, April 1, etc. At the inauguration of Franklin Pierce, Georgia students took the day off and were duly fined two dollars each. To avoid detection when attending a circus, they disguised themselves as Negroes and sat with the slaves. Delaware students had better luck; the faculty permitted them to go to one after ten-o'clock classes.

Harvard students went, not always in a reverent spirit, to Boston for the festival known as the Artillery election. Motte describes it thus:

It is the anniversary of that "ancient and fish-like" association called the Ancient and honorable artillery. . . . After dinner, I went to the Common, to see the Governor perform the august ceremony of sitting down on a chair. I think it would add considerably to the effect, if he would order the band to strike up. . . .

Motte also liked auctions. With some friends he attended one where he bought nothing, "but put on a conoisseur-like look, and tried all the wines that were sold." It was an unhappy Saturday when the Harvard student awoke to find it raining so that, instead of a good dinner and promenade in Boston, he faced the prospect of "cod-fish in commons, and solitude in his room."

As has been noted, Amherst students made excursions over to the seminary at South Hadley. But they also turned out en masse, along with faculty and villagers, to attend a cattle show where young Hammond was impressed by the many "countenances marked only by sordid meanness or beastly passion." Perhaps this is only collegiate cynicism; perhaps a realistic glimpse into the American past.

A near-by city was always an attraction. With the growth of fraternities, delegates from local chapters began to attend conventions. Hammond went to Providence for such an occasion. A Delaware college student came back from Philadelphia full of stories about the shooting galleries, theaters and shops, and with his initial tattooed on his arm. All this suggests a certain naïveté both on the part of the raconteur and of his audience.

Perhaps this lack of sophistication is the greatest difference between the pre-Civil War students and those of later times. The early student might drink, gamble, or read Byron, but he was often from the country or small town, had perhaps never attended a dance or a theater, had not seen a first-rate work of art or heard good music. To a large degree before the 1830s he came from a locality within horseback range of the college. In fact, one of the most characteristic features of the American college was that it tended to spring up in response to demands based on local pride or sectarianism.

Obviously boys from the larger cities and wealthier families would have more sophistication than their country-bred fellows. The sons of planter aristocrats, especially in Virginia, would have experienced cultivated manners. But in the early nineteenth century the revival of orthodoxy and puritan taboos made suspect such things as fiction, the theater, and art. Foreign travelers were not impressed with the cultivation of Americans. Beginning with Washington Irving, American writers and scholars turned to Europe for the elements of culture they found lacking at home—a spiritual and physical exodus which culminated in Henry James, and includes such belated pilgrims as Ezra Pound, Gertrude Stein, and T. S. Eliot.

Perhaps this return to Europe had some bearing on the gradual relaxation of puritan restrictions in the colleges. In the days when a college professor's salary equaled or exceeded that of a judge, faculty members often managed at least one European tour. By mid-century they took their families along. But as early as 1826 Longfellow began a three-year European sojourn in order to fit himself for teaching languages at Bowdoin. In the early 1830s Emerson, on a trip abroad, heard the *Miserere* sung in St. Peter's, attended an opera and commented —unfavorably—on the ballet. The point is not that he took his puritan prejudices with him and came home more an American than ever; it is rather that this lay preacher to the nation talked familiarly of Goethe, Wordsworth, Coleridge and Carlyle—the last three of whom he had met. Who, after hearing and reading Coleridge, could regard the theater and especially Shakespeare as dangerous?

The causes of the gradual change of moral climate are complex, but certainly the European travels of cultivated Americans, especially teachers and writers, had something to do with it. So too, no doubt, had growing wealth. But with the revolt against Calvinist theology led by Channing and Emerson came a more gradual relaxation of Calvinistic taboos. In the 1830s William Motte complained that his dancing pumps were unfashionable and hurt his feet. He decided to wear them out as fast as possible. At the University of Georgia dancing, which, as an agency of the devil, had been forbidden between 1819 and 1829, became so common in the thirties that a commencement ball was a regular feature. The trustees annually appropriated a hundred dollars for commencement music. Hammond of Amherst went to the theater in Boston—not however to a Shakespearean play. In fact, he was a bit shocked by the extensive displays of white pantalettes and petticoats, and by a vaudeville act involving characters in the wrong bedrooms— "not positively indecent" but not just his "beau ideal of delicacy." Even in puritanical Oberlin two faculty members attended a theater in Columbus while acting as delegates to a teachers' convention. True, they were forced to resign, but after prayer and heart-searching were reinstated. As Abe Martin remarked: "We're all purty much alike when we git out o' town." And before long the Oberlin ban on reading Shakespeare in mixed classes was lifted.

In so far as there is a consistent pattern it is one of relaxing puritanism in the colleges, accompanied by bitter attacks from a fundamentalist clergy. We have seen (Chapter II) how Presidents Holley and Tappan suffered from this. With the election of Alonzo Church as president of the University of Georgia in 1829, the Methodists and Baptists launched a ferocious attack in the press and the legislature on the "infidel" college. Although church members in the state numbered about 75,000 as against 533,000 nonmembers, they persuaded the legislature to pad the board of trustees with sectarians who promptly forbade students to engage in political discussion either in debates or commencement orations. Between 1836 and 1838 the sectarians set up three rival colleges: Emory (Methodist), Mercer (Baptist), and Oglethorpe (Presbyterian).

Thus at the very time when the older schools and the state universities were growing less puritanical, a wave of reaction created a new set of colleges. The process helped to develop class distinctions between colleges. Increasingly the less provincial elements in the population sent their sons to the more liberal institutions while the country boys and ministers' sons went to ill-financed sectarian colleges.

It might seem at first glance that the creation of small, local colleges brought higher education within reach of people otherwise denied it. Yet oddly enough the percentage of boys going to college declined steadily before the Civil War. After all, even at the local colleges, most students lived in dormitories and ate in the commons—the cost of which did not vary greatly within a given region. Because of low pay scales and too few jobs, the manual-labor feature of many smaller places did not meet student expenses to the degree advertised. It is true, however, that at such places the scale of student living was likely to be simpler and even austere.

On the debit side was the fact noted by Tappan that the scattering of money and effort prevented the development of strong, well-financed colleges and universities. The old curriculum was cheaper than a more diversified one. Thus the puritan reaction against the growing liberalism of many colleges was also uneconomic. It delayed the development of strong institutions with courses designed for a changing America.

Even the attempt to create a stricter moral climate for students was not a success. As Andrew White pointed out, struggling sectarian schools had to wink at behavior which would have brought expulsion elsewhere. In addition to the carousing and rioting he found in one such institution, he noted that most of the students relied on ponies and promptings instead of study. Boredom from uninspired teaching, rote recitations, and the lack of social activities at the early colleges were important causes of their riots and disorder; yet these were the very things likely to be preserved at pious, poverty-ridden institutions. Nor does the history of American colleges give any evidence that more rigid rules produced better behavior.

Certainly it appears that the early students were no more honest than those of later generations. Neither the official at-

mosphere of piety nor the allegedly wholesome home training
of former days prevented lying, cheating, forging excuses or
stealing. The first three appear constantly in faculty records of
discipline. Students told lies about their own infractions of the
rules or to protect their friends. If caught with liquor in their
rooms, they alleged that it was only for medicinal purposes;
overheard references to hearts or spades had nothing to do with
a card game; absences were, as now, due to illness. Students
with low grades have always been remarkably unhealthy.

Cheating in the days of rote recitations in Greek and Latin
usually took the form of purchased or homemade ponies. Motte
refers to a Greek examination at Harvard where students were
forbidden to bring any books: "There were therefore, no assistants, in the shape of *ponies, interliners, cut-down editions of
Clarke &c.*" In the 1860s, at a time when the college was unable
to pay their salaries, the faculty of Lafayette voted to buy, at
college expense, clean copies of Greek texts for use in examinations. The famous honor system of the University of Virginia
grew out of a rule adopted by the faculty in 1842 requiring
each student to sign a pledge on his honor that he had received
no aid during examinations. This at first did not take the place
of professorial supervision; it merely supplemented it. Before
long, however, the students began to take it on themselves to
call up suspected cheaters and, if a man could not successfully
defend himself, to request him to leave—a "request" which
was never disregarded.

Stealing in college dormitories tends to be a sporadic evil,
and one which does not necessarily get into faculty records because students often deal with it in their own way. Therefore
the absence of official records is not a sure indication of the
nonexistence of theft. For instance, when Jacob Motte went to
church, he carefully locked his room and hid the key behind
the stove in the entry so that "some light-fingered rogue may
not behave bad by paying his devotions to my chattels in my
absence. . . ." At Delaware College in the fifties there was a
rash of thefts of coal, kerosene (an expensive item), and cloth-

ing from dormitory rooms. Cleaver on one occasion found his "fluid" gone and the can filled with water; he was forced to get a new lid and lock for his coalbox, and he reported numerous thefts throughout the dormitory. Someone rifled the cashbox belonging to his literary society.

It is probably impossible to determine whether these various misdemeanors were more common before the Civil War than today or less so. Faculty records of cheating give no sure indication of the extent of the practice for the same reason that police records of arrests are no accurate gauge of the extent of crime. A cheating scandal, like a well-publicized crime, can set off a wave of enforcement. And as with other law-enforcement agencies, faculties vary in skill and alertness. At Pennsylvania in 1807, a graduating orator who got his speech from a friend later found the whole thing in a magazine. Apparently the faculty did not read magazines. Certainly there is no evidence that there was less student lying, cheating, and stealing in the period of intense religiosity than there is today. The best guess is that student morality in these matters has on the whole remained fairly constant, but there is considerable evidence that individual institutions experienced epidemics of low morality at times of low morale. A weak president, a tyrannical faculty, or a financial crisis in an institution often contributed to student misdemeanors.

Oddly enough, hazing does seem to have been an extensive activity. In some places, as at Yale, there were elaborate rules for freshmen, and these must have been to some extent enforced by the punishment of nonconformists. Interclass "rushes" and contests were the rule, and pranks such as the bucket of water balanced over a door victimized the uninitiated. But in all the ample records of early college disorders, misdemeanors and crimes there are few references to organized hazing. The apparent scarcity of this form of misbehavior cannot be attributed solely to the system of resident proctors in dormitories; after all, they were unable to prevent illicit wine parties, card games, or even the smashing of doors and windows. Organized hazing as a student folkway seems to be of relatively late origin in America.

However, one folkway especially characteristic of the United States appeared very early—the custom of working for all or part of one's college expenses. The British novelist J. B. Priestley, noting the prevalence of the working student in contemporary America, spoke of the revival of a healthy medieval custom. Rather it was an indigenous growth. Some of the same causes operated to produce this similar pattern: a scarcity of money in an agricultural economy and an educational system designed less for gentlemen than for the clergy. Perhaps most important of all in America has been the respectability of working for a living, even by manual labor. It never hurt the political fortunes of Franklin that he began as a printer or of Lincoln that he split rails. Equally significant is the frequent combination of high intellectual achievement with practical skills. Franklin is variously famous as an essayist, political thinker, and the inventor of lightning rods, bifocal spectacles and a stove. He also founded a college. Jefferson's reputation as a political philosopher and creator of the University of Virginia has sometimes obscured the fact that he invented among other things a new type of plow. The earliest professor of Fine Arts at New York University was a Mr. Samuel F. B. Morse, also something of an inventor. The first pipe-laying machine was invented by one of our most original thinkers in the field of higher education: Ezra Cornell.

It was a Harvard graduate of the class of 1837 who, on the basis of his own experience with manual labor, damned the whole system of theoretical education: "If I wished a boy to know something about the arts and sciences," wrote Henry Thoreau, "I would not pursue the common course, which is merely to send him into the neighborhood of some professor, where anything is professed and practiced but the art of life. . . ." Instead, he suggested the laboratory method:

Which would have advanced the most at the end of a month— the boy who had made his own jack-knife from the ore which he had dug and smelted, reading as much as would be necessary for this,—or the boy who had attended the lectures on metallurgy at the Institute in the meanwhile, and had received a Rogers' penknife from his father?

The pertinence of Thoreau's remarks must not be obscured by the accounts of early chemical laboratories such as Professor Silliman's in a Yale cellar in 1804. Professor Silliman, a lawyer who knew nothing about chemistry, had been selected by President Dwight to teach the subject, and in preparation had been sent to Philadelphia for five months of study at the medical college.

A less theoretical approach to science characterized Harvard Professor John White Webster, who in the 1850s murdered a creditor, dismembered the body and tried to burn it in his laboratory. Unfortunately for Professor Webster, the experiment was not entirely successful: he was hanged. Early scientific instruction, including that of the homicidal professor, was conducted by means of textbooks and lectures. Students did not work in the laboratory; they witnessed experiments. Long before his professor became famous, Motte noted: "At 10 o'clock a lecture from Dr. Webster on chemistry, during which he produced some diabolical smells."

However if the prevailing academic tradition failed to provide the kind of practical experience demanded by Thoreau, the folkways of America did furnish it—informally through the jobs which students got for themselves, and more officially through the development of "manual-labor" institutions. A Harvard student writing to a friend in the summer of 1790 reported that he had employed his vacation working with the ax, the plane, the saw, and the hammer. The following winter this same student petitioned the president and Overseers to extend his midwinter vacation three weeks because of his "embarrassed condition." This petition being granted, Jonathan Fisher was able to teach school for seven weeks for a total of thirteen dollars plus board and room.

This practice of vacation teaching was common in a time when rural schools operated sporadically whenever a teacher could be obtained. Whittier described a Dartmouth student

of the 1820s who, like Fisher, could turn his hand to all sorts
of occupations:

> Brisk wielder of the birch and rule,
> The master of the district school
> Held at the fire his favored place,
> Its warm glow lit a laughing face
> Fresh-hued and fair, where scarce appeared
> The uncertain prophecy of beard.
> He teased the mitten-blinded cat,
> Played cross-pins on my uncle's hat,
> Sang songs, and told us what befalls
> In classic Dartmouth's college halls.
> Born the wild Northern hills among,
> From whence his yeoman father wrung
> By patient toil subsistence scant,
> Not competence and yet not want,
> He early gained the power to pay
> His cheerful, self-reliant way;
> Could doff at ease his scholar's gown
> To peddle wares from town to town;
> Or through the long vacation's reach
> In lonely lowland districts teach . . .
> Happy the snow-locked homes wherein
> He tuned his merry violin,
> Or played the athlete in the barn,
> Or held the good dame's winding-yarn,
> Or mirth-provoking versions told
> Of classic legends rare and old,
> Wherein the scenes of Greece and Rome
> Had all the commonplace of home,
> And little seemed at best the odds
> 'Twixt Yankee pedlers and old gods. . . .

There is no better description extant of the self-supporting
American college student of the period—perhaps of any period.
Here too is a foreshadowing of the elements in American life
which doomed the traditional classicism: Whittier's student
had learned at least as much from experience as from formal
teaching; for him American life was as filled with epic qualities
as Homer's Greece.

Emerson, too, saw that when he wrote in *The Poet:*

We have yet had no genius in America, with tyrannous eye,
which knew the value of our incomparable materials, and saw,
in the barbarism and materialism of the times, another carnival
of the same gods whose picture he so much admires in Homer.
. . . Banks and tariffs, the newspaper and caucus, Methodism
and Unitarianism, are flat and dull to dull people, but rest on
the same foundations of wonder as the town of Troy and the
temple of Delphi . . .

Emerson and Thoreau were preaching doctrines which most
colleges were not ready to accept, but which the college student had discovered for himself.

It is significant that Whittier's self-supporting student came
from Dartmouth, the first college to officially encourage manual labor. Here all students were expected to spend vacations
working on the land, in the mills, or in shops. It was forbidden
"at any time to speak diminutively of the practice of labor."
From as far away as Connecticut men came to the college, paying their way by working in sawmills.

Of course students at other colleges often worked to earn
expenses. As has been noted, the Harvard president and Overseers were sympathetic to Jonathan Fisher's plea for a three
weeks' absence so that he might teach. A generation later
President Kirkland put impecunious freshmen into jobs as
bell ringers, tutors, etc. and gave Emerson a job in his own
house. The employment of student waiters in college commons
was a widespread practice.

At Dartmouth, however, student employment was regarded
not merely as a necessary makeshift for poor students; it was a
part of his education. Thus Dartmouth is the ancestor of the
"manual labor" institutions which flourished in the 1830s.
Students in such schools and colleges were required to spend
two or more hours a day at manual labor either on the college
farm or in workshops. The system had two objectives: to enable
a student to earn all or part of his expenses, and to produce
better discipline. This was the era of Carlyle's gospel of work

and the theory that Satan finds work for idle hands. Like so much else in the period, work became a moral issue, frequently to the advantage of the employer.

The manual-labor plan seems to have originated with Reverend George W. Gale, who tried it first at the Oneida Institute in 1827. Writing to Finney, of Oberlin fame, Gale said, "Depend upon it, Brother Finney, . . . this System of Education . . . will be to the moral world what the lever of Archimedes, could he have found a fulcrum, would be to the natural." With Lewis Tappan and others he founded the Society for Promoting Manual Labor in Literary Institutions. One of the enthusiasts, Theodore Weld, traveled 4,500 miles, much of the way on horseback, giving 200 lectures on manual labor and temperance. Among the numerous manual-labor colleges that sprang up in the 1830s were Mercer, in Georgia; Davidson, in North Carolina; Randolph-Macon, in Virginia; Knox, in Illinois; Marietta and Oberlin, in Ohio; Lafayette, in Pennsylvania.

Despite the missionary zeal with which the movement started off, the results were disappointing. There was not enough market for the brooms, cane-bottomed chairs, and other products of the workshops; college farms were not efficiently operated; and the wage scale was so low that it took a student many hours to earn even part of his expenses. Both students and college officials found that the labor interfered with study.

At Oberlin, where the system persisted longest, it was officially estimated in 1834 that a study year of forty weeks would cost from fifty-eight to eighty-nine dollars—which, like all such official estimates, was too low. One of the oldest undergraduate proverbs is: "Nothing lies like a college catalogue." But even though Oberlin fees and expenses were low, students would have had to work an astronomical number of hours to pay them. At a time when oats and potatoes sold for twenty-five cents a bushel, the wage scale for students was from two and three fourths to ten cents an hour. Girls earned between two and a half and three and a quarter cents for domestic labor. Thus at three cents an hour a girl would have had to work 600 hours to earn the eighteen-dollar tuition fee—over 2,900 hours to earn the total expense of eighty-nine dollars. To earn her full college expenses a girl would have had to work over ten hours a day during the forty-week school year. Nor could all the boys find work on the college farm, which didn't pay anyway and was eventually leased out. Wheat produced a mere ten bushels an acre; only one out of ten fruit trees lived; a silkworm scheme did not pan out; and sugar beets were raised not for economic reasons but to prevent the purchase of slave-produced sugar from Louisiana. Thus during the 1840s and 1850s the manual-labor system faded out, even at Oberlin.

It would thus appear that official schemes for student employment were less successful than the undergraduate's habit of going out during vacations to fell trees, teach school, and peddle goods or Bibles.

At the older Eastern institutions the working student was probably in the minority. During this same period of the manual-labor colleges, Jacob Motte pictured the vacation activities of Harvard students:

. . . some lounging in the fashionable streets of fashionable cities, others will be pursuing their sports in the country with dog and gun. Some will spend their time in pouring over old mathematical or metaphysical books, while others are skimming over new novels.

Obviously there was a great social and economic difference between a fashionable young Southern gentleman like Motte and an Ohio farmer's son at Oberlin. The one complained of the fit of his dancing pumps and paid his tailor eight dollars more for a coat than the other spent for a year's tuition. The girls at a Harvard commencement wore expensive clothes; those dated by Oberlin men earned their way through college by washing and ironing the men's shirts at thirty-seven and a half cents a dozen. By the 1840s a year's expenses might be about $100 at Oberlin, $195 at Yale, $226 at Princeton, $245 at Harvard and $332 at Virginia.

Despite these differences, the American colleges have never been one-class institutions. Even at expensive Virginia the faculty asserted that in 1844-1845 the great majority of the students belonged to the middle ranks of society, people who had to husband their finances scrupulously. It was claimed that a considerable number of those in attendance had earned their own money for expenses. Even after the general increase of prices in the fifties, the total expenses for a year at the University of Georgia in 1860 were between $178 and $213—almost exactly the same as those of the same period at Oberlin. At Georgia, as at Virginia, the sons of wealthy planters rubbed elbows with boys from middle-class families. The fashionable Jacob Motte graduated from Harvard a few weeks before the entrance of Henry David Thoreau, son of a small farmer who also painted signs. Ten years before, it had graduated a poverty-stricken young man named Emerson.

Social distinctions existed of course. In seventeenth-century Harvard students were listed according to the rank of their families in the state, and those of the upper rank had the best rooms and the privilege of helping themselves first at table. But between the Revolution and the Civil War, class distinctions seem to have been lightly felt: a student's loyalties and friendships centered around his literary society and his class. The small size of most colleges and the dormitory system contributed to this social democracy. At Amherst, well-to-do William Hammond was equally at home with his landlady's daughter and the young ladies of faculty families. A classmate gave a party to which he invited faculty wives, the "reigning belles," and the whole class. "Was astonished to find how well our class could appear in emergencies," commented Hammond.

Even the development of Greek-letter fraternities during the forties and fifties did not follow any clearly marked lines of social class. The early official opposition to them was not based on charges of social discrimination but grew out of the widespread distrust of secret societies which found political expression in the Anti-Masonic Party. Another very good reason for faculty suspicion and antifraternity rules was that meetings were often the occasion for a spree. The *Yale Lit* of 1856 ironically reported:

. . . a dignified company regularly straggling into Morning
Prayers, directly from their hebdomadal gathering, looking dull
and sleepy, and, as a matter of course, totally unfitted for the
duties of the day.

Another cause of opposition to fraternities was their habit
of controlling college politics. William Hammond, a member
of Psi Upsilon, spent an immense amount of his time politicking for campus elections. The *Yale Lit* charged:

No office "in the gift of the people," whether important or
trivial, can by any possibility be filled acceptably without a
long course of dabbling by five or six enterprising Societies.

However, campus politics was not invented by the fraternities; they merely took over what had been an activity of the
literary societies. After all, the students were practicing in a
small arena the arts and crafts they had observed in American
life and would later exercise in that larger setting.

The college fraternity, whether it operated *sub rosa* or with
official sanction, was undoubtedly something of a nuisance, but
in its early stages seems not to have been an agency for social
discrimination based on wealth. The day of palatial clubhouses
was yet to come; pre-Civil War meeting places were likely to
be in rented rooms over a tobacco store or barbershop. The
popular but impecunious student has seldom been excluded
from the American college fraternity.

In this the fraternity reflected an aspect of the college scene
which lasted until colleges became too large for intimate association among all classmates, and the sons of the plutocracy
arrived with huge allowances of spending money. The *Yale
Lit* of 1857 was probably not greatly exaggerating when it
stated:

It matters not what one has been or has done, before he entered
College. His standing here is gained by what he *does,* and what
he *is,* in College.

Most boys found a college atmosphere congenial. It is not
only in the rainbow-hued memories of alumni that college life

was a happy time; the students themselves realized that they were hugely enjoying themselves. Despite his disapproval of student revelry and his worry over difficult studies, Jonathan Fisher summed up his first year at Harvard: ". . . yet at this Seat of the Muses, all things considered, I think I have spent the happiest year in my life." Forty years later Jacob Motte, whose diary is a consistent record of enjoyment, described the college scene with that sentimental love which echoes throughout the songs and stories of generations of students:

Nothing can equal the beauty of a moonlight evening within the walls of Harvard, during the stillness of a vacation. The large and unoccupied buildings spreading their dark shadows across the college yard, the tall trees through whose branches the moon sheds her silvery light upon the surrounding objects, the beautiful walks where silence rules in the midst of uninterrupted repose, are objects that inspire the mind with a solemnity of feeling, most delightful in improving the soul.

The future naturalist John Muir, a student at the University of Wisconsin in the early 1860s, endured a life of hardship, living for fifty cents a week on a diet of bread, molasses, graham mush, and baked potatoes roasted on the hot ashes of the basement furnace. Nevertheless, when he was ready to graduate, he climbed a hill overlooking Lake Mendota to take a last, fond look at the campus where, as he said, "I had spent so many hungry and happy and hopeful days. There with streaming eyes I bade my blessed Alma Mater farewell."

And when the four years were over, they came to a handsome climax in a commencement where students could display their literary and forensic skills. In the days of small college classes every graduating senior had some part in the program, which might run for two days. These occasions, frequently called "Public Day" or "Exhibition Day," often attracted large audiences. The first commencement at William and Mary (1700) drew visitors from New York, Pennsylvania and Maryland—even a number of Indians. Compared to this large audience the whole student body numbered about sixty.

By the latter part of the eighteenth century, commencements had taken on some of their modern character with returning alumni, lights in every window, songs in the yard. At Yale's of September 1795 a recent Harvard graduate was waked at dawn by the uproar:

It seemed as if the earth shook from its centre, and the foundation of the hills was removed. A fit of trembling seized me, and tears bedewed my cheeks. My first impression was that the end of all things had come. . . .

It was the firing of a cannon which had so upset the clergyman from Cambridge.

Harvard commencements were equally gala but less violently masculine. In the 1830s a junior noted with pleasure:

The college yard presents a lively scene—ladies crossing in every direction with fur-belows and fur-aboves—bare heads and *almost* bare legs—but looking very handsome.

For a Delaware College student of the 1850s the exhibition by the literary societies was the high point of the occasion. This was held the day before the official graduation exercises. Two days earlier the boys had cut greens for decorations, which the July heat withered before the celebration, necessitating the redecoration of the hall. A returning alumnus of the society took the whole crowd to supper at an inn; the ladies served cakes and lemon drinks and passed out fans and programs. "The Oration," noted the student, "will be remembered by the Athenaean and The Delta Phi Literary Societies of Delaware College as long as there is a man alive."

By comparison commencement was tepid: "The speeches were good; beautiful music; weather improved and the ladies in very fine array. Flowers and applause and a refrained emotion." One reason things went off well was that "the town boys and our own ruffians were kept down both last night and this morning." Delaware students and faculty were not always so fortunate. Boys from the mills often disturbed lectures and tried to break up exhibitions.

It was all quite different from the modern stuffed-shirt performance with honorary-degree recipients and a visiting speaker taking the limelight. No doubt the long series of student speakers became boring, but they were what the parents and sweethearts had come to hear. Four years of practice in the literary and debating societies lay behind this final public demonstration of learning and skill. To a considerable degree this learning and skill was the product less of the formal instruction than of the student's own enterprise.

5

Death and Transfiguration

The Civil War transformed American college education. As might be guessed, the first effect was destructive: a large proportion of the student body went to war. But colleges are hard to kill. During the Revolution they had kept going even when on occasion they had to get out of town as did Harvard, Yale and Rutgers. In the Civil War some Southern colleges had to suspend, but others kept open, among them Virginia and the University of North Carolina. Northern colleges, although not menaced by invading armies, often operated under extremely difficult conditions. And both North and South colleges had to cope with a flood of returning veterans.

If one fact emerges more clearly than any other it is that the American college was no ivy-covered retreat. Oberlin, as has been recorded, was in the thick of the antislavery fight from the beginning. At most other colleges the students at first contented themselves with debating the questions of slavery, secession, etc., in their literary societies. But as the nation became more inflamed, so did the students. In 1858 at the University of Michigan there were few abolitionists, but one student became one after reading *Uncle Tom's Cabin* and seeing the lacerated backs of some runaway slaves who told of "Legree whippings." Even as late as 1860 Michigan students chased an antislavery speaker out of a church and smashed the windows. But a year later when Wendell Phillips came to speak, the senior class armed themselves with clubs to protect the meeting.

At Yale, Moses Coit Tyler wrote home about "a tremendous speech" by Henry Ward Beecher, who appealed to the citizens of New Haven for rifles to equip a "Colony" going to Kansas in 1856. The venerable Professor Silliman stood up and pledged the cost of one rifle, twenty-five dollars. When two more were pledged, Beecher said that if the audience made it twenty-five, he would get an equal number from his church. In the gallery young Tyler arose and promised to raise twenty-five dollars from the junior class. An uproar of applause followed. Before he went to bed he had raised nearly the whole amount. Then the Southerners in the class raised a hullabaloo about the commitment to an Abolition Emigrant Company—"a sufficient ground for dissolving the Union."

When Brooks caned Sumner in the United States Senate, Georgia students raised money to buy the assailant a new cane. At Virginia the Washington and Jefferson societies declined an invitation from Yale to join in the publication of an undergraduate magazine until that institution would exclude Negroes. But even in 1860 the student publication was still opposing disunion.

Then came the election of Lincoln. The Virginia faculty rescinded the ban on student military companies, and two were immediately organized with about seventy members between them. Two months before the state seceded, some students had climbed at midnight to the dome of the Rotunda to unfurl the Confederate flag. At far-off Michigan, when the news of Fort Sumter's surrender came on Sunday morning, church services became impossible. President Tappan addressed the students and said he had arranged for military drill. As at other colleges the campus quickly took on a military aspect; sports were abandoned for military drill, and the nights echoed to the sound of patriotic songs.

All over the nation the same pattern was repeated: students organized military companies or enlisted in the armies while faculties tried to restrain them. The Lafayette faculty instructed the president to ascertain by what means guns had been furnished to students by the state. They directed that all guns be stored under the supervision of a professor and that students be permitted to use them in their drill only if no gunpowder was "burned" in them. At Georgia the faculty reminded students that their first duty was to their books, but one after another quietly enlisted. Chancellor Lipscomb, hoping for an influx of Southern students from Northern colleges, decided to keep the university open on a wartime footing. To make this possible the trustees promptly reduced faculty salaries twenty per cent. But by 1863 the enrollment had dropped from about one hundred before the war to twenty, and with the calling out of the State Guards in which most students were enrolled, the college suspended entirely. At Lafayette the enrollment dropped from over a hundred to thirty-nine. With Lee's invasion of Pennsylvania the college was left with so few students that no commencement was held in 1863.

That colleges were able to operate at all was due largely to the early age at which many students entered. At Pennsylvania most of those in the Arts department were between fourteen or fifteen and eighteen or nineteen. This meant that student military organizations were little more than cadet corps. It was the older students who enlisted. The Pennsylvania commencement in 1863 was held on the third of July in a city almost in panic because of the approach of Lee's army. Earthworks were being thrown up, and one of the speakers, as noted on the program, was "excused—gone for defense of the State." Another, on a one-day leave from the army, took his degree in his lieutenant's uniform covered by a scholar's gown borrowed from the Reverend Phillips Brooks. While the ceremonies were in progress, one of the absent members of the class, William Brooke Rawle, was taking part in cavalry charges at Gettysburg and wondering whether he was "an idiot for permitting myself to be just where I was" or whether he "would rather give up half his lifetime than to have missed having a hand in it."

In the Civil War, faculties set a precedent for the future by granting credits and degrees to students in service. At Lafayette the faculty granted a student petition to allow men in the service to be continued in their classes without examination, and voted to award each his full average grade. The Pennsylvania trustees promised undergraduates who would volunteer "to serve their country in her present noble efforts to crush a

136 ACADEMIC PROCESSION

wicked rebellion" and those who were drafted that they might graduate with their classes if they were not absent more than a year.

The percentage of students and recent alumni who served in the armies was probably greater in the South where the military tradition was stronger. About three fourths of the graduates of Emory (founded 1836) entered the service. Approximately 2,500 University of Virginia men—about twenty-seven per cent of all the matriculates—served the Confederacy, and about 500 of these lost their lives. However, the relatively new University of Michigan furnished 1,205 men to the Union army, among them 151 surgeons, 85 assistant surgeons, and 406 commissioned officers. Twenty-three per cent of the graduates of New England colleges served in the Union army. Young businessmen like Jay Gould and Jim Fiske might purchase substitutes, but the college men trained for the professions fought and died along with the laborers, farmers, and artisans.

With the close of the war, the American colleges experienced for the first time that peculiarly American phenomenon of a mass return of veterans. Nothing comparable had occurred at the end of the Revolution: then the colleges went through a period of poverty and depleted enrollments. But with the end of the Civil War, Michigan, which had 526 students in 1860, found itself with 1,255 in 1866—400 of whom had seen active war service. By 1869 Harvard had jumped from a prewar 366 to 1,147. Even in the war-ravaged South, colleges found themselves with substantial enrollments. In 1866 Virginia had 490 students—only about 110 fewer than the whole student body of 1860, and far above the mere 138 of 1845. When the University of Georgia reopened in 1866, there were seventy-eight students as compared to less than a hundred in all classes before the war. The forty-four students who finished in 1869 composed the largest graduating class in the history of the university up to that time. Only institutions wrecked by the Union armies or taken over by carpetbaggers, like North Carolina, were unable to operate.

The returning veteran of 1866 was far more like his counterpart of World War II than like the riotous playboy of the Mademoiselle-from-Armentières era. At Oberlin and other Western colleges, a British traveler of 1865 saw the veterans "bearded like pards" and wearing old military jackets, sitting in classrooms with mere youngsters, "their equals in book learning." But the veterans went about their work "with an ardour and simplicity in no wise lessened by their warlike experience." At the University of Georgia, where most of the 1866 crop of students had been in the war, Chancellor Lipscomb described them as:

. . . much more manly in their sympathies and aspirations; much more obedient as to the real spirit of submission to discipline and consequently much more thoughtful and prudent as to matters of personal control; much more under influence and requiring less stern authority for their government than we ordinarily find in this class of persons.

Thus in the stately prose of the nineteenth century we find a description of the type of veteran so familiar to educators ninety years later.

The returning veteran also brought with him an enthusiasm for baseball. As has been noted, the pre-Civil War college had almost no organized sports. Crew races, which required both a suitable body of water and expensive equipment, had appeared at only a few schools. The early football was apparently more allied to interclass rushes than to a team sport. At Oberlin in 1859 there had been a brief rage for cricket, a game introduced also at Michigan. But during the war, in both the Northern and Southern armies, baseball became immensely popular; in the colleges of the 1860s it became a mania. Probably the first intercollegiate game was that of a Harvard class against one from Brown, played in Providence on June 27, 1863. That same year Michigan students wrote to Colonel Abner Doubleday for information, and the next year organized a baseball club. By 1867 the university was in the grip of baseball fever. The Lafayette faculty of 1866 voted to permit the baseball club a day's leave of absence for an intercollegiate game, but resolved to permit no further excuses from classes for baseball players. Two months later the faculty found it necessary to admonish students for playing during study hours. A year later at the University of Georgia, three baseball clubs were organized, and soon became nomadic. Oberlin experienced the same fever. With the coming of baseball, organized athletics became a central feature of college life.

In a still more important way the Civil War regenerated American education. It was a war which had been won not only on the battlefield but by the factory, the railroad, the technician. The American public understood this better than did the professors. A large part of the history of higher education in the sixties and seventies is the story of community pressure on the colleges to meet the needs of a new age. It is perhaps no accident that the rise of Germany and the United States as world powers coincided with a revolution from classical to scientific studies in the universities; whereas England, where Matthew Arnold and his kind helped to prevent such a revolution in the universities, lost out in the technological race with Germany and the United States. It is also perhaps no accident that British poets from Housman to Auden have found the classical world much more comfortable than the age of the motorcar, antitoxins, and sanitary plumbing.

Much of the educational revolution was of course the inevitable result of the needs of expanding industrialism, but part of it was due to the dry-as-dust nature of classical education. As has been suggested in previous chapters, a system dominated by the Yale doctrines of 1827 failed to provide the kind of scientific, humanistic, and social studies which could help a student understand nineteenth-century America. Like Henry Adams, most people who wanted such understanding had to seek it in European universities, in books not included in American college courses, or through actual experience.

In view of the prevailing classicism of college education before 1861 it is not surprising that many of the postwar inventors, industrialists, financiers and political leaders were not college-trained. But the real failure of that education is perhaps best indicated by the fact that between 1850 and 1900 American literature was largely created by people not trained in our colleges. This was not true of the earlier period. Despite such conspicuous exceptions as Franklin and Irving, it is college-trained men who largely make up the roster of our early writers: Cotton Mather, Jonathan Edwards, Thomas Jefferson, James Madison in theology and politics; James Fenimore Cooper and the "Connecticut Wits" (all Yale men) in early attempts at fiction and verse; Emerson, Thoreau, Hawthorne and Longfellow in New England's golden summer. But with *Moby Dick* in 1851 and *Leaves of Grass* in 1855 the roster of greats and near greats reads: Melville, Whitman, Mark Twain, Emily Dickinson, Lowell, Holmes, Howells and Henry James. Only two, Lowell and Holmes, were college men, although James, after picking up an education in foreign travel, did enter Harvard Law School. More literary greats of the last half of the century were graduates of printing offices than of colleges.

There had been prophetic voices to warn the traditionalists that they were not providing a vital education. "Why," asked the Amherst faculty in 1827, "such reluctance to admit modern improvements and modern literature? Why so little attention to the natural, civil and political history of our own country and to the genius of our government?" Fifteen years later President Wayland, of Brown, took up the demand for a more realistic approach to higher education. In the West the early state universities had made some moves in the direction of vocational education for teachers and farmers, but often on a subcollegiate level. In the college departments there was a tendency to imitate the curriculums of the older institutions. Harvard and Yale had introduced scientific schools, but segregated them from the college.

With the coming of peace, the demand for a more practical kind of education could not be denied. The returning veterans were mature men, many of them married, who had immediate vocational aims. Wealthy industrialists and businessmen were often ready to give large sums for departments of science and engineering. Faculties, long deaf to ideological arguments, began to listen to the language of money. After all, many of them had almost literally starved during the war.

The experience of Lafayette is a case in point. At one period, members of the faculty, including the world-famous philologist Francis A. March, instead of receiving salaries were permitted to requisition food from the supplies bought for the college commons. Since its founding in 1832, the college had operated on a shoestring. Then a wealthy canalboat operator, Asa Packer, gave the money to found Lehigh University, a non-sectarian institution specializing in science and engineering, only fifteen miles distant at South Bethlehem. That same year, 1865, the Lafayette faculty petitioned the trustees to set up a scientific course leading to a B.S. degree, stating:

The number of students in our country is great, and rapidly increasing, who wish to study the natural sciences, Philosophy, and modern literature . . . and who would be glad to enjoy the cultivation, and the learned habits and associations of college life, but who will not study Greek and Latin.

The last clause is significant: it was a moribund classicism which led to the alternative of vocationalism. In the next sentence the Lafayette faculty added the corollary:

Polytechnic Schools, Commercial Academies and Agricultural Colleges are springing up around us in answer to this want, and most of the great Universities and Colleges have added to the old classical studies a parallel Scientific Course.

Within a year a wealthy coal-mine operator gave Lafayette an endowment for the course, and soon after donated $300,000 for a scientific building—a sum greater than the cost of all the then existing structures on the campus. Thus began a process which at most colleges eventually relegated the humanities to the dusty back rooms of Old Main while the sciences moved into million-dollar laboratory buildings, and the schools of business became the largest divisions of universities. Eighty-seven years later the humanities are trying to recover the ball lost on this play. The followers of the Robert Maynard Hutchins system are still using the Yale formations of 1828.

The new "scientific course" at Lafayette and elsewhere was rapidly followed by more specifically vocational curriculums in various branches of engineering. For one thing, the so-called scientific course was so like the traditional curriculum that it did not satisfy the demand for scientific and vocational studies. At Lafayette in 1875 the percentage of recitation time devoted to the principal areas in the scientific course was approximately twenty-five for mathematics, including physics and mechanics; sixteen for the natural sciences; but thirty-five in Anglo-Saxon, English, French, and German. Economics, political science, and history all told were assigned a mere three per cent of the recitation time. A student in the classical course devoted about twenty-four per cent of his time to mathematical subjects, thirty-four per cent to ancient languages, fourteen per cent to modern languages, and seven and one half per cent to natural science. Thus in both courses language and mathematics were the staples of the curriculum.

It must always be remembered that course labels are not a sufficient guide to an understanding of a curriculum. Just as the early "classical" or "liberal" education was in fact largely a training in translation and grammar, so the new "scientific" course was essentially the traditional curriculum with the substitution of Anglo-Saxon and modern languages for Latin and Greek. It is true that more time was given to the sciences in the new course, but even so a student at Lafayette spent only 154 hours on chemistry, 140 on botany and zoology—fewer than the number now spent in classes and laboratory in a freshman course in either subject. The student in the classical course of the same date got a mere twelve hours of history, thirty-six of chemistry. These figures are for the total time spent in class; calculated in terms of credit hours this would mean about two for chemistry and less than one for history. Ten years later at Amherst, freshmen and sophomores in the classical

course attended classes seventeen hours a week. Of these, between fourteen and sixteen, depending on the semester, were
devoted to languages and mathematics.

It is against the background of these typical college programs
that we can better understand the demand for vocational training and for the elective system. The scientific course had too
little science to be vocationally useful; the liberal-arts course
was not liberal and had no relation to the arts.

Even English was studied in the traditional manner which
had stultified the classics. As described in the Lafayette catalogue:

An English classic is taken up. The text is minutely analyzed,
the idioms explored, and synonyms weighed; the mythology,
biography, history, metaphysics, theology, geography, are all
looked up. The rhetorical laws of English composition, and
the principles of epic, and dramatic art are applied to Milton,
Shakespeare and the other English classics, *line by line*. [Italics
mine.]

This is not cited as an egregious horror; college courses and
methods in every period have been remarkably standardized.
In planning a curriculum, a faculty's first question is always:
"What is customary elsewhere?" It is small wonder that the
graduates of this system of education produced few important
works of literature. Lafayette College had in Professor Francis
March one of the most famous professors of English in America
during the last quarter of the nineteenth century; it graduated
not a single writer of even minor importance. Certainly neither
Lafayette nor Syracuse can take credit for Stephen Crane: he
stayed but a year at each place, and before and during his college days worked as a journalist. He upset his professors by
calling Tennyson's poetry "swill" and turned to Tolstoy and
Flaubert—neither of whom was then studied in college
courses. As one recent textbook on American literature states:
"His fragmentary college career was distinguished only in baseball." Like Walt Whitman, Mark Twain, Bret Harte and Wil-

liam Dean Howells, Stephen Crane was an alumnus of the newspaper office.

It is true that in the hands of a personality like George Lyman Kittredge this method of minute textual analysis inherited from the classicists could come alive. But Kittredge brought into play both histrionics and a vast store of humanistic learning. Most practitioners of the method have been neither such good actors nor such good raconteurs; even Kittredge's own disciples have often turned out to be practicing pedants. Whether applied to the classics or to English literature, the method, except in the hands of an unusually brilliant teacher, is a stultifying one.

The natural result of this persistent traditionalism was that the public began to take matters into its own hands. A Maine congressman, Justin Smith Morrill, who had quit school at fifteen to clerk in a village store, introduced a bill in 1857 which donated public lands in states and territories "which may provide colleges for the benefit of agriculture and the mechanic arts." President Buchanan vetoed it, but Morrill introduced a similar bill which Lincoln signed in 1862. Although the full effects of the bill were slow in developing, it eventually became one of the chief forces in the revolution from classicism to vocationalism.

With the passage of the act, the scramble for its largess began. In New York there was a struggle, to be repeated elsewhere, between advocates of a single strong institution and the lobbyists for about twenty small sectarian colleges. A state senator with little formal schooling, after discussing the matter with Andrew White, became the champion of the plan for a great educational institution at Ithaca. Ezra Cornell, who had successively been a teacher, potter, carpenter, mechanic, and operator of a flour mill, had also invented devices for improving telegraph wiring, and was one of the founders of Western Union. This typically American graduate of the school of experience gave $500,000 and two hundred acres of land at Ithaca to bring the new institution into being.

With White at its head, Cornell University began operation in 1865. One of the great college presidents in America, Andrew White had, as we have seen (p. 72), turned down an appointment at Yale for the freer atmosphere of the University of Michigan. At Cornell he introduced the elective system, student self-government, and stated the radical doctrine that "a professor should not be called upon to be a policeman."

One of the most difficult problems was the recruiting of a faculty capable of teaching in a modern university. According to White, there were in America no young men holding graduate fellowships, with the exception of two or three at Harvard. He had to sail to Europe to purchase scientific equipment and find professors equipped to handle the technical divisions. In order to get superior teaching in an era when well-qualified men were scarce, White devised the scheme of nonresident professors and lecturers to supplement the instruction by the resident faculty. Twenty lectures by Agassiz drew large numbers of the ablest students in science; those of James Russell Lowell attracted students interested in literature. From England came James A. Froude, Godwin Smith and Edward A. Freeman, a *regius* professor at Oxford who wore a shooting jacket to class. As White described the functions of the nonresident lecturers and the resident faculty: "The former shook the bush and the latter caught the birds."

There were three general programs from which to choose: the arts course with Latin and Greek, the general course with Latin and modern language, and the scientific course. During the first two years the work was prescribed; after that a student was given a wide latitude in the choice of subjects. Like Folwell of Minnesota, White developed a division between the work of the first two years and that of the junior and senior years—a pattern which has recently been widely adopted.

Following the all too familiar American pattern, the sectarians and the educational traditionalists attacked the new institution. So violent was the sectarian press that the governor of the state, who had been in Ithaca the day before Cornell opened, found it politic to be absent from the inaugural ceremonies. Commented White: "His excellency was a very wise man in his generation. . . ." Following the opening in 1865, the sectarian press led a violent campaign against Ezra Cornell. When there was dancing at a Founder's Day celebration, a number of clergymen protested on the grounds that dancing was "destructive of vital godliness." The matter was brought before the faculty, but no action was taken. A candidate for a professorship in the technical department had excellent recommendations from Harvard except that a bishop complained that the man was a Unitarian. White replied that if the professor were the best man for the position he would appoint him if he were a Buddhist—a remark which upset the bishop, who expressed doubts that a layman should be permitted to teach at all. From conservative educators came attacks on the elective system and on the combining of scientific and technical study with the hallowed classics.

As a matter of fact the classics flourished. White's theory was that by getting the uninterested students out of the course, the work could be carried further than was usual in American colleges. The results supported the theory: a few years after the university opened, Cornell students took more first prizes in intercollegiate competition in Latin, Greek, and mathematics than were garnered by all the other competing institutions put together. Furthermore, there were improved relations between students and classical professors. In the old days students had made fun of such faculty members as eccentrics and pedants—a condition which changed at Cornell.

The manual-labor features advocated by the founder failed here as they did elsewhere; students proved so unskillful that it was cheaper to put them in a hotel and hire laborers. On the other hand the course in electrical engineering—probably the first in America—aroused the students' enthusiasm. They built a dynamo which lighted the whole college.

In 1878 White traveled abroad, studying the courses in economics and political science offered by European institutions. At Cornell he established lectures in sociology for all students. They studied such topics as crime, poverty, alcoholism, insanity, and made field trips to state institutions. This essentially modern approach to the subject, though lacking the exactness of natural science, was a long step away from the academic theorizing of the old course in moral philosophy which had once offered the students only glimpses into this area of knowledge.

Similarly White introduced work in American history. According to him there was not a single course in that subject offered in the United States; students had to go to France for it. At first, visiting lecturers were brought in; then White's former Michigan student, Moses Coit Tyler. It is significant that this pioneer professor of American history and first historian of our literature did not come from one of the older colleges but from a Western state university.

Like Cornell, the Western universities developed rapidly in the period after the Civil War—and for the same reasons. Public funds provided the necessary financial support, and public pressures led to the development of new types of education. The Morrill Act added federal aid to state appropriations, and required the development of departments of agriculture and engineering. As has been noted, Michigan, with an enrollment of 1,255 in 1866, became the second largest university* of the period. Its historian, Kent Sagendorph, writing of the 1870s, states:

Throughout America, the University of Michigan led the nation's colleges in three important aspects—it had the highest attendance, enjoyed the biggest income, and offered the greatest number of undergraduate and professional courses.

To a large extent Michigan became the pattern for the other great state universities, particularly Wisconsin and Minnesota. Both of these were founded before the Civil War, but Wisconsin developed slowly, and Minnesota's first building, Old Main, stood empty until 1867. The man chiefly responsible for getting the University of Minnesota on its feet was a hardware mer-

---

* As Michigan's enrollment included a preparatory department, Harvard was actually the largest university.

chant, J. S. Pillsbury, to whom the institution owed $5.50 for locks and $1,000 for other supplies. Pillsbury and others traveled over the state settling the claims of bondholders by means of sales of some of the university's landholdings. With the passage of the Morrill Act, Pillsbury, by that time a senator, successfully advocated a single strong institution rather than a college and a separate school of agriculture.

In 1867 the squatters occupying Old Main were chased out, and the university reopened, this time on a coeducational basis. However, because the regents thought of it as chiefly a place for instruction in the humanities, there was a fifty-year period of hostility on the part of the farm community. A lady of the early faculty did not help matters with her composition of a song for the farm-school division:

So it's back to the farm, boys, for luck, luck, luck,
Hear the neighing, mooing, and the cluck-cluck-cluck.
Our sheepskins wrapped by Ceres will be our mascots true;
Our motto: Scientific farming, cock-a-doodle-do!

Twenty years after the reopening, the farmers, acting through the Grange and the Farmers' Alliance, were still fighting for a separate school of agriculture not controlled by the "snobs and theorists" on the faculty.

Again Pillsbury came to the aid of the university with a gift to build a science hall, provided that the land grants were kept intact—a stipulation which prevented the legislature from splitting off the School of Agriculture. It will be remembered that Pillsbury was not a college man. Shortly after he started as a hardware merchant, his store had burned, leaving him $38,000 in debt. He became one of the founders of the great milling industry, then senator, then governor of the state. Yet, like Thomas Jefferson a half century before, he especially valued his work in the creation of a university. Speaking at the dedication of his statue, he stated: "There is no spot on earth I more prefer to be remembered than on this campus."

For J. S. Pillsbury, as for so many Americans, there has been a strange fascination in the development of a college. One of the striking features of the post-Civil War college is the part played by the noncollege man. Men like Pillsbury, Ezra Cornell, Matthew Vassar, Johns Hopkins, Ario Pardee, Asa Packer, in the sixties and seventies, not only gave large sums of money; they gave them to further various educational philosophies or, rather, various aspects of the same philosophy: the ideal of an education to meet the needs of American life. In the tradition of Franklin, this education was to be utilitarian, but not narrowly so. Usually these noncollege benefactors of colleges recognized the cultural values in the traditional system; perhaps they envied somewhat the lawyers and clergymen who exemplified these values. As we have seen, Lafayette, Cornell, Minnesota all preserved the study of the classics at the same time they introduced scientific and vocational studies. Rather, these millers, inventors, brewers, miners, businessmen and canalboat operators saved the colleges from a sterile specialization in a minor aspect of learning.

And perhaps their interest in higher education saved these men from being engulfed in the corrupt materialism of their era. Like the church of the Middle Ages, the college of the post-Civil War decades became the symbol of an ideal. In the midst of constant war men built cathedrals dedicated to a woman, the mother of the Prince of Peace; in the most brutally materialistic half century in America, the graduates of the school of hard knocks helped to transform the colleges from parochial prep schools into great universities.

Their allies in this great endeavor were a group of brilliant intellectuals, most of them rebels against a moribund classicism. The same two decades made notable by Ezra Cornell, J. S. Pillsbury, Asa Packer, Matthew Vassar, and Johns Hopkins were also the period of Andrew White of Cornell, William Watts Folwell of Minnesota, Charles W. Eliot of Harvard, Daniel Coit Gilman of Johns Hopkins, and Frederick A. P. Barnard of Columbia—probably the most brilliant constellation of college presidents ever seen in America. For these were the days before boards of trustees selected ex-generals and displaced politicians as the titular heads of great universities.

Like Cornell of the same decade, Minnesota was unusually fortunate. Among those who recommended William Watts Folwell as the first president were Professor Thomas Lounsbury of Yale, and President Andrew White of Cornell. In 1869 the regents elected him at the age of thirty-six. Folwell, a graduate of Hobart, had studied, in addition to required subjects, the violin, law, and the science of sailing. He had then gone to Europe to take up Sanskrit and Arabic, and to make a pilgrimage to see Jacob Grimm, whom he called the "father of modern philology." However, Folwell objected to the nature of German education: "I cannot endure to have learning piled on me. I do not want to be instructed but to be informed."

In the Civil War he became an army engineer, and built bridges so well that he emerged as a colonel. In his Civil War uniform Folwell was romantically handsome. He had thick hair parted at the side, a short silky beard, and the eyes of a mystic. Sixty years later, in his nineties, the beard had become a white Vandyke; the hair had receded, showing a handsome forehead; the eyes had become shrewd and wise, but still looked off into distant horizons.

They looked into distant horizons when he made his inaugural address. A university, he said, is not "merely an overgrown college," but "a federation of professional schools." Quoting Ezra Cornell, he stated that it should be "an institution in which any person can find instruction in any subject."

Such a federation of schools . . . embracing potentially all subjects of practical interest, teaching always with reference to principles, occupying ever an attitude of investigation, knowing no favorite subjects, thoroughly imbued with the scientific spirit: that is the university.

Folwell therefore preached the elective system. It was absurd, he said, to compel a student "to drudge and agonize over a study as a mere gymnastic. There should ever be held out a worthy reason, a noble and practical motive for all the lessons and exercises of a school." He argued that "the close of the sophomore year is a well-marked era in college life." Grammar, drill, paradigms, construing, and "blackboard drudgery" should then give way to "humanizing, literary, and reflective subjects."

Folwell planned, however, the eventual sloughing off of undergraduate work. Like Jefferson and Tappan, he thought in terms of a university superimposed on a system of colleges. According to Folwell, a college might be denominational; a university must be secular. The former could assume the burdens of discipline; the latter should expect students to be ready for adult effort. Long before the doctrine was accepted in America, he spoke of the need for pure research:

We purchase a telegraph, the photograph, a new motor, the spectroscope, the lucifer match, or chloroform at the price of fifty years of seemingly fruitless laboratory work. The university should be the natural resort and recourse for counsel and information.

Like so many educational pioneers, Folwell was attacked by the traditionalists, in this case his own faculty. Wrapping themselves in the American flag and clutching their classic textbooks, they said that the old system was basically American and would never be changed. Folwell answered that the old colleges did not meet the demands of a great number of young people preparing to be merchants, engineers, architects, chemists, miners, metallurgists, pharmacists, manufacturers, journalists, naturalists, astronomers, horticulturalists, and farmers. Many distinguished educators came to his support, and for a time the regents upheld him.

Next he set about bringing the secondary schools and the university into a co-operative relationship. He recognized that the schools must be concerned with the "great body of youth" who could not reach college; nevertheless, he insisted that the state must develop "a complete, continuous and effective system of schools" ready to "offer every child in Minnesota a liberal education."

However, a combination of the classicists, disgruntled students, the denominational colleges and a depression defeated Folwell. A faculty group, described by Folwell as "the Bourbons," presented to the regents a report designed to overthrow his ideas. According to a recent historian of the university, they wanted to establish the point that institutions of higher learning existed to teach Latin and Greek; the natural and social sciences were relatively unimportant. The regents abolished physics and history. Following the depression of 1879, enrollment began to plunge at the same time that denominational schools were gaining public support. Some recently disciplined students put on Ku Klux Klan costumes in order to stage a demonstration against the president. Folwell resigned under pressure.

Unlike Tappan, who fled to Europe, Folwell refused offers to go elsewhere, and he taught political science at Minnesota from 1884 to 1906. A man interested in everything "from Plato to hog cholera," he next devoted himself to writing a four-volume history of the state, a project he completed just before his death in 1929 at the age of ninety-six.

His successor, Cyrus Northrup, was a type more congenial to faculty and regents: a genial, pedestrian administrator. Northrup did succeed in gradually breaking down the hostility of the farming community to the university, but the brilliant pioneering begun by Folwell was laid aside.

At the same time that Western institutions like Minnesota, Michigan, and Oberlin were becoming more traditional in their collegiate programs, several Eastern colleges, especially Harvard and Columbia, embarked on radical reforms. It was in the first two decades following the Civil War that Harvard emerged as the greatest of all American institutions of learning. Before that time it had been a small college, always surpassed in enrollment by Yale, and at times by Union, Dartmouth and Virginia. In 1856-1857 it had a mere 366 students. In 1869 it enrolled 1,147, making it the largest university in the country. Michigan came next with 1,111. Excluding the professional schools of law, theology, and medicine, Harvard had 655 students, Yale 644, and Michigan 462.

In his 1870 report to the trustees of Columbia, President Barnard attributed the growth of Harvard directly to a more liberal curriculum than that of any other Eastern college. In support of this theory he pointed out that despite an increase in population, the total enrollment in New England colleges other than Harvard had decreased six per cent in fifteen years. However, Barnard's proposals for a liberalization of the Columbia curriculum were long resisted by a conservative board of trustees. Harvard under Eliot embarked on a program of innovation far more radical than the relatively minor changes which had begun under President Quincy forty years before.

Charles William Eliot was only thirty-five when he was elected president of Harvard in 1869. The choice was not without opposition. The classicists feared his liberality to new subjects; scientists, chiefly Agassiz and Pierce, were afraid he would sacrifice the humanities to science. Even after his election by the Corporation, the Board of Overseers refused to ratify the action. When the Corporation returned the same nomination, the Overseers finally accepted it. A prophetic editorial in the Boston *Post* stated: "His administration will prove a turning point in the history of Harvard."

In a period when college presidents were most often clergymen, Eliot was a chemist. He had entered Harvard at fifteen, had remained after graduation as a tutor in mathematics and chemistry, then had been promoted to assistant professor. Rejected for a professorship, he traveled in Europe where he attended some lectures in French and German universities. He seems to have been more interested in their methods and organization than in scholarly work in chemistry. On his return he was called to a professorship at Massachusetts Institute of Technology. Something of the low level of American scholarship can be gathered from the fact that a man of thirty-one without any degree beyond the A.B. could become a full professor in a respected institution.

Two reasons for his election to the presidency of Harvard four years later were his impeccable Harvard lineage and two articles on "The New Education" written for that equally impeccable New England institution, *The Atlantic Monthly*. His father had been treasurer of Harvard College, and thus a member of the Corporation; back of his father extended a line of

Lymans and Eliots, many of them members of early Harvard classes.

In the *Atlantic* articles Eliot reviewed the various attempts to introduce scientific courses and pointed out the failure to provide a scientific training as respectable as the classical training. He then discussed preparatory-school education, advocating more emphasis on English, modern language and science. He insisted on the need for teaching American history. Most important in his discussion was his insistence on discovering a boy's innate aptitude. "The natural bent and peculiar quality of every boy's mind should be sacredly regarded in his education. . . ." This was particularly important both for the happiness of the individual and because of the increasing specialization of modern society.

Here then was the foundation of Eliot's belief in the elective system. As we have seen, Eliot was not the first advocate of elective studies; the idea goes as far back as Franklin and Smith's College of Philadelphia; it was developed by Jefferson, and more recently preached by Wayland, White, and Barnard. In this, as in much else, Eliot was not an original thinker nor a very learned man. His genius was for educational statesmanship.

Eliot's inaugural address outlined the task of the great university he hoped to see in America. When it came time for him to read it, he stepped up to the desk, an erect, athletic young man wearing sideburns and holding his head tilted upward. In a clear, strong voice filled with feeling and intense sincerity, he began:

The endless controversies whether language, philosophy, mathematics, or science supplies the best mental training, whether general education should be chiefly literary or chiefly scientific have no practical lesson for today. The University recognizes no real antagonism between literature and science, and consents to no such narrow alternatives as mathematics or classics, science or metaphysics. We would have them all, and at their best. . . . It will be generations before the best American institutions of education will get growth enough to bear pruning.

He went on to speak of methods of instruction, of standards of examination, of college discipline, of scholarships, of higher education for women. Although Harvard could not admit them on a coeducational basis, some other device might be found. He discussed the elective system. "The young man of nineteen or twenty ought to know what he likes best and is most fit for." At least he would know what he hated. "When the revelation of his own peculiar taste and capacity comes to a young man, let him reverently give it welcome, thank God, and take courage." As for the State, it was variety, not uniformity of men's minds which was needed.

He spoke of the need for a true university in America, but one which should copy no European model:

A university must be indigenous; it must be rich; but, above all, it must be free. The winnowing breeze of freedom must blow through all its chambers. It takes a hurricane to blow wheat away. An atmosphere of intellectual freedom is the native air of literature and science. . . .

Emerson, right in front among the Overseers, smiled, for much of what the earnest young man was saying about the individual and academic freedom was his own doctrine. Professor John Fiske wrote to his wife that he had never heard a speech so grand and impressive; "The old arches rang with thunders of applause." Mrs. Elliot Cabot came home, emotionally stirred as if she had been to the opera.

Certainly she had heard the overture to a great work. To an incredible degree Eliot achieved during the next forty years almost every item of the program he had outlined. When he retired in 1909, Harvard was the great, indigenous university he had envisioned; it was rich and, to a degree unknown elsewhere in America, it was free.

Eliot's first great step was not the introduction of the elective system (that came gradually over a period of fifteen years), but the strengthening of the faculty. He did this in three ways: by increasing salaries, by setting scholars free from the traditional dull routine, and by seeking unusual men from all over

America and even in Europe. Almost his first act was to increase professorial salaries from $3,000 to $4,000. Before the Civil War, $2,000 was a good professorial salary; even as late as 1867 Michigan paid only $1,500. The same year that Harvard professors went up to $4,000, those at New York University were advanced from $1,500 to $3,000. By means of this one action Eliot had placed Harvard in a position to get almost any man it wanted in America.

When Eliot became president, Francis J. Child, then forty-four, a scholar famous on both sides of the Atlantic for his work on the ballads, was teaching chiefly required classes in composition and spending his time reading themes. In 1868 he had one elective section. Five years later he was teaching elective courses in Anglo-Saxon, History and Grammar of the English Language, and a new elective in Chaucer, Shakespeare, Bacon, Milton and Dryden. By 1879 Eliot said that the recitation method of conducting classes had largely given way to lectures, "conversational instruction," and the discussion method. Thus, under Eliot, students and faculty were set free from the routine which had stultified both for over two centuries.

It would be easy to attribute to Eliot the roster of brilliant men added to the faculty during his time. Certainly he had an eye for talent: witness his appointment of Henry Adams and the famous anecdote in which Adams boasted that he knew nothing about medieval history and Eliot replied: "If you can point out anyone who knows more, Mr. Adams, I will appoint him." But it seems to have been Dean Ephraim Gurney who suggested Adams for the job. However they were suggested, the men appointed by Eliot during his first five years included John Trowbridge, William James, O. W. Holmes, Jr., Charles Eliot Norton and George Herbert Palmer. All were young and all became distinguished or famous. It is probably impossible to determine the extent to which Eliot was responsible for the choice of these and other brilliant men appointed later—such men as Josiah Royce, George Lyman Kittredge, George Santayana, Albert Bushnell Hart, Barrett Wendell, George Pierce

Baker, Bliss Perry, Henry P. Bowditch, Roscoe Pound—these and others like them who made up by far the most distinguished faculty in America for a period of fifty years. Some of them, like Adams, Norton, Holmes, Wendell, and Kittredge, because of their ancestry and Harvard connections, were almost inevitable choices, no matter who had been president. Even before Eliot, Harvard had attracted Asa Gray, Francis J. Child, Louis Agassiz, Evangelinus A. Sophocles, George M. Lane, Henry Wadsworth Longfellow, James Russell Lowell—a distinguished faculty in themselves.

The point is that Eliot created an environment in which brilliant men could develop. One of the great tragedies of American education is that so many able scholars and teachers have been condemned to a dull routine of teaching ill-prepared students. Until late in the nineteenth century only a handful of institutions had the facilities, wealth, and atmosphere which are necessary to scholarly growth. A few great personalities like the elder Dwight, Mark Hopkins and Benjamin Silliman transcended their environment, but many another cherished name in college histories represents a local celebrity distinguished only in the provincial world of small colleges and magnified in the beery eyes of returning alumni.

The whole story of the environment created or fostered by Eliot is at least a book in itself. But two points should be mentioned here: his reorganization of the college along modern departmental and administrative lines, and his development of genuine graduate and professional schools.

Among the measures for reorganizing the college were the appointment of Ephraim Gurney as its first dean to relieve the president of disciplinary duties; the appointment of a dean for each department with its own faculty; the establishment of a university calendar governing all departments; and an overhauling of the university statutes—a revision which gradually cut forty pages of rules down to a booklet of five pages. Increasingly students were treated as adults. What Eliot himself regarded as the most important administrative change was his practice of presiding over the meetings of the faculties of every department. During his first year he presided at thirty-four meetings of the Corporation, forty-five of the College Faculty, and thirty-eight or thirty-nine of those held by the smaller faculties of the Divinity School, Laurence Scientific School, Medical School, Dental School, School of Mining and Geology, and Zoological Museum. It was through this means that he unified the heterogeneous units into a university and brought his influence to bear on each of them.

His reform of the Medical School was typical. Although the School was regarded as one of the best in the country, its standards were low. As was then the custom, the faculty depended for their income on student fees, a system which tempted lecturers to strive for popularity at the expense of standards. There was no regular sequence of courses; students could attend lectures by the same man year after year. At the end of the course each student underwent an oral examination covering nine subjects and lasting an hour and a half. If he passed five of the subjects, he was graduated. William James remembered Oliver Wendell Holmes asking him one question. When James answered correctly, the Autocrat announced: "If you know *that*, you know everything; now tell me about your family and the news at home."

In his fight for higher standards of medical education, Eliot was supported by Charles Francis Adams, chairman of the Board of Overseers. It was Adams who used as an argument the story of the young Harvard doctor who had killed a patient with an overdose of morphia. "I suppose," concluded Adams, "this young doctor was one of those graduates who were required to pass only five examinations out of nine to obtain the degree." Written examinations were introduced; a progressive course of three, and eventually four, years was adopted; and clinical work was made the rule.

To rejuvenate the Law School Eliot brought in a brilliant former student as dean, Christopher Columbus Langdell. It was Langdell who introduced the case method of study.

Much more closely allied to the undergraduate education was the creation of a graduate department in the college. The usual custom in American colleges had been to award the M.A. to any Bachelor of Arts who maintained a good moral character for three years after graduation, and who paid a five-dollar fee for it. The development of a genuine graduate department at Harvard was closely linked with the system of granting honors in various fields of study at graduation, a practice which encouraged what is now called "majoring." The graduate department, organized in 1872, had courses leading to the degrees of Master of Arts, Doctor of Science, and Doctor of Philosophy. Even after the change in 1890 from a graduate department to a separate Graduate School of Arts and Sciences, there was no clear-cut separation of undergraduates and graduate students. At Harvard they have always sat side by side in the classroom. Along with the abandonment of the old recitation method, this custom helped to produce a genuine university level of instruction.

To further encourage faculty scholarship Eliot introduced the sabbatical leave and exchange professorships with France and Germany.

In any organic body the whole is always greater than the sum of its parts. Thus no listing of the changes brought about under Eliot will tell the whole story of the transformation of an old-fashioned college loosely affiliated with some professional schools into a modern university. Most important of all was the atmosphere created by Eliot. It was an atmosphere of freedom. For the faculty it included freedom from the boring routine of hearing recitations in prep-school subjects; a freedom of inquiry little known in more orthodox academic communities; and that even rarer freedom conferred by adequate salaries and sabbatical leaves. For the students it meant increasing freedom of choice of subjects and freedom to be self-directing individuals. As Eliot had discovered at M.I.T., students not harassed by petty regulations were more orderly and responsible than those under the old system. The traditional antagonism between students and faculty largely disappeared. Eliot introduced the M.I.T. system at Harvard. Like the elective system this too had wide influence on other colleges.

Of course there were flaws in the picture. Eliot was often domineering, especially as the years went on; people found him cold, and students disliked him; the elective system developed excesses of its own; and academic freedom was occasionally sacrificed to expediency as in the dismissal of Professor John Fiske, an eminent historian, but the target of the religious press. The growing wealth and prestige of Harvard attracted to it the plutocracy which created the Gold Coast and the snobbery of exclusive clubs. But some of these are matters for a later chapter. The Harvard of Eliot's first decade as president became probably the most vital force in American college education. Michigan, Cornell, Minnesota were all important, but in the first two decades after 1865 Harvard took the position it has held ever since as the greatest of American universities.

Nothing, perhaps, could better illustrate the point that success is as much due to circumstances as to ability than the history of Eliot's contemporary, Frederick A. P. Barnard. As an educational thinker Barnard was at least the equal of Eliot, perhaps his superior. But the Columbia of his day was a small college with a stodgy board of trustees who consistently disregarded some of the most brilliant reports ever written by a college president.

Barnard was fifty-five when he was called to the presidency in 1865. A Yale graduate, he had become a teacher of the deaf and dumb, then a professor at the University of Alabama and, next, president of the University of Mississippi. With the coming of the Civil War he declined a post in the Confederate government and came north. Originally he had accepted and preached the Yale doctrine of a traditional classical education. But Barnard was one of those rare individuals who grow after reaching middle life. Until his death in harness at eighty, he preached increasingly liberal educational doctrines to his unimaginative board of trustees.

It was the modern University of Columbia which Barnard

sketched in a series of reports to the board. These reports add up to one of the most searching and comprehensive discussions of college education written in America. The prose style is heavy and academic; the content is alive even today. Barnard was one of that increasingly rare breed of college presidents who are educators rather than mere executives of a corporation.

When Barnard arrived, Columbia had only 150 students, an enrollment which shrank to 116 seven years later. The arts faculty consisted of seven or eight professors. The librarian was on duty only about an hour and a half daily, and became enraged when anyone suggested that he buy a book. Thus he spent only about half the annual appropriation of $1,500. In 1876 a new professor described the students as "rich loafers with no appreciation of anything scientific or intellectual." Another professor remarked that he did as little as possible for "these dunderheads," but devoted his time to research. Barnard himself soon became so deaf that he was forced to conduct faculty meetings by means of an immense ear trumpet with speaking tubes running to each seat at the conference table.

In this unpromising situation Barnard immediately began to preach the idea of a great university. Three years before Eliot's call for an indigenous, wealthy university, Barnard advised his trustees:

Universities are a want of the country which must and will be supplied; but they cannot spring into being full panoplied like Minerva from the head of Jupiter. They must grow by gradual accretion. . . .

He spoke of the dream of educators for an American university combining the best features of British and European institutions. He estimated such a project would cost ten or fifteen million dollars.

He also anticipated Eliot in proposing that students be treated as adults and that the faculty be freed from the job of acting as policemen. Written examinations were substituted for the time-honored system of daily grades based on the instructor's estimate of a student's performance in oral recitation.

D. S. WILLETTS PRESENTING DIPLOMAS TO THE GRADUATES OF THE WOMEN'S MEDICAL COLLEGE AT STEINWAY HALL, NEW YORK, 1873

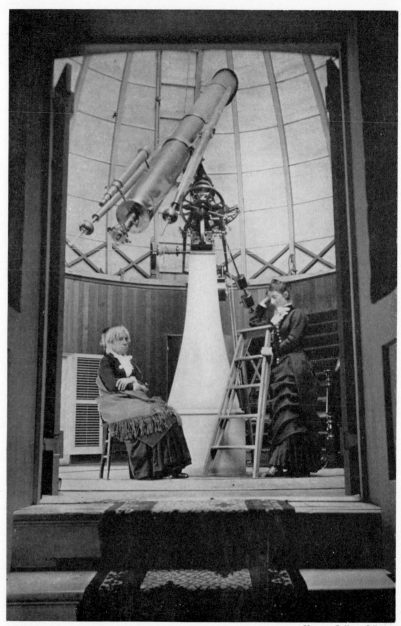

MARIA MITCHELL AND MARY WHITNEY IN OBSERVATORY,
VASSAR COLLEGE, ABOUT 1888

Miss Mitchell (1818-1889), who had discovered a comet in 1847, was surprised when Matthew Vassar offered her a position as professor of astronomy.

Barnard believed that the fairest system was a combination of monthly reports and final examinations. Because students sometimes came to the examination room "fortified with instrumentalities which enable them to defeat the object of the exercise," he argued for a development of a sense of honor among them.

In 1870 Barnard took up the proposition advanced twenty years before by Francis Wayland that the American people were increasingly rejecting the traditional education. This became a recurring theme in his reports. "It is idle," he argued, "to prove to a people that they ought to prefer a species of culture which, upon evidence satisfactory to them, they have deliberately made up their minds not to prefer." He pointed to Cornell and the University of Michigan which, because of their modern programs, had attracted throngs of students at a time when enrollments elsewhere were declining in proportion to the population.

But Barnard did not argue merely on the basis of making colleges popular; he demanded change on educational grounds:

If . . . we consider the success of those institutions which offer to their students a considerable latitude in the selection of their studies, we shall see that it is not an inferior grade of education which the popular voice demands, nor a diminished amount of education. It is rather that education shall be varied to suit the varying capacities of individuals; and further, that, in place of limited and necessarily superficial attainments in many things there shall be thoroughness, or at least the opportunity for thoroughness, in a smaller number.

As with most of his arguments he supported this with statistics. He pointed to curriculums so expanded by additional subjects that many of them were allotted an amount of time adding up to only two or three weeks. Most subjects were not pursued beyond their elements. Of all attacks on the traditional system Barnard's is one of the most damning.

To a small degree he was able to introduce elective subjects, but because these demanded additions to the faculty, he was limited by the small income of the college. In 1865 he advocated honor courses; in 1866, uniform entrance examinations for all colleges; in 1868, the study of modern languages; in 1871, a generous program of fellowships and scholarships. After meeting a charming suffragette, Mrs. Lillie Devereux Blake, he took up her idea that women should be admitted to Columbia. Thus at seventy, he began a series of annual pleas on the subject.

Here again he supported his arguments with statistical evidence: after the admission of women to Cornell, student mortality dropped from twenty-six to sixteen per cent. Cornell had not dropped one woman for poor scholarship. In answer to an eminent medical authority, probably Dr. Weir Mitchell, who said women lacked the physical stamina for higher education, Barnard replied that if the argument proved anything, it was that women should not be educated at all. For "valueless as the teaching at many young women's 'finishing schools' may be, it is usually heaped up upon its victims." He asserted that the solution of a problem in algebra or the interpretation of a passage in Homer was no more exhausting than bending over a drawing table or "drumming on an ill-tuned piano."

As for the possible distraction of men from their studies, the elderly gentleman replied:

. . . The comparative freedom of school intercourse tends far less to excite the imaginations of irrepressible youth, and clothe for them the objects of their possible admiration with unreal charms than does separate education.

In subsequent reports he referred to the "Harvard Annex" and prophesied that Harvard would eventually give up the education of women or else admit them to the same classrooms. Separate colleges for women were uneconomic: they involved a duplication of facilities.

While continuing to press for coeducation, he next proposed a school of engineering, a school of commerce, and a school of architecture. He also wanted departments of political and civil history, philosophy, and philology. "These and other analogous educational wants of the country it is the obvious mission and the manifest destiny of Columbia College to supply." A year later he became even more prophetic of Columbia's manifest destiny in proposing a chair of Education. Apparently unaware of pioneering work in this field at Oberlin, he said that no American institution had apparently made education a subject of investigation and instruction. He cited work in Germany and at Edinburgh as models, and looked forward to the time when training in this field should be required of all teachers in America. Such work should include a history of education, the theories of the great educators, and an inquiry into the psychology of the growing mind. This last should attempt, through experiment, to estimate the mode, rate, and kind of growth. Thus for better or worse, Barnard anticipated the Columbia Teachers College.

A scientific study of education was greatly needed; the excesses and mountebanks in the field were yet to come. However, Barnard did foresee the excesses in intercollegiate athletics. By 1888 he was arguing that they should be prohibited on the ground that only a few students benefited from the physical training and the others were distracted from their studies. The system had become "a perversion of what was intended."

The reports contain much else: proposals for a closer link between preparatory and college education; for student self-government; for sections classified according to ability; for work in adult education. Like White and Folwell, he proposed a uniform curriculum during the first two years, followed by specialization, a plan adopted at Harvard after Eliot's free elective system had proved chaotic.

When Barnard died in office at the age of eighty, he had not realized most of his program. Unlike the more fortunate Eliot he had not the advantage of an already large and successful institution or of a community ready to support a great university. Had their roles been reversed, Barnard might have been the greater of the two. Even without Eliot, Harvard had in 1869 sufficient momentum to make it a great university. Barnard was able to be only the prophet of a great university, a man looking toward the day in a "not too distant future"

. . . when no seeker after knowledge shall fail to find here what he requires, and no department or branch or ramification of human learning or human science shall want here its living expositor.

And in that day and even earlier, it is earnestly to be hoped that no sincere and earnest seeker after knowledge, of whatever age, sex, race, or previous condition, shall be denied the privilege of coming here to seek.

Thus ten years after thirty-five-year-old Eliot made his famous inaugural address, seventy-year-old Frederick Barnard spoke a more daring prophecy. In Barnard's vision of 1880 we see the portrait of the education to come in America.

The institution which did much to make this vision possible was the Johns Hopkins University. Like so many other important educational institutions of the post-Civil War era, it was greatly indebted to a noncollege man. Johns Hopkins, the son of a Quaker planter, had been withdrawn from school to work on the plantation when the family, as a matter of principle, freed their slaves. When a merchant uncle in Baltimore asked the parents to permit young Johns to come to the city, the boy went to work in his uncle's store. Later he went into business for himself where through excellent management and shrewd investments, especially in real estate and railroads, he built a fortune of about $8,000,000. Of this he left perhaps $7,000,000 for a university and hospital.

It is not certain how clearly Johns Hopkins envisioned the kind of institution to be created. But in the last years of his life he carefully selected a board of trustees to bring it into being. It was a board made up of prominent Baltimore business and professional men, four of them related to Hopkins. At least ten had had some college or university training and one had studied abroad. As the institution was to be nonsectarian, they represented various denominations, but with a large proportion of Friends.

Except for its completely local membership, it seemed like a typical board of trustees; however it did not behave like one. When Hopkins died in 1874, the men he had selected seven years earlier set about the task of creating the university he had endowed. They worked in no perfunctory fashion. It would have been easy and natural, and certainly less productive of local controversy, to set up an institution modeled on the so-called university of the time—that is, a college offering some postgraduate instruction, plus a medical school. Instead, they looked about for new ideas. For one thing, they purchased for their own information a collection of books on education, most of them recent and reflecting the current controversies on the subject. The list included Matthew Arnold, Horace Mann, Josiah Quincy, Herbert Spencer; it included college histories, discussions of women's education, works on British universities, and books on educational theory.

Perhaps an even greater influence on their thinking came from the university presidents they invited to their meetings: Charles W. Eliot of Harvard, Andrew D. White of Cornell, and James B. Angell of Michigan. The list is significant: these three institutions represented the most advanced educational developments of the 1870s and were the three most nearly of university grade. One of the Hopkins trustees visited Michigan where he sat up until midnight with President Angell and ex-President Frieze discussing the future of the new institution. Both Angell and Frieze argued against a college similar to four hundred others, and in favor of a genuine graduate university.

In the selection of a president they acted with equal sagacity. It was Andrew White who proposed that they invite the then president of the University of California, Daniel Coit Gilman. When Gilman came east to discuss the matter, the Board asked him to state his views. He replied that he would attempt to establish not another college but a university designed to promote scholarship of the first order. He would select a faculty of outstanding men, offer them good salaries, give them students advanced enough to keep them stimulated, and expect them to publish the results of their investigations. The Board met the next afternoon and elected Gilman as president.

Before the new president took over his duties, the Board encouraged him to visit educational institutions in America and Europe. During his travels, Gilman consulted with such men as Tyndall, Huxley and Herbert Spencer. He also scouted for suitable faculty members. Of the first six full professors, three were English and two were Americans trained in German universities.

Gilman was inaugurated in February 1876. Johns Hopkins, one of the few institutions which is honest about its date of origin, uses this as its founding date, although it could easily claim 1867 when the original trustees were incorporated at the request of Johns Hopkins.

The early university was not, as is often supposed, only a graduate school. Gilman, recognizing the need for undergraduates oriented toward graduate study, included a college department. This too did not follow the conventional American pattern. Students entered at the sophomore level for a three-year course, which however could be completed in less time if the student did the necessary work. Within four years the president and faculty developed a group system of studies for eight different fields: the classics; mathematics and engineering; general science; literary training not rigidly classical; premedical; pretheological, and prelaw courses; and a course leading to the A.B. for those planning to enter business. Hence the programs, although not narrowly vocational, were planned for various vocational objectives. This method of organization avoided on the one hand the rigidity of the usual curriculum and on the other the anarchy of completely free election of unrelated studies. All groups included a core of subjects such as English, French, German, history, philosophy, and a laboratory science. Thus in the 1880s the Johns Hopkins curriculum was more like that of today than it was like that of Eliot's Harvard.

But Johns Hopkins is more famous for its contributions to the modern university. Speaking at Gilman's retirement in 1902, President Eliot said:

. . . The creation of a school of graduate studies . . . has lifted every other university in the country in its departments of arts and sciences. I want to testify that the graduate school of Harvard University started feebly in 1870 and 1871, did not thrive, until the example of Johns Hopkins forced our faculty to put their strength into the development of our instruction for graduates. And what was true of Harvard was true of every other university in the land which aspired to create an advanced school of arts and sciences.

The chief reason for this was, of course, that whereas graduate study and research at other institutions had been by-products of the undergraduate department, they were at Johns Hopkins the main objective. Gilman was the first university president to promote learned societies and learned journals. Apparently he was disappointed in the societies; such organizations did not become important until the development of interuniversity organizations like the Modern Language Association and the American Historical Association. But under Gilman, Johns Hopkins began the publication of the *American Chemical Journal,* the *Journal of Physiology,* the *American Journal of Philology,* and *Modern Language Notes.* Dr. Herbert B. Adams in 1882 founded a monograph series, the *Johns Hopkins University Studies in Historical and Political Science.*

Most important of all was the flow of men trained in scholarly research who went out to staff the faculties of the nation. The roster from Johns Hopkins is a long and honorable one. These scholars and those trained in the universities which followed the Hopkins pattern were to transform the whole nature of undergraduate instruction. Men and women so trained could not be content with the old system of rote recitations based on the same texts year after year. Nor were they willing to try to teach half a dozen different subjects; they were specialists with both the virtues and limitations of their kind.

Undoubtedly Johns Hopkins under Gilman performed an important service in developing scholarly work, but it may also have done an immense disservice. Some of the excesses of the method did not appear until a later date, and therefore belong to subsequent chapters. But it may be that in following too closely the German pattern of training college teachers primarily as research specialists, the Johns Hopkins University and its imitators failed in part to meet the needs of the United States. There is no question that such specialized training is essential to men and women who will devote their lives to research; it is less certain that it is the best preparation for the teachers of undergraduates. It may be that in leading American universities to develop along the European pattern, Johns Hopkins failed to create the type of institution envisioned by Eliot when he said, "A university must be indigenous."

In its close link between undergraduate teaching and graduate study, Harvard developed along more characteristically American lines as did Columbia in its explorations of the problems of teaching and its hospitality to both men and women of all races and conditions. Too often the graduate school has emphasized a type of scholarship unrelated to the needs of its own time. In science and in medicine, as at the Johns Hopkins Medical School under Dr. William H. Welch, pure research has been immensely fruitful; it has been less fruitful in the field of the humanities. It is unfortunate that graduate study in literature followed the German model of philological research, source hunting, and manuscript collation. In its way a *Journal of Philology* can represent as sterile an approach to literature as the gerund-grinding of the early colleges.

It would be unfair to blame all of the excesses and mistaken directions on any one institution. In a generation when many American scholars had studied in European universities, it was inevitable that their methods should be brought to America. This country needed research and advanced study. To the Johns Hopkins' everlasting credit, it led the way in providing for this need. But the United States needed too the more characteristically American developments at Michigan, Cornell, Minnesota and Harvard. Taking them as a whole, the first two decades following the Civil War were a period of immense progress in education. And it was an unusal group of men who led and guided this progress, a magnificent roster which included Folwell, White, Eliot, Barnard and Gilman.

6

High Seriousness in Bloomers

Higher education for women had to wait until there was a place in society for the college-trained woman. Thus most of the early hullabaloo over the question of woman's mental abilities was beside the point. Before the 1820s or 1830s there were almost no jobs open to an educated woman. Even schoolteaching, except of very young children, was in the hands of men. As we have seen, the teachers in the early schools were often male undergraduates who were earning their college expenses.

Even had women been admitted to the colleges, there was little in the traditional curriculum which bore any relation to their function in life as wives and mothers. After women began to teach, they could have gained little to their purpose from the drill in Greek, Latin, and mathematics. To a greater degree than is usually realized, women in colonial and early nineteenth-century America were gainfully employed. They operated taverns and mercantile establishments; they became tailors, dressmakers, and midwives. But such occupations, even for men, required nothing more than common schooling. This was available to girls in the middle colonies, and to a lesser extent in New England. The Quakers and Moravians opened their schools on a relatively equal basis to both boys and girls. The old-fashioned academy, like Dwight's at Greenfield Hill, often accepted girls, and, as we have seen, carried on an educational program which rivaled that of the early colleges.

Before 1860, however, the chief agency for women's education beyond the elementary stage was the female academy or seminary. Perhaps no educational institution in America has been so universally attacked. Certainly it was vulnerable on a number of accounts: it was usually operated for the profit of its proprietor; its academic work was superficial; it stressed "accomplishments"; its teachers were ill paid and ill trained. Most of its weaknesses were due to the community which produced it. It was weak financially because Americans would not appropriate public funds for women's education; it stressed "accomplishments" because that was what parents wanted their daughters to learn; it could not develop any educational program for the great majority of its students because they rarely stayed more than a few months. In a typical school of this kind nearly a third of the pupils entered after regular classes were formed or left before they were completed. In another, half of those who entered left before the expiration of six months; in another nearly three fourths failed to remain that length of time. This was the pattern at even the best schools. Over a fifteen-year period, out of 1,600 pupils who entered the schools run by Zilpha Grant, only 156 completed the three-year course. The proportion of graduates at Troy, Milwaukee, and South Hadley —all superior institutions—was likewise small. Before 1860 the American public simply refused to pay for a good education for women.

This refusal to give anything like adequate support to women's education did not prevent people from extensive and acrimonious discussion of the topic. Between 1830 and 1860 almost every editor in the country expressed views on the subject— usually unfavorable to the prevailing system. Probably the most famous attack on the female seminaries was the long satiric poem in *Harper's New Monthly Magazine* for September 1858. This described the school of Madam Cancan with "her morals infernal, her manners elysian," and concluded:

Madam Cancan still lives and still ogles and teaches,
And still her lay sermons on Fashions she preaches;
Still keeps of smooth phrases the choicest assortment;
Still lectures on dress, easy carriage, deportment;
And spends all her skill in thus moulding her pets
Into very-genteelly-got-up marionettes.
Yes! Puppet's the word; for there's nothing inside
But a clock-work of vanity, fashion and pride!
Puppets warranted sound, that without any falter
When wound up will go just as far as the altar;

But when once the cap's donned with the matronly border,
Lo! the quiet machine goes at once out of order.

A few years earlier, Professor Silliman of Yale had made
women's education the subject of a Phi Beta Kappa address in
which he had stated that the best diploma for a woman was a
large family and a happy husband. She should place "He" before the "Arts" to obtain the degree of "Mistress of Hearts."

In this nineteenth-century world of socially ambitious mothers and condescending men it is not strange that the female
seminaries were often superficial. Yet they had certain healthy
qualities. To a degree beyond that of the men's colleges they
strove for a functional education. Even the much-criticized
emphasis on "ornamental" subjects—drawing, painting, dancing, and music—had some point. In nineteenth-century America women became the chief guardians of the arts and the amenities. That the standards of taste and achievement in the arts
were trivial and sentimental is as much the fault of the age as
of the academies. By relegating these subjects to the female
seminaries staffed by poorly educated teachers, the era reaped
a harvest of filigree and sentimentality in art, music, and literature. On a higher level the seminaries taught English composition and rhetoric, modern language, science, mathematics,
history, and moral philosophy. Before 1830 the emphasis was on
elementary and secondary-school subjects. With the increase in
national wealth and the decline of very early marriages, girls
remained in school longer. After 1830 the curriculum, at least
on paper, contained a high proportion of courses at the junior-
college level or even beyond. A sampling of Thomas Woody's
findings in *A History of Women's Education in the United
States* shows that, of 107 schools tabulated, the percentages of
institutions offering certain subjects then found chiefly in colleges were as follows:

Algebra	83%
Plane trigonometry	40%
Evidences of Christianity	50%
Moral Philosophy	80%

Natural Philosophy	80%
Chemistry	90%
Astronomy	85%
Political science	34%
Ancient history	44%
Modern history	41%
United States history	45%

By comparison, the percentages for painting, drawing and music were 43%, 50% and 30%—all less frequent than physiology with 55%.

Leaders of the seminary movement, such as Emma Willard, Catherine Beecher and Joseph Emerson, argued that the female schools, by trying to teach too many subjects, failed to teach much in any one. But Eliot and Barnard were able to bring the same charge against the colleges. At Wethersfield, Joseph Emerson established a three-year course with a definite regulation of the number of studies to be pursued. To a large extent the three-year course became standard in the seminaries.

Thus before the development of genuine collegiate education for women, the academies and seminaries had worked out a program of mixed secondary and collegiate studies emphasizing English, science, modern language, history, moral philosophy, and utilitarian subjects such as hygiene and pedagogy. The great difference between their curriculums and those of the colleges was that the seminaries paid much less attention to Latin and Greek and allowed much greater flexibility in choice of studies. These things were symbolic of a much more fundamental difference: the seminaries were more frankly utilitarian in their aims. They stressed such things as domestic training, maternal influence, social usefulness, and preparation for teaching. Like the colleges they emphasized religious and moral training. But they spoke too of the values of accomplishments, health, and intellectual enjoyment. Increasingly as college training grew out of touch with the needs of American life, its apologists talked about liberal education and cultural values. The seminaries, less committed to a traditional system, were freer to develop an education designed to meet specific needs and demands.

The other great difference between them and the colleges was in the quality of their work. For this the seminaries were less to blame than were the mores of the time. The haphazard nature of student attendance has been noted. But the most basic weakness was that in the absence of endowments or public financing, the seminaries were of necessity operated by their proprietors for profit. It will be remembered that almost all of the early colleges had financial aid from the states or from religious organizations—frequently from both. They became endowed corporations. Conversely many of the female academies and seminaries were the lengthened shadows of their founders and proprietors, and often disappeared with the death or retirement of these entrepreneurs. A school might be excellent because of a single teacher or headmistress, and might sink into obscurity under a successor. Schools often had not even a permanent location.

Catherine Beecher, seeking endowment for institutions in the West, tried to interest religious denominations. Knowing the prejudice against women speakers, she got her brother Thomas or some other gentleman to deliver her addresses for her. She got money for buildings but little more. Emma Willard went with her husband to present to the New York legislature her "Plan for Improving Female Education." Despite a letter of recommendation from John Adams and an appeal by Governor Clinton, she got little encouragement in Albany. As a result her school moved from Middlebury to Waterford, and from there to Troy in response to the encouragement of local groups. Mary Lyon raised the first funds for Mount Holyoke Female Seminary by popular subscription. Less able and less idealistic women operated on a catch-as-catch-can basis in rented buildings and with half-baked assistants. Like Madam Cancan's, their manners were likely to be better than their educational morals.

Seen in this context the pioneering coeducational work at

Oberlin and Antioch becomes all the more significant. For the first time women could get a college education equal to that afforded the men. This was not the case in the earliest colleges for women only.

The women's college movement began in the South. In 1839, two years after the first women were admitted to the collegiate department at Oberlin, the Georgia Female College in Macon opened its doors. Although it was authorized to "confer all such honors, degrees, and licenses as are usually conferred in colleges or universities," the evidence is that both in entrance requirements and curriculum its standards were well below those of near-by men's colleges. This was due not to intention but, as President George F. Pierce pointed out, to lack of money. In order to pay faculty salaries, the college had to admit poorly qualified students. That Pierce had in mind a genuine college is clear. He stated: "Girls can learn, and they deserve to be taught." If the necessary facilities were provided, "there will be advancement corresponding in grade, and equivalent in effect to anything ever realized from the most generous for the Lords of Creation." Proudly he called attention to the pioneering nature of the Georgia Female College. Before it opened, "the notion of a female college was laughed at as a Platonic idea—a mere dream—an impractical fancy. . . ." But there had been an increasing demand, to which society had at last responded. "The project is novel; it stands out on the map of the world's history alone—isolated—a magnificent example of public spirit. . . ."

The college stood apart also in its system of discipline. At a time when both colleges and seminaries had a multiplicity of rules, the Georgia Female College had few. It was thought that many rules would simply "multiply offences" and that better results could be obtained by developing confidence and affection between teacher and pupil. As a result, the only acts of disorder were of "the mischievous kind rather than the rebellious—ebullitions of playful feeling. . . ."

During the 1840s and 1850s other women's colleges sprang up in Ohio, Illinois, Tennessee, Pennsylvania, and New York.

On the basis of a study of their curriculums, Woody states that Mary Sharp (1851) in Winchester, Tennessee, was the earliest college for women only which required both Latin and Greek (though in meager amounts) in a four-year course, and gave an A.B. degree comparable in form and significance to those of men's colleges. In New York the Elmira Female University (1855) even more nearly approximated the work of contemporary men's colleges. For one thing Elmira was better endowed than most women's institutions: it received $10,000 from the legislature and $80,000 from Simeon Benjamin.

Although New England was slow in joining the national movement for women's colleges, it was a New England woman who had much to do with the development. It hardly counts that Catherine Beecher was born on Long Island, so completely was she of the Brahmin caste. Her father, Lyman Beecher, had studied theology under Timothy Dwight; her brother was Henry Ward Beecher; her sister wrote *Uncle Tom's Cabin*. When Catherine was ten, the Beechers moved back to Connecticut, where she was educated, and where she subsequently taught. She became engaged to a Yale professor. After he lost his life in a shipwreck, she devoted her energies to the founding of women's educational institutions in the West and to propaganda for the cause of female education.

In charateristic Beecher fashion Catherine paid less attention to theology than to the practical elements in life. At Mount Holyoke Seminary, her younger contemporary, Mary Lyon, thought in terms of an education designed to win converts to religion and to train recruits for the mission fields of the East. Catherine Beecher believed the two great callings of women to be those of mother and teacher. Both Emma Willard and Mary Lyon belonged to the female-seminary school of thought. In fact, Mrs. Willard declared the "absurdity of sending ladies to college" must "strike everyone."

The institutions founded by Miss Beecher at Hartford, Cincinnati and Milwaukee were seminaries because in the twenties and thirties America was not ready for women's colleges. It was even difficult to raise funds for a seminary. At Hartford when

Miss Beecher sought funds for a study hall, lecture room, and recitation rooms, many of the city fathers were, in her words, "surprised and almost dismayed at the 'visionary and impractical' suggestion." It was then that she discovered the influence of the leading women in a community—"my chief reliance ever since."

It was this discovery which led to the organization of a permanent body, the American Women's Educational Association, in 1852 with the objective: "To aid in securing to American women a liberal education, honorable position, and remunerative employment *in their appropriate profession*, by means of *endowed* institutions, on the college plan of organization. . . ." Its program was an outgrowth of Catherine Beecher's book of the year before, the *True Remedy for the Wrongs of Women*, in which she set forth the chief needs: permanence, the college system, endowment, equipment, and division of responsibility among teachers. The president was to be merely the presiding officer, not a paternalistic autocrat.

Although Catherine Beecher founded no important women's college, she broke the ground for those who followed her. It is impossible to determine the extent to which her work influenced the development of the Elmira Female College and the ideas of Matthew Vassar, Henry Durant, the founder of Wellesley, and Sophia Smith, who endowed Smith. Certainly many of her ideas were embodied in the women's colleges founded in the fifties and sixties. For one thing, her emphasis on the vocational element in woman's education—domestic science and teaching —helped to overcome male prejudice against women's colleges. As we shall see, she later became involved in the controversy over the true function of a women's college. But her great contributions were her organizing ability and her effective propaganda for a college education for women.

She also took a leading part in the development of physical education for women. In the mid-nineteenth century everyone seems to have agreed that the health of the American girl was bad. Medical journals, educational periodicals, and newspapers joined in complaining that girls spent too much time in their studies and too little in the open air. Part of the criticism no doubt grew out of the current prejudice against intellectual training for women, but that does not account for the criticism from such people as Elizabeth Blackwell, Catherine Beecher, and Dio Lewis. After attending a commencement at a female seminary, Dio Lewis thought it would be more accurate to say "the girls themselves were *finished*" not that "their *education* is *finished*. Pale, thin, bent—they had been outrageously humbugged." Catherine Beecher declared that the "standard of health among American women is so low that few have a correct idea of what a healthy woman is."

The reformers preached exercise and a more sensible form of dress. The fashion of tight lacing enforced by socially ambitious mothers came in for particular attack. Emma Willard, Catherine Beecher, and Mary Lyon all developed systems of physical education for their pupils. The course of calisthenic exercises invented by Miss Beecher was widely copied, and was probably the foundation of the system used at Mount Holyoke from 1835 until 1862 when the New Gymnastics of Dio Lewis were substituted. It was the early Holyoke methods which so much amused an Amherst student. William Hammond noted in his diary:

Saw some of the young ladies exercise in calisthenics, a species of orthodox *dancing* in which they perambulate a smooth floor in various figures, with a sort of sliding stage step; not unlike children's plays, all except the kissing part. . . . The whole movement is accompanied by singing in which noise rather than tune or harmony seems to be the main object. By a species of delusion peculiar to the seminary they imagine that all this [is] very conducive to health, strength, gracefulness, etc.

Granting that this smacks of male undergraduate condescension, it none the less points up a kind of solemn artificiality in the early attempts at physical education for women. Outdoor exercise was usually confined to walking and botanizing.

The system introduced by Dio Lewis at his Family School for Young Ladies and soon copied at Elmira Female College and

elsewhere was more strenuous. It included thorough instruction in anatomy and physiology, plain and nutritious food, regular hours, two to four half hours of gymnastics, regular walks,
indoor sports and amusements, and loose-fitting clothing. The
girls wore no corsets, ate but twice a day, and square-danced
from two to four evenings a week. Apparently young men joined
in the dancing, for the "round" or the "German" were forbidden because "the rotary motion is injurious to the brain and
spinal marrow" and "the peculiar contact between the man and
the woman *may* suggest impure thoughts." Whatever Lewis'
system did for the marrow or the morals, it at least developed
the muscles: chest measurements increased two and a half
inches, and arms one and a half inches, all within eight months.
It remained for the institutions such as Vassar and Wellesley
to introduce genuine outdoor sports for women.

As with the men's colleges the great period of development
in women's colleges came after the Civil War. The twenty-five
years before it had been filled with discussion and had seen
perhaps a dozen pioneering experiments, all poorly financed.
Nevertheless, these early colleges furnished useful models when
in 1861 Matthew Vassar provided an endowment such as no
women's college had yet enjoyed. The first president, Milo
P. Jewett, bombarded the president of Elmira with questions
about organization, faculty, etc. And Jewett's first plan of
studies at Vassar suggests links with Mary Sharp College and
the University of Virginia. This is understandable in view of
Jewett's experience at Judson Female Institute in Alabama.

Matthew Vassar seems a most unlikely person to have under-
taken a radical educational experiment. He was born in England in 1792 and was brought to America at the age of four.
His father, a Baptist farmer, was one of those who fled the reactionary England which tried moderate reformers like Thelwall
and Tooke for treason, drove Priestley and Paine from the
country, and caused the outspoken William Blake to veil his
political ideas in obscure symbolism. That James Vassar came
to America in search of political liberty suggests a kind of intel-

lectual independence which the son seems to have shared. The father shifted from farming to brewing, but a fire wiped out his business.

Thus Matthew Vassar, with little education, built up his own brewing business from almost nothing. By 1845 the Poughkeepsie brewer was wealthy enough to make a nine-month tour of Europe. During his travels he talked much about what to do with his fortune, and was greatly impressed with Guy's Hospital, an institution endowed by a remote relative. Apparently he determined on a similar institution in America. However a niece, Lydia Booth, who ran the Cottage Hill Seminary in the village of Poughkeepsie, talked to him about the need for better educational opportunities for women. After her death the seminary was taken over by Professor M. P. Jewett, who had been head of the Judson Female Institute in Alabama. Jewett joined the Baptist congregation to which Vassar belonged and became an intimate friend. He too preached the idea of founding a women's college, but on a grander scale than Miss Booth had dreamed of—something comparable to Yale or Harvard.

Matthew Vassar was not a man who moved hastily. He discussed the idea with leading educators; he employed an architect to draw up plans and estimates. At last in 1860 he decided to go ahead with the scheme. He selected Jewett as his chief adviser, obtained a charter, and appointed a board of trustees. As soon as the act of incorporation became a law, Vassar read to the trustees a statement of his views:

. . . It occurred to me, that woman, having received from her creator the same intellectual constitution as man, has the same right as man to intellectual culture and development.

I considered that the MOTHERS of a country mold the character of its citizens, determine its institutions, and shape its destiny.

Next to the influence of the mother is that of the FEMALE TEACHER. . . .

It also seemed to me that if women were properly educated, some new avenues of honorable employment . . . might be opened to her.

He then went on to outline a curriculum including science ("with full apparatus"); economics; political science; aesthetics; domestic science; hygiene; "Moral Science, particularly bearing on the filial, conjugal, and parental relation"; the classics, so far as may be demanded by the spirit of the times; and systematic reading and study of the Bible. Despite his Baptist affiliations, he insisted that "all sectarian influences should be carefully excluded. . . ." For that reason he had selected trustees of various denominations, and he recommended that the faculty be chosen in "a like catholic spirit." The college was not to be a charity school, but a considerable number of scholarships were to be provided for needy students who showed "decided promise."

When he had finished reading his statement, Vassar handed over to the trustees a tin box containing stocks, bonds, mortgages and a deed for 200 acres of land—a gift totaling more than $400,000. Up to that time no woman's college had had an endowment of over $100,000.

Most of the newspaper notices praised the gift, though expressing the hope that education would not unfit women for their proper duties. The *New York Times* was quite tolerant:

What do you think of a woman's college? And why not? After Allopathic, Hydropathic, Homeopathic and patent pill colleges, universities and all that sort of thing, why not let the girls have one?

Vassar himself broke the ground for the first building, a mammoth five-story affair designed to house under one roof living quarters for nearly 400 girls, laboratories, library, chapel, and social rooms. Although on a larger scale than usual, this was the firetrap design which in the interests of morals and economy had become almost standard for female institutions in the nineteenth century. The widespread incidence of colds and sore throats in women's schools of the time is testimony to the impossibility of heating these sprawling four or five-story monsters with their miscellaneous towers. But the nineteenth-century neurosis about female morality dictated that girls must be

gathered under one roof where they would be under the supervision of as many faculty as possible.

A combination of kerosene lamps, poor water supply, and
the inability of local fire companies to pump water above the
second floor has largely deprived posterity of these monuments
to nineteenth-century mores. Mr. Vassar, however, provided
against some of the more obvious disadvantages of this design.
All the partition walls were of brick from cellar to attic. The
580-foot corridors were provided with eight iron doors set into
four double fire walls so that the building could be quickly
divided into five separate parts. Iron water tanks, with pipes to
fire hoses on each floor, were installed in the attic. There were
nine stairways, two of them in between fireproof walls. On the
roof were 6,000 feet of lightning rods and cables. Among the
most modern features of the building were gas lighting, indoor
plumbing, and steam heat, the latter furnished by a separate
power plant. For its time it was probably the most modern and
completely equipped college building in America.

Soon after its completion, Vassar added other buildings: an
observatory and a gymnasium containing rooms for calisthenics, a riding school, and a bowling alley, plus apartments for
five families. The thirty by eighty-foot calisthenic hall was
furnished with all the appliances used in the system of Dio
Lewis. It was not until five years later that Princeton had a
gymnasium.

The main building was ready for occupancy in 1865. When
the college opened, there was a faculty of eight men and twenty-
two women, a student body of 353. The emphasis on women
faculty members was an idea of Vassar's. In 1864 he told the
trustees:

It is my hope—it was my only hope and desire—indeed it has
been the main incentive to all I have already done, or may
hereafter do, or hope to do, to inaugurate a new era in the
history of the life of woman. . . . I wish to give one sex the
advantages too long monopolized by the other. Ours is, and is
to be, an institution for women—not men. In all its labors,
positions, rewards, and hopes, the idea is the development and

exposition and the marshaling to the front and the preferment of women—of their powers on every side, demonstrative of their equality with men—demonstrative, indeed, of such capacities as in certain fixed directions surpass those of men. . . . We are especially defeated if we fail to express, by our acts, our practical belief in her pre-eminent powers as an instructor of her own sex.

Thus a seventy-two-year-old provincial brewer, who had left school at fourteen, wrote the declaration of independence for women's colleges. Even thirty years later some eminent physicians and educators—male, of course—were still debating whether or not women were intellectually and physically capable of college education—or if they were, if it did not somehow or other destroy their womanhood. Matthew Vassar told his trustees that it could be done "without the slightest hazard to the attractiveness of her character." He was not even daunted when a pious graduate, who had gone through the college on a scholarship, wrote: "A college foundation which is laid in beer will never prosper." A student, who happened to be in the lower office when Mr. Vassar received this missive, reports that he shouted, "Well, it was good beer, wasn't it?" Then the humor of the thing struck him and he joined the students in a roar of laughter.

Like Matthew Vassar the girls and the faculty had a sense of participating in a revolution—"a new era in the history of the life of woman." So poor was the education then usually available that fewer than half of the early students qualified for full standing in the college department. As with the other early colleges admitting women, a preparatory department was necessary. Despite Mr. Vassar's desire to employ women teachers, seven of the first nine professorships had to be given to men: there were not enough qualified women. The women on the first faculty were chiefly instructors and "teachers." Seven of them taught music, the subject having the largest enrollment. In such circumstances a good bit of self-conscious feminism developed. Maria Mitchell, Professor of Astronomy, judged everything from the standpoint of "How is this going to affect women?" The "Lady Principal," Miss Lyman, impressed on the girls that the higher education of women was an experiment, that the world was looking on. "The good of the college! The good of the college!" was constantly reiterated. But it was not a somber atmosphere. Frances Wood, who joined the faculty in 1867, summed it up forty years later: "It was a wonderful thing when Vassar opened for a girl to have a chance to go to college. . . ."

Much of the same pattern was repeated at Wellesley. Here too, one wealthy man endowed the college, outlined the course of study, and personally supervised the construction of the mammoth building designed to put it entirely under one roof. However, unlike Matthew Vassar, Henry Fowle Durant was something of a scholar. At Harvard he had laid out a course of study to prepare himself to be a writer, preferably a poet. In his career as a lawyer he was often employed as junior counsel by the prominent Rufus Choate, but his fortune came chiefly through a series of shrewd investments. His wife was the sort of person who detested "Mother Goose" and taught their son his letters by readings from the Bible. When the boy died at fifteen (a daughter had died at the age of two months), Durant underwent a religious conversion, gave up the law—but not business —and for nine years engaged in evangelistic preaching.

His interest in women's education was undoubtedly stimulated by his wife, Pauline, who had wanted to go to Holyoke, but instead had been sent to a boarding school. The religiosity of both Durants was apparent at every stage of the development of Wellesley Female Seminary. The original statute states: "The College was founded for the glory of God and the service of the Lord Jesus Christ, in and by the education and culture of women." It was required that every trustee, teacher, and officer be a member of an Evangelical Church and that the study of the Bible should be pursued by every student throughout the entire college course. Workmen on the building were forbidden to swear or speak in loud voices. Both Durant and his wife supervised the work daily. At the laying of the cornerstone Pauline put in it a Bible bound in gold-tooled leather and inscribed: "This building is humbly dedicated to our Heavenly Father, with the hope and prayer that He may always be first in everything in this institution. . . ."

College Hall was finished in 1875 after four years of work. A contemporary account described it as "one great art gallery . . . not a girls' school but a palace." In appearance it somewhat resembled Vassar College, but with the addition of more towers, porches, pavilions and spires. Built in the form of a double Latin cross, it was 480 feet long, 166 feet wide at the wings, and 80 feet high. What was considered the beauty spot of the building was the Center where the two main corridors crossed. Ten granite pillars carried a series of arches to support the four stories of balconies which surrounded an open well reaching to the glass roof. In the center a marble basin was surrounded by exotic plants and life-sized statues of the Niobe-protecting-her-daughter variety. The reception parlor, finished in carved teakwood, was decorated with bronzes and autographed portraits of Longfellow, Bryant, and Tennyson. Within the building were rooms for 350 students and faculty, plus a chapel, library, gymnasium, dining hall, museums, classrooms and lecture rooms. Despite the provision of fire walls, the Center was in effect an immense flue, and a ventilating system carried ducts to all parts of the building. It was totally destroyed by fire in 1914.

This nineteenth-century firetrap design necessarily influenced the nature of student life in women's colleges. For all the lavish equipment—even student rooms were carpeted and provided with walnut furniture—the design was institutional: it hinted supervision and enforced confinement. The rules at Vassar and Wellesley provided for every hour of the student's day. The first schedule at Vassar was similar to those of men's colleges twenty or thirty years earlier:

Rising	6:00 A.M.
Morning prayers	6:45
Breakfast	7:00
Arrangement of rooms	7:30

Silent time	7:40
Morning study hours	9:00-12:40
Dinner	1:00 P.M.
Recreation period	2:00-2:40
Afternoon study hours	2:45-5:45
Supper	6:00
Evening prayers, followed by silent time	6:30
Evening study hour	8:00-9:00
Retiring	9:40-10:00

All sorts of minor matters were supervised. Miss Lyman, the lady principal, insisted that every girl change for dinner. "You may take off one calico frock and put on a fresh one of the same kind, if you can do no better, but some sort of change is essential." She attempted to make the girls wear gloves for every college function, even for the reading of an essay or poem in chapel. "If there is a student here who cannot afford white gloves—even of lisle thread, I shall be glad to provide a pair." A freshman strolling in the corridor before class one morning was joined by Miss Lyman, who without saying a word walked arm in arm with her until the bell rang. Taking her leave, the principal remarked, "My dear, you do not walk quite properly. You should turn your toes out a little more." At commencement time, each senior was summoned to Miss Lyman's room for an inspection of the gown to be worn at graduation. The student mounted a table and revolved slowly while Miss Lyman pointed out to a maid any slight alteration which she deemed desirable.

Students were not permitted to visit one another's rooms during study hours without Miss Lyman's permission. They were not allowed to use the main entrance hall, but had to come in and out by rear doors. Their visitors were received in the parlor by Miss Lyman or an assistant, and students were expected not to enter until summoned. The custom was that even members of the faculty informed Miss Lyman before going out of an evening.

At Wellesley the Durants themselves took over this sort of moralistic supervision. "Mr. Durant rules the college, from the amount of Latin we shall read to the kind of meat we shall have for dinner," wrote the president of the first class to her parents. A handsome man with flowing white hair, he dressed always in a black broadcloth Prince Albert and wore a silk hat. Active and vivacious, he was forever flitting about the corridors on some errand, for he kept in touch with every detail: the dinner menu, the dishwashing, sports, the decoration of rooms, and especially what he considered the spiritual welfare of his students. During a scarlet-fever epidemic in 1877 he brought bunches of grapes to the ill girls and sat by their bedsides expounding his views on the evils of the theater and the opera.

One of his phobias was eating between meals. Students were forbidden to have any food except fresh fruit in their rooms. As supper was a very simple meal consisting of bread, butter, cookies, molasses and milk, students often complained of hunger. But one of Durant's favorite dictums was that "pies, lies, and doughnuts" should never have a place at Wellesley. A student letter of 1877 reported: "There is considerable sickness now. The girls seem to be giving out. I suppose it must be from studying too hard . . . so much has been said on the subject of eating between meals that most girls would as soon almost take poison as do it. . . ." Thanksgiving was no exception to the rule against receiving food from home. The first college physician stated: "I have known some fine roast turkey, rolls, jelly, pie, cake, etc., coming at Thanksgiving time, finding their way down the dust shaft because the conscientious daughter would not violate the college regulations."

Incidents such as these suggest that the college girls of the sixties, seventies and eighties were far more different from their brothers and sweethearts at Amherst, Harvard and Yale than were the young women of a later period. The institutional architecture and organization of the early women's colleges produced a corresponding psychology. A contributing factor was that many of the girls stayed more than four years. Close-knit institutions, even vastly freer ones than nineteenth-century Vassar or Wellesley, put a brand on students who remain a long time, witness a Princeton or Virginia Ph.D. who has done his undergraduate work at the same place. As at Vassar, a preparatory department was necessary at Wellesley; only fifty-eight of the first 314 students qualified for college work. Thus a girl who earned the A.B. degree was likely to have spent five or six years in the same highly regimented environment. Because of cost and distance, many of the students did not even get away for holidays. When they did, they carried with them the marks of their training. A Wellesley girl returning by train to Virginia for the Christmas holidays happened to look at her watch. "It's silent time at Wellesley now," she said. Instantly a hush fell over the Wellesley girls traveling with her.

It is understandable that the pioneers in women's education like Vassar and Durant wanted women on the faculty. Both men were deeply concerned with the preparation of teachers, and logic required that if women were to be given a higher education, they must be given opportunities for putting it to use. Durant took the radical step of providing that the president and all members of the faculty should be women. Ada Howard, Wellesley's first president, came from Holyoke, which, along with Oberlin and Michigan, provided most of the original faculty. From Holyoke too came the idea of the moral value of requiring students to do their own domestic work.

However laudable the motives, the effect was to preserve some of the worst features of the boarding school: an overemphasis on refinement, on conformity and piety, on the giggly kind of schoolgirlishness satirized in W. S. Gilbert's three little maids from school. Susan Maria Hallowell, professor of botany at Wellesley, known as "Our Lady of the Flowers," wore a little flowered bonnet in academic processions. Katherine Lee Bates, of the class of 1880, wrote *America the Beautiful*. Even the sensible Alice Freeman, finding her room filled with flowers, said they had been "sent by my rosebud garden of girls." One of her problems as president was to deal with an epidemic of hysteria: there were frequent screams over trifles, and gossip ran riot. Her method was to call the seniors together and say that she would hold them responsible for the continuance of such nonsense. The fuss stopped.

This sort of thing was of course the feminine counterpart of the more violent uproars at men's colleges. And the white-gloves refinement had its opposite in the male assumption of the mucker prose: the drinking and the kind of humor represented by nailing shut all the privy doors on the campus. But one fact must be taken into account: almost all the women faculty members were spinsters in an era which rigidly limited the social activities of ladies. Professors in men's colleges had opportunities for a fuller life as husbands, fathers, pillars of the community. It is perhaps this difference as much as any other which produced a high percentage of unmarried college women. From Mary Lyon to Ellen Fitz Pendleton, female educators were likely to be a formidable type, suggesting in their manner a considerable hostility to men. It will be remembered that the brash William Hammond feared a meeting with Miss Lyon or "the assistant dragoness."

Of course men could be pretty silly in the era when Tennyson's poetry was continually quoted as the model for women's education. Alice Freeman complained, apropos of an address at Wellesley:

It does seem impossible for a man to come here and speak in a sensible way to sensible women. As usual, our orator talked in a superior way about woman's nature and condition, health, etc. He said he "knew the depths of a woman's heart." If I live to be a thousand years, I hope I never make that remark about any man.

It is significant that Miss Freeman was a graduate of Michigan, where she had enjoyed hikes, picnics, and sleigh rides. All her life she considered herself fortunate to have gone to a coeducational college. She believed that such places gave a healthier attitude toward sex and produced more suitable marriages. Her own marriage to George Herbert Palmer seems to have been a most happy one. Not a particularly original thinker on education, she nevertheless brought to Wellesley a healthy sanity which to some degree counteracted the religiosity of the

Durants. Thus despite her deep interest in religion and her admiration for Henry Durant, she refused his request that she try to convert a senior who was not a Christian. One of her first acts as president was to abolish the daily Bible classes on the grounds that they encouraged sentimentality, and to substitute a college course in the Bible.

Despite his religious fanaticism Henry Durant was an extremely intelligent man. It was he who picked Miss Freeman, a twenty-six-year-old history teacher, as the person to succeed the ailing Miss Howard, a lady who outlived her successor by five years. Miss Freeman proved to be one of the ablest presidents Wellesley ever had. When she became acting president in 1881, she had to guide the college through the financial crisis following Durant's death. It was Durant who introduced the teaching of science through the laboratory method. He brought to the college such speakers as Longfellow, Howells, Holmes, Whittier and Matthew Arnold. To encourage outdoor sports he donated three boats for student crews: the *Argo*, the *Mayflower* and the *Evangeline*. The combination of athletics and aesthetics sometimes proved trying to visiting lecturers. At the age of seventy Longfellow was unable to avoid an excursion on Lake Waban with the crew of the *Evangeline*, which culminated in a climb up a steep bank under an arch of crossed oars. On his next visit the poet confined himself to reading in chapel.

When Vassar and Wellesley were chartered, the word *Female* appeared in their titles. This practice was immediately attacked by those who felt that it suggested a special and inferior type of education for women. "Let the misnomer be corrected," urged a writer in *Godey's Lady's Book*. In response to the protest the trustees of both institutions asked the legislatures for a change of names. Thus in 1867 Vassar Female College became Vassar College, and Wellesley Female Institute even before it opened became Wellesley College. Smith, which opened the same year as Wellesley, was Smith College from the start.

All this went deeper than mere nomenclature; it was in accord with the theory that a woman should be given an education like a man's. The first circular issued by the trustees of Smith College stated:

The object of the Institution, as stated by the founder, is "The establishment and maintenance of an institution for the higher education of young women, with the design to furnish them means and facilities for education equal to those which are afforded in our colleges to young men."

There is every reason to believe that the idea attributed to Sophia Smith had been put in her mind, or at least into her mouth, by the real founder of the college, the Reverend John M. Greene, a graduate of Amherst. It was to him Miss Smith came for advice when she unexpectedly inherited a large sum from her brother. At first he demurred but she burst into tears and pleaded, "I did not want this money . . . but it has come to me and I must dispose of it, and you must help me." Greene first proposed gifts to Amherst and Mount Holyoke, a suggestion she stubbornly refused to accept despite further urging by an Amherst professor. Greene later proposed the endowment of a woman's college and, with her consent, presented the plans to professors W. S. Tyler and Julius H. Seelye for criticism. They took up the idea with enthusiasm. Miss Smith agreed, and in her will named all three to the board of trustees.

After her death, Greene, Tyler and another trustee, Professor Edwards A. Park of Andover, undertook a campaign for additional funds so that the new college would start off on a sound basis. Of one prospective donor Professor Park wrote to Tyler, ". . . he has an immense property, and it will do him good to endow Smith College." By the time the college was started, there was about $500,000 in principal, interest and contributions. Miss Smith's will provided that not more than half of her bequest should go for buildings, and the trustees also had "no desire to repeat the too common mistake of investing the greater part of their funds in brick and mortar." Henry Durant had been less wise; a few years after his death, President

Freeman was struggling to keep the immense building at Wellesley from being forced to close.

The all-male board of trustees at Smith stated further that "the requirements for admission will be substantially the same as at Harvard, Yale, Brown, Amherst, and other New-England Colleges."

Thus the chief difference between Smith and the other women's colleges was in the emphasis on the classics. Vassar and Wellesley did not at first require Greek for entrance, and Vassar offered a scientific course leading to an A.B., but requiring no Greek and less Latin than was demanded in such courses at men's colleges. It is significant that an education like a man's should have come to mean the classical curriculum. The evidence suggests that at Vassar and Wellesley the amount and difficulty of the work was at least equal to that of Amherst or Harvard. In fact there is considerable evidence that with the extreme development of the elective system under Eliot, a man could get a degree at Harvard with a lot less effort than was required of a girl at Wellesley. By 1883 the only required courses at Harvard were freshman English, French or German, sophomore and junior themes and forensics, and an easy half-year course in chemistry and one in physics. Even these could be "anticipated in prep school, and an A.B. could be obtained by passing 18.4 courses (about 110 hours), one fourth of these with grades of C or better. Not until ten years later was a student required to get C or better in at least half his work.

It was understandable but perhaps unfortunate that the women's colleges should pattern themselves after the more conservative men's institutions. The classical curriculum had come to stand for the best in education; the newer "scientific" courses were generally regarded as easier, and probably were. As has been pointed out above (p. 141), they were less scientific than nonclassical. Whereas the classics had some relation to male professions such as law or the ministry, their only vocational usefulness for women was to prepare teachers who would teach the classics to future teachers of the classics.

Their chief justification, therefore, had to be their cultural value. Thus at a time when men's education was becoming increasingly vocational, women's developed along cultural lines. Vassar, Wellesley and Smith all started off with well-equipped departments of fine arts; both Wellesley and Smith emphasized English literature. Henry Durant told Katherine Lee Bates that perhaps a new school of Lake poets might spring up on Lake Waban, whose banks (with fine symbolism) proved so difficult for Longfellow to climb.

One result of this emphasis on a cultural education for women was to intensify the American male's notion that culture was somehow effeminate. In coeducational institutions, the boys increasingly deserted classes in literature which attracted the girls. It is probable this tendency toward a cultural education for women and a vocational one for men was the result —not the cause—of a profound dichotomy in American life. Henry James noted the same thing in social life; business was the province of men, the amenities were left to the women.

The irony was that both Matthew Vassar and Henry Durant had thought in terms of vocations for women, primarily motherhood and teaching. It would seem that the colleges were better at preparing teachers than wives and mothers. By 1892, among the 734 graduates of Wellesley, 540 were teachers, 12 practicing physicians, 15 librarians, and 20 missionaries. As such figures suggest, marriage was not a favored vocation. A study by Margaret Shinn in 1895 showed that of 1,805 college women, only 28.2% were married as compared to 80% for women over 20 in the population as a whole. The figures for college women went up in the later age groups: 32.7% of women over 25; 54.5% for women over 40. As a considerably larger proportion of graduates of coeducational colleges married than did those from women's colleges, it is evident that the Eastern women's institution tended to produce spinster schoolteachers. And as Miss Shinn pointed out, a resident teacher in a girls' boarding school had few chances to marry. In the West where women taught in high schools, more of them married. To some extent the colleges were unfairly

WELLS COLLEGE CREWS, 1878

HIGH SERIOUSNESS IN BLOOMERS

A University of Nebraska coed of about 1900 goes out for sport.

blamed for the small percentage of marriages. As one writer put it in 1890: "If only half of the college women marry it is because they come from a social class in which only half of the women marry."

In any discussion of marriage and fecundity of college women, it must be noted that the percentages for college men were also low. A study in 1903 came to the conclusion that "considering the facts that in our social system man makes the advances and that woman is by nature more prone than man to domesticity and parenthood, it is not impossible that men's colleges do more to unfit for these than do those for women."

Even if that was true, the fact remains that in our social order the woman as mother or teacher is given chief responsibility for the care and education of children. It was doubly unfortunate, therefore, that the women's colleges emulated those features of male education which most unfitted men for domestic life: sex segregation, delayed marriage, and the classical curriculum. Women needed less Greek and more child psychology.

As early as 1851 that warrior for women's education, Catherine Beecher, complained that the higher seminaries "too closely copied" the curriculums of men's colleges. In her *Reminiscences* (1874) she wrote:

The curriculum . . . is very nearly the same as that of Yale or Cambridge and nothing is withdrawn or added with reference to the preparation of woman for her distinctive profession as housekeeper, mother, nurse, and chief educator of infancy and childhood.

Other critics spoke along similar lines. Catherine Beecher blamed the situation on "the fact that there is no university in the United States *the intellectual* interests of which are managed by the professors, but *always by a corporation outside.* . . ."

The theory that boards of trustees are the source of academic ills is always attractive to the academic mind, but there is little evidence that educators in 1875 were any more realistic about the curriculum than faculties had been for a century. Both

Matthew Vassar and Henry Durant had envisioned the training of women as mothers and teachers; it was the academic experts who introduced and entrenched the classical curriculum. At Smith the first curriculum was largely the work of Amherst graduates and faculty. The first president, L. Clark Seelye, was an Amherst professor whose brother became president of Amherst. The belief in woman's right to a higher education was to be demonstrated by her ability to master Latin and Greek. After all, Eliot of Harvard insisted on the difference between the minds of men and women; and as late as 1895 Dr. S. Weir Mitchell, the most eminent psychiatrist of his time, argued that most women would sacrifice mental and physical health. M. Carey Thomas of Bryn Mawr reported that a student of 1908 was "terror struck" after reading G. Stanley Hall's *Adolescence,* lest she and other college students were doomed to live as pathological invalids. Elsewhere Hall stated: "It is utterly impossible without injury to hold girls to the same standards of conduct, regularity, severe moral accountability, strenuous mental work, that boys need." It is not strange that the best answer to this sort of male paranoia seemed to be a demonstration that women could excel in the sanctified classical curriculum. Thus it was fifty or sixty years before the women's colleges really faced the problem of a curriculum designed to meet the social and economic needs of women.

Some of these needs seem to have been better provided for at coeducational institutions. As early as 1846 Oberlin set up a Teachers' Department, in which there was much discussion of teaching methods and theories of discipline. By 1879 Michigan had a chair in the History, Theory and Art of Education. As has been noted, coeds married in larger proportion than did their contemporaries at women's colleges. And they were less likely to develop activities of the daisy-chain variety.

Certainly coeducation had a civilizing effect on the men. In 1867, reporting on Oberlin's experience, President James H. Fairchild said that it makes "men of boys and gentlemen of rowdies." As Ezra Cornell hoped to see at least 5,000 boys and girls studying at the university he planned, Andrew White visited Oberlin and Michigan to see how coeducation worked. At Michigan, where it had been introduced since his day, he noted that the men were no longer slouchy and unkempt in class. "It was," he said, "the difference between the smoking car and the car back of it." The most convincing testimony came from a janitor, who reported that students no longer pushed one another up and down stairs or held boxing matches in the lobby.

President Fairchild effectively answered the critics of coeducation and of higher education for women. Were not women a handicap to the progress of men? Not in his experience as a teacher of Latin, Greek, Hebrew, mathematics, and philosophy. Strong and weak scholars were equally distributed among men and women. Nor did women's health break down more often than men's. Women were neither coarsened nor caused to disdain the usual lot of women. Most of them married. As for foolish love affairs, he argued that monastic institutions were more likely to heighten the imagination of youths, filling their minds with fanciful creations unlike actual men and women. An Oberlin professor told the Honorable Dudley Campbell of Cambridge, "Nothing acts as a better antidote for romance than young men and women doing geometry together at eight o'clock every morning." But did not the acquaintances formed at school lead to matrimony? "Undoubtedly," answered Fairchild, "and if this is a fatal objection, the system must be pronounced a failure." Were there not occasional immoralities? Yes, but were the best Eastern colleges and seminaries free from these?

Male students were often less enthusiastic about coeducation. At Oberlin it had existed long enough for men to get used to it, but when introduced at Michigan, it was unpopular until after the turn of the century. Cornell men tried to exclude coeds from elections, publications and committees. A professor who sympathized with the boys is reported to have said at a student banquet, ". . . the girls have a civilization and interests of their own and do not share in those of the boys. . . . Enforced association under the circumstances is irksome. It is promised in regard to coeducation that it will 'refine' the boys, but college boys want their fling and don't wish to be refined. They prefer congenial savagery." When girls were admitted at Wisconsin to keep the institution going during the Civil War, the handful of remaining men felt deeply humiliated and refused to recognize in any way the presence of women. The girls retaliated by paying no attention to the boys.

But Western men found it less necessary to demonstrate their masculinity than the Cornell men of the 1870s or University of Pennsylvania men of more recent date. By 1864 Wisconsin students held a mixed social gathering at the exhibition of the women's literary society. And by 1874 the student paper was commenting favorably on the part taken by girls in chapel rhetoricals and other exercises. The freshmen even petitioned the faculty to permit women to attend class meetings. The only squawk was over the disproportion of women selected as commencement speakers. The trouble was that the selection was based on class standing, and in this the women outranked the men.

The conflicting attitudes within the colleges only reflected those in the community. Ignoring the experience of colleges like Oberlin, the opponents of coeducation spent seventy-five years arguing that it would coarsen women and ruin their health and morals, that it would lower the standards of work and thus debase men's education. Many of the arguments were the same as those used against women's colleges. In 1874 Dr. E. H. Clarke, an ex-Harvard professor, prophesied that if present trends continued, "the mothers of our republic must be drawn from transatlantic homes. The sons of the New World will have to react, on a magnificent scale, to the old story of unwived Rome and the Sabines." Henry Maudsley, in a book *Sex in Education,* 1880, attacked coeducation on the ground that "identical education of the two sexes is a crime before God and humanity, that physiology protests against, and that experience weeps over." As late as 1903 the eminent psychologist G. Stanley Hall wrote: "Coeducation in the middle teens tends to sexual precocity. This is very bad, it is one of the subtlest dangers that can befall civilization."

As a rule the proponents of coeducation did not command such gaudy rhetoric. Like Fairchild of Oberlin, they pointed to the record of women's health and achievement. They argued that coeducation was in accord with democratic ideals and that it avoided the duplication of facilities. In 1884 H. S. Tarbell made a significant point when he wrote: "Coeducation is at present a necessity for those young ladies who desire to be accredited with thorough scholarship. A diploma from Michigan University is of much more value to a lady than one from any of the colleges for women." This is borne out by the experience of Henry Durant, who had difficulty finding qualified women for the first Wellesley faculty. Those who came from Michigan were so satisfactory that he wanted more from there. Among them was Alice Freeman, who at twenty-six became the second president of Wellesley. It must be remembered that until the late eighties there were only seven women's institutions doing genuine college work. Bryn Mawr received its college charter in 1888, Holyoke not until 1893.

As had happened with men's education, the American people went ahead despite the experts, and developed the kind of institutions they needed. Notwithstanding the horrendous warnings of learned physicians, psychologists, psychiatrists, and educators—whose objectivity was conditioned by the fact that they were male and usually from the East—coeducation was rapidly extended. By 1870 women had been admitted to 30.7% of all colleges other than technical schools and those for women only. Ten years later the proportion of coeducational institutions was 51.3%, and in 1890 it was 65.5%. By far the largest number were in the West.* Between 1875 and 1900 women in coeducational schools increased 600%; whereas the number in women's colleges went up about 60%. By that time there were nearly 20,000 coeds compared to not quite 16,000 in all-

* In 1873, of ninety-seven institutions five were in New England, eight in the middle states, seventeen in the South, and sixty-seven in the West.

girl colleges. Yet the Republic remained on its foundations; women continued to bear children; and American men did not participate in a rape of the Sabine women. Even President Eliot somewhat grudgingly accepted coeducation with the statement that although young men and women between fifteen and twenty are not "best educated in intimate association . . . this method may nevertheless be justifiable in a community which cannot afford anything better."

It was such views that produced at some men's colleges a co-ordinate college for women. The pattern for these was suggested by Queens College, London, and Girton College, Cambridge. Harvard at first dipped a very tentative toe in the water by giving examinations, but no courses, for women. Eliot's attitude has been described as that of a mother who, though not encouraging her daughter's education, did not prohibit her to read. After the examinations had been in operation four years, Arthur Gilman suggested to Professor Greenough that professors repeat some of their courses for women. Greenough and several other professors, among them Child, Goodwin, and Gurney, took up the idea with enthusiasm. Mrs. Agassiz helped to raise $15,000. Thus in 1879 the Harvard Annex began operation. As it had no power to grant degrees, those who completed the course received certificates stating that they had "pursued a course of study equivalent in amount and quality to that for which the Bachelor of Arts is conferred in Harvard College, and had passed in a satisfactory manner examinations on that course, corresponding to the college examinations."

This pedantic makeshift was naturally unsatisfactory to the ladies. The Woman's Educational Association began raising funds for an endowment. Mrs. Agassiz was elected president in 1882 and a building was obtained three years later. It was not until 1893 that the semiofficial name *Annex* was changed to Radcliffe College, and the power to grant degrees was not obtained until 1894. Yet, despite the somewhat makeshift character of the Annex during its early years, it had one enormous advantage—the services of members of the most distinguished faculty in America. No other women's college of the time could boast scholars and teachers remotely approaching such men as Agassiz, Child, Greenough, Dean Briggs and Kittredge. Although Vassar, Wellesley and Smith developed some brilliant scholars in their own faculties, it must be remembered that the first staffs were usually women who had had little opportunity for advanced study. Some of them, even at Wellesley, Holyoke and Smith, had no college degrees. Many of them were very young. Alice Freeman, for instance, came to Wellesley at twenty-four as head of the History Department, and was made president at twenty-six. Thus Radcliffe became a useful laboratory for proving the theory that women could do college work equal to the best. By 1909 Eliot admitted that they often surpassed the men.

The development of Barnard was similar to that of Radcliffe. As has been noted above (p. 162) Frederick A. P. Barnard advocated coeducation beginning with his report of 1879. As in Cambridge, a citizens' organization took up the cause, in this case the Association for Promoting Higher Education of Women, whose primary object was to secure the admission of women to Columbia. The Association and President Barnard continued to bring pressure until, in 1883, the trustees established "a course of collegiate study equivalent to the course given to young men in the college." This was less than Barnard and the Association wanted, but it went further than Harvard had done; the course led to a degree. Furthermore, it was organized according to the plan proposed years before by Folwell of Minnesota, and later by Barnard. The work of the first two years was required; that of the last two was entirely elective. As in modern institutions, the courses were arranged in groups: English language and literature; modern languages and foreign literature; Latin language and literature; Greek language and literature; mathematics, history and political science; physics, chemistry and hygiene; natural history, geology, paleontology, botany and zoology; moral and intellectual philosophy.

Co-ordinate colleges were set up elsewhere: Sophie Newcomb Memorial College for Women, affiliated with Tulane, in 1887;

and the Women's College at Brown in 1891. With the reaction against coeducation around the turn of the century, a few places like Chicago and Stanford tried to segregate the girls in separate colleges. Tufts, which had admitted women in 1892, set up a separate women's division: Jackson College, in 1910. But as the figures on p. 197 show, coeducational institutions outnumbered other types as early as 1880, and attracted an increasing proportion of the women attending college.

Thus, during the quarter century following the Civil War, the pattern of women's higher education in America was established. Vassar, Wellesley, Smith and Bryn Mawr were all founded during those years; coeducation was introduced at Wisconsin, Michigan, Cornell, Minnesota and many other places; Harvard and Columbia set up co-ordinate colleges which became distinguished in their own right. Most important of all was the recognition of women's right to a college education. Some notion of the revolutionary nature of the change can be gained from the experience of M. Carey Thomas, who, before she entered Cornell in 1873, had seen only one college woman in her life. "I had heard that such a woman was staying at the house of an acquaintance. I went to see her with fear. Even if she had hoofs and horns I was determined to go to college all the same." Miss Thomas became the first woman to receive a Ph.D. at a European university. In 1894 she became president of Bryn Mawr.

Women's education of this period reflected and intensified a characteristic of American society: a tendency to put culture and morals in the wife's name. One indication of this was the adoption of the classical curriculum by women's colleges at the very time when men's education was becoming increasingly specialized through the development of technical schools and the growth of the elective system. It is significant that a number of the most distinguished faculty members taught literature, people like Vida Scudder of Wellesley; M. Carey Thomas of Bryn Mawr; William Allan Neilson, who taught English at Bryn Mawr, Harvard and Columbia before becoming president of Smith. In the coeducational institutions the tendency

was for women to outnumber the men in liberal-arts departments. Writing in 1907, President Charles R. Van Hise of Wisconsin reported that in thirteen universities 52.7% of the students in liberal arts were women, although there were many
more men than women at these institutions.

It was to be expected that the rules for women should be
stricter than those for men. The whole pattern of Western civilization since Penelope held off the suitors while Odysseus
dallied with Circe and Calypso has set a high value on female
chastity. Thus at all colleges admitting women there were
rigid regulations about social life, going out of the building
after dark, early bedtime, etc. Almost every detail of social life
was supervised, and the forbidding and very public dormitory parlor was a standard feature. Coeducational institutions
adopted the spirit if not the unfortunate wording of a regulation at Swarthmore, which provided that "Intercourse of the
students is under the care of the Dean and her assistants."

When Cornell girls, objecting to the greater restrictions
placed on them and the presence of a "lady warden" in the
dormitory, demanded the same freedom to come and go enjoyed by the men, President White "showed them that a firm
public opinion was an invincible barrier to the liberties they
claimed." As a rule, although they occasionally objected to
specific restrictions, college women seem to have cheerfully
accepted the rules—and to a large degree to have obeyed them.
(Cf. p. 186 above.)

A much more controversial result of putting the nation's
conscience in the keeping of women was the development of
social consciousness. The ruthlessness, exploitation and corruption of the Gilded Age need no repetition here. It was
the period of which Henry Adams wrote: "One might search
the whole list of Congress, Judiciary, and Executive during the
twenty-five years between 1870 and 1895, and find little but
damaged reputation. . . ." All Boston, all New England and
respectable New York, including Charles Francis Adams the
father and Charles Francis Adams the son, agreed that Washington was no place for a respectable young man. "All Wash-

ington, including Presidents, Cabinet officers, Judiciary, Senators, Congressmen, and clerks expressed the same opinion.
. . ." By the turn of the century Mark Twain noted: "I believe
the entire population of the United States—*exclusive of the
women*—to be rotten, as far as the dollar is concerned." Thus
to intelligent college women the field of missions seemed to be
less in foreign fields than in the American jungle.

The Durants had thought in terms of training missionaries
and Christian workers on the early nineteenth-century evangelical pattern exemplified by Oberlin. Louise McCoy North,
1879, remarked that in Durant's time the whole college was a
Christian Association. The Missionary Society, begun in the
first year of the college, undertook the support of missionaries
who went out from Wellesley.

Allied to the work for missions were the activities for the
benefit of factory girls and women prisoners. For years Wellesley students went to South Natick on Saturday evenings to lead
meetings and entertainments in a clubroom they had fitted up
for girls employed in the shoe factory. On Thanksgiving nights
students gave entertainments for prisoners in a women's re-
formatory. The Temperance Society, one of Durant's enthusiasms, brought lecturers to the college and circulated total
abstinence pledges. Under Alice Freeman, who had been active
in Christian work at Michigan, the various organizations at
Wellesley were merged.

From such activities it was a natural·step to more practical
and informed work for social welfare. Professor Katherine
Coman, of the Economics department, publicized figures from
the census of 1880, which showed that factory girls had an
average income of $5.77 a week, and expenses of $5.64. The
student publication, *Prelude,* in its editorials praised the awak-
ening interest in political economy classes as a tendency toward lessening the gap between students and the world. At a
later period Katherine Coman wrote:

College women cannot rest content in ignorance of the woes
of the world, and once conscious of the part they must play

as consumers, employees, investors, or wage-earners, they will not shirk responsibility.

In the English department young Vida Scudder in 1890 originated a course, "Social Ideals in English Letters." She considered it her "most original and significant contribution to the teaching of English literature."

A year before, women from Smith, Vassar, Wellesley and Bryn Mawr opened a settlement house at 95 Rivington Street in New York. Two weeks later in Chicago, a twenty-nine-year-old graduate of Rockford College joined with Ellen Gates Starr to start Hull House. Jane Addams was later to help form the Progressive Party, to become vice-president of the National Woman's Suffrage Association, and to share with Nicholas Murray Butler the Nobel Peace Prize. Vida Scudder brought to Wellesley a fiery young labor leader, Jack O'Sullivan, to speak to the younger members of the faculty. To their horror he attempted to organize a teachers' union. At one time Miss Scudder belonged to fifty-nine organizations bent on reform. She even joined the Socialist party at a time when such a step was regarded by respectable people as equivalent to moral turpitude.

Much of this story belongs to a later chapter, but it is clear that by 1890 college women were becoming deeply aware of American social problems and intended to do something about them.

This too was part of that revolution which makes the quarter-century following the Civil War the miraculous years in American higher education. It was the period which saw the rise of true universities; the reformation of the curriculum; the development of universities for all the people; the founding of Cornell and Johns Hopkins, Vassar, Wellesley, Smith, Bryn Mawr, Radcliffe, and Barnard; the introduction of coeducation at Wisconsin, Michigan, Minnesota, and a host of other places. After more than two centuries of stagnation, higher education came alive and began the task of revitalizing the intellectual, economic, and social life of America.

7

The Golden Age and the
Gilded Cage

It is ironic that the most fruitful period in American higher
education sowed the seeds of three of its greatest evils: commercialized athletics, domination by the business community,
and a caste system symbolized by the Gold Coast. These grew
out of the very forces which had produced the revolution. Thus
the development of great universities brought with it a mass
audience for athletic spectacles; a moribund classicism and the
free elective system both permitted the athlete and the playboy to reduce academic effort to a minimum; the munificent
gifts of men like Cornell, Vassar and Durant, and later by the
oil, pork, soap, steel, and railroad barons, brought with them a
shift in control from the professional classes to the new rich.

This shift in control was foreshadowed by a change in the
social and intellectual life of the colleges. A smaller percentage
of students came to prepare for the ministry, law, and teaching;
they came to prepare for entrance into the business community,
especially that part of it concerned with big business and
finance. And it was the sons of big business, finance, and corporation law who dominated the life of the campus in the older
Eastern colleges. To an amazing degree the pattern set by
Harvard, Yale and Princeton after 1880 became that of colleges all over the country. The clubs, the social organization,
the athletics—even the clothes and the slang—of "the big
three" were copied by college youth throughout the nation.
In its totality the system which flowered between 1880 and
World War I reflected the ideals of the social class which
dominated the period.

Thus in the immensely popular novel *Stover at Yale* a turn-of-the-century student says:

I say our colleges to-day are business colleges—Yale more so, perhaps, because it is more sensitively American. Let's take up any side of our life here. Begin with athletics. What has become of the natural spontaneous joy of contest? Instead you have one of the most perfectly organized business systems for achieving a required result-success.

He goes on to cite musical organizations, student publications. "We are like a beef trust, with every by-product organized, down to the last possibility."

It should be noted that the student was talking about things entirely outside the curriculum and the official organization of the college. For it was in the three decades, 1880 to 1910, that the faculty lost control of American college education. This was not originally due to boards of trustees, tyrannical presidents, or alumni interference—none of the bugaboos described by Thorstein Veblen and his imitators. It was not the organization of the American college which pushed the faculty out of the driver's seat; it was the nature of American life.

Veblen's naïve notion, shared by many teachers, that the problems of higher education could be solved by turning it over to the faculty ignores both the history of its development in America and the complexity of the social processes that produced its most characteristic features. It is significant that the most extreme development of the side shows took place at Yale where by tradition the faculty was exceptionally powerful in determining academic policy. In the seventies and eighties this meant the hegemony of the classicists. Scientists and social scientists had been largely relegated to the poorly supported Sheffield Scientific School. Under President Noah Porter, 1871-1886, the faculty adhered to the concepts laid down a half-century before in the famous report of 1828. As President Porter stated it: "The student often most needs the discipline to which he is least inclined." Like his colleague, Thomas A. Thatcher, Porter believed that "no kind of intellectual athletics is more useful . . . than the reflective analysis of classic sentences." A freshman of the class of 1879, Poultney Bigelow, once asked his instructor to recommend readings in history. The reply was "Young man, if you think you came to Yale with the idea of reading, you will find out your mistake very soon."

By the time very limited elective choices were offered in the late eighties and nineties, a pattern of student folkways had already crystallized. One important effect of the standardized curriculum was to develop an intense unity in college classes. For four years the students in each class lived and worked as a unit; they developed the same enthusiasms and the same dislikes. In 1892 George Santayana, commenting on the compulsory routine at Yale, stated: "Common grievances are a greater bond than common privileges."

The grievances were against a dull routine under teachers who expressed their own boredom and frustration through biting sarcasm and a "tariff of black marks." Outside the classroom the students enjoyed life immensely. As Santayana put it:

The relations of one Yale student to another are comparatively simple and direct. They are like passengers in a ship or fellow countrymen abroad; their sense of common interests and common emotions overwhelms all latent antipathies. They live in a sort of primitive brotherhood, with a ready enthusiasm for every good or bad project, and a contagious good humor.

Professor Bernadotte Perrin testified to the same thing in the 1890s:

Where three or four hundred men are forced through the same course of study, regardless of their individual preferences or tastes, there results a kind of collective or mass individuality. . . . And so this lower undergraduate life at Yale fosters mass movements of every kind; keeps alive the old "class-spirit" . . .

It was even felt that the grinding routine of the classroom helped to develop the hardihood and self-discipline of Yale athletes. Certainly it helped to turn the energies and interests of students into extracurricular channels. As Henry Seidel

Canby says of his student days in the nineties: "College life was at least 90% of our felt experience, and therefore 90% of the college as we knew it."

It would be a mistake to give the classical curriculum the entire credit for the vast development of extracurricular life. Nevertheless this development seems to have been most extreme at those institutions with the most conservative curriculums. Certainly the development was not confined to wealthy places. A comparatively poverty-stricken small college like Lafayette produced a team in 1896 rated next to Princeton's as the best in the country; three years later Lafayette beat both Penn and Navy; the college swarmed with fraternities; students devoted a large proportion of their time to activities and organizations. Most small colleges, because of conservatism and lack of money, stuck to the classical curriculum. A little college of the period was likely to be a smaller version of Yale or Princeton. Nor was the development confined to the East. In the late 1880s, with an enrollment of about 500 in college courses, the University of Wisconsin had thirteen fraternities. By 1894 ten of them had their own chapter houses. As we shall see, football became immensely popular from Yale to Stanford during the eighties and nineties.

Canby, who saw the system at Yale both as student and teacher, came to the conclusion that the faculty's "actual conflict was not with ignorance but with college life and all that it implied; and behind it the ideas and ideals of an American society in which materialism dominated action and governed thought." An intensely competitive spirit prevailed in all student activities.

Yet paradoxically the college of the late nineteenth and early twentieth century was also a refuge from the drabness of the commercial and moral life of the period. Canby himself notes that the largest group came for college life, a romantic, golden interlude of song, sport, activities, drinking, and glory either on the athletic field or in some organization. The glamour is reflected in many a college story: Owen Wister's *Philosophy 4*, Charles Flandrau's *Harvard Episodes*, Owen Johnson's

Stover at Yale. Between 1897 and 1914 the Frank Merriwell stories of Yale ran through a series of 800 installments. Flandrau wrote additional Harvard stories for *The Saturday Evening Post*; *Stover at Yale* appeared first in *McClure's Magazine*. As Canby says, college life was for many "an intoxicating dream." Of students: "We were naïvely yet arrogantly aware that we belonged to America's golden girls and boys."

Over and over students sang:

> Oh, father and mother
> Pay all the bills,
> And we have all the fun.
>
> Hooray!
> That's the way we do,
> In college life.

Father and mother did not always pay the bills; many a student waited on table and did manual labor in the summer. If a boy could play football, he might get to be a big man in college, no matter what his background. But in the famous Eastern colleges it was the prep-school graduate who set the pattern, a pattern imitated all over the country. At least several chapters could be written of the influence on student attitudes and mores resulting from such "church schools" as Andover, Groton, Phillips-Exeter, Lawrenceville, Hill and Hotchkiss. As Stover discovered at Yale, there was an Andover clique, one from Exeter, etc. His own chances for making various societies were hurt by the fact that he came from Lawrenceville, which was much better represented at Princeton than at Yale.

Here again the influence of the classical curriculum operated. Public high schools rarely provided enough training in Greek to meet the requirements of the better Eastern colleges. Poor students often entered with conditions in Latin or Greek; they had to sweat extra hours in college to make up their deficiencies. Thus they became the "grinds" or "greasy grinds"—fellows who did not go out for football or activities. It is quite possible that the tradition that all students, rich or poor, had an equal chance at college honors is an American myth. Stover's friend Regan, who earned his way and made the team —without being subsidized—is a character more common in fiction than in college. An observer noted that the 1927 Princeton football squad of forty-four men contained not a man from a public high school. But most of the great preparatory schools were represented.

For one thing, a famous prep school gave a man a head start for college honors. When Stover first comes to Yale, he is represented as looking up a friend, who tells him: "We've got a corking lot in the house—best of the Andover crowd." Stover is introduced to a student named Hunter:

He was face to face with the big man of the Andover crowd, measuring him and being measured. . . . This man could not help but be a leader in the class. . . . He examined, analyzed, deliberated. He knew what lay before him. He would make no mistakes.

A green boy from a public high school was more likely to make mistakes, to get in with a crowd of "fruits." So strong was the tendency of boys from fashionable schools to congregate that it nearly wrecked President Lowell's attempt to introduce a more democratic system in Harvard dormitories. When the new freshman halls were opened in 1914, it was found that applicants from the fashionable New England schools, almost without exception, had selected rooms in the same hall. An appeal to the heads of the schools was necessary to obtain the desired scattering of students. Before 1914 college authorities had not attempted to check the tendency of prep-school boys to flock together.

A man's prep-school background was especially important in his election to one of the student clubs. And in most colleges, clubs or fraternities controlled undergraduate life. In small colleges, and west of the Alleghenies, a high-school graduate had a good chance of joining a fraternity; in the older Eastern colleges, his chances were slim. For one thing, club life was expensive. An exceptional athlete might find his way eased by wealthier students, but as a rule the clubs were composed of wealthy men.

It was not merely a matter of dues and fees; the whole scale of living set by the leaders was expensive. To get elected to sophomore societies, rich and socially ambitious students at Yale congregated in "The Hutch," an expensive private dormitory. Such men patronized good tailors; they dined well; they made five and ten-dollar bets on all sorts of things; they ordered fine cigars by the hundreds; they ruined expensive suits and shirts in the course of pranks, rushes, and sprees. Yale tradition was that what a man did in college determined his standing, a tradition which is perhaps stronger than the evidence. Certainly a poor boy could go to college there. Between 1888 and 1914 tuition was $155. For five dollars a month Stover's friend Regan occupied a rathole over a bakery; weekly board at four dollars was still possible in the 1890s. Flandrau describes a Harvard student who subsisted on oatmeal cooked over the gas jet in his room. But a man who tended a half-dozen furnaces or acted as night clerk in a hotel had not the time for both studies and activities.

These activities, as all accounts agree, took up a fearful amount of time. At Yale, where student life was fiercely competitive, a man might take singing lessons in order to compete for leadership of the glee club; another would make drawings during the summer in order to make the *Record*. "There are fellows in your class," Le Baron told Stover, "who've been working all summer to get ahead in the competition for the *Lit* or the *Record,* or to make the leader of the glee club." At the end of the football season a player was expected to go out for some other sport. A freshman tried to make the sophomore societies, the first step toward the all-important senior societies. To do this he had to be careful to join the right eating club. It was important to belong to the right crowd—"the crowd you'll want to know through life." As Le Baron instructed Stover:

You come from a school that doesn't send many fellows here. You haven't the fellows ahead pulling for you, the way other crowds have. I don't want you to make any mistake. Remember, you're going to be watched from now on.

At a time when classes numbered about 300, the sophomore societies elected only fifty-one; the junior societies, and the three senior societies—Skull and Bones, Scroll and Key, and Wolf's Head—only fifteen each. The percentage of men "tapped" for senior societies at Harvard was even smaller. However, because of a much less closely knit student body, the pressures of competition were less than at Yale or Princeton. Small Eastern and Southern colleges developed a pattern similar to Yale's; large state universities had, like Harvard, a core of the elite, the big men in college, within a diverse and loosely organized student body. Perhaps nowhere else were most students freer from social pressures than at Harvard. But for the elite, as at Yale, the thought of Tap Day dominated the first three years. On that fatal afternoon in May juniors gathered tensely in Harvard Yard or near the Yale fence. As the clock struck five, men issued from the society buildings and moved about among the white-faced juniors. Each of the chosen felt a slap on the shoulder and heard the words, "Go to your room." Those others who had hoped for the honor were broken men; sometimes one of them fainted.

For a few days a man might be congratulated, but ever after no one was supposed to mention the sacred name of his society or even to notice the identifying pin in his tie. At Yale, tradition forbade the noninitiated so much as to glance at the jaillike sanctuaries of Skull and Bones, Scroll and Key, or Wolf's Head or notice the mysterious midnight processions of the priesthood.

At other colleges, Greek-letter fraternities dominated activities and social life. These usually selected their members from the freshmen during a frantic rushing period at the start of the year. However, almost any man who distinguished himself during his college life was likely to be invited to join some fraternity. At many places half the student body were Greek-letter men. At Princeton the eating clubs combined the worst features of both systems. Lacking national connections, they developed the provincial snobbery of the Yale societies; like the fraternities they segregated their members from the rest of the student body. A fraternity brother or Princeton clubman lived, ate and slept in company with a small group throughout most of his college years. The same was true of a Harvard clubman, but it affected a much smaller percentage of the student body. The evils of the system led Woodrow Wilson to make his ill-advised attempt to abolish the clubs at Princeton. His bullheaded methods nearly tore the university apart and brought down on his head the wrath of powerful alumni. It was simpler, he discovered, to resign and go into New Jersey politics. Lowell's freshman house plan was more successful because it was a less negative approach to the problem and because he enlisted alumni support. In state universities the periodic legislative attacks on fraternities usually proved as futile as Wilson's methods. The fraternities simply went underground until the storm blew over.

The club and fraternity problem has never been completely solved, but several factors have mitigated some of the worst evils. Freshman dormitories and sensible college regulations governing rushing have helped, but most important has been the changed atmosphere of college life. A modern student body is much more representative of the whole population than was the case before World War I, and community pressures have increasingly operated against social snobbery. The system of the period 1880 to 1917 was a product of the ruthless economic and social competition of American life of the period.

A related feature of college life before 1917 was the development of the Gold Coast at Harvard and its equivalent at Yale— luxurious private dormitories inhabited by the plutocracy. Claverly at Harvard, and Hutchinson ("The Hutch") at Yale were the university counterparts of the vast mansions of the Morgans, Vanderbilts, Fricks, and Carnegies. With the importation of a taste for the Gothic of Oxford and Cambridge, both Yale and Princeton undertook the building of luxurious, if somewhat ill-lighted dormitories. Under the second Timothy

Dwight, 1886 to 1899, Yale pulled down most of the Brick Row to replace it with handsome stone dormitories. The change was symbolic. Brick Row belonged to the barracks style of college architecture still preserved in the older dormitories in Harvard Yard, a style reflecting the poverty and simple life of the early colleges. James Gamble Rogers' neo-Gothic design for Yale's Harkness and Ralph Adams Cram's for the Princeton Graduate College are only sophisticated editions of the Romantic period in American colleges. They combine its two great forces: wealth and romance. The wealthy men who endowed them were products of collegiate generations which went in for both ruthless competition and uncritical emotion. Canby explains the *fin de siècle* Tudor Gothic in terms of the sentimental imagination of the alumni who paid for it. It can also be explained in part by the failure of the nineteenth-century American college to give its graduates any feeling either for their own national past or the values of their own time. Only Harvard took as its models the colonial buildings in the Yard. And not even the city colleges discovered the functional vitality of steel and concrete. Even as late as the 1930s the universities of Pittsburgh and Temple were clothing steel office buildings with Gothic exteriors. Recent Princeton buildings are poured concrete within a Gothic shell.

It is not strange that the men who went to college between 1880 and 1917 tried to return to a nostalgic past. In most colleges the faculty talked to them chiefly about the glories of ancient times. Literature, fine arts and architecture were all things which had happened long ago. And student life existed in a golden never-never land. Graduation was more of a tragedy than an achievement. Canby, remembering his own student days, says, "The youth stepped out into the world trailing clouds of memory behind him. He took on a new identity as clerk, law student, or office assistant, yet held desperately to his affiliation with a caste of men whose memories were like his own."

The caste system was an intricate one reaching back into the prep school and forward into business and professional life.

First of all there was a social hierarchy of colleges: "The Big Three"; then the older New England group including Amherst, Williams and Dartmouth; anomalous universities like Cornell, Columbia and Pennsylvania with their own caste systems; the older Eastern colleges such as Lafayette, Dickinson, Franklin and Marshall; Southern institutions with their own hierarchy ranging from Virginia and William and Mary down to tiny provincial sectarian strongholds; the large Western universities; and finally the horde of fresh-water colleges. Naturally the order of the hierarchy differed somewhat, depending on the sectional viewpoint. Thus a Wisconsin graduate would rank higher in Chicago than in Boston; a Virginia man was an aristocrat below the Mason-Dixon line. Every engineering school in the country considered itself next in rank to M.I.T.

Within each institution there were the two main groups: fraternity (or club) men, and nonfraternity men. Fraternity loyalties could reach across the continent. In *Stanford Stories* (1900) a student's choice of a fraternity is governed by the fact that his rich uncle belonged to the same one at Amherst. It seems to have been somewhere in the eighties or nineties that student slang began to develop derogatory terms for the non-elect. In that era they were "fruits"; later "drips," "black men," "meat balls," etc. Not every nonfraternity man was a "fruit," but fruits were almost certain to wear no mystic pin. A man who tried to ingratiate himself with the elect was a "swipe." Of course fraternities and clubs developed hierarchies of their own, with the earliest organizations on a campus usually at the top, although this could be modified by the over-all standing of a national fraternity. At institutions like Harvard, Yale and Dartmouth, which had a class-club system, the small senior societies were the pinnacle of the pyramid. Thus at Yale the very tip was Skull and Bones. For these, achievement, rather than mere wealth or fashion, was the criterion, but the more purely social "eating clubs" at Yale, Princeton and Harvard became havens of an aristocracy of wealth and privilege. At Princeton the hegemony of the clubs seems to have come later than elsewhere, apparently after 1895.

For a chronicler of the nineties Harvard is

. . . the five small clubs . . . whose influence is the most powerful, the farthest reaching influence in the undergraduate life
of the place. . . . The club . . . rather prided itself in not
being a reward for either the meritorious or energetic. It was
composed of men drawn from the same station in life, the similarity of whose past associations and experience, in addition
to whatever natural attractions they possessed, rendered them
mutually agreeable.

Their influence reached into the faculty. For the tutor,
Thorn, "They were everything that made the world, as he knew
it just then, interesting and beautiful." In another story a
freshman elected to Dickey, a sophomore club, is for that reason
taken into the confidence of Professor Fleetwood, who nostalgically remembers his own younger days in the club. At one
point Thorn, without reading the examination paper, passes a
lazy fellow club member, only to discover that the boy had
turned in a blank blue book. The point of the story is that an
older man can't step back into the world of youth without making a fool of himself. But it also illustrates the group consciousness in so close knit a society.

Owen Wister, Harvard 1882, is contemptuous of Oscar Mai-
roni, a student employed to tutor the two playboy heroes of
Philosophy 4. "Calculation was his second nature . . . like the
socialists, merit with him meant not being able to live as well
as your neighbor." But "money filled the pockets of Bertie and
Billy; therefore were their heads empty of money and full of
less cramping thoughts." For such as Bertie and Billy it was a
luxurious world. A roommate comes in from a dinner of soft-
shell crabs, broiled lobster, salmon, grass plover, dough birds,
and rum omelette. Flandrau's club men dine frequently in
Boston on a "bird" or a duck apiece. It was a world where
boots were put out at night, where a man might keep a servant,
and at his club ask a steward to call a horse cab to take him
to an early exam. Drinks were served openly at clubs.

Gone were the days reflected in Hammond's diary when a

whole college class participated on an equal basis in social functions, dated and danced with the same girls, lived in the same dormitories and ate at the same table. The closing of the Yale commons and the demolition of Brick Row were symbols of the change. At Harvard, Hasty Pudding had started in 1795 as a relatively democratic group which ate corn-meal mush together in preference to the food in commons. Porcellian ("Pork") had more aristocratic beginnings, being first called the Gentleman's Society, and very early excluding anyone not "blooded" or closely affiliated with the Boston or banking elect. Thus, although Harvard social distinctions began early, the "select" clubs never had over eighteen per cent of the students, and by 1950 included only five per cent. This represents exclusiveness to a high degree, but it also means that the nonelect at Harvard have usually been in a less invidious position than elsewhere. There were always too many of them, and the tradition of individualism even in the eighties and nineties left a student vastly freer from group pressures than at tightly organized Yale. Between these two extremes lay the social organization of other colleges, although in this period the Yale pattern was more often imitated.

A more sinister social cleavage developed during these years, one growing directly out of American society—that of race. As early as 1895, A. Lawrence Lowell became concerned over the lack of proper housing for the poorer students. In 1902 he wrote President Eliot on the "tendency of wealthy students to live in private dormitories outside the yard," and spoke of the "great danger of a snobbish separation of the students on lines of wealth." In a committee report drafted the same year he pointed to a related evil: Hastings Hall, one of the best college dormitories, suffered in reputation because a large number of Jews lived in it. The building had become known by such names as Little Jerusalem. It was to break up both Gold Coasts and Little Jerusalems that Harvard, under Lowell, developed the system of freshman dormitories and commons.

In colleges where Greek-letter fraternities governed the social and political life, the rules against non-Aryans and a reluctance to admit Catholics automatically excluded such groups from much of the life of the campus. A traveling representative for a famous national fraternity noted that at colleges like Princeton and Williams, "considered sacred to the Anglo-Saxon type," the students kept down the proportion of Jews by making them uncomfortable. Thus developed the tendency of Jewish and second-generation Americans to flock to the city universities. Added to these were the students who, because they lived at home, took little part in university life outside the classroom. As early as 1881 President Barnard spoke of 120 Columbia students who had to use the ferries daily. All these forces tended to produce one set of colleges for the elect, another for the "unwashed" and the "fruits."

Just as prep-school connections helped to govern the success of a man in college, so his college connections operated when he went into the world. The American college throve on the myth that any poor boy who worked his way through had an equal chance with the others to become rich and famous. Thousands of young men came for that reason. But the development of hierarchies among and within colleges made this increasingly difficult. The famous law firms, the big banks and brokerage houses selected young men only from certain colleges, and preferably from certain clubs. Only the boys from select groups had the opportunity to meet and marry girls from the privileged classes. In an earlier day more than one "self-made" man had got his start by marrying the daughter of the leading merchant, banker or lawyer. It still happened, of course, but the barriers were probably growing higher until the social upheavals following 1917.

An extreme development of the system is illustrated in Charles Flandrau's *Diary of a Freshman* (1900). A fellow student remarks:

"Now, take Bertie," he said. "Bertie knew who his classmates in college were going to be at the age of five. They're the same chaps he's been going to school with and to kid dancing-classes . . . and at all these morns and noons and dewy eves they dance with the same girls that two years from now they'll meet in society, and subsequently marry, just because it's part of the routine. After they get out of college they'll all go abroad for a few months in groups of three and four, and when they get back they'll be taken into the same club (their names will have been on the waiting list some twenty-odd years) and they'll join a lunch club down town in order not to miss seeing one another every day at noon for the rest of their lives.

So tight a social group is of course more characteristic of Boston or Philadelphia than of other cities, but a Bones or Pork man found his way eased in New York or even Chicago. An unusually brilliant or ruthless man could succeed without such connections, but he had to work much harder and more cleverly than rivals who got off to a head start. For as has been often recorded, wealth in America during these years was concentrated in relatively few hands. Great fortunes like Henry Ford's could be made by developing industrial processes, but they were often made by the graduates of the machine shop rather than of the college. For the college man the usual road to wealth lay through the law offices, banks, and industrial empires of the big cities.

The graduate of a small college or of a Western university might aspire to a judgeship or bank presidency in the smaller cities and towns; he might get to Congress, become a physician or college professor. Particularly west of the Alleghenies he might become a governor or senator. But he was unlikely to be taken into the inner social and financial circles of Boston, New York or Philadelphia. In the first half of the twentieth century five of our eight Presidents were graduates of Harvard, Yale, Princeton and Amherst. A sixth came from Stanford, "the Western Harvard," where the social system most resembled that in the East.

Some of this might suggest that the famous Eastern colleges provided the best education. No doubt some or all of them were superior. But all accounts agree that between 1880 and 1917 college standards were low, not so much through the failure to provide good instruction as through the failure of the students to take it. It was the period which developed the philosophy of "the gentleman's grade." This meant a C, and in the eighties a Harvard student was required to make even that mediocre grade in only one third of his courses. In the eighties and nineties wealthy students paid as much as five dollars an hour to a grind or three dollars and a half for a "seminar" at a tutoring school to cram for examinations.

Wherever the classical course prevailed, ponies or trots were common. The Yale Class Book of 1900 published the answer to the question: "Have you ever used a trot?" Yes, 246. No, 15. By the turn of the century the use of purchased themes at Yale had become so common that the price fell from five dollars to two dollars. On three floors of one large dormitory, not a single student wrote his own themes. A faculty committee in 1903 reported: "Scholarship has apparently declined throughout the country; certainly at Yale. . . . In fact, in late years the scholar has become almost taboo at Yale." That same year a Harvard committee discovered that students worked only three and a half hours per course per week, and in lecture courses only two and a half hours. Under the elective system they flocked to the easy courses. At Yale cribbing was so general that younger instructors felt it "undesirable for them to report cases of cheating to the faculty." In the mid-nineties the Wisconsin faculty, plagued with numerous cases of cheating, adopted various methods to curb the evil. But after two years of effort a committee declared: "Very careful investigation has led to the conclusion that 'cribbing' in examinations is deplorably common in the University. . . ."

To support their contention that "hard study has become *unfashionable* at Yale," the committee under Irving Fisher reported that of the nine valedictorians after 1893, not a single one had been elected to a senior society. This contrasted with twenty-six out of thirty-four who had been tapped between 1861 and 1894. Class averages had been declining since 1896-1897, the low point coming with the class of 1905, whose yearbook boasted:

Never since the Heavenly Hosts with all the Titans fought
Saw they a class whose scholarship approached so close to
naught.

Four years later Woodrow Wilson, then president of Princeton, wrote a famous article for *Scribner's* in which he stated:

The born leaders and managers and originators are drafted
off to "run the college" (it is in fact nothing less), and the
classroom, the laboratory, the studious conference with instructors get only the residuum of their attention. . . . The side
shows are so numerous, so diverting—so important, if you will
—that they have swallowed up the circus. . . .

The most alluring of all the side shows was football. The
baseball fever of the sixties was mild compared to the football
psychosis which developed during the eighties and nineties. In
a period like the present when the disease has become endemic,
it is difficult to realize the extent to which football transformed
the American college. Very early it ceased to be a game and became a profession; it pulled into its orbit the whole college,
from freshman to college president, and beyond that the
alumni, townspeople—the nation itself. Controversies about
professionalism and brutality resounded throughout the nation's newspapers and magazines. By 1905 a President of the
United States took it on himself to intervene in the riot.

Such startling phenomena as those connected with college
football have presented irresistible temptations for sociological, economic, and psychiatric interpretations. Certainly social
forces, economics, and abnormal psychology have all played a
part. Among them was the growing materialism which substituted the grandstand for the camp meeting. Another was the
increasing ability of the nation to afford an expensive sport.
Possibly the puritan and evangelical tradition which had
frowned on art, literature, and sex helped to channel emotional
drives into an enthusiasm for combative sport.

Within the college framework there were additional social,
economic, and psychological pressures. The shift of student
objectives from the professions to business brought an increas-

ing proportion of undergraduates more interested in competitive activities than in books. Before long, college authorities found that football was big business and, for a time at least, good advertising. In the psychological area it is clear that football and its attendant uproar were only a variant of the student violence of earlier periods—a tradition reaching back into the Middle Ages when colleges began. It was characteristic of Americans to transform random violence and noise into team play and organized cheering. All this was not imposed from above: the students, not the faculty, created organized sports.

It was inevitable that Yale, where mass mores were most powerful, should have been the first great football college. Perhaps it is also typical that Yale did not originate intercollegiate football. That dubious honor belongs to Rutgers and Princeton who in 1869 played a game somewhat similar to soccer, and with a round ball. Unorganized football was much older. Columbia students had kicked a ball around the campus as early as 1824, and football "rushes" at Harvard went back to 1826. In fact, early college football bears great resemblance to the ancient game played by British apprentices in the streets of London. Very early the American versions developed a good bit of ferocity. In the class combats of the late fifties Yale men painted their faces to look fierce and produced such lyrics as:

> Let them come on, the base-born crew!
> Each soil-stained churl-alack!
> What gain they but a smitten skull,
> A sod for their base back!

When Rutgers played Columbia in the 1870s, there were twenty men on a side. They kicked not only the ball but each other. Jumping on an opponent's stomach with both feet was not frowned on. As no substitutions were permitted, a man left the field only if carried off. Some of these practices were later revived.

The modern Rugby game seems to have come from England by way of McGill University, which in 1874 played a two-game series with Harvard—one game with the round ball and its rules, the other with the oval ball and Rugby rules. The Rugby game caught on; Harvard, Tufts and Yale adopted it. The first Harvard-Yale game was played, November 13, 1875, at New Haven. Harvard won. But, beginning in 1878, with Walter Camp on the team, Yale began a series of victories not broken until 1890. (There was no game in 1885, and Harvard forfeited in 1888.)

In the eighties and nineties football became synonymous with Yale. In illustrations for stories and advertisements, an athletic hero was usually shown with a Y on his turtle-neck sweater. And with reason. In the eighteen years between 1883 and 1901, Yale teams went through nine undefeated seasons. The teams of 1888, 1891, and 1892 were not even scored on. In the thirteen games played in 1888, Yale ran up the fantastic total of 700 points against 0 for her opponents. From mid-season of 1885 until the end of 1899, Yale teams won 46 straight games, scoring 2,018 points to their opponents' 29.

Next in line came Princeton with four undefeated teams; Harvard with three, and Penn with two. In 1905 Charles Eliot Norton upset Dr. Weir Mitchell, then a Penn trustee, by describing football as "the chief industry of the University of Pennsylvania." It had also become the chief industry of a number of smaller Eastern colleges and of Western universities. In 1901 Michigan broke through the hegemony of the Ivy League to become the national champions. Four years later it was Chicago.

The uniformity of college mores and enthusiasms throughout the nation is well illustrated by the rapid spread of football. As early as 1881 Michigan sent a team east to play Harvard and other colleges. About four years later Wisconsin had interclass games although it did not have a regular intercollegiate schedule until 1890. Six years later the schedule included Grinnell, Beloit, Chicago, Northwestern and Minnesota. The postseason game racket had already begun: Wisconsin played one game at Chicago with the Carlisle Indians. The Indians won 18 to 8. In 1892 Stanford and California took up football under the leadership of Yalemen Walter Camp, 1888, Lee McClung, 1892, and C. O. Gill, 1889.

In the 1830s Yale missionaries had carried culture to the West; sixty years later they carried football. Parke H. Davis of Princeton, coach at Wisconsin, estimated that at least forty-five former Yale players, thirty-five from Princeton, and twenty-four from Harvard were coaching in the nineties. At the new University of Chicago, President Harper brought in Amos Alonzo Stagg, Yale 1888, as Director of Physical Culture and Athletics on professorial tenure. The title was a euphemism for "football coach." Years later when the chief industry of Notre Dame had become football, someone asked Knute Rockne if a Yale coach might not learn something in South Bend. Rockne is reported to have said, "Why, I've learned everything I know about football from Yale. Lonny Stagg taught it to me."

Yale men were also active in other sports. In 1894 Professor A. T. Hadley, later president of the college, noted that there were hundreds of men in training for a handful of positions on varsity teams. Until 1880 Harvard crews had usually won over Yale, but beginning in that year Yale won eighteen out of the next twenty-three races between the two colleges.

But it was football that everywhere became the most popular and most controversial feature of the colleges. It began on modest budgets. At the start the players paid for their own uniforms, consisting chiefly of canvas pants, wool stockings, and a heavy sweater protected by a canvas jacket. The Harvard-Columbia game of 1881, played before what was then considered a large crowd, brought in gate receipts of $342. A decade later Ivy League games drew crowds of thirty to forty thousand. Newspapers began to give much publicity to college games, and in 1889 Walter Camp named the first All-American team. College football had become big business.

As in the business life of the period, few holds were barred. There were no eligibility rules. A University of Wisconsin player who graduated in 1892 was still playing on the team in 1896. He was on the faculty. Big colleges recruited athletes from small colleges. The Columbia team of 1899 contained only three undergraduates; the rest were graduate students who had played elsewhere. In 1895 the student paper at Wisconsin charged that Beloit, Michigan, Northwestern and Chicago were employing professional athletes, and defended Wisconsin against charges of subsidizing players and dirty playing. Elsewhere similiar charges and defenses became the rule.

The game got out of the hands of both students and faculty. College presidents like Eliot of Harvard, and Hadley of Yale, nostalgically remembering their own athletic prowess, were tolerant of the sports-loving boys. Other college presidents, with their eyes on wealthy alumni and the public, hired smart coaches. Michigan got a tramp athlete, Fielding H. (Hurry Up) Yost, who had played at West Virginia, 1895, Lafayette, 1896, and Virginia, 1897. (He got a law degree at Virginia.) Yost had coached at Ohio Wesleyan and Stanford before coming to Michigan in 1901. Soon he was more famous than any of the scholars at the university. The team of 1901 was the best in the country, making 550 points against 0. It played in a post-season game with Stanford on New Year's Day at the Tournament of Roses. Although the grandstand seated only 5,000, every press association in the country ran in a wire.

Professional coaches accelerated the transformation of a game into a military campaign with strategy planned long in advance of a contest, and with scouts sent to learn the secrets of the enemy. In 1902, Wisconsin students ducked a Minnesota spy in the lake. Under attack by the press, presidents of universities in the Western Conference in 1906 stated that coaches like Yost and Stagg had built up a national craze which had gone far beyond the original concept of college athletics. Walter Camp, athletic adviser to President Hadley, attributed Yale's success in athletics to "the Czar principle" backed up by Yale loyalty.

Under professional coaches trickery became a factor in football success. For the first Tournament of Roses game, Yost was permitted to bring only fifteen players to face the forty on the Stanford bench. With the temperature at 85° the Stanford coach insisted on thirty-five-minute halves. Nevertheless, the men from Michigan ran up a score of 45 to 0 by the middle of the second half. Coach Fisher took the Stanford men off the field. Perhaps most famous of all were the devices of Glen Warner with his Carlisle Indians. Playing against Harvard in 1903, the Indians executed the notorious Warner play of stuffing the ball into the back of the runner's sweater. Five years later Harvard's new coach, Percy Haughton, learned of a Warner trick against Syracuse: each Indian end and back-field man had an imitation half-football sewed to his jersey. But when Warner was offered the conventional choice of one of three footballs before the Harvard game, he found that all of them had been dyed a deep crimson to match the Harvard jerseys. "You win," said Warner. Harvard did, on that occasion, 17 to 0.

More disturbing to those faculty members who did not confuse football prowess with excellence in algebra, and to that part of the public which managed to retain some sanity despite such heady stimulants, were the casualty lists. A patriotic historian claims for Harvard the invention of the flying wedge in 1892. It had evolved out of Princeton's straight wedge, 1884, and Yale's shoving wedge, 1889. Vanderbilt developed a chessboard play (1892) similar to the flying wedge. That same year came the turtle or turtle back, although Stagg claimed to have used it earlier. In this formation ten men formed a mass with their bodies bent over, forming a "turtle back." The ball was snapped into the mass, which then moved down the field in what looked like a flying wedge. As the opponents massed to stop it, a lone man left behind ran with the ball down the other side of the field. Such plays, involving mass momentum, produced a considerable mangling of the participants. After seeing Yale play Harvard, John L. Sullivan, certainly no softy, stated: "There's murder in that game." Public outcry led by the *Nation* and the New York *Evening Post* caused the cancellation of the Army-Navy game in 1893. The Columbia team of 1899 had so many injuries that it was forced to cancel a game with Navy. In 1903 the slaughter reached a peak of forty-four dead.

Professionalism invaded both baseball and football. In 1894

Professor George Wharton Pepper, of the University of Pennsylvania Law School, charged: "There is . . . but little which bears the semblance of sport for sport's sake. In baseball and football the evils are most conspicuous." He deplored the "strengthening of the athletic army by the addition of mercenaries who stand ready to give their time and skill to the college which retains them." Pepper was later to become a United States Senator and a trustee of Pennsylvania, but the system was too much a part of the whole fabric of higher education to be much affected by the most influential critics. At the time when Pepper made his remarks, Penn had recently acquired a tract of land for a new athletic field; ten years later it had invested over half a million dollars in fieldhouses, grandstands and gymnasium. In 1903 Harvard opened its stadium seating over 57,000. By 1906 Michigan had stands seating 25,000; others built of concrete were added in 1910. The Yale Bowl, seating nearly 75,000, was dedicated in 1914. Football had become a vested interest with a huge capital investment.

By 1905 it had also become a national scandal. The *Outlook,* publishing a series of articles on the subject, quoted *The Harvard Bulletin* (the athletic organ of Harvard graduates):

Something is the matter with a game . . . which takes the time and attention, not only of the players, but also of the undergraduates as a body, until for weeks they talk and think nothing but football; which requires the constant attendance of skilled surgeons, who conduct on the field what one of the most eminent has called "a hospital clinic." . . . Why are men coached to slug? . . . We know that players are so coached.

President Eliot, heretofore rather tolerant of sport, was quoted as saying, ". . . the game of football has become seriously injurious to rational American life in schools and colleges."

In the same magazine and in *The Saturday Evening Post,* Dr. J. William White, Professor of Surgery at the University of Pennsylvania, and head of its Department of Physical Education, defended the game. In the *Post* White argued that, though

Samson lacked discretion, he was a judge in Israel. However, he gave no statistics on the number of football players, similarly qualified, who became judges. So closely linked were football and finances that Dr. Weir Mitchell, a much abler physician, was restrained from publishing an answer on the grounds that it might hurt a campaign for a gymnasium. In the *Outlook,* White quoted from President Theodore Roosevelt's address to an alumni banquet:

I believe heartily in sport. I believe in outdoor games, and I do not mind in the least that they are rough games, or that those who take part in them are occasionally injured. I have no sympathy whatever with the overwrought sentimentality which would keep a young man in cotton-wool, and- I have hearty contempt for him if he counts a broken collar bone as a serious consequence when balanced against the chance of showing that he possesses hardihood, physical address, and courage.

In an editorial the *Outlook* pointed out that Dr. White had failed to quote that part of Roosevelt's address which deplored brutality and low cunning. The editors referred to sports writers who complained of semiprofessional and unsportsmanlike methods. They pointed out that President Roosevelt himself had called to the White House a group of leading coaches to discuss methods of reducing the number of casualties. Out of this conference came an agreement to "reduce the elements of brutality in play." Soon after this, President Hadley and Walter Camp of Yale got together with President Eliot and Percy Haughton to open up the game by introducing the onside kick and forward pass. But the reform party in the Yale faculty lost the battle to get at the basic evils of overemphasis and huge gate receipts. Throughout the country the story was much the same; public protests and faculty rules on eligibility brought minor reforms, but alumni, graduate managers, and coaches controlled the machine. Within the college and university structure athletics became a separate state under the nominal rule of the president and trustees. Aside from its baneful effect on student life and scholarship, big-time athletics therefore contributed greatly to the growing split between faculties and adminstrative officers.

The most tragic result of overemphasis and commercialization in athletics was that colleges lost their moral leadership. Students and the public, seeing the chicanery and hypocrisy involved, became cynical about the honesty of college officials who winked at or connived at professionalism, fake eligibility rules, and unsportsmanlike play. Certain members of every faculty and administration became notorious for their willingness to relax academic standards for athletes. Idealistic chapel talks by such officials sounded pretty phony. The emotional and often alcoholic binge of autumn Saturdays was not the best preparation for the Sunday sermon on the spiritual life. In fact, preachers often took up the "get in there and fight" theme. The athletic field became the most powerful forum on the campus, and the doctrine preached there was "Win at any price."

It is a sad commentary on the colleges' loss of moral leadership to note that public journals were often the most insistent voices demanding reform. Largely because of an attack on subsidized athletics by the press, Michigan withdrew from the "Big 10" for ten years, 1907-1917. Journalistic criticism was largely responsible for other attempts at reform, including that by President Theodore Roosevelt.

The excesses were not confined to the game itself. Yost had a part in the development of large, well-trained bands to parade between halves. The development has done more for gate receipts than for musical education. During the nineties the whole machinery of mass hysteria developed: cheer leaders, pep rallies, train loads of returning alumni, victory parades. The night following a game was likely to be filled with drinking and riot. A Lafayette football song of the period is typical:

> Ring the bell of old South College,
> Paint the town as ne'er before.

At most colleges the victory bonfire was a standard feature. The fuel included not only the boxes donated by local merchants, but privies, wooden doorsteps, and street signs. The residents of college towns learned to dread a football victory.

A perennial defense of football has been that it developed college spirit. However, as earlier chapters indicate, there has rarely been a dearth of college spirit. Such spirit as was generated by athletics has not always been of an admirable variety. But one thing football *did* accomplish: it broke the pattern of snobbishness based on race, religion, and wealth. Students and alumni alike recruited team candidates from all ranks and races. In 1893 the captain of the Harvard team was William H. Lewis, a Negro. American Indians from Carlisle played against the most aristocratic teams in the East. The sons of Polish immigrants shared locker rooms and training tables with Princeton Anglo-Saxons. The many jokes about the unpronounceable names of football players are only testimony to the prevalence of second-generation Americans on college teams. And because of the prestige of football heroes, such men tended to become big men in college. Perhaps football's greatest achievement is its contribution to social democracy in the colleges.

Nor were athletics responsible for all the college uproar of the period. Much of it was the traditional student license spread over a somewhat larger area. Even as late as the eighties, faculty members at Yale and Princeton were still required to act as policemen. In his student days at Yale, Phelps said it was not uncommon to see a nightgowned professor hiding behind a tree and taking down the names of boys involved in an uproar. By the nineties rules and supervision had considerably relaxed at many places. For one thing, a considerable number of students no longer lived in proctored dormitories: they lived in rented rooms, boardinghouses, fraternity houses or even private dormitories. The growing size of colleges made it more difficult for faculty members to recognize individual culprits. Many college towns had ceased to be villages. One result was that college drinking was much harder to control. All accounts indicate that there was a good bit of it.

College students have ever been given to mass demonstrations. In Europe these have often been inspired by politics; in America they have usually been for the hell of it. At Harvard the cry of "Rinehart!" would bring shouting students to the windows or into the yard. On a warm evening in May, Yale students held "bottle night" when, in a wild orgy of destruction, the water bottles traditional in a Yale room would be hurled from hundreds of windows. At Pennsylvania the yell "Rowbottom!" would cause students to pour from dormitories and fraternity houses onto the streets to stop traffic, upset carriages, and pull trolley poles off the wire. If a Rowbottom brought out the police and fire engines, it was a success. In the larger college towns the local vaudeville theater was likely to be the scene of a mass raid in which students overwhelmed the doorman, paraded down the aisles onto the stage and interrupted the show.

In 1899 Wisconsin students staged probably the first "panty raid." (The term was to come a half century later when the sport was revived on a national scale.) The Wisconsin affair began with a Halloween nightshirt parade. When it reached Ladies' Hall, someone hit on the idea of looting the laundry room. The story got into the Chicago papers. At a convocation the president announced that 204 articles of clothing had been taken "as trophies of the escapade." He added the highly debatable statement: "No man has any right to be called a gentleman who will keep an article of ladies' wearing apparel as a trophy." The faculty acted according to form and suspended some of the ringleaders. But the girls' response was far different from the one their granddaughters would adopt: the young ladies of 1899 resolved to have "no social relations with the men of the University until the faculty or men of the University have satisfactorily dealt with the offenders." The historians of the university suggest that this indicates some knowledge of Aristophanes. A more likely explanation is that the college girl of 1899 was far more unlike her counterpart of 1951 than the male of her era was different from his grandson.

Probably in no period in the history of the American college has men's student life been so carefree, so much a world in itself. The old puritanism had relaxed; the passions of the Civil War had subsided; the later concern over social and economic problems had—at least at men's colleges—not yet impinged. "We toil not, neither do we agitate, but we play football" was the boast of the Yale class of 1901. All over the nation students could have made the same statement.

The college man's mode of dress was symbolic. He probably came to college wearing a stiff-bosomed shirt with starched cuffs and high collar; his suit had matching coat and trousers; he wore a derby hat. Before long his usual costume included faded corduroy trousers, shirt with turned-down collar, a turtle-neck sweater, and a cap. Or because of the prevalence of bicycles, he might wear golf knickers and wool stockings. In season he sometimes replaced the cap with a stiff straw hat with a club hatband. For afternoon social affairs he wore white flannel or duck trousers. For informal evening wear he chose a loud shirt—hand-tailored if he could afford it—and flowered silk or a bow tie. His tattersall or buckskin vest contrasted with his tailored suit. A rigid requirement was that a topcoat must be loose fitting. The costume seems to have come in late in the eighties and lasted until about 1914, with periodic changes in the cut of coats and trousers, and in the size of hatbrims and crowns. A horrid style of short, peg trousers came in after the turn of the century. But always, from coast to coast, he could be recognized at once as a college boy, a creature apart from the herd.

Student mores required that he fill his room with a collection of knickknacks, including an array of steins, pipes, tobacco jars and humidors. On the walls were pennants; on the lounge a pile of pillows embroidered by various girls. To get them he had used cajolery, flattery, nepotism, and bribery. In a similar manner he had accumulated a "harem": photographs and snapshots of as many girls as possible. Some he scarcely knew; they were his sister's friends. The street signs he had stolen.

The quality and condition of the furniture depended largely on the wealth of the student, but a Morris chair was *de rigueur,* as was some sort of table. This last was commonly kept bare for a card game or the brewing of punch. In an emergency it could be used for the writing of a theme or letter. Textbooks and notes could be piled on a chair. A banjo or mandolin was almost a must.

Every college had a mandolin club—even Quaker Swarthmore. One advantage was that a mandolin club could travel about with the glee club giving concerts and attending social functions. For that purpose a member had to own or borrow a dress suit. As early as the eighties students wore formal clothes (then the Prince Albert) to class dances at Wisconsin, although some legislators frowned on this as undemocratic. The student paper protested: "The sweet co-ed who intrepidly winds her way up the campus to recitations through all the vicissitudes of Madison weather, must needs be borne to her scene of conquest in Library Hall by a two-dollar hack."

At coeducational institutions there was much more dating and mixed social life than at most men's colleges. Amherst, because of its proximity to Smith and Holyoke, was an exception. In the stories of men's colleges of the time one is struck by the small part girls played in students' lives. Drinking was a much more common practice than dating. The fashionable attitude toward girls was one of amused condescension. One product of the system was the college widow, the girl who for a decade or so went to dances with boys who had a girl at home or who aspired to a society marriage. Seniors, bringing a debutante to the prom, would pass the local girl on to a freshman without a partner. With the careless cruelty of youth the other older boys would tell the youngster about the years she had been going to dances, the boys she had kissed. The cards were stacked against her. If a coed did not find a mate in college, she moved on into a world of her contemporaries; the college widow remained in a society of ever younger men.

There is a good bit of truth in the remark in the satire, *Old Siwash,* about "those paradises in pants, where they import a carload of girls from all over the country to one dance a year and worry along the rest of the time with chorus girls and sweet

young town girls who began bringing students up by hand about
the time William H. Taft was a freshman." Even the sexually
reticent college novels of the period represent wealthy students
taking chorus girls or vaudeville actresses to late dinners, or
show students picking up lower-class town girls for a carriage
ride into the country. There seems to be little question that in
men's colleges a considerable proportion of the boy-girl relationships were not of the type that lead to marriage or mutual
respect.

In clubhouses and dormitories, as in London coffeehouse
society of the eighteenth century, the legend grew up that
women were feather-brained creatures incapable of understanding really important matters. Naturally this close-knit male
society developed rituals, cant phrases, and private jokes which
put outsiders at a disadvantage. No girl was supposed to be
capable of understanding football; college jokes have rung the
changes on that theme for seventy-five years. Men were the "in"
group; women the "out." On the Yale campus the appearance
of a girl would bring the cry of "Fire!" and a crowd of yelling
students to the windows. One of Flandrau's Harvard students
talking about Class Day speaks of "the vast army of women
from Heaven knows where, who came early and stayed until
they were put out." Mothers are commonly represented as being
stupid about their sons. It was all partly a pose, but a long-held
pose can become a psychological habit. When the defenders of
women's colleges contended that men's colleges were the more
guilty of unfitting students for marriage and family life, they
had a point.

To an amazing degree the man's college of 1880-1917 absorbed the whole emotional life of the student. If he lay awake
of nights, it was out of concern over his chances for the team,
the paper, the glee club, the social club. His idea of a big
evening was to join his fellows for beer and song at Mory's or
one of its scores of equivalents in other college towns. His sentimental attachments were for the college, the fraternity, the
"best friends he would ever know." The phrase "I'd die for
dear old Rutgers" could raise a laugh, but it caricatured a

real feeling. Coming back to the campus on a May evening, he would raise his voice in sentimental song, his eyes dim with alcoholic tears. The Lafayette "Alma Mater" catches the mood:

> We'll gather by the twilight's glow
> In front of old Pardee.
> In all the world no other scene
> So fair, so dear to me.

Any reading of college stories makes clear the basic unsophistication of the college student before the First World War. He often gambled and drank; he sometimes wenched; he knew more about good food and wines than his successors, but for him the world was relatively a simple place. He had an accepted code. He might use a pony, but he was not supposed to lie; he could break an opponent's collarbone in football, but he must not alibi a defeat; he could get drunk but he went to church and "heeled" for the Y.M.C.A. There were good women and "fast" women. He might queer himself by going with the latter, but that was a less serious offense than taking the smallest liberty, especially in speech, with a good girl. It was amusing to hide out from a tradesman's dun, but unforgivable to welch on a gambling debt. His ideal was that of the gentleman—as defined by Rudyard Kipling.

It is no accident that the famous Whiffenpoof song is a reworking of Kipling's "Gentleman Rankers." In the nineties and early 1900s Kipling was the favorite author, followed by R. L. Stevenson. When William Lyon Phelps was a Yale undergraduate in the eighties, his essay on *Wilhelm Meister* was rejected for the *Lit* because no one had ever heard of the novel. But in the nineties there was a Kipling Club and a Stevenson Club. Perhaps this had something to do with the fact that Phelps was the first man who ever taught English literature to Yale freshmen. Phelps himself regarded Browning's *The Ring and the Book* as "the most precious and profound spiritual treasure that England has received since the death of Shakespeare." Flandrau's Harvard students around the turn of the century also went in for Kipling and Stevenson, but they also read

Balzac and Henry James. It is also perhaps no accident that T. S. Eliot was a Harvard graduate (1909).

All the evidence suggests that in the intellectually sterile period under consideration Harvard was one of the few colleges which gave its undergraduates some culture beyond a narrow classical or technical training. In 1877 Bliss Perry discovered that his first Latin assignment at Williams was identical with that given to his father in 1848. And in 1916 his son started with the same assignment. As Perry says: "For sixty years at least, and probably longer, it was the same squirrel in the same cage." Perry was talking about students, but the really caged squirrel was the instructor who went through the same routine with the same texts year after year. There was small incentive to scholarship or originality of thought to a man who knew by heart the passages his students would recite each day. Thus when William Lyon Phelps left Yale for graduate study at Harvard, he found "a vitality indescribable. Bliss was it in that dawn to be alive." There were lectures by such men as Child, Briggs, Baker, Wendell and Kittredge in English; William James, Royce, Santayana, Palmer and Münsterberg in philosophy; Norton in fine arts. No such constellation existed elsewhere in America. But as a teacher at Harvard, Phelps found the work too demanding, and returned to become a celebrity at Yale.

The experience of Bliss Perry is a case in point. After a somewhat stultifying period as student and teacher at Williams, he went to Princeton in 1893. Here he felt a sense of freedom because a faculty member "could smoke a pipe on Nassau Street without losing caste." Looking back, he believed "there was more substantial work done at Princeton in that epoch of the golden nineties than is generally supposed." In support of this he cited the attempts of students to emulate Booth Tarkington and Jesse Lynch Williams, both recent graduates. But when Eliot invited him to come to Harvard after the turn of the century, he found it "a teacher's paradise. . . . Its fascination . . . lay in its freedom. I do not mean merely that academic freedom. . . . That very lack of cooperative team-work . . .

left us free, as individuals, to teach in our own fashion and to try, within reason, any experiments we pleased."

Nevertheless, the students of the time had developed a heroic resistance to culture. Speaking of his own student days in the eighties, Phelps wrote:

The younger generation in my time had a narrow and provincial outlook. They were interested mainly in affairs of their little world. They were mainly Philistines: they had little respect for scholarship, were innocent of culture, knew nothing of good music or art, and cared not at all for international affairs.

Canby, a student in the nineties, paints the same picture:

We resisted the intrusion of abstract ideas because our skin was full to bursting of our own affairs and our minds hot with our own enthusiasms.

A decade later Owen Johnson has a Yale student tell Stover and his friends, all seniors:

You don't know the big men in music; you don't know the pioneers and the leaders in any art; you don't know the great literatures of the world, and what they represent; you don't know how other races are working out their social destinies; you've never even stopped to examine yourselves. . . . You have no general knowledge, no intellectual interests, you haven't even opinions, and at the end of four years of *education* you will march up and be handed a degree—Bachelor of Arts! . . . Do you wonder why I repeat that our colleges are splendidly organized institutions for the prevention of learning?

Almost at the same time Princeton's President Wilson was writing of the faculty:

. . . those who perform in the main tent must often whistle for their audiences, discouraged and humiliated.

Obviously thoughtful men were beginning to question the golden age.

Nevertheless, gold of a substantial kind flowed into college coffers. When in the early eighties Leland Stanford and his wife were considering the endowment of a college as a memorial to their son, they visited Harvard in company with an up-and-coming young Columbia professor, Nicholas Murray Butler, to get ideas. How much, asked Mrs. Stanford, would it cost to duplicate the buildings and equipment? Dr. Eliot estimated $15,000,000. The lady turned to her husband and exclaimed gleefully, "We can do it, Leland, we can do it!" It had taken just 250 years to build Harvard; the Stanfords set out to duplicate it overnight. The money had come from a ruthless use of political power as governor and senator to advance the fortunes of the Central and Southern Pacific railroads. But it was the colleges which had caught the imagination of America. By 1896 the widowed Mrs. Stanford was selling her jewels to keep the new university alive during a financial crisis.

During its first 185 years Yale had built up its permanent funds to about $2,000,000. In the thirteen years (1886-1899) of Dwight's presidency these increased to $4,500,000. In addition, the college rebuilt much of its plant: at the end of Dwight's reign there were twenty-three old buildings and seventeen new ones. And new college buildings are nearly always built on a larger scale than the old.

In 1894 Columbia moved to a two-million-dollar tract of land in Morningside Heights, and President Low gave $1,000,-000 for a library building. Seth Low was an unusual college president. Before becoming head of Columbia he had been a reforming mayor of Brooklyn; in 1901 he defeated the forces of Tammany Hall to become mayor of New York. In his ten years as president of Columbia he transformed it from a small college into a university; he raised $5,500,000; he brought into the faculty outstanding men from other colleges, among them Henry Fairfield Osborn in biology, and John Bassett Moore in law. Like Eliot, Low recognized that an outstanding faculty is the basis of a great university.

Just as outstanding men on a faculty attract other able men, so does money attract money. Whatever their limitations in directing education, business leaders have tended to place their bets on those institutions which attracted able men. In the decade after Low's resignation, Butler was able to raise about $16,500,000, and between 1911 and 1921 another $20,000,000. At Harvard where Eliot built up the finest faculty in America, he was able to increase the endowment from $2,387,000 to $22,-716,000 during his forty years as president. Nearly $16,000,000 of this came between 1889 and 1909.

When John D. Rockefeller was considering the endowment of a large Baptist college or university, he was introduced to a remarkable young professor of Hebrew in the Yale Divinity School, William Rainey Harper. Although Harper was something of a scholar, he was the sort of scholar a businessman could understand: a go-getter. At the age of eighteen he had taken his Ph.D. at Yale. During the next twelve years he had taught at Morgan Park Theological Seminary in Chicago, published several Hebrew textbooks, developed correspondence courses, organized summer schools at four or five places, founded and edited two journals of Hebrew studies, organized an association of professors of Hebrew, and built up the Chautauqua Summer School of Liberal Arts to the point where it had about 2,000 students. When at thirty he came to Yale as a full professor, he continued the same fantastic scale of activities and added others such as lecture courses in Brooklyn, Vassar, Boston and New Haven—all during a single winter. Four universities—Brown, Rochester, South Dakota and Iowa —sought him as president.

When President Dwight of Yale learned of the plans to make Harper the head of Rockefeller's proposed university at Chicago, he sent him abroad for a rest, and devoted himself to fighting off "all intending and approaching Baptists . . . who from time to time are disposed to assail the tabernacles of the blessed saints and run off with their professors." But Dwight lost his battle, as in a way did the advisers of Mr. Rockefeller. The advisers thought in terms of a college which might grow into a university. From the first Harper insisted: "It is not a college, but a university that is wanted, a university of the highest order." This idea appealed to Rockefeller and in 1890 Harper was invited to become the president of the new institution. Initially Rockefeller had pledged $600,000, but within five years Harper had wangled gifts of $9,000,000, most of it from Rockefeller. By 1910 the latter had given nearly $35,000,-000.

From the start, Harper set his sights high. By offering high salaries—$7,000 for department heads in 1891—he attracted a brilliant faculty. To get Alice Freeman Palmer for dean of women he offered $12,000 to her and her philosopher husband George Herbert Palmer. As president of Wellesley, Alice Freeman's salary had been only $4,000. When Palmer declined to leave Harvard, Harper again offered the deanship to Mrs. Palmer, stipulating that she need do no teaching and spend only twelve weeks a year at Chicago. She took it for a tentative year, then for two more. Before the university opened, nearly a thousand people applied for faculty posts. Because of controversies at Clark University, Harper was able to get almost the whole scientific faculty for Chicago's graduate school—including such men as Michelson, Donaldson, and Loeb. Hearing of the construction of the world's largest telescope, Harper appealed to Charles T. Yerkes, who obtained the telescope and built an observatory to house it.

Yerkes, like the husband of the donor of the great Widener Library at Harvard, had got his start by some highly odorous deals in Philadelphia streetcar franchises. Later Yerkes had shifted his center of operations to Chicago. Unwittingly he was to do perhaps as much for literature as for science: he furnished the model for Frank Cowperwood in Dreiser's novels, *The Financier, The Titan* and *The Stoic*.

Despite the fact that Harper obtained vast sums from some of the most notable pirates in America, he seems to have used them in the public interest and to have resisted the pressures of money to curtail freedom of inquiry and teaching. To make the university a service institution he introduced the four-quarter system, which made the summer session a regular part of the program. Students could thus complete their work in less time than usual, or could interrupt it to work for funds to continue. To encourage scholarship he established in 1893 a well-financed university press—the first in the country to remain in continuous operation. In answer to pressures from the wealthy he stated that "no donor of money to a university . . . has any right, before God or man, to interfere with the teaching."

But the vast revolution in college and university finances had its price. Not all presidents possessed backbones as well supported by muscle as William Rainey Harper's. And the public, after reading the revelations of Ray Stannard Baker, Ida Tarbell and Lincoln Steffens, and the novels of Frank Norris, often wondered if institutions like Stanford and Chicago were not purchased at too great social cost. The oft-spoken phrase, "tainted money," is a sign of a public moral consciousness becoming queasy from the stink of corruption. Faculties and public alike wondered if the pure fountain of truth could come from universities tainted at the source.

Even when the money came from unimpeachable sources it too had its price. President Arthur Twining Hadley of Yale said that when he called on President Noah Porter (1871-1876) he usually found him reading Kant; when he called on President Timothy Dwight (1886-1899) he found him reading a balance sheet. In 1897, Charles F. Thwing, president of Western Reserve, wrote:

The scholarship of our instructors is constantly growing richer but the scholarship of the superintending bodies is declining. . . . The demand for money and the consequent financial responsibility may *not* lessen, but the undue emphasis on our having business men in our administrative bodies will presently give place to a wiser policy. . . . It would be well to have our governing bodies composed more generally of teachers, of authors, of editors, and of men of leisure who are sympathetic with and appreciative of the ends and the methods of scholarship.*

President Thwing's *presently* was somewhat premature. Businessmen on boards of trustees were prone to regard

* Charles F. Thwing, *The American College in American Life* (New York: G. P. Putnam's Sons, 1897).

faculty members as employees whose duty it was to obey orders and who could be dismissed at the pleasure of the employer. About 1870 the courts began to support this view. In 1899 J. H. Raymond stated in the *Chicago Tribune:*

As to what should be taught . . . they [the faculty] should promptly and gracefully submit to the determination of the trustees. . . . If the trustees err, it is for the patrons and proprietors, not for the employees, to change either the policy or personnel of the board.

The trustees of seven well-known universities, when interviewed, approved this statement.

A year later Mrs. Stanford, egged on by former business associates of her husband, insisted on the dismissal of Professor Edward A. Ross, who had written in favor of free silver, municipal ownership of utilities, and against the importation of cheap labor from Japan. Because Professor Ross had a national reputation in the fields of economics and sociology, the case became a *cause célèbre.* Several other faculty members resigned in protest. As there was already much resentment over the Central Pacific's control of state politics, many California papers came to his defense. The usually liberal president of Stanford, David Starr Jordan, was then jockeyed into firing the head of the history department, Dr. George Elliott Howard, who had spoken out against the dismissal of Ross.

No faculty firing up to that time had so dramatized the issue of wealth versus academic freedom. The American Economic Association appointed a distinguished committee to investigate the case, thus initiating a procedure which was to be followed by other learned societies in similar instances. The academic community had begun to organize in its own defense. All too often the enemy seemed to be the business community.

By tradition college presidents were part of the faculty. Therefore a number of them threw their weight on the side of the professors in defending the rights of freedom of inquiry and teaching. When Stanford dropped Professor Ross, Chancellor E. Benjamin Andrews promptly invited him to join the faculty of the University of Nebraska. A few years before, Andrews, then president of Brown, had resigned when the trustees asked him to desist from speaking on the money question. Although the alumni had persuaded him to withdraw his resignation, he had accepted the Nebraska position when it was offered. Another defender of academic freedom, President Eliot, invited Ross to give a series of lectures at Harvard. And when Ross went to Wisconsin in 1906, he began a service of thirty years under three presidents, "all with the scholar's point of view."

However, the problem was not merely a question of the personality of the college president. With the growing wealth and complexity of colleges and universities came an increasing division of functions between teaching and scholarship on the one hand, and management and finance on the other. The shift in control of athletics was merely another symptom of the same thing. Because the historical development of the American college had produced a monarchial form of organization, the president was in a strategic position to dominate both finances and faculty. The vast increases in endowments and gate receipts gave strong administrators an immense power over academic policy. In the hands of educational statesmen like Charles W. Eliot, A. Lawrence Lowell, and William Rainey Harper, the power was devoted largely to valid educational aims—often larger and more far-seeing than those of the faculty. But the power of money was there also for the incompetents, the mountebanks, the political timeservers, and the tyrants.

Somewhere around 1906 Thorstein Veblen wrote a bitter account of the divergence in aims between faculties and administrators imbued with the philosophy of business. He told of a college president who argued that faculty members were employees, and as such had no right to criticize management. And faculty members in various institutions had begun to describe presidents in such terms as "a large person full of small potatoes," "a four-flusher," "half a peck of pusillanimity," or "the only white thing about him is his liver." In a novel about the University of Chicago, Robert Herrick, who joined the faculty in 1893, pictured a president referred to as "His Majesty." Justified or not, such remarks were signs of a growing dichotomy. The days were passing when President Eliot rode his bicycle to market and dropped by at 7:15 in the morning to invite a new member of the faculty to lunch.

Although President Harper of Chicago may have been His Majesty, he had nevertheless respected the intellectual freedom of his faculty. He had even promoted an instructor who had bitterly attacked him in a faculty meeting. But in Herrick's novel, a successor, President Doolittle, was of the "Hanna-McKinley breed, ardent about nothing, industrious, methodical, believing in a smug orderly world run by people like himself, who were neither brilliant nor 'erratic' but kept their accounts in order, and never offended those in power." Outside his door a group of faculty members wait for a chance to talk with him. The time is before World War I:

Here in epitome was the drama of American university life, in the figures of these mature, intelligent—in some cases . . . distinguished men—sitting in a row in the black office chairs, like clerks waiting their chance to defend themselves and their life effort before the autocrat of their destinies.

Nowhere else in the entire modern world it seemed to Clavercin was there such an example of pure autocracy as in the American university. . . . He tried to think why it had come to this point of one man control, for it had not always been like this, and he concluded that it was because the trustees self-chosen for the care of the university funds were busy and ignorant men, depending on their agent to inform them and administer their great trust.

In 1915 the gap between teaching staffs and administrations had become so great that faculty members all over the country organized for their own protection The American Association of University Professors. Administrative officers were excluded from voting membership. The split had become formalized.

Just before World War I there were faint signs of improvement. Academic standards and performance had begun to rise from the low point around 1905. By 1913 a Yale student, Richard A. Douglas, stated in the *News* that "to take a book out of the library—legitimately—no longer brings ostracism." He suggested further that "utterly shiftless bipeds" should not be treated as equals with enquiring scholarly minds. In *Harper's Magazine,* Assistant Professor Henry Seidel Canby expressed the view that Yale and other universities were "on the eve of a 'growing-up' of our student body." Three years later at Pennsylvania a student named George Kearney wrote an essay for the *Red and Blue* on the theme, "Burn the Stadium." The American Association of University Professors laid down definitions of academic freedom and of professional responsibility. At Harvard, President Lowell set about the abolition of the Gold Coast. A larger proportion of the nation's young people were going to college. Increasingly the institutions catering to the general public were developing new programs to meet varied needs. This was deplored by men trained in the German tradition of scholarship or the British one of a gentleman's education. The profits and losses of this trend are still to be assessed.

Yet despite some glimmerings of a new dawn, the portents of storm were ominous. The conflict between activities and education had not been resolved. And there were growing tensions between the academic world and the business community, tensions reflected in the split between faculty and administration. As in the nation itself, no adequate controls had been developed for the vast new wealth of the colleges. Things were in the saddle and threatened to ride higher education. Much of the golden age turned out to be gilt.

8

The Age of Conflict and
Coonskin Coats

On March 4, 1913, a former college president entered the
White House. His two immediate predecessors had carried into
public life the collegiate forces of their time: Theodore Roosevelt, the muscular morality of the gridiron; Taft, the domi-
nance of wealth and big business. With the election of Wilson
it seemed that the idealistic and intellectual forces in American
life and education were to come into their own. Instead the
colleges were to be involved in the tragic epic of Wilson's
administration.

In no previous era of American history had the colleges been
so closely linked with the larger national drama. College presidents were leaders in the debate over American intervention
in the war; college professors were among the first victims of
the growing national intolerance of dissent; college campuses
were turned into vast training camps; experts from college
faculties became Wilson's chief advisers at the peace conference;
and the college professor came to symbolize the dangerous
radical hunted down by Wilson's Attorney General, A. Mitchell
Palmer.

As in a prologue to a play the defeat of academic idealism
by the brutal, materialistic forces of the time had all been foreshadowed in Wilson's experience at Princeton. His attempt
to destroy the club system in the interests of democracy had
alienated the student body and brought down on his head the
concerted wrath of the alumni. His attack on the side shows,
particularly football, had made him the hero of the academic
profession, but had made no dent in the problem. His plan

to develop a graduate school as an integral part of the university had been defeated by the dean of that school, Andrew West, who obtained millions from a wealthy donor to set up the graduate college as a separate unit a mile away from the campus. Even Wilson's development of campus housing in the interests of greater democracy had established a kind of gothic Gold Coast under university auspices: Princeton became the rich man's country-club college of the F. Scott Fitzgerald era.

No doubt Wilson's misadventures were in large measure due to his personality, his ability to arouse passionate enmity. But one wonders if he ever recognized the nature of the enemy. His attempt to destroy the aristocratic club system was an attack on the symptom, not the disease. The leaders who brought democracy into higher education had been men like William Watts Folwell, Andrew White, Frederick A. P. Barnard and Charles W. Eliot, who had thought in terms of educational programs designed to meet the needs of a nation, not a class. In the larger arena of national life Wilson allowed idealistic vision to blind him to the activities of the munitions makers, international bankers, and the nationalistic European politicians. Perhaps, as Mark Sullivan suggests, "Wilson all his life had dealt with words, thought in terms of words as distinguished from things." If so, his failure was the special failure of the mind trained in the old academic tradition of learning almost exclusively from books, of debating abstractions. It was this academic tradition which had been attacked by both Emerson and Thoreau. Only the scientists had successfully developed a new technique. In other disciplines the word was all too often substituted for the referent. Thus the crusade to make the world safe for democracy nearly killed democracy in the United States.

In the colleges, as in the nation as a whole, the first great conflict of opinion was over pacifism versus preparedness. There is considerable evidence that most advocates of preparedness believed that the United States would or should enter the war on the side of the Allies. As early as August 9, 1914, ex-president Eliot wrote to Wilson:

Has not the United States an opportunity at this moment to propose a combination of the British Empire, the United States, France, Japan, Italy, and Russia in an offensive and defensive alliance to rebuke and punish Austria-Hungary and Germany for the outrages they are now committing by enforcing against those two countries non-intercourse with the rest of the world by land and sea? . . . The proposal would involve the taking part by our navy in the blocading process.

A year later President Hadley of Yale, declaring his belief that military training had a place in college education, began negotiations for the establishment of an artillery battalion on the campus. In answer to faculty objections to giving A.B. credit for military training he argued its value in training for citizenship. As very few men were likely to make the Army a career, "it is not a professional study." Hadley seems to have been unaware of the ironic implications of this criteria for a liberal education.

At Harvard, Lowell urged students to join the R.O.T.C. at Plattsburg. On the other hand, David Starr Jordan, ex-president of Stanford, toured the country speaking against American intervention. Before 1914 Nicholas Murray Butler had been active in promoting peace through the Carnegie Endowment and the Association for International Conciliation; however the moment war began, he became an aggressive nationalist.

Students, caught up in the excitement of activities and club life, were slow to develop strong feelings about the war. At F. Scott Fitzgerald's Princeton the Triangle Club rehearsed for its musical show from two in the afternoon until eight the next morning. With the approach of club elections, "the campus became a document in hysteria." At Yale, Stephen Vincent Benét described Hold-off Night when the sophomore dormitories became "tense and sweltering as the air before a thunderstorm." The motorcar had appeared on the campus early in the century; now men went roaring off into the night in Locomobiles and Stutz Bearcats. In Fitzgerald's *This Side of Paradise*, Amory Blaine's friend Hungerford was killed driving back to Princeton with a drunken crowd.

Both the petting party and the flapper had arrived. On a pre-war Triangle Show trip "Amory had come into constant contact with that great American phenomenon, the 'petting party.'"

None of the Victorian mothers—and most of the mothers were Victorian—had any idea how casually their daughters were accustomed to be kissed. . . .

Amory saw girls doing things that even in his memory would have been impossible: eating three-o'clock after-dance suppers in impossible cafés, talking of every side of life with an air half of earnestness, half of mockery, yet with a furtive excitement that Amory considered stood for a real moral let-down. But he never realized how wide-spread it was until he saw the cities between New York and Chicago as one vast juvenile intrigue.

Benét, writing also of prewar students, estimated that two thirds of them would have been willing to go on a "petting party."

"Why on earth are we here?" Amory asked a girl he had taken to a parked car outside the country club at Louisville. She answered, "I don't know. I'm just full of the devil."

College humor magazines began to publish sexy jokes. The most remarkable feature of these was the prevailing theme of "girl leads boy on." Thus in the Penn *Punch Bowl* under a drawing of a couple dancing was the typical joke of the time:

"Jack, you've been making love to some other girl."
"How do you know?"
"Because you've improved so."

As in Fitzgerald's novel, the preoccupation with sex, and the changed concept of women was not confined to the Eastern seaboard: from Dartmouth to the University of Texas, and in the "cow colleges" of the Midwest, student magazines re-peated the theme. In bull sessions students had always talked of sex and had boasted of their exploits, but between 1912 and 1917 they began to debate the validity of the moral code. Some of them read Rupert Brooke, D. H. Lawrence, H. G. Wells and Freud. "The problem of evil had been identified for Amory into the problem of sex. He was beginning to identify evil with the strong phallic worship in Brooke and the early Wells." In the college stories of the eighties, nineties and early 1900s the central incident was always the winning of a game, the making of a club, or the achievement of some other collegiate goal. The central incidents in the lives of Fitzgerald's Amory Blaine (Princeton 1914-1917) and Benét's Philip Sellaby (Yale 1912-1916) are their relations with women.

To some degree this may represent a change in literary fashion, but the evidence of student publications suggests that it is also a reflection of a changing social order. In his last years at Princeton, Fitzgerald noted that the students around the small tables in the Nassau Inn "began questioning aloud the institutions that Amory and countless others before him had questioned so long in secret." They discussed sex and socialism, and the "social barriers as artificial distinctions made by the strong to bolster up their weak retainers and keep out the almost strong." In "a fury of righteousness" 100 men resigned from their clubs. A year out of college Benét's Philip Sellaby dreamed of "a samurai order of science ruling the world from aeroplanes with the lucid unintelligence of a chemical law. Toward a Whitmanesque submergence in 'The People,' largely connected with heartier handshakes and fewer baths."

One symbol of the revolt was that girls began to use cigarettes. By 1918 Wellesley found it necessary to officially ban smoking. The terms "parlor snake," "necking," and "petting party" were all in use before America entered the war. In the eastern United States at least, almost all the elements of the postwar era were already features of college life. It required only prohibition to bring in the hip flask and drinking in parked automobiles. The war was therefore less a cause than an accelerating force in a social revolution.

At first the war in Europe only added another excitement to the heady stimulants of college life. As Benét described it:

The war came, watched by Philip and most of his class with the fascinated interest of spectators before a burning house, but its cloud was no bigger than one's personal convictions.

Men took sides, ally or German, some from reason but more from the fun of taking sides, a fun comparable to that of backing the Cubs against the Giants. A handful left for ambulance service, two or three to join various armies, to the others no warning came at all that each casual step taken was on earthquake ground.*

Throughout the country as a whole the popular song was "I Didn't Raise My Boy to Be a Soldier." In November 1914, William Lyon Phelps declared: "From the standpoint of Christianity, there is no such thing as a foreign war. Every war is a civil war. . . . War means murder and destruction on the largest scale. There is nothing beautiful about it; nothing fine; nothing admirable; nothing noble."

In 1914 the standing army numbered about 80,000, and the ill-trained National Guard about 127,000. Because much of the regular army was required in posts from the Philippines and Alaska to the Canal Zone and Puerto Rico, and to man Coast Artillery, the "mobile army" consisted of 24,602 men. Ex-President Roosevelt demanded greater preparedness, and General Leonard Wood recommended universal military training. By 1915 Wilson had changed his view that "preparedness was not a pressing question." Finding the majority sentiment in Congress still opposed to any substantial increase in the armed forces, he made a speaking tour of the country in 1916, frankly stating his change of view but reiterating his "resolution to keep . . . out of the war." By 1917 David Starr Jordan, a pacifist, was forbidden to speak at Princeton and elsewhere. Only because of his own immense popularity with students was Phelps able to gain a hearing for Jordan at Yale.

Partly as a lark, partly with serious purpose, college students took up the demand for military training. When, in November 1915, the University Senate at Michigan voted for compulsory military training, the regents refused to authorize it, but the student paper, on the basis of a straw vote, found the student body overwhelmingly in favor of immediate training. That same

---

* From *The Beginning of Wisdom,* published by Rinehart & Company, Inc. Copyright, 1921, by Stephen Vincent Benét.

fall President Hadley of Yale made arrangements with the Connecticut Militia for the organization of a Field Artillery Battery. It was hoped that 138 undergraduates and graduates would apply; instead nearly 1,000 undergraduates alone tried to sign up. Eventually four batteries were organized, but Hadley had immense difficulty in getting the War Department to provide a qualified instructor. It was not until the following March that guns, caissons and other necessary equipment could be obtained. Then in May, Congress cut off the appropriation for the proposed National Guard encampments at Tobyhanna, Pennsylvania. Only the troubles with Mexico reactivated Tobyhanna. In colleges all over the nation similar conflicts and confusions resulted from attempts to introduce military training.

In the summer of 1916 the National Defense Act made possible the setting up of Reserve Officers Training at colleges. Only sixteen institutions applied for R.O.T.C. units, but not until January 1917 was the War Department able to come through with the necessary instructors. With the entry of the United States into the war the R.O.T.C. program was greatly expanded. Then in 1918 it was dropped in favor of the ill-conceived Student Army Training Corps. Thus, instead of using the special skills of the colleges, the government turned them into vast army camps. Faculties did their best to maintain a semblance of academic work, but the long hours of drill left students little time or energy to study. And the program brought in thousands of boys unfitted to profit from even a dilute form of higher education.

In its brief semester of existence the S.A.T.C. nearly wrecked the colleges. Academic instruction became a farce, and rowdy trainees tore up the buildings. A favorite sport was running bayonets through doors in dormitories and fraternity houses. The army reduced the faculty to underlings. At Michigan classes were often canceled by an order that all students were to come out to drill, and were to disregard any instructions from the faculty on pain of court-martial. President Hutchins had estimated that the university could handle 200 trainees; the army sent 800 immediately, and eventually 3,600. By October they were being quartered in fraternity front yards. In one day they built a mess hall 110 by 20 feet, and fed 1,450 men there that evening. Faculty members everywhere were stopped by campus sentries demanding passes. President Hadley wrote the Yale faculty asking them to take in good part the inconvenience of obeying orders from students in uniform.

With the end of the war, the S.A.T.C. was disbanded, to the relief of college officials everywhere. In its brief two months of existence it had proved a crude, and perhaps disastrous, makeshift. Dean Johnson of Minnesota spoke for the teaching profession when he called the experiment "an unequivocal failure." The professors went back to their classrooms disillusioned about war and the military; thousands of the trainees left college to join the American Legion and participate in witch hunts against the colleges. Many of the boys who remained were of a different breed from former generations of students: they were not well prepared for college work, and they came from social classes with no intellectual traditions. They remained in college to raise hell.

The S.A.T.C. was not the worst disaster that befell the faculty; they became victims of the growing intolerance in American society. Not many had been pro-German, but with America's entry into the war even mild pacifists were likely to be accused of being traitors. With the country engaged in a hysterical spy hunt it was inevitable that professors of German should come under attack. At Minnesota a woman teacher was accused of disloyalty because of her alleged failure to contribute to the Red Cross. Faculty members were of course not the only victims. In Madison, Wisconsin, Senator LaFollette was burned in effigy. Citizens with German and Scandinavian names were roughly handled by vigilantes demanding that the victims buy Liberty bonds. Brown and Wisconsin revoked the honorary degrees previously conferred on Ambassador von Bernstorff.

Despite this and the fact that large numbers of Wisconsin faculty and students were in war service, the superpatriots made the university a target because of utterances by Senator LaFollette and another alumnus, Louis Lochner. A complaining alumnus, after listening to President Van Hise's enumeration of the war services of the university, stated that they did "not carry great weight with industrial organizations who have turned over their entire staffs and resources to the public welfare." Van Hise retorted that as far as he knew no industrial concern "has made any arrangement with the government which has not yielded very handsome profits."

More serious were the charges made by two speakers who denounced Wisconsin students for being apathetic to patriotic addresses. The first of these disgruntled orators was Assistant Secretary of Agriculture Carl Vrooman, sent as Wilson's representative to review the university cadets. "Has the University the right kind of patriotic leadership?" he demanded later. "Is it guided by a milk and water patriotism? . . ." He overlooked the possibility that students who had listened to a series of patriotic addresses plus two faculty lectures a week on war issues might be a bit bored. It is quite possible that Vrooman's charges heightened the perceptions of Princeton Professor Robert McElroy, of the hyperthyroid National Security League, who spoke at Wisconsin the following April. To the *New York Tribune* he described in detail an audience made up of students wearing their country's uniform: "They sat with folded arms, staring wearily up at the ceiling. From time to time they'd turn and look at each other and smile superciliously, sort of pityingly." Finally the speaker had said, "Do you know what I think of you from your conduct tonight? I think you're a bunch of damned traitors." This was to an audience of cadets who had marched two and a half miles in the rain and who were forced to sit in a cold hall listening to such talk. Of such stuff were charges of treason made in 1918.

In this atmosphere of hate and hysteria Nicholas Murray Butler, never one to do things in a small way, became a leading executioner. As the most recent historian of Columbia describes him: "Dr. Butler had always the bearing of a Roman emperor." As a man who "worked night and day to identify himself with persons of wealth," Nicholas the Miraculous was not one to put academic freedom before more tangible considerations.

Even when he did not force out a nonconformist, he had the ability to make him sufficiently uncomfortable to resign. Thus, even before World War I, he had lost by resignation such prominent men as the composer Edward MacDowell; the poet and professor of English, George Edward Woodberry; and the classical philologist, editor and critic, Harry Thurston Peck. Peck, founder of *The Bookman*, had been forced out when, after a second marriage, a woman had sued him for breach of promise. When the scholarly literary critic Joel E. Spingarn offered a resolution at a meeting of the English faculty expressing admiration for the scholarship of Peck, he too was suddenly fired.

No one of these cases was an entirely clear-cut example of a violation of academic freedom. There were questions of administrative organization, moral turpitude or unwise statements to the press. But with the approach of American entry into the war, academic freedom at Columbia became definitely the issue. In the days when Butler was working for peace, he gave an instructor in economics, Leon Fraser, an extracurricular assignment to organize courses in pacifism and international conciliation throughout the country. But in 1917 when Fraser criticized the Plattsburg Officers' Training Program, Butler told the department not to renominate him. (Fraser later became president of the First National Bank of New York and a Columbia trustee.) On October 1, 1917, Professor J. McKeen Cattell was dismissed from the chair of psychology he had held for twenty-six years. His offense was that he had addressed a letter on Columbia stationery to members of Congress, asking them to support a bill against sending draftees to Europe against their will. Also dismissed was an English instructor, Henry Wadsworth Dana, for making anti-war speeches. A week later the historian Charles A. Beard resigned with the statement:

Having observed closely the inner life of Columbia for many years, I have been driven to the conclusion that the university is really under the control of a small and active group of trustees who have no standing in the world of education, who are reactionary and visionless in politics, narrow and medieval in religion. Their conduct betrays a profound misconception of the true function of a university in the advancement of learning. . . .

I am convinced that while I remain in the pay of the trustees of Columbia University I cannot do effectively my honorable part in sustaining public opinion in support of a just war on the German empire. . . .

As I think of their [his colleagues'] scholarship and their worldwide reputation and compare them with the few obscure and wilful trustees who now dominate the university and terrorize the young instructors I cannot repress my astonishment that America, of all countries, has made the status of the professor lower than that of the manual laborer who, through his union, has at least some voice in the terms and conditions of his employment. Holding his position literally by the day, the professor is liable to dismissal without a hearing, without the judgment of his colleagues who are his real peers.

Beard ended by demanding that legislative bodies should "strip boards of their absolute power over the intellectual life of the institutions under their management."

In professorial language Beard had stated the fundamental issue: the conflict between professional competence and lay control. Somehow faculty members have never been able to make the public understand that professors, like physicians, cannot have laymen writing the prescriptions. What Beard overlooked was the implications of his reference to the happier lot of union labor. Or he could have mentioned a craft union called the American Medical Association.

Lacking a strong organization, faculty members experienced elsewhere the insecurities described by Beard. At the University of Minnesota, Professor William Schafer, head of the Department of Political Science, was accused of pacifism. When he appeared before the Regents, he found no formal charges and faced no accusers. He said he considered himself a loyal American citizen, but had no enthusiasm for the war. He wished to see his country win, but did not believe that "the Hohenzollerns should be wiped out root and branch." He was promptly fired.

President Wilson asked his commission on labor conciliation to try to get the case reopened, but to no avail. Felix Frankfurter told his associates on the commission that in his opinion the action of the Regents constituted "a plain case of czarism, the very thing America is fighting." In colleges all over the country the pattern was repeated.

However, Lowell of Harvard refused to join in the lynching bee. When Hugo Münsterberg, professor of psychology, continued to defend the German viewpoint, students and alumni demanded his scalp. In London, Clarence Weiner, class of 1900, allegedly threatened to withdraw a ten-million-dollar bequest to the university unless Münsterberg was dismissed. Münsterberg offered to resign if Weiner would immediately remit half the amount promised. Lowell rejected such theatrical martyrdom, and ended the matter with a classic statement on academic freedom:

If a university or college censors what its professors may say, if it restrains them from uttering something that it does not approve, it thereby assumes responsibility for what it permits them to say. This is logical and inevitable, but it is a responsibility which an institution would be very unwise in assuming. . . .

The ironic feature of the popular and official attack on college professors was that never before had they been so important in the winning of a war. Many went into the armed forces. From Wisconsin alone 187 faculty members were granted leave for war service. Of these, 126 were in the army, 11 in the navy, 10 in the Red Cross, and 40 in civilian service. The pattern was typical of all colleges. In September 1918, Yale had 75 faculty in war service and 125 others assigned to instruction in S.A.T.C. and other units. Less glamorous but perhaps more important were the technical services performed by faculty members. They offered courses in aeronautics, bacteriology, French, history, military science, political science, and wireless telegraphy. From Harvard an instructor of chemistry, James B. Conant, went to turn out poison gases for the army and to set up models

YALE FOOTBALL TEAM, 1888

WON 13   LOST 0   YALE POINTS 700   OPPONENTS 0

Thomas McClung (holding ball) Captain. Named All-time All-American in 1904 by *N. Y. Evening World.*

Amos Alonzo Stagg (at far left) End.

Walter Heffelfinger (rear, third from right) Guard. Probably the greatest player of all time.

PRINCETON–YALE GAME
at the Berkley Oval, New York City, 1889.

for gas-mask production. Fifteen members of the Wisconsin faculty were similarly engaged. In the first great technological war the college professor was indispensable.

His role in making the peace is more debatable. Wilson sailed for the peace conference at Versailles accompanied by a corps of professorial "experts" on European problems. There was Professor Charles H. Haskins of Harvard, specialist on Alsace-Lorraine; Professor W. L. Westerman of Wisconsin, specialist on Turkey; Professor Clive Day of Yale, specialist on the Balkans; Professor W. E. Lunt of Haverford, specialist on Northern Italy; Professor Rolland B. Dixon of Harvard, specialist on ethnography. In the words of William Allen White:

Down the gangplank walked this Yankee knight errant followed by a desperate crew of college professors in horn-rimmed glasses carrying text books, encyclopaedias, maps, charts, graphs, statistics, and all sorts of literary crowbars to pry up the boundaries of Europe and move them around in the interests of justice as seen through the Fourteen Points.

No doubt this caricature had a considerable element of truth. Wilson and his "experts" must have seemed naïve to the European statesmen and their advisers long familiar with the intricacies of Old World politics and ethnography. Certainly Wilson's doctrinaire approach to the establishing of nations and boundaries showed an appalling ignorance of economic necessities. The plight of an Austria cut off from its economic roots is only one case in point. But the great failure was not that of the professorial experts; they at least tried to apply reason and knowledge to the problems. The real failure was that of the American ruling class.

It was the captains of business and industry, the journalists and political leaders who failed to grasp the meaning of the First World War. Wilson and his professors had at least a grip on the main issue: the world was literally one world, and a cancerous spot anywhere affected the whole organism. Events in Manchuria, in the Ruhr, and in Sudetenland were to give tragic proof of the main point.

It was not at Versailles that the professors failed; it was in the forty years before Versailles. On the one hand the traditionalists had clung to a moribund classicism giving almost no understanding of the modern world; on the other the vocationalists in schools of agriculture, engineering, business and the like had largely contented themselves with developing technical skills. Thus the leaders of America trained in the intellectually soft era of the colleges lacked the kind of education they desperately needed. Their college courses had given them only the most superficial knowledge of European history, politics and languages, and almost no understanding of economic and social forces.

The upper middle class which ruled the nation could speak neither French nor German, knew no European literature, little modern history, little economics beyond Adam Smith, no sociology, and had never heard of cultural anthropology.

Thus for most Americans *socialism, anarchism* and *Bolshevism* were interchangeable dirty words. Trade-unionism at home and abroad was regarded as merely the work of radical agitators. Probably not one college graduate in ten could have defined a cartel. Before 1917 only a slightly larger percentage could have identified Karl Marx. Theodore Roosevelt's attack on "malefactors of great wealth" was characteristic of the naïve approach to economic forces. His novelist friend, Owen Wister, Harvard A.B. and LL.B., had pictured socialism as merely envy of one's wealthier neighbors—an almost universal view among his class. In a series of magazine articles in 1921 Vice-President Coolidge equated internationalism with un-Americanism. He pictured professors who had joined the American Federation of Labor as dangerously radical. Coolidge had graduated from Amherst with high honors in 1895.

One of the ironies of the situation was that the general increase of faculty scholarship had often increased the gap between learning and life. With the growing insistence on the doctorate for faculty members, they had become specialists in some small area of learning. The old-time college president who could, and sometimes did, teach all the courses in the curriculum was also able to integrate whatever learning he had into a unified whole. This he tended to do in the course in moral philosophy. Moreover, he made practical applications of philosophy, ethics, religion, sociology, economics, and politics to the world of his time. Certified Ph.D.s have not always been able to do this.

Thus students in philosophy came away with more knowledge of trends and influences; those in history, with more exact information—at least until after the examination—those in science, with more technical skills. The growth of the elective system had intensified this fragmentation of education. Perhaps the overemphasis on activities had been partially due to the student's inability to relate scattered bits of specialized learning to anything he recognized as important. He was given Philosophy 4 or 104, but no philosophy of life. And the passionate discussion of contemporary problems in the old literary society had given way to fraternity-house bull sessions on athletics and campus politics. Apparently it was the women's colleges which made some attempt to apply the study of literature or Christian ethics to contemporary social and economic problems such as the living conditions of factory workers. It is no accident that in the postwar era the reactionaries particularly attacked the women's colleges.

With the end of the war, the United States experienced the most concerted attack on civil liberties since the days of the Alien and Sedition Laws. Just as the more ruthless elements of the property-owning class in the early 1800s had used the press and pulpit to brand Jeffersonian liberals as Jacobin traitors, so the business community of the 1920s mobilized all the forces of propaganda to prove that liberals, labor unions and college professors were "Reds." It was the period when organizations of superpatriots pointed in alarm to the National League of Women Voters, the Federal Council of Churches, and the Foreign Policy Association. A woman speaking for the Better America Federation objected to *Main Street* on the ground that it "created a distaste for the conventional good life of America." The same speaker called Professors John Dewey and James

Harvey Robinson "most dangerous to young people." Mr. Whitney, of the America Defense Society, charged that Professors Felix Frankfurter and Zechariah Chafee, of the Harvard Law School, and Frederick Wells Williams and Max Solomon Mandell, of Yale, used words which "publicly uttered and even used in the classrooms, are to put it conservatively, decidedly encouraging to the Communists." S. Stanwood Mencken, of the National Security League, estimated that there were 600,000 Communists in the nation.

In 1921 Vice-President Calvin Coolidge wrote for the *Delineator* a series of articles entitled: "Enemies of the Republic." The first of these was subtitled: "Are the Reds Stalking our College Women?" As evidence, he cited the report in the Vassar *Miscellany News* by a girl who had attended a Senate committee hearing. In horrified italics Coolidge quoted her remark that she was *"quite impressed by the Soviet ambassador,"* and *"struck by his moderation and intelligence compared to the narrowness of some of the committee."* Under a subheading, "Hotbed of Bolshevism," he quoted from the Radcliffe *News* which reported a speech before a Socialist Club. The remark which particularly disturbed the Vice-President was *"Every society must have a state, and we must not stop with the United States of America, but go on and achieve the United States of the World."* He further cited as dangerous the statement in the *News* that *"A genuine democritization of industry must be brought about,"* and an editorial criticizing the expulsion of five Socialist members of the New York Assembly. (It was an action which had been criticized also by Theodore Roosevelt, Jr., and Charles Evans Hughes.) At Wellesley, Coolidge learned of a professor who was "said to have voted for Debs." In his next installment Coolidge reported that an investigator in the Midwest had talked to a college professor's wife who told of attending a dinner where several instructors were present. "Do you know," the lady said, "they were all Bolsheviks?" Thus, in a popular magazine, a Vice-President of the United States, a man who had been a lawyer and a state governor, used as evidence against the colleges the alleged opinion of a provincial woman making vague general charges.

What Coolidge did not say was that the lady's remark had been quoted from the *New Republic* where it had appeared in a quite different context. As reported there, her remark had been picked up by a local businessman, who replied:

It is too bad it is that way. But it is true and we are meeting the situation. We are keeping a watch on these people and are gradually having them dismissed from the university, but not on that ground, of course.

Nor did Coolidge add that his source reported that faculty men of the same university had been followed about town by stenographers sent by a local business group to take down their speeches. That this was not an isolated incident is suggested by the report of a luncheon speech of Harry Haldeman, founder of the Better America Federation of California. He was quoted as saying:

Through the children of the best families throughout the land, who are attending universities, we are having students of radical tendencies watched. We are receiving reports of what is going on both as to students and teachers that uphold radical doctrines and views.

What the Federation regarded as radical views is suggested by their sponsorship of a legislative bill providing the cancellation of the license of any teacher who in discussing the Constitution with a pupil "shall express to such pupil any opinion or argument in favor of making any change in any provision."

In this atmosphere of spying and suspicion when a remark taken out of context or a student's distortion of a classroom lecture might bring headlines and alumni uproar, most faculty members learned to keep their opinions to themselves, with the result that students often regarded them as mealy-mouthed hypocrites. At Minnesota in December 1919, the *Foolscap* charged that the professors followed prescribed orders on what they might say. The American Association of University Professors asked President Burton to call a general faculty meeting to discuss the problem. In a secret ballot, thirty-three faculty members said, "Restraints upon complete freedom did exist at Minnesota." A faculty committee appointed to investigate found the problem "psychological in its nature." Four things limiting academic freedom were listed: "a post-bellum intolerance and its concomitant fear; a certain readiness [by university officials] to receive criticism of faculty members whose long service should act as a presumption in their favor; an aggressive and impudent willingness of men representing forces outside the university to spy on teachers and to exert pressure on the authorities; a tendency in the university to succumb to the idea that a university's function is an institution for the indoctrination of opinion." Upton Sinclair later charged that the report was never allowed to come before the faculty, and the instructor most active in preparing it was dropped. From Massachusetts to California, Sinclair heard from faculty members such phrases as "It's like a slow strangling."

In January 1923, Katherine Fullerton Gerould, an eminent essayist and story writer, told in *Harper's* of a trip to Canada which by contrast had revealed the fear-ridden atmosphere of the United States. "What you found there was startling in its unexpected relieving of a pain that had been chronic." Certainly she was no radical: she believed the *Nation* and the Rand School of Social Work to be un-American institutions "which can do nothing but harm." But suppressing them would, she said, be even more un-American, a bowing to the mob rule she found everywhere.

The only way in which an American citizen who is really interested in all the social and political problems of his country can preserve any freedom of expression is to choose the mob that is most sympathetic to him, and abide under the shadow of that mob. At that he will have to hold his tongue a great deal. . . . We have returned to the spirit of the Inquisition. . . .

It is worth noting that Mrs. Gerould was the wife of a college professor.

In this period of national psychosis some college presidents strove against community and alumni demands for faculty scalps. Mrs. Gerould's husband kept his job at Princeton despite the flood of vituperative letters sent to *Harper's*. After surveying the colleges of the nation, Upton Sinclair wrote: "The University of Wisconsin has the reputation of being the most liberal institution of higher learning in the United States, and on the whole I think the reputation is deserved." The testimony of another controversial figure, E. A. Ross (p. 242), and the history of the university (1949) by Merle Curti and Vernon Carstensen furnish evidence that Wisconsin maintained academic freedom to a remarkable degree. Wellesley also stood its ground. Despite the Coolidge attack on the socialistic views of Professors Mary Calkins and Vida Scudder, they remained on the faculty. This sort of thing was old stuff at Wellesley. Back in 1912 the *Boston Transcript* had denounced Professors Scudder and Ellen Hayes for speaking at a meeting sponsored by the Progressive Women's Club of Lawrence during a strike. Miss Scudder freely acknowledged her membership in the Socialist Party and offered her resignation. The college trustees took no action on the offer. Not only that, but in 1922 Henry Raymond Mussey was brought into the Department of Economics. Five years before, Mussey had resigned from Columbia in protest against the limitations on academic freedom under Butler. In the interim before his appointment at Wellesley he had been managing editor of the *Nation*. At Harvard, Lowell resisted the alumni demand, backed by threats of withdrawal of endowments, for the scalp of Professor Harold Laski, who had expressed sympathy for the Boston police during their strike. When the Overseers were about to approach him on the matter, Lowell is reported to have prepared the answer, "If the overseers ask for Laski's resignation they will get mine."

The student response to all this furor was what might have been expected. As a group, young people value fair play and are quick to see through cant. The excesses of the Palmer Red hunt, which, in the words of Frederick Lewis Allen, "set a new record in American history for executive transgression of individual constitutional rights," stirred up feeling for the underdog. Many students of course did not much concern themselves with such matters, but public attacks on their own professors were something much closer to home. Student newspapers were quick to defend their institutions against charges by businessmen, patriotic societies, and newspapers. Frequently the faculty member under attack was especially popular; it was likely to be the stimulating, thought-provoking lecturer who raised the blood pressure of the superpatriots. And students were quick to recognize the distortions, the phrases taken out of context, which characterized the attacks. The balderdash of much of the conservative oratory and publication turned the stomachs of the more intelligent students. For instance, Coolidge ended his exposé of the women's colleges with the statement:

Adherence to radical doctrines means the ultimate breaking down of the old sturdy virtues of manhood and womanhood, the insidious destruction of character, and the weakening of the moral fibre of the individual, the destruction of the foundations of civilization.

This sort of thing sounded even more empty three years later when the scandals of the Harding administration began to come to light. In the meantime some students were reading *Main Street, Babbitt, Spoon River Anthology* and *Winesburg, Ohio.* The "old sturdy virtues" began to look like a myth.

It would be a mistake to overemphasize the intellectual elements in the student revolt against the opinions of their elders. Much of the reaction was a much more spontaneous kicking over the traces. A social and moral revolution was under way, a revolution against everything the older generation preached— but by no means universally practiced. Great political, religious, or social revolutions are prefaced by a decay of the old order, a period when the codes and creeds no longer represent the inner reality. Thus without intellectualizing it, a host of boys and girls in the early 1920s instinctively knew that the platitudes about honesty, democracy, chastity and religion did not represent the truth about American life. They knew that kikes and wops and niggers were outside the pale—in fact, many of the college students agreed that they should be. In their own homes they had learned the gospel of getting and spending. With the coming of prohibition they knew of the liquor in country-club locker rooms or in the family cellar. The World War had taught them that the world was a brutal place; those who had been in the army knew that it was a bawdy world. What the defenders of the established order overlooked was that youth has an instinctive hatred of bunk.

As an example of radicalism Coolidge had quoted a student's remark in the Vassar *Miscellany News:* "I'm not pessimistic. I'm not optimistic. I'm just antagonistic." His comment was "There one has it." For once he was perceptive. There, indeed, one did have it, the spirit of student revolt in the 1920s. But the reasons were not, as he supposed, radical professors, agitators, or Socialist clubs. These were only the symptoms. The revolt took two main channels: a gaudy binge with sex, bootleg gin, and automobiles; and, on the part of some, an intellectual revolution. Often enough the two streams flowed together as they had in Fitzgerald's prewar Princeton.

On the intellectual level the reaction against the witch hunters took the form of the Socialist clubs so much deplored by the Vice-President, and of various social science clubs not committed to any particular dogma. In colleges all over the nation these groups plagued the authorities by inviting speakers on controversial subjects, people like Scott Nearing (whose fame rested in no small degree on his being fired from the University of Pennsylvania), Upton Sinclair, William Z. Foster and Lincoln Steffens. Of course, in that era all sorts of people could be considered dangerous speakers. At the University of Michigan, Jane Addams was barred from speaking on women's suffrage. Wisconsin students in particular plagued the administration with demands for permission to bring in controversial figures. Always the issue of free speech came into the controversies. Students demanded the right to hear all sides of every question; conservative alumni, trustees, and citizens objected to colleges becoming forums for radical views. Administrators, caught in the middle, tried to strike some sort of balance such as permitting speakers to address limited groups or requiring administrative approval of speakers. No doubt college authorities were often too timid, too ready to give in to pressure groups, but in their defense it should be pointed out that propagandists are ever ready to make a college or university the sounding board for their views. It is not merely a matter of speaking to students; it often involves the publicity and free advertising which result from the use of a university platform for the expression of controversial views.

The moral revolt of the jazz age has been variously attributed to the war, the motorcar, Freud, and bootleg gin. No doubt all played a part. But what is often forgotten is that American puritan mores had been relaxing for at least a generation. As has been pointed out in the preceding chapter, student life from 1880 to 1914 had been a pretty gay affair—for the men. The most important new feature of life in the jazz age was the change in feminine mores. The girls joined in the party. The raccoon-coated Princeton student of 1920 was far more like his father of the turtle-neck sweater era than was the short-skirted Vassar girl like her well-swathed mother. In this connection clothes are a useful symbol. Dressed for a date the male of 1920 wore almost exactly what his father had worn—only the cut was slightly changed. The girl who accompanied him had discarded corsets and petticoats; as she climbed into the car, her skirts revealed bare knees and more than a glimpse of thigh. In 1890 many a man had married before he saw so much of the female body. For the women it was a revolution, for the man a revelation.

And it was a temptation. This lightly dressed girl often accepted a cigarette and a pull from a hip flask. Even if she did not smoke, she danced in the conventional close embrace. The music had developed from erotic savage dances and in the sporting houses of New Orleans. Between dances couple after couple wandered out to the cars parked around the country club or college gym. As always, the young followed a group pattern—everybody was doing it. A girl who didn't pet, at least to some degree, was a "flat tire." No longer was the popular girl a belle; she was a "hot number," a "jazz baby."

The war is too simple an explanation of this vast revolution in mores. In war-ravaged Europe the *carpe diem* attitude of youth could be explained largely in terms of the social and economic dislocations of the war. Men could not get or could not settle down to civilian jobs; a generation of girls far outnumbered the eligible men; there was chaos everywhere. All these forces touched America lightly. The generation which entered college between 1919 and 1929 had in most instances never been in the army; the girls had lost no lovers at the front. This is not to say that the war had no influence; undoubtedly there was truth in the song, "How Ya Gonna Keep 'Em Down on the Farm after They've Seen Paree?" But the vast majority of "flaming youth" had never seen Paree except in the movies. And speaking of the movies, it should be noted that the vamp and the bathing beauty had already appeared on the screen before 1917. The divorce rate had been rising steadily; *petting* and *necking* were already in the vocabulary. New Orleans jazz had developed before the war. It is probable that the jazz age in America would have come, war or no war.

Certainly flaming youth was no creation of the colleges. Judge Ben Lindsay of the Denver Juvenile Court horrified the nation with an account of high-school girls carrying contraceptives in their vanity cases and of a vast amount of promiscuity among teen-agers. Here we must take into account the question of class mores. Although Dr. Kinsey's investigations were made in the 1940s, there is every reason to believe that his discovery of differing sex patterns between college students and non-college youth of the same age represents a social phenomenon of long standing. Kinsey found that among that part of the male population which quit school before college, premarital intercourse was much more common than among college students; whereas petting without intercourse was much more characteristic of the college population. The collegiate sex code permitted extensive petting but frowned on sex relations with "nice" girls. This is exactly the code reflected in college stories of the 1920s: Percy Marks, *The Plastic Age* (1924), Lynn and Lois Montross, *Town and Gown* (1923) and *Fraternity Row* (1926). It was essentially the code of the prewar students pictured by Fitzgerald and Benét.

To a great degree then it would seem that the revolution as far as college students were concerned was one of manners much more than of morals. In so far as there was a change in morals, it was one among the girls rather than among the men. Dr. Kinsey's interviews with older men led him to conclude that over a period of fifty years there had been little change in the percentages of men with premarital sex experience. However, studies such as Terman's showed an increasing proportion of women with such experiences. Kinsey dates the revolution in the 1920s.

Thus in college stories we find such typical characters as the lounge lizard who pets, but does not try to seduce the coeds; the flapper who is a hot necker but manages to retain a precarious technical virginity; the woman-chaser who seeks his fun among the town "bags" and "broads"—not necessarily professional prostitutes, but simply girls with the mores of the noncollege class; and finally there is the upper-class girl with a code "like a man's." In *This Side of Paradise* she is Eleanor; in *The Plastic Age,* Cynthia. A commentary on the era is the relationship between Hugh Carver and Cynthia Day. Hugh, an essentially nice boy, gets drunk at a dance and takes the flapper, Cynthia, to a dormitory room. Their rendezvous is interrupted before anything happens. Hugh, really in love with Cynthia, later apologizes, but Cynthia breaks off their friendship—not because of the incident, but because, although she loves Hugh, she feels that her previous sexual adventures have made her unworthy of the inexperienced boy.

A more typical incident is the first seduction theme. In *Town and Gown* it is called "First Man," a story of a boy and girl who let a petting party get out of control. In this story, the boy is apologetic; the girl takes the loss of virginity in her stride. Many a confessional freshman theme tells a variant of the story. Such statistical evidence as is available suggests that the picture given in novels is fairly accurate. Thus, instead of the sexual orgy attributed to the "flaming youth" of the colleges, there was increased premarital experimentation, often "monogamous," by the girls except for a few who went in for promiscuity, and about the usual amount of downtown sex activity by the boys.

The revolution in manners was something else. The spirit of revolt against the older generation, of being antagonistic, made life miserable for student deans and faculty chaperones. Added to this was the motorcar, which spread student social life over an area with a radius of a hundred miles. Students crashed dances at other colleges; they took dates to roadhouses thirty miles away; they dashed off after classes to attend shows in distant cities; they followed en masse after the football team. On week ends, those who had no cars, or friends with cars, hitchhiked. Ancient Fords broke down miles from home; hitchhikers failed to get return rides or allowed themselves to be taken far off their course. Late Sunday night or early Monday morning weary students straggled back to the campus to sleep through, or in, early classes.

Instead of getting drunk downtown and disturbing the peace with song as they staggered back to their rooms, they now got drunk at dances and set off in automobiles to the consternation of the countryside. Monday-morning papers carried stories of smashups and deaths. At Princeton it was considered desirable to have an imported roadster, but one could get by with a Cadillac or Packard phaeton. Even at less aristocratic colleges students turned up with expensive cars. Michigan had trouble with students driving Stutzes, Mercers and a Mercedes-Benz. President Little persuaded the University Senate to ban cars for freshmen and sophomores. Similar prohibitions went in elsewhere. In 1927, after two students were killed and a number injured, President Little forbade all student driving and employed a detail of motorcycle police to enforce the rule. At most colleges officials just shut their eyes and pretended not to notice; they had their hands full with other problems. After all, the possession of a motorcar was becoming almost an Amer-

ican constitutional right. Students could pick up Model T
Fords in running condition for between $25 and $75. The
next step was to decorate the "tin lizzie" with such epigrams as
"capacity ten gals," "four wheels, no brakes," "don't laugh, your
daughter may be in here."

The all-engrossing faculty problems were drinking and student behavior at dances. The actual amount of drinking was
probably less than a generation before, but it caused more
trouble. The traditional college tipple, beer, gave way under
prohibition to bootleg concoctions which often produced gas-
tric distress and embarrassing scenes. Furthermore, the drinking
often took place on campus and especially in connection with
dances. Because of the cut-in dance, at least half of the men
came stag. With no responsibility for a girl, and with a good
bit of free time on their hands, stags tended to resort to the
washroom for periodic swigs. Another new feature of college
dances was the girl who passed out in the ladies' room or even
more publicly. As coeds were likely to be careful on their own
campuses, the girl who got "stinko" was usually an import—
perhaps from another college, but more or less outside the disciplinary powers at the scene of her exploit. At most she could
be sent home before the close of a house-party week end.

The cut-in dance, imported from the South, where a girl's
social success was traditionally measured by the number of fraternity pins she could accumulate, tended to depopulate college
dances of quiet and sedate girls. If a girl danced ten minutes
with the same man, the stags avoided her in droves, with the
result that her partner became acutely unhappy. Knowing that
he would be kidded or, as the phrase was, "ridden," he overlooked any charm the lady might have in his desperate desire
to get rid of her. College humor magazines developed an infi-
nite number of variations of the gag about the boy waving a
five-dollar bill behind his partner as they danced by the stag
line. Many a girl retired to the ladies' room on some pretext
or other, never to emerge for the rest of the evening. Under
the pressure of this cruel system, girls used every device to
attract the stags: daring dresses, lascivious styles of dancing, a

line of risqué jokes. If a boy returned to the stag line to report, "Boy, does she really put it up against you!" or, "Man! the jokes that baby knows," the line formed on the right.

One result was that boys tended to "drag" the "hot numbers" of their acquaintance—if possible, models or show girls. Thus a considerable amount of the flapper's reputation for outrageous behavior was due to the highly selected type of girl brought to college dances. A boy might be seriously dating a home-town girl, but did not necessarily bring her to college dances unless they were engaged and did not mind dancing together the whole evening. Male students had chased after chorus girls before 1920 but did not often bring them to college dances. Not that all prom trotters were chorines; it was only that the less inhibited girls set the pattern for social success. A famous musical-comedy star of the period was reported to have boasted that she had slept in every dormitory at Harvard. And Dorothy Parker cracked that if all the girls who attended a Yale prom were laid end to end, she wouldn't be surprised.

Girls from conventional families found themselves in a social milieu for which their training had not prepared them. If they were coeds, the more homely or inhibited flocked together to play "wholesome games" and gossip about girls who smoked and drank! The more pious or pimply boys were active in the "Y" and pledged themselves never to marry a girl who used cigarettes. In all periods there have been social cleavages between the more and the less pious students, but the rapid social changes of the 1920s probably widened the gap between these groups. Some swam gaily with the current; others held desperately to the rafts of traditional morals and manners.

The greatest gulf, however, was that between generations. Parents, and faculty members over thirty, found the younger generation incomprehensible, while youth regarded their elders as either hopelessly incompetent or as pious hypocrites. Probably never in American history had two generations found it harder to communicate. One of the most characteristic lacunae in the work of F. Scott Fitzgerald is the absence of characters

over thirty. His world is the world of youth and the young mar-
rieds. In an introduction to a collection of Fitzgerald's short
stories, Malcolm Cowley explains this gulf on the ground that
"the elders were discredited in their [the younger generation's]
eyes by the war, by prohibition, by the Red scare of 1919-1920,
and by the scandals like that of Teapot Dome."

That may have been true of the more intellectually aware
young people. But a host of others cared little about Red scares
or Teapot Dome. They came to college dances too late to go
through the receiving line; they avoided speaking to faculty
chaperones who might detect the whiff of gin; in dormitories
girls smoked cigarettes at open windows to thwart suspicious
proctors; in ladies' rooms they shed the corsets and petticoats
insisted on by their mothers. Maternal advice against kissing
before a formal offer of marriage made no sense in a world
where "everybody does it." In a Montross story there is a savage
portrait of a dean of women trying vainly to enforce a rule that
couples must dance six inches apart. The young people knew
just enough Freud to attribute all adult admonitions to sexual
frustration. And adults too often regarded smoking and bobbed
hair as moral issues. Frequently the older generation confused
the new freedom of speech with sin. Others were simply baffled, like the father who said that his daughter would talk about
anything, and usually talked about nothing else.

In the past the more understanding members of a faculty
could always recognize a student prank as something not unlike
some event of their own undergraduate lives. But to even the
most tolerant, student behavior of the twenties seemed incomprehensible. A member of the class of 1923 remembers discussing *The Plastic Age* with a brilliant professor who taught with
gusto the plays of the Elizabethan and Restoration eras. To the
recent graduate the novel was a photographically realistic picture of the college life he had known; to the professor at the
same college it was a strange world. "Things weren't like that,
were they?" he asked.

In this great war between the old and young, undergraduate

publications became a battleground. Editorials in student papers attacked sacred cows like prohibition, big business and traditional religion. Writers defended faculty members who had incurred the ire of business leaders or superpatriots. Literary magazines published stories imitative of Hemingway, Cabell, Mencken and Lewis—the writers most objectionable to the pious and the conservative. And it was the heyday of the college humor magazine. The Dartmouth *Jack o' Lantern*, *The Harvard Lampoon*, *The Penn Punchbowl*, *The Cornell Widow*, *The Lafayette Lyre*, *The Princeton Tiger*, *The Lehigh Bur*, the Texas *Longhorn*, the *Wisconsin Octopus* and hordes of others published the most risqué jokes and drawings they could get past the harried faculty advisers. Drawings of bathing girls and near-nudes abounded. Students swelled with pride when their own colleges produced a number "almost as raw as *The Punchbowl.*" Even college yearbooks occasionally put one over on the censors. At militantly Presbyterian Lafayette, the *Melange* for 1920 memorialized in thinly veiled language the occasion when a celebrated local prostitute named Violet had been the guest of the boys on the second floor of a certain dormitory. Elsewhere in the same publication the editors enshrined those who carried mementos of the occasion. Another local lady and her patrons were also immortalized. As has been noted, students had brought prostitutes into dormitories long before this, but probably never before the 1920s had they brought them into a college yearbook.

In his commencement address that same year, the president of the college, John Henry MacCracken, preached the ideals of sectarian instruction and the superiority of the Anglo-Saxon race. This all too typical combination of student license and official bigotry flowered in college graduates like Fitzgerald's Tom Buchanan of *The Great Gatsby*.

At Wisconsin the business manager of the *Octopus*, the student humor magazine, had the grace to apologize to President Birge for an offensive advertisement in the *Cardinal*. The president accepted the apology but remarked that "it had never occurred to him that it was notably below the standards of the *Octopus* as regards either taste or wit." A national magazine, *College Humor,* carried such standards to a titillated public.

Student publications were only reflecting the mood of the more intellectually alert element in the nation, a mood described by Frederick Lewis Allen as "the revolt of the highbrows." It was the period of the debunking biography, of the novel satirizing or deploring American life. In the *American Mercury,* founded 1924, H. L. Mencken led a raucus crusade against pious cant, prohibition, the "Bible Belt" and the "booboisie." An elderly professor at the University of Chicago spoke for alarmed conservatives when he said, "The one thing that makes me fear for the future is the number of our students who read the *American Mercury;* on the campus you see it under every arm; they absorb everything in it." It became a point of pride to keep the conservatives in a state of alarm—a not very difficult feat in any age, but in the twenties particularly easy. In 1925 some of the best wits in America launched *The New Yorker* with the slogan "not for the old lady from Dubuque."

Looking back, some literary-minded persons have suggested that Eliot's "The Waste Land" was the key poem of the era. Perhaps it caught the mood of postwar European intellectuals and of some American expatriates—the mood reflected in *The Sun Also Rises* and the early novels of Aldous Huxley. But the American college student was more likely to find in Masters, Dreiser, Lewis and Mencken the spirit of his own revolt against the decadent puritanism of William Jennings Bryan and the prohibitionists; against the sort of religion represented by Bruce Barton's *The Man Nobody Knows,* which pictured Jesus as a super salesman; and against the business and social ideals of George F. Babbitt. In student publications there was little of Eliot's longing for a spiritual sanctuary, but rather the slap-happy iconoclasm of H. L. Mencken which went after the idols of respectability with a baseball bat. The collegiate world was not a wasteland but a shooting gallery at a carnival.

Through it all, however, ran an undercurrent of seriousness. College bull sessions usually came around to religion and sex.

Sex as smut had always been an element in student conversation, but in the twenties sex became as never before a topic for serious discussion. Freud and the new freedoms of women and literature supplied a body of material for endless discussion. Boys and girls were genuinely puzzled by the social revolution they were living through. Most of them had been brought up under a code which no longer seemed to apply. Like Hugh Carver in *The Plastic Age,* a boy might get drunk at a dance and experiment with sex; a girl might quote Edna St. Vincent Millay's "What lips my lips have kissed" or "My candle burns at both its ends," but each was more than a little uncertain. The actual revolt required gin to dull the sense of guilt. In fraternity houses and women's dormitories the questioning went on till long after midnight.

Similarly the traditional religious ideas no longer made sense. Why required chapel? In college after college, students petitioned and wrote editorials against it. A number of institutions dropped or softened the requirement. Nevertheless, a considerable amount of testimony agrees that, despite a skepticism about conventional creeds, students of the twenties were more deeply concerned about religion than the prewar college generation had been. Yet all too often chapel speakers preached a return to orthodoxy or inveighed against cigarettes, liquor and bobbed hair. At sectarian colleges, teachers of required courses in Bible used quack scientific ideas to combat the teachings of departments of biology and geology. As a result, student religion of the 1920s tended to be a jerry-built affair constructed without much help from the older generation.

Generalizations about trends and tendencies must not obscure the fact that there was a great variety of student behavior. For many boys and girls, social life consisted of such staples as the movie date followed by a malted milk at the drugstore; a Saturday-night doggie roast or a Sunday hike; a dance to Victrola music at a girl's home. Informal dances in the college gym were often rather sedate affairs, "high-hatted" by the more sophisticated. At Wellesley, by investing thirty-five cents, a girl could bring a date to a Saturday-night dance presided over by

the stately Ellen Pendleton. Such dances closed promptly at
10:45, and the train for Boston left at 11:15. Even so, scores of
Harvard and M.I.T. men as well as others from more distant
colleges turned up for such restrained revelry. Particularly at
coeducational institutions there was an immense amount of informal and nonalcoholic social life. Nor was the good-night kiss
an invention of the twenties; as Hammond's diary shows, it was
a standard feature of the 1840s. And petting under other names
had existed wherever boys and girls went sleigh riding or driving in the country. No doubt there was more of it in the twenties, but it was no new feature of college life.

As for the revolt against business and religion, that too
touched many students lightly. Numbers of them attended non-
required evening services on Sunday, partly for the same reason
their ancestors had done so—that is, to walk home with a boy
or girl.

At most colleges infinitely more men were looking forward
to making money than were hoping to destroy the capitalist
system. The great increase in enrollments following the war
was particularly marked in schools of engineering and business. Even students in liberal-arts courses at a place like Princeton, which had no school of business, were often looking forward to the lush pastures of Wall Street. Every spring the
representatives of big corporations went into the academic
groves on the annual ivory hunt. In club and fraternity houses
seniors debated the question of salary versus commissions. Men
who knew how to dress well, who had connections, who had
spent their week ends in wealthy homes and who knew the fathers of debutantes, were siphoned off in droves to become customers' men for brokerage houses. From the less swanky colleges
and universities they went into insurance and real estate. The
studious boy preparing for graduate school was regarded as a
sort of freak. Law or medicine made sense, but not scholarship
or teaching.

For this attitude there were sound reasons. It was not only
the lure of big money in the stock market or Florida real estate;
it was the starvation salaries and low social status of teaching

and research which tipped the scales. The witch hunt for radicals in college faculties was partly a symptom of the low social status of teachers. As a class they no longer sat at the dinner tables of the local business and professional leaders; they could not afford to return the hospitality. They wore shabby clothes, and they often lacked that badge of respectability, a motorcar. In 1893, President Harper of Chicago, after making a study of more than a hundred institutions, found that the average salary for a year's teaching was about $1,470. When in 1908 the Carnegie Foundation for the Advancement of Teaching studied 100 leading institutions, it found that the average salary of a full professor was between $1,350 and $4,800, with the average somewhere near $2,500.

With the inflation during and after World War I, the cost of living went up about eighty per cent while faculty salaries went up little or not at all. On the basis of questionnaires, Trevor Arnett, of the General Education Board, found that by 1920 the average increases in salaries amounted to between twenty and thirty-five per cent of the increased cost of living. A later study by Trevor Arnett, published in 1928, showed the pattern during the boom years:

	Nominal averages	Real averages
1914-1915	$1,724	$1,724
1919-1920	2,279	1,114
1926-1927	2,958	1,825

In the early twenties an instructor, even at wealthy institutions, often started at $1,000—an amount perhaps half or a fourth of the spending-money allowance of some of his students. If the instructor had a Ph.D., he had invested between $5,000 and $8,000 in his own education.

The result of all this was to drive a wedge between college teachers and the community. A man trying to support a family on starvation wages was not only unable to take his place in the life of the influential part of the community; he developed compensatory resentments. From his point of view the capitalistic system was a failure. Often his revolt went no further than a contempt for the social and cultural values of the business community, but sometimes it took the form of an intellectual flirtation with radical views.

It was this atmosphere which fostered the growth of radicalism among the student intellectuals like Scott Nearing, John Reed, Granville Hicks, Max Eastman, Eugene Lyons and all those who worshiped the god which failed. All of them, even the others who became Communist agents, were motivated by a political idealism for which there was small market in the America of Harding, Coolidge and Hoover. The professors did not need to teach radical views; the abler students saw in the shabby scholars a symbol of what capitalism did to the intellectual. At commencement time the honorary degrees went to the wealthy and the powerful so frequently that they had little meaning as accolades for intellectual achievement. This was not a new phenomenon in America; between 1830 and 1928 the percentage of political leaders receiving degrees remained almost constant. But a study by the American Association of University Professors in 1917 showed that only 8.06 per cent of 447 LL.D.s from thirty-seven institutions went to scholars and investigators. Not so large a proportion went to businessmen as faculty members were inclined to suppose; nevertheless, the habit of honoring benefactors and potential benefactors was sufficiently notorious to be the subject of cartoons in newspapers and magazines.

Faculty members became most cynical when degrees went to men who symbolized forces deplored by the academic community. Economists and political scientists might question the growth of vast holding companies which manipulated public utilities for speculative purposes, but in the twenties there were countless instances where honorary degrees were conferred on some of the most powerful executives of holding companies. Between 1919 and 1921 three institutions, Swarthmore, Lafayette and George Washington, gave LL.D.s to A. Mitchell Palmer.

The class war between the intellectuals and the conservatives who ruled the nation came to its climax with the Sacco-Vanzetti case. This became the key symbol of the era. At first it was the leftist and radical press, particularly in Europe, which raised questions about the justice of the trial in which these two anarchists were convicted of a pay-roll murder in 1921. Thus, when writers and college professors began to voice similar doubts, it seemed to many conservatives only another proof of dangerous radicalism among the intellectuals. And the writers and professors, bringing out fact after fact which showed the prejudice and perjury involved in the conviction, came increasingly to feel that the leaders of business and government were not interested in evidence but only in teaching the radicals the brutal lesson that there was no room for dissent in America. So much did the case become the symbol of the conflict between power and intellectual freedom that it became the theme of plays, poems, and novels by such diverse writers as Maxwell Anderson, Edna St. Vincent Millay and Upton Sinclair. It is no accident, therefore, that in Nugent and Thurber's comedy, *The Male Animal,* a timid college professor demonstrates his manhood by reading, in defiance of a reactionary trustee, Vanzetti's powerful last letter.

The history of the case itself is much too long and complex for inclusion here but its relation to the college community is a vital part of the story of higher education in the 1920s. It became so much a part of the history of Harvard that a recent historian of the university devotes several pages to it in a brief book covering the events of over 300 years. It was a Harvard professor of law, Felix Frankfurter, who published in the *Atlantic* a review of the case and cast great doubt on the guilt of the defendants. Dean Roscoe Pound, of the same law school, defended those who demanded a reconsideration of the case, and attacked the view that it was better to execute obnoxious persons than to admit a mistake by the courts. President Lowell apparently took a different view.

The intellectuals began to discover that those in power were not to be moved by thoughtful articles in even the most respectable periodicals. As they had done in the fight against slavery, the intellectuals began to enter the arena. Harvard graduate

Heywood Broun devoted so many of his columns in the *New York World* to the case that he was fired. A Seattle lawyer, Edward Holton James, Harvard 1898, a nephew of William and Henry James, was arrested for participation in a mass meeting on the Boston Common. However, he denied the charge that he had shouted "Down with the cops," and insisted that he had said, "Down with the police." Among the writers arrested for parading in front of the State House were John Dos Passos, Dorothy Parker and Edna St. Vincent Millay. Sixty-seven-year-old Ellen Hayes, head of the English department at Wellesley, stated, "I feel I must voice a protest." She too was arrested for picketing the State House. In a final appeal a group sent a telegram to President Coolidge, signed by David Starr Jordan, Oswald Garrison Villard, Glenn Frank, Alexander Meiklejohn, Benjamin B. Lindsey, Arthur Garfield Hayes, Ida Tarbell, Rockwell Kent, Carl Van Doren, John F. Hylan, Floyd Dell and Otto Soglow. Three of these were, or had been, college presidents; one was a Columbia professor. Their alliance with writers, artists, liberal lawyers, and a New York mayor was prophetic of the social alignments of the next decade.

The case also emphasized the dichotomy between the professors and the powers which ruled the academic community. Alexander Meiklejohn had been forced out of Amherst by conservatives on the faculty and board of trustees; David Starr Jordan had been debarred from speaking at Princeton and other colleges in 1917; Glenn Frank, president of the liberal University of Wisconsin, had brought in Meiklejohn to develop an experimental college. Thus they were hardly typical of their kind. After all, it was two college presidents who did much to send Sacco and Vanzetti to the electric chair.

A. Lawrence Lowell was appointed by Governor Fuller as chairman of a three-man committee to review the case in order to determine if executive clemency was warranted. The other members were President Stratton of M.I.T. and Judge Robert Grant. A few weeks later, they reported that they believed Sacco and Vanzetti guilty even though they deplored Judge Thayer's indiscreet remarks such as his reference to the defendants as "anarchist bastards." Although the committee made a careful study of the case, they seem to have been more concerned with the procedures at the trial than with the possible innocence of the defendants. So, despite appeals by conservative newspapers, the men were executed on August 22, 1927. The Episcopal Bishop of Massachusetts, William Lawrence, spoke for his class as he had in 1901 when he called strikes a form of brigandage, and said that it is only to the man of morality that wealth comes." He congratulated Governor Fuller, and expressed "admiration for the way in which you have done your duty in the Sacco-Vanzetti case." Only a year later the conservative *Outlook*, after a long investigation, stated that it "had, finally, become morally convinced that the trials of these men as carried on were open to question and that more than a possibility existed of one of the greatest miscarriages of justice in history." More than twenty years later two Harvard Law School professors published *The Legacy of Sacco and Vanzetti*, exposing the whole history of blunder and hysteria involved in the verdict and execution.

And so for at least a generation the scars were to remain. The socially and politically aware members of the academic community were imbued with a deep distrust and hostility to the conservative elements in the church, business, and government. A. Lawrence Lowell will go down in history not as the man who tried to introduce greater democracy among Harvard freshmen or as the defender of academic freedom, but as the man who sent Sacco and Vanzetti to death.

For hundreds of professors and students this long agony had brought an awareness of the world outside the colleges. Increasingly academic life shifted from books and football to a concern with the social, political and economic order. Many a student who knew nothing about the trial of Socrates became deeply stirred over that of Sacco and Vanzetti. Only a few of the million boys and girls in college saw any point in learning the Latin word for *shoemaker* or *fish peddler*, but thousands of them came to believe it important to know more about shoemakers and fishpeddlers. The Sacco-Vanzetti case was not a cause of this but a symbol.

It would be absurd to attribute any substantial part of this changed attitude to a single incident, even a single cause such as the growing democratization of the student body. Ever since the Civil War, Americans had demanded a "practical" education. To some this meant simply a vocational education for engineering, farming, dentistry, accounting, journalism, or salesmanship. To the more thoughtful and better-educated part of the community, *practical* meant *contemporary*—an emphasis on the understanding of the complex forces in modern life: science, politics, economics, social forces, human psychology. Educators tried to build curriculums which would combine training for a job with preparation for citizenship. But they also recognized another objective often overlooked by both the public and students—that is, an understanding of the cultural heritage.

The failure of so many Americans to understand and value this cultural objective represents the great failure of the classicists and the traditionalists. The example cited by Bliss Perry was all too typical: the Williams College Latin assignment which had remained unchanged from 1848 to 1916 or longer—"the same squirrel in the same cage." For a hundred years the traditionalists had defended the classical curriculum on the grounds of mental discipline. But in 1890 at Pennsylvania, J. McKeen Cattell, working along the lines of Galton's *Inquiries into Human Faculty* (1883), published a paper on "Mental Tests and Measurements." By 1920 the psychologists had demolished the arguments for a mental training universally valuable.

Cattell's work at Pennsylvania and Columbia (until Butler fired him) became the foundation for further studies by Thorndike, Terman, and a host of others. Perhaps no other single field of research since Darwin has produced such a revolution in the colleges. The development of intelligence and aptitude tests gave an entirely new basis for the selection of students. Such tests put the applicant from a poor school on a more equal footing with his wealthier or luckier contemporaries; they provided a measure of the achievement to be expected; they became an invaluable tool for guidance counselors and a guide for students in the selection of courses and vocations; they even helped to measure effectiveness of courses and teachers. Thus, if the tests showed that a group of students had ability, an instructor could not excuse poor results by alleging the stupidity of his class. Traditional disciplines could no longer be justified as mental gymnastics; they were re-examined for possible values as tool or cultural subjects.

Because it is usually inadvisable to inform students of their intelligence or scholastic aptitude scores, the tests were sometimes used as a pretext for refusing admission to applicants who were not white, Protestant Anglo-Saxons. On the whole, however, they were a powerful force in the democratization of the colleges. By demonstrating that enormous numbers of boys and girls had the intelligence to do college work, they helped to counteract the pressures of social and academic conservatives for limiting enrollments. Faculty members faced with the problems of a rapidly mounting college population were quick to say that the quality was going down and that further extension of democratic education would produce hopeless mediocrity. Those professors whose subjects were avoided by students were especially fond of this line of reasoning. Speaking of the state university, Professor Norman Foerster wrote: "Whom it can provide for should properly be decided by an entrance examination, though this expedient is regarded as an anathema even by educationists, enthusiastic over the new science of testing and measurement."

By entrance examinations Foerster of course meant subject-matter examinations of the College Board type. These had greatly favored the graduates of private preparatory schools which made a specialty of drilling their pupils for College Boards. The more prosperous graduates of public high schools often paid for special tutoring to cram for the examinations. Harvard, Yale and Princeton were surrounded by cramming schools. Foerster's hostility to the newer aptitude tests is not unrelated to his dislike of subjects having vocational usefulness and of humanitarianism, which he regarded as the antithesis of humanism. Apparently in his lexicon the social sciences were humanitarian and therefore damned. It was in the Middle Ages "that the intellect itself . . . attained an astonishing keenness and penetration which it has since progressively lost."

This intransigent attitude for which Foerster was a leading spokesman helped to produce the very excesses of vocational education against which the conservatives were protesting. Instead of participating in and guiding the educational developments of the time, they braced their feet and called names. An increasing proportion of American young folk were determined on a college education; they and their parents wanted that education to lead to some goal less vague than culture or intellectual development. The psychologists supported them in their view that the mind had to be educated for something, that mental discipline for its own sake was too much like training a runner by means of setting-up exercises.

The conflict had been developing for a long time before the postwar flood of students brought it to a showdown. How steady and rapid was the increase of both numbers and percentages is illustrated by the following table:

Year	Enrollment	Per cent of population 18-21 years of age, inclusive
1890	156,756	3.04
1900	237,592	4.01
1910	355,213	4.84
1920	597,880	8.14
1930	1,100,737	12.37

Faced with such a steady and continuing trend, the conservatives who demanded limitation of enrollments should have recognized instead the similarity of such an attempt to that of King Canute—a person they ought to have known about even if they were contemptuous of statistical measurement.

The inhospitality to students usually took the form of a refusal to expand course offerings in liberal-arts curriculums. Thus courses in journalism, denied a place in English departments, proliferated into separate departments; statistics, finding no place in traditional mathematics, went over to schools of business or developed independently; even public speaking, traditionally a part of literature and rhetoric, was forced to set up in business for itself. Perhaps the most tragic divorce was that between learning and pedagogy which produced the separate domiciles of the liberal arts and the teachers' colleges. The fantastic anti-intellectualism of Columbia Teachers' College and its progeny, both legitimate and bastard, throughout the nation is largely the result of the refusal of traditional educators to make adequate provision for the training of teachers. Professors of traditional subjects insisted that if a college graduate knew mathematics or French or English literature, he was adequately equipped to teach those subjects in high school; they refused to see that a knowledge of calculus, Racine, or Chaucer did not have much bearing on the high-school curriculum. And the professors of liberal arts were completely oblivious of the huge proportion of high-school students who were not going to college, who needed not French or trigonometry, but bookkeeping, typing, and civics.

Teachers' colleges, cut off from the genuine values of a cultural education, chased after every fad and fancy dreamed up by the so-called progressive educators. They studied English by carving Macbeth's castle out of soap; they did theses on dishwashing and janitorial work; they adopted meaningless slogans such as "teaching pupils, not subjects"—which implies that a progressive educator can teach a pupil without teaching him anything. They developed a trade language "pedagese"; their research turned up such truths as the discovery that pupils of different size need seats of varying height; they dealt in large generalizations about government and society like George Sylvester Counts's assertion that "Capitalism no longer works," or William Heard Kilpatrick's analogy of the yearly change of automobile models to demonstrate that the Constitution was obsolete. Even their patron saint, John Dewey, denied some of the heresies promulgated in his name.

Because the attitude of the liberal-arts colleges suggested that of the father in *East Lynne* turning his daughter out into the snow, the spurned daughter retaliated by setting up a house of ill fame on the same street. By the 1930s and 1940s the teachers' colleges had become a national scandal for low standards, for overemphasis on technique, and for the proliferation of repetitious courses in "education" to a point where these occupied a third or more of the curriculum. As had happened with football, popular magazines published exposés and demanded reform.

Professors of liberal arts also became perturbed. In trade journals such as the academic quarterlies and the *Bulletin of the American Association of University Professors* they published scores of articles attacking vocationalism and defending liberal education and the humanities—not always clearly defined, but alleged to produce such results as "stimulating . . . a critical and aesthetic taste"; "teach hope, love, and courage"; "recognize or retrieve those eternal truths which are above the stream of evolution and change." However students, trustees, and alumni were inclined to demand evolution and change on the grounds that hope, love, and courage were an inadequate preparation for modern life. They could have added that the traditionalists more often talked about aesthetics than taught or practiced them. With the development of specialized vocabularies, even specialized styles for each discipline, scholarly writing became incomprehensible to anyone but the elect. Between 1900 and 1928 the annual output of Ph.D.s went up from fewer than 400 to nearly 2,000. The quality of learned prose went down in about the same proportion.

The inability of scholars to write in an intelligible style and their unwillingness to relate their work to the contemporary world led to bitter and sometimes shortsighted attacks from alumni. At Yale, even before the end of the war, the *Yale Alumni Weekly* stated: "We are through for good . . . with the old aimless college course." In February 1919 the Alumni Committee on a Plan for University Development reported ". . . the structure of the University needs changing to meet new problems. . . ." This Committee appointed by the Corporation brought in such recommendations as:

That a definite course of instruction, or that a curriculum consisting of a consistent and largely prescribed character be provided . . . leading to each of the several professional schools, or towards the life work of various students.

That emphasis among the instructors in such undergraduate school be laid on teaching rather than on research work.

The bitter and complicated controversy which followed also involved problems of organization within the university structure. Of more general significance was that faculty intransigence led to an alumni revolt which not only forced reforms over faculty opposition, but brought with it an attack on permanent tenure for professors and a demand for limitation of their powers over appointments and promotions. Midwestern alumni in particular were bitter against entrance requirements which favored the graduates of Eastern prep schools. As a result, Yale for the first time dropped Latin as an absolute requirement for admission. But after assessing the real values of the reorganization of the university, chiefly the more efficient integration of its various units, the Yale historian, George W. Pierson, comments:

Nevertheless . . . it becomes plain that the years 1917-21 did mark an unhappy turning point in the career of the College Faculty. . . . In ways only dimly understood the war had brought the whole value of a liberal education into question. Then, in ways only too obvious, this imposed Reorganization had reduced the independence of the College and shaken the Faculty's morale. Authority and confidence in itself were undermined.

A few years later Amherst underwent an even more violent upheaval over some of the same issues. With the forced resignation of Alexander Meiklejohn as president in 1923, the conservatives on the faculty won a tactical if not a moral victory. In his inaugural address in 1912 Meiklejohn had attacked the fragmentation of knowledge into a series of unrelated courses, and had proposed a program of general education for freshmen and sophomores, planned and taught as a unified whole. In outlining his theory of the function of a liberal college he had argued against training for specific vocations, but had insisted on the practical aim of giving the student "some kind of interpretation of his own experience and of the world in which he lives."

Valid as was much of the criticism, the tone of the address had a certain sharpness; it suggested a schoolmaster lecturing a recalcitrant class. In the controversies which developed during Meiklejohn's administration, it is more than usually difficult to separate issues from personalities. On paper, especially as described by the liberal educators and journalists who espoused Meiklejohn's cause, the issues seem to be the old ones of faculty resistance to academic change and of alumni alarm over "radicalism." But especially in a small community, a college president's relationship with his faculty is not only a matter of shared or conflicting views; it involves social groupings and loyalties; it depends on the tone of official and personal conversations; even the gossip of faculty wives is important. A young faculty member wrote in *The Nation* that a neighbor of his thought that the controversy centered on the failure of four of the new men to keep their lawns mowed.

Certainly the older members of the faculty resented what seemed like Meiklejohn's favoritism to new men and his tactless remarks about the older faculty. On the other hand, it was the new men who were willing to try new methods and to introduce more effective teaching. The president was not an Amherst man, and into a close-knit academic community made up largely of alumni of the college he brought other outsiders. In the curriculum he gave prominence to what he called humanistic science, a field still viewed suspiciously by scholars in the older disciplines. Probably a professor of Greek could have left his lawn unmowed with impunity.

Meiklejohn put his finger on the basic problem of all those who would reform college education: "The Faculty find it

PRINCETON–YALE FOOTBALL CROWD, NEW HAVEN, 1915

REGISTRATION: TEMPLE UNIVERSITY, 1950

An important development after 1900 was the growth of city colleges, both public and private.
Most students lived at home, and many worked after classes.

exceedingly difficult to improve themselves, and they find it exceedingly objectionable to have anyone else do it to them." At Amherst, as at Yale, the changes resisted by the faculty were to be rather generally adopted in colleges and universities within the next twenty-five years: such things as a common freshman year, an integrated curriculum of general education, greater emphasis on the social sciences. As had happened with earlier modifications in the curriculum, the changes came largely because of community pressures or administrative leadership. To believers in a more democratic system of university control it is disturbing to note how often faculties have resisted or blocked necessary changes. Meiklejohn's own belief was that boards of trustees should be abolished, and that a college should be governed by its faculty with the president as an officer of the faculty.

In the Amherst controversy the faculty gained the support of the type of alumnus and trustee who as a rule is unsympathetic to academic freedom. One alumnus brought up an incident of six months before American entry into the war when Meiklejohn had insisted on representation of those opposed to war at a meeting to discuss preparedness. Said the alumnus of the president: "His attitude [was] against what all red-blooded Americans were thinking at that time." Meiklejohn was further criticized for establishing classes in collaboration with labor unions in Holyoke and Springfield, and for saying that a man's moral beliefs had nothing to do with his fitness for a professorship because morality was "a debatable subject."

As so often happened in the 1920s, students found themselves at loggerheads with their elders on the faculty and board of trustees. In an attempt to keep Meiklejohn the senior class sent a delegation to New York for a conference with the trustees. For a time it seemed as if the whole class might refuse their degrees; in the end thirteen actually did refuse. Whatever mistakes the president may have made, the most damning testimony against the faculty conservatives appeared in an article in the *Amherst Student* which said of the president:

Under his inspiration men who before saw education as a cut and dried compulsory affair of dull facts and duller figures have seen it take on color and meaning until it has become for them a living thing fraught with all the significance of life.

The uproars at Yale and Amherst thus dramatized some of the fundamental issues in higher education. The fact that both institutions were among the best in the nation is all the more evidence of how far higher education had lost touch with the felt needs of students and alumni. At dozens of other colleges where no alumni or presidential prodding materialized, the faculty slumbered on while the students found color and meaning not in the classroom but on the football field and in the fraternity house.

Nevertheless a new air had begun to blow through some musty college halls. Attacks from conservative and reactionary groups in the community tended to shift faculty sympathy from those groups and their administrative appointees, to the liberal or occasionally radical elements in the intellectual world. Professors began more often to read *The Nation, The New Republic* and the *American Mercury*. Even magazines with a conservative background increasingly spoke for liberal views: *Harper's* carried Mrs. Gerould's attack on thought control through fear; *The Atlantic* published Professor Frankfurter's defense of Sacco and Vanzetti; the *Century* opened its pages to President Meiklejohn.

When Glenn Frank, the editor of the *Century*, became president of the University of Wisconsin, he invited Meiklejohn to join the faculty, and in 1926 the two men laid plans for an experimental college within the university. Here Meiklejohn was permitted to develop an integrated program of study for freshmen and sophomores. An experimental college of a different type, Sarah Lawrence, opened in 1928, drew on the theories of John Dewey in developing an educational program which attempted to relate study more closely to the student's experience in the community, and to use the student's interests as the foundation on which to build individualized programs of study.

Less drastic but perhaps more important because of their

wider adoption were the various modifications of existing curriculums to permit and encourage the superior student to take
more responsibility for his own education. By 1924 President
Aydelotte of Swarthmore found forty-four American colleges
and universities which had honors courses. Most of these based
honors on work taken in addition to the ordinary requirements,
but nine provided honors courses which took the place of the
regular program. At Columbia such work took the form of the
great-books course developed after the war by John Erskine.
Smith College developed an honors course in 1921 and Swarthmore in 1922. The Swarthmore plan permitted the superior
student to omit a considerable amount of classroom work in
order to undertake an extensive program of individual reading
in preparation for comprehensive examinations. Rollins College, under Hamilton Holt, dropped the lecture system entirely
in favor of conferences and discussions which required the
student to hunt up his own information. In 1924 Princeton
adopted the "Four Course Plan" designed to give juniors and
seniors more freedom in their reading, converging on a particular subject, and terminating in a thesis and comprehensive
examination.

Still another type of development was the co-operative plan,
first applied to engineering and later to business. Although it
originated at the University of Cincinnati, it was developed
most fully by Arthur E. Morgan at Antioch, where it became
the standard program. A number of other institutions adopted
it as an alternative to the regular four-year course. Under the
co-operative plan a student usually alternates five weeks in
classes and laboratories with five weeks in industry. The long
summer vacation is dispensed with, and the whole course requires five years.

Of all the various experiments, the co-operative plan is most
characteristically American: it combines practical experience
with theoretical knowledge; it enables the student to earn much
of his own educational expenses; and it leads directly to a
vocation. Its roots lie in the manual-labor colleges of the 1830s
and in the doctrines of Emerson and Thoreau. To the Ameri-

can scholar Emerson had preached: "Years are well spent in country labors; in town; in the insight into trades and manufactures. . . ." And Thoreau had argued that the man who made his own jackknife from ore he had smelted himself would learn more about chemistry and metallurgy than he could get from lectures and textbooks. John Dewey's doctrine of learning by doing is in the same tradition.

The programs introduced at Sarah Lawrence and later at Bennington (1932) stem directly from the theories of John Dewey. Because of high tuition Sarah Lawrence has tended to be a posh school drawing its faculty and students from a sophisticated elite. Thus it is likely to go in for *avant-garde* literary, sociological and political ideas—an important service, but not always a useful pattern for the college education of the nation as a whole. Experimental colleges are valuable as laboratories, but laboratory results cannot always be reproduced in ordinary life. For one thing, the faculties of such institutions are likely to be unusually alert, vivid personalities. Just as a Mark Hopkins could bring classical curriculum to life, so a brilliant scholar-teacher can bring intellectual discipline into "progressive" education. Almost any system of education is effective in the hands of superior teachers. Conversely, when conducted by run-of-the-mill faculty a plan like that at Sarah Lawrence was a comparative failure at one institution—even though the students were highly selected.

At Minnesota, President Lotus D. Coffman's committee on Educational Guidance issued in 1923 what the university historian, James Gray, calls a Magna Charta of students' rights. The report insisted that the freshman be told precisely what the university could do in preparing him for a profession or vocation, and what the opportunities were in various fields. It recommended special vocational guidance for women. For those students who needed it there should be psychiatric help. It suggested a "quality credit rule" for superior students. By 1928 the university had developed techniques for classifying all freshmen according to abilities. Four years later it set up an educational testing bureau under Edmund G. Williamson, who believed it "a terrific indictment of the educational system that fine intelligences were being leveled down to mediocrity because no one quite knew what to do with them." Scientific measurement also provided a means to salvage many a weak or floundering student. This work at Minnesota became the model for similar testing and guidance throughout the country during the next decades. Its roots lay, of course, in the pioneering work of men like Cattell and Thorndike. Testing and guidance were one of the great developments of the era. They provided the means for bringing into mass education some of the values of the old small college.

The importance of developments such as honors programs, reading periods, tutorials, comprehensive examinations, and senior theses is that they preserved the values of a liberal education, or rather, brought them into American higher education. They got away from emphasis on routine lectures and drill; they encouraged individual effort, respected individual interests and aptitudes; and they provided an excellent training for later graduate and professional study. To a considerable degree they changed the wealthier institutions from country clubs into educational enterprises.

These varied innovations and experiments all led to important developments in the next two decades: in fact, almost the entire pattern of higher education for the next era had been sketched in outline. Thus the period which ended with the crash of 1929 was greater in prophecy than in performance. For a large proportion of the students it had been the biggest party in the history of the colleges. In their yellow slickers and coonskin coats they had driven Stutzes, Mercers and tin lizzies to the most gaudy football spectacles ever produced; they had thumbed their noses at their elders to indulge in necking and bootleg gin; they had fox-trotted cheek to cheek to the best dance music ever written in America; some of them had experienced the heady excitement of an intellectual revolution. For the faculty it had been a time of uncertainty, conflict, poverty, and persecution, but they too had felt the impact of new ideas, new projects. The excesses, the materialism of the war years and the jazz age had forced the intellectuals to re-evaluate their function in society. Despite all the stresses, the conflicts, the tragedies, the colleges were probably healthier in 1929 than in 1914, more ready to participate in the rebuilding of the nation.

9

Question Period

The depression touched the colleges lightly. This fact is not immediately observable in the voluminous and sometimes agonized faculty publications dealing with the subject. The professors had not shared in the boom and many were therefore not inclined to feel the justice of being asked to share the hardships of the bust. But at least statistically the colleges fared better than business and industry. For one thing the depression was slow in reaching the campus, its real impact being delayed until 1932. In fact, during 1930 and 1931 staff members enjoyed the benefits of fixed salaries in a time of rapidly falling prices. Even when salary cuts became the rule (eighty-four per cent of the colleges made such cuts) the profession as a whole was more affluent than it had been during the boom. A sampling of the figures compiled by Committee Y of the American Association of University Professors will indicate what happened:

Year	Index of university salaries	Cost of living	Purchasing power of median university salaries
1913-1914	100.0	100.0	100.0
1917-1918	108.7	135.6	80.2
1919-1920	135.3	196.3	68.9
1923-1924	169.0	175.1	95.5
1927-1928	180.3	173.6	103.9
1930-1931	187.7	160.4	117.0
1932-1933	174.1	135.9	128.1
1934-1935	160.2	140.6	113.9

Thus it was not until 1927 that faculty salaries bought as much as they had before World War I, but even in the depths of the depression they bought more than in 1914.

A comparison based on somewhat incomplete data indicates

that in terms of dollars, the academic profession suffered a smaller percentage decline than did five other professions: *

	Loss, per cent
Consulting engineers	62.2
Dentists	47.3
Physicians and surgeons	42.9
Lawyers	30.2
Clergymen	26.4
College faculty members	15.0

Over-all figures do not of course tell the whole story. Some institutions (sixteen per cent) made no cuts at all; a few cut salaries by over twenty-five per cent. In general the magnitude of the cuts was least at the private institutions and in the East. On the other hand, legislatures often made reductions in salaries mandatory in state-supported institutions. Some colleges reduced salaries on a straight percentage basis, others on a differential basis, such as a provision that the first $1,000 be exempt from reduction.

Painful as were the more drastic salary cuts, the worst effect of the depression was unemployment. Here too the colleges fared better than other enterprises. In Philadelphia and vicinity, for instance, fifty banks closed, but no colleges. Throughout the country, student enrollment dropped in 1933-1934 to 92.1 per cent of the peak year of 1931-1932, and faculties shrank to 96.4 per cent during the same period. But percentages are not people. Some 80,000 students who would have gone to college did not get there, and several thousand teachers either lost their jobs or failed to find employment on the completion of graduate work. As the A.A.U.P. study reveals, the lowest rank in the faculty heirarchy suffered worst. Professors kept their jobs; instructors were dropped when reductions were made in staff. Promotions were slow in coming or brought "dry raises" —improvements in rank but not in salary. However, in reviewing the situation as a whole, Committee Y of the A.A.U.P. stated that "the pinch of depression was more acute in some

---

* By permission from *Depression, Recovery and Higher Education*, by Malcolm M. Willey. Copyright, 1937, McGraw-Hill Book Company, Inc.

other professions than among college faculty members. . . .
Times were hard and ambitions may have been blocked, yet
the adjustments required of teachers at the college level cannot be said to be more devastating or disrupting of morale and
standards of living than in other professions." Thus despite individual hardships and squawks, faculty members as represented
by their chief organization maintained an objective calm not
always characteristic of other groups.

A less admirable professorial trait was revealed in their comparative failure to act together either in their own interest or
in organized attempts to deal with university problems created
by the depression. In the entire country the chief professional
organization, the American Association of University Professors, had only 300 chapters and 13,377 members in 1937. Yet
there were in the country over 900 colleges, universities, inde-
pendent professional schools, and teachers colleges, with faculties totaling over 90,000. Thus only about one out of every
fourteen faculty members was willing to join with his fellows in working for their mutual welfare. Unionization made
scarcely a dent; the Federation of Teachers had a mere twenty-
eight locals in 1936. In analyzing the reasons for this situation,
Committee Y of the A.A.U.P. lists "a tradition of dignity"
which holds that the profession has nothing in common with
labor, a timidity or inertia, and a spirit of individualism. In
some institutions faculty members feared to discuss openly any
view which might run counter to administration practice. Even
at those places which had chapters of the A.A.U.P. only twenty-
three per cent held meetings between 1930 and 1936 to discuss
salary cuts or restorations. A particularly unhandsome phase of
this sort of behavior is the spirit of every-man-for-himself reflected in the rivalries between ranks and between departments.
In the words of Committee Y: "The prevailing departmental set-up has tended to make staff members departmentally
minded, with each division seeking to advance its own interests." The Committee could not find convincing evidence that
the depression changed the situation.

This failure to work together for mutual welfare in an emergency helps to explain the larger failure of faculties to work together for comprehensive educational goals. Despite the characteristic faculty lunch-table griping represented by Veblen's *The Higher Learning in America,* the professors have shown small aptitude or willingness to undertake university statesmanship. They have seldom followed Franklin's advice that "We must hang together or we shall each hang separately," or pondered Madison's prescription for the control of faction.

The effect of the depression on student mores was probably greater than on those of the faculty. The studies conducted in 1936 by the A.A.U.P. and *Fortune* both agree that student radicalism was negligible, but there was a new seriousness of purpose. College polls showed students voting for the Democratic or Republican candidates of their fathers' choice; but in bull sessions, economics became the chief topic of discussion. A new type of college leader emerged. The old-style campus big shot no longer dominated the scene: the football star, the "muscular Christian" from the college "Y," the smoothie from the big prep school who became a track manager, ran the yearbook and organized class banquets and proms. These did not disappear but they yielded ground to the editorial writer for the student paper, the organizer of forums and discussion groups. Students followed the pattern of Walter Lippmann rather than Walter Camp. They demanded courses in Communism, Fascism, and the works of Thomas Jefferson, but did not often join a *Bund* or Communist cell.

They did, however, develop typically undergraduate organizations like the Jacobin Club at Minnesota and the Veterans of Future Wars at Princeton. The Jacobin Club held mock political conventions, and discussed Fascism, Communism and the Oxford Oath. Inspired in part by the revelations of historians about the Allies' share of responsibility for World War I, and the investigations of the Nye Committee of the Senate into the shenanigans of munitions makers, students tended to be pacifistic. Robert Sherwood's play, *Idiot's Delight,* shows the mood of the times. At Yale, Walter Millis' *Road to War* was a popular book, and helped to create an anti-foreign-entanglement sentiment. At institutions where military drill was compulsory, there were student protests and, at a number of places, revolts. Wisconsin made drill optional, and DePauw abolished it. Throughout the country a few dedicated students took the Oxford Oath against participating in war.

The leftist American Student Union, capitalizing on the sentiment against war and Fascism, attracted many liberal and progressive students who had no enthusiasm for a collectivist society and who were not aware of the behind-the-scenes Communist domination of the organization. When in April 1936 the A.S.U. organized a Peace Strike, the leaders claimed that 500,000 undergraduates in school and college cut classes. However, as *Fortune* points out, the sincere strikers were outnumbered by those who turned out to see the excitement and to find an excuse for a holiday. It is worth noting that, despite peace sentiment at Yale, students refused to join the Peace Strike because it was run by the "black men" or "meat balls."

The Veterans of Future Wars, dreamed up by a Princeton student, Lewis J. Gorin, Jr., although related to pacifistic movements, was mainly a satiric attack on soldier bonus bills. In its brief life the Veterans of Future Wars flourished chiefly at the wealthier Eastern colleges.

Despite the alarm of the American Legion and the D.A.R., most students maintained a wait-and-see attitude. Only the hired patriots of college football squads were likely to throw tomatoes at pacifistic speakers like Oswald Garrison Villard. To what extent they were acting as administration goon squads, as some liberals charged, has never been revealed. And when war actually came in Europe, it was only the small Communist-front organizations which painted walls and sidewalks with the slogan, "The Yanks aren't coming."

Because of the interest in the problems of the depression and the growing world crisis, there was a shift in student leadership, a change which *Fortune* called "so clear and striking that it amounts to a structural change in the undergraduate world." The new type of leader with his skill in debating or editorial writing began to resemble the Oxford or Cambridge undergraduate preparing for a career in the civil service. Students began to ask how to get into politics, to invite such speakers as Harold Laski, Norman Thomas, Hugh S. Johnson, Arthur Krock, Raymond Moley, Fiorello La Guardia, Edmund Wilson and Jouett Shouse. They flocked to courses in economics, sociology, and political science. No doubt the prominence of intellectuals in the New Deal had much to do with this shift in thinking. Gone were the days when a Henry Adams could write that there was no place in Washington for respectable young men of promise, that the government didn't want them. For the second time since the Civil War there was a place for the highly educated civil servant. The screams and cartoons against the "Brain Trust" which filled the Hearst press and its sort were testimony to the importance of the college-trained expert. And although liberal professors and students rarely joined radical organizations, they united in a hatred of the die-hards of the Hearst-McCormick press, the D.A.R. and the American Legion. Every time one of these groups attacked a textbook or a professor, they made hundreds of students aware of the cause of academic freedom. By the end of the decade student polls went increasingly for Roosevelt; more and more students set their sights on government service. At Princeton, which in the 1920s had been the great training ground for bond salesmen and bankers, the School of Public and International Affairs, established 1930, grew so rapidly that by 1941 it acquired a building of its own, and in 1946 became the Woodrow Wilson School of Public and International Affairs with a separate endowment.

People who had attended college with Stover or remembered nostalgically the excitements of the ivory hunts were inclined to deplore the undergraduates' interest in security as represented by salaried jobs in government, education, or industry. Students tended to view the good life in terms of the permanent job with a $10,000 or $15,000 ceiling and a retirement plan, rather than as a speculative scramble for the big money. They rarely discussed the theme of "the first million." In large part this was a natural reaction to the spectacle of the wonder boys of the classes of 1900-1920 jumping out of tenth-story windows and of the bond salesmen and engineers of more recent classes taking twenty-dollar-a-week jobs or working on "projects" for the W.P.A. Security looked very attractive to the boy whose elder brother had lost his job or to the girl whose sister with two babies had moved in with the home folks. But the nostalgic critics who saw a weakening of the pioneering spirit of Daniel Boone, Buffalo Bill and Henry Ford often failed to recognize a certain idealism in the shift of values. Government, education, research, and technology held the promise of a better world. The remaking of a whole region through a TVA challenged the imagination; it was much more in the pioneering tradition than the finagling of a Samuel Insull in utility holding companies. The president of the nation's second largest bank went to jail; the President of the nation talked of solving the problems of one third of the population who were ill housed, ill clothed and ill fed. Whatever the final verdict of history will be on the wisdom of Franklin Roosevelt's policies, it cannot be denied that in the 1930s he fired the imagination of a host of young Americans. A job in a government bureau was not merely a safe haven; it was for many the enlistment in the cause of humanity.

Furthermore, the Federal Government played a more important part in college education than at any time since the first Morrill Act. At a time when private donations were at a low ebb and state legislatures were curtailing appropriations, the Federal Relief Administration, followed by the National Youth Administration, stepped in with financial aid to college students. In 1936-1937 the NYA, through its program of grants to colleges for student employment, aided 124,818 undergraduate and graduate students. Although this was but eight per cent of college enrollments, it nevertheless set a pattern for the more far-reaching G.I. aid for the veterans of World War II.

The twenty-dollars-a-week maximum under the NYA program was specifically allocated to able students who otherwise could not attend college. This qualification was not always synonymous with the requirements for the jobs to which the colleges assigned them. Untrained girls working at odd hours for college libraries messed up the stacks; graduate students in economics did a poor job correcting freshman themes or exercises in Spanish. Somehow the Spanish or English major desired by those departments either failed to qualify for aid or was requisitioned by the dean's office as a file clerk. Many students regarded the aid as a sinecure, as indeed it often was. The supervision of untrained personnel available only a few hours a day at such intervals as did not conflict with classes often proved more bother than it was worth. Faculty members found it easier to shoo off the NYA workers than to pick up after them. The scheme, although it met some emergency needs, was not an unqualified success.

Another method of federal aid took the form of building funds from the Public Works Administration. Beginning in 1933 the program was designed to stimulate employment in the construction industry. At first the grants were thirty per cent of the expenditure for labor and materials; in 1935 they were increased to forty-five per cent. Additional federal funds could be borrowed. Under the PWA grants and loans the colleges undertook construction costing $58,834,048. Undoubtedly some of this was vitally needed, but faculty members, alarmed at falling salaries and curtailed expenditures for educational services, raised questions about the wisdom of putting so much into stone and mortar. Such criticism was not motivated solely by selfish interest; faculty members know that reduced library budgets can do damage reaching far into the future. Books go out of print and back numbers of periodicals are often hard to find. The effect of overcrowded classes and canceled courses is even more difficult to assess. A new dormitory may be more impressive than the continued purchase of books or the continuance of small classes, but it may be less important.

The controversy over plant versus personnel is an old one. Obviously some sort of balance must be struck between them, and specific projects must be weighed in terms of the situation in a particular college. In this area of policy making, however, most faculties have a valid complaint over their inadequate share in making decisions. The laymen on boards of trustees have often been more concerned about buildings than services. All too seldom are the chemists or physicists asked which they need more—new laboratories or a larger staff.

The effect of the depression on buildings and budgets is easier to assess than its effect on students. Even such measurable data as increased enrollments in economics, sociology, and political science is not conclusive evidence; the development was under way before 1930. We can only assume that the depression stimulated the trend. As for changes in student manners and mores, it can only be said with assurance that they took place. The causes of such changes are so complex as to tempt one to resort to concepts like *Zeitgeist*.

Take for instance the disappearance of the raccoon coat early in the thirties. This might seem an obvious result of the depression, but it was also a change of fashion which would have come anyway. With it went also the cheap yellow slicker decorated with autographs, slogans and bathing girls. The automobile did not disappear from the campus but it no longer was painted with odd designs and wisecracks. In so far as that fashion survived, it was the mark of the high-school jalopy. The point is that it was no longer smart to be collegiate.

The men adopted an informal style resembling that of Oxford and Cambridge: tweed jacket and gray slacks (the American rarely called them bags). Shoes were almost invariably white saddle oxfords which in no circumstances could be cleaned. No matter what the weather a hat was not permitted, although in very cold regions a skating cap could be worn. In the East the typical college girl wore a tweed skirt and a sweater, often knitted by herself. (Tolerant instructors sometimes permitted knitting during lectures.) Her low-heeled shoes resembled her brother's; she used no make-up and little lipstick. Girls in the South and Midwest were less untidy and more dressy. At city colleges both boys and girls tended to follow the fashions of the varied social groups from which they came. Styles ranged all the way from Third Avenue models to copies of Princeton and Bryn Mawr.

In place of the nose-thumbing unconventionality of the twenties there was a quiet sophistication. If a student drank, he no longer made an issue of it. Among the girls, cigarettes had become as much an accepted part of life as the Coke or milk shake. Dormitory rules commonly forbade smoking in their rooms, but sometimes permitted it in a lounge room. Around the tables of the campus sweetshop, the girl who did not smoke was the exception. The *Fortune* survey found that both men and women took sex much more calmly than in the jazz age. Sexual matters were regarded as one's own business. The majority of students did not put any particular premium on virginity or at least thought that they did not, but they did not regard promiscuity as very pretty. As *Fortune* summed it up: "The code seems to indicate: reasonable restraint, particularly on the part of the girls, before marriage, and fidelity on both sides after marriage." Only in those Pacific Coast universities under the Hollywood influence did the investigators find a lingering of the jazz-age experimental attitude.

By the end of the decade the patterns of dating and dancing had changed. In the twenties a girl might go to college dances with a new man each time; in fact, the man who brought her was not necessarily the man who drove her home. Stags played the field. This free-for-all pattern had been most highly developed in the South where a girl at a college house party often made a series of dates: lunch with one boy, tea dancing with another, a quick one at eight, the prom with her host, and one or two late dates after it. But in the thirties boys and girls more often went steady. If they broke up, each might find a permanent or semipermanent partner. The cut-in dance declined in popularity. By the 1940s a couple might dance together for the whole evening, or possibly exchange one or two dances with the couples they had come with.

This change reflected the less hectic quality of student social life. One contributing cause, especially after World War II, was the growth of student bodies. Except at the smaller colleges, there was the growing impersonality of the city. During the depression fraternities could less often afford to put on a big party with an orchestra imported from New York or Chicago—a "name band." There were sophomore hops, junior and senior proms, but much of the time a couple bent on dancing went to a roadhouse or juke-box joint, either alone or with a double date. At many places, for the price of a few beers or Cokes, they could spend an hour or two dancing to a small orchestra or a coin-operated record player. Even the development of jitterbugging around 1940 contributed to this dance floor monogamy: a boy and girl practiced intricate steps and acrobatics until they became a team of skilled performers. However, at the more sophisticated colleges jitterbug dances had only limited vogue.

As so often happens, the novel of college life catches the atmosphere of a period. Probably the best of all college novels is George Anthony Weller's *Not to Eat, Not for Love* (1933). Although the time of the story is the late twenties, the psychological climate is more characteristic of a later student generation. Just as F. Scott Fitzgerald's Princeton foreshadowed the jazz-age college, so Weller's Harvard was a preview of student life elsewhere. The culture lag between manners and mores of the wealthy Eastern colleges and those elsewhere seems to be about a student generation—roughly four years.

The seeds of undergraduate culture are carried from the fashionable institutions by college publications, by boys and girls returning to their home communities, by recently graduated teachers, and by a certain amount of visiting back and forth. In Weller's novel, two Harvard sophisticates make subtle sport of some naïve fraternity men who have followed their college team to Cambridge. Speaking of one of the visitors named Galt, Wells Fargo remarks, "He's the last of a strange race. They never can come again. He ought to be kept intact and perfect and original, and by taking him in we are doing our share for posterity." More aware visitors than young Galt quickly caught on to the fact that they were becoming museum pieces.

An important but unsung culture carrier is the attractive, wealthy "transfer student." Dropped from some fashionable institution for poor scholarship, the transfer enrolls at a less prosperous and more tolerant college or university, bringing along well-tailored clothes, a swank car, and social graces. Boys and girls of this type tend to associate with the social leaders of their adopted campuses, and thus become models for the manners and dress of those arbiters of college society. It is a generally accepted principle of American life that the owner of a Cadillac convertible can never be wrong.

Not all the spread of student fashion is from East to West; a fad like the swallowing of live goldfish can originate anywhere. From the Pacific Coast came the cultural contribution of the drum majorette. Although this innovation was not well adapted to colder climates, it spread, despite chapped knees and goose pimples, to coeducational institutions all over the country.

The sex mores and dating habits of students are only to a small degree academic products; rather, they are an adaptation of community behavior. The "going steady" pattern seems to be a characteristic phenomenon of the American high school; whereas debutante parties, with hostess lists of eligible men, foster variety in social relationships. Thus in college, boys and girls from fashionable schools are likely to date and dance with a larger number of partners than are students with a public-school background. At any given college or university the class which predominates among the student leaders sets the tone of social life. Differences between student behavior at Princeton and Minnesota are probably due less to the influence of those institutions than to the differing proportion of prep-school and high-school graduates in their respective student bodies.

However, a growing sophistication can be noted among students at most institutions except perhaps at the jerkwater colleges. The schoolteacher discovered by *Life* who had never heard of *Harper's* or the *Atlantic* was no doubt a product of some shabby normal school turned into a half-baked college. The prevailing increase in sophistication appeared in college dramatic productions, in the choice of music by glee clubs, in the serious literary magazines. It was a trend which began in the twenties, but which became much more general after 1932.

An unlamented loss was the disappearance of many of the college humor magazines—victims of an improvement in student literary taste, and the loss of cigarette advertising during the depression. The campus sale of *College Humor* dropped to almost nothing. Especially in the East, good prints and etchings displaced pennants as dormitory decorations.

George Weller's Harvard students of 1929 are more mature emotionally and intellectually than the brash boys and girls of the college novels covering the preceding era. Fitzgerald's Amory Blaine, Marks's Hugh Carver, and the boys and girls of *Town and Gown* seem five years younger than Wells Fargo, Severn Beed, and Epes Todd of *Not to Eat, Not for Love*. In the Montross stories there is Andy Protheroe, described as "a gentleman of the school variously known as Slickers, Lizards, Fussers, Snakes, Tea-Hounds, Neckers, or Sheiks." As one might expect, his "line" to a girl runs like this: "I don't ask it for myself. . . . I ask it only in respect to our elders—Mrs. Lampeer and the deans and the older generation would be so disappointed if we didn't pet just a little." On the other hand, Weller's Severn Beed, a practiced Don Juan, is much more subtle. After a too-hasty attempt to seduce a girl,

He got up, fearful that he would say something severing. He walked slowly across the room, and as he reached the fire and put out his hands he thought, now I am really playing, at last. . . .
Already he knew Ruth Wheeler well enough not to expect that she would turn avengingly formal on his hands, but he was a little afraid that she might think the right thing would be to scatter sunbeams. She did neither. She simply let him pace the recovery and responded completely to it at each point.

No doubt Weller is a more skilled writer than the Montrosses, but the difference in sensibility of the two books reflects also the difference in sensibility in students of different eras. A Montross student who bought a ticket to a symphony was kidded so unmercifully by his fraternity brothers that he gave it away. In Weller's novel one of the bonds between Beed and Ruth Wheeler was that "their taste in the indisputably great music proved to be strangely similar." Another student, Epes Todd, took a girl to a program of Christmas carols in Appelton Chapel:

When they came out, they were in the predicament of those who have never spoken unguardedly with each other; the music had exposed them. They walked toward Sever. One of the French hymns had brought up words in Epes from another carol he had known, *The first Noel the angel did say,* and they repeated themselves over so steadily that it seemed she must hear them and remain silent out of fear of interruption.

They walked around the romanesque fortress of Sever. They caught sight of the Chapel again, with someone locking the side door, and she said, "My trouble, after evenings like this, is to find out which music I heard and which was my own."

By the mid-1930s glee clubs everywhere were abandoning "The Bull Frog on the Bank" in favor of Bach. When students could afford it, they bought classical records and visited one another's rooms to hear them. In library browsing rooms and the lounges of student union buildings, boys and girls sat in silence listening to recordings or argued about the merits of Toscanini, Menuhin or Rachmaninoff. The change in taste as represented by improved glee-club programs stems in large part from the work of Dr. Archibald T. Davison, who made the Harvard glee club into one of the great musical organizations of the country. Students elsewhere who heard it sing Gregorian chants or old English madrigals recognized the barbershop quality of much of the usual campus music. A similar change took place in regard to chamber music, orchestras and bands. A study prepared in 1935 for the Association of American Colleges found that serious interest in instumental music was widespread and carried "a prestige unthought of in the days when banjo and mandolin clubs were the only instrumental release that college afforded."

Some of this of course was closely related to the formal study of music which had become a part of the curriculum at over seventy per cent of the institutions in the Association of American Colleges. However, music courses often carried degree credit only for music majors, or to a very limited extent for the A.B. Therefore, developments like *a cappella* choirs and college symphony orchestras were usually linked to the professional training of musicians and music teachers. Their importance to other students was in their influence on musical taste. The growth of interest in good music generally was a part of a change in national taste reflected in the spread of symphony orchestras and the sale of classical recordings. It is noteworthy, however, that the interest in good music was particularly marked at urban universities with a high proportion of second-generation Italian, Jewish and Slavic students.

The influence of such groups on the American college is a topic worthy of separate investigation, but it seems probable that they played a part in the relaxation of traditional Anglo-Saxon puritanism, in widening artistic interests, and in lowering the standards of spoken and written English. Their alleged greater willingness to work hard for an education has not always been apparent in the classroom. As a group they have evidenced the effectiveness of the melting pot; they show the traditional American student traits of good-humored resistance to books and overstudy, a fondness for "activities," and the tendency to treat the faculty with amused tolerance. A respectful "Herr Professor" attitude or a background of wide reading is an almost sure indication of an upbringing abroad.

Whatever the effectiveness of the American high school as a melting pot, it has not been notable since 1930 as a preparatory school. In justification the professors of education have argued that the vast increase in high-school population has forced a shift of emphasis from preparation for college to education for life. Whether or not this latter end is effectively served by organized activities and life-adjustment courses in place of intellectual training is debatable. But it is generally agreed that college preparatory work has suffered.

This caused the development of prefreshman courses and "remedial" work, especially in English and mathematics. State universities and city colleges took over some of the functions of the high school. This lack of adequate preparation has been a recurring problem in American higher education: most of the early state universities, the Western colleges, and the first women's colleges had found it necessary to maintain preparatory departments. Among the reasons for the situation have been the unwillingness of Americans to pay decent salaries to high-school teachers, the intellectual poverty of a large part of the population, and the failure of the colleges to train teachers—a dual failure of the traditionalists and of the quack doctors who infest the teachers' colleges. Perhaps such failures were the inevitable result of an era of vast expansion in both secondary and higher education. Nowhere else in the world had a nation built so fast for so many.

By 1930 college education had become big business with over 1,100,000 students;* annual receipts of $567,618,000; and productive endowments of $1,347,676,000. This last represents an increase of 2,700 per cent over the estimated productive funds of all the colleges in 1800, an amount which Thwing put at less than $500,000. In that distant day the total worth of collegiate property was about $1,000,000—or about one half the value of the present-day athletic plant at Minnesota or Ohio State. There were about 100 professors and perhaps 2,000 students. Thus about one person in 2,500 was in college as contrasted with one in 125 in 1930.

Such figures are one indication of the enormously increased impact of the colleges on American society in terms of money, power, and influence on human lives. Under the pressures of American life, higher education had been increasingly geared to the activities of the whole community in business, technology, finance and politics. It was not merely a matter of vocational emphasis; it involved research in science, economics, sociology,

* The growth of the colleges is best illustrated by the following table:

Year	Enrollments
1889-1890	156,756
1899-1900	237,592
1909-1910	355,215
1919-1920	597,857
1929-1930	1,100,737
1933-1934	1,055,360

and government—matters of concern to all the people. The classical scholar or Anglo-Saxon philologist could live out his life talking and writing about things which touched the lives of most men not at all. But when an Oberlin professor of chemistry developed a cheap process for producing aluminum, his work reached into every kitchen and eventually made possible the bomb-carrying airplane. As has been noted, college professors helped to design the weapons of World War I, and afterward to draw the map of Europe. From university laboratories here and abroad in the twenties, thirties and forties came vitamins, insulin, sulfa drugs, and antibiotics. The professor became so important in public life that the cartoonist's old symbol—a fat man in a high hat and a dollar-marked vest—gave way to the untidy man in a cap and gown. In the 1930s people talked not of "the trusts" but of "the brain trust." Except at some jerkwater colleges or for a few lingering philologists the cloistered, ivy-covered retreat had ceased to exist.

All this had its price. The vast increase in the number of students brought with it an increasing popular concern about what the colleges were teaching; legislatures and private donors of millions asked how the money was being spent; politicians and businessmen resented the intrusion of academic people into their bailiwicks. By participating in the hurly-burly of business and political life the colleges got some black eyes and bruises. But they also gained some valuable laboratory experience: theoretical scholarship was tested on the proving grounds of business, industry, and government. English professors tried to help their students to write salable stories and novels; economists were asked to advise on interest rates; sociologists told prison wardens how to operate a jail; political scientists on labor mediation boards helped labor leaders and employers in settling industrial disputes.

Again as in the Harding-Coolidge era the colleges became the targets of the reactionaries. Between the beginning of the depression and 1936, fourteen states enacted legislation requiring loyalty oaths of teachers. Seven other states and the District of Columbia already had similar legislation, passed in the early

1920s. Such laws always applied to teachers in secondary schools, and in fourteen states to those in colleges. In a study prepared for the American Federation of Teachers, Henry B. Linfield found that the chief promoters of this kind of legislation were the D.A.R., the American Legion, and the Veterans of Foreign Wars. Committee Y of the American Association of University Professors noted that the attacks on higher education came also from the Hearst and Macfadden press. The Hearst organization sent reporters posing as students into classrooms to obtain from professors statements which could be interpreted as subversive. Other publisher patriots like Colonel McCormick of the *Chicago Tribune* joined the pack to chase Eliza across the ice.

The reasons for selecting the schoolteacher and college professor as scapegoats in times of crisis in America must be sought partially in the realm of abnormal psychology, but there is room for an ugly suspicion that attacks on publicly supported schools and colleges have an economic motive. A loyalty-oath bill not only costs the taxpayer nothing, but may even stir up enough suspicion of education to keep down appropriations. The delicate academic statement by the A.A.U.P.'s Committee Y suggests: "The philosophy that underlies loyalty legislation for college teachers . . . is a philosophy that misconceives the world of the present and the function of education in that world. . . . Homogeneity will never be achieved by the passing of laws, least of all laws that seek to impose the values of one group upon another. That this can be done is one of the erroneous assumptions of those who press for oath bills."

Whatever the motives and misconceptions of those who promulgate loyalty oaths and spying on teachers, the fact remains that a disturbingly large part of the American public is ever ready for a witch hunt. Such people demand conformity to what they regard as orthodoxy and have a deep-rooted suspicion of the educator who tries to keep an open mind. Loyalty oaths catch few Communists; they operate against free inquiry and open discussion of controversial problems. As a group, schoolteachers and college professors have been on the side of traditional American values as defined in the Constitution and as embodied in literature and life. It is one of the tragedies of the nation that the other conservative elements in the population have often employed, or condoned, the most venal publishers and the least-educated organizations in the attempt to brand any dissent as disloyal. It is an act in the tragedy which in the 1930s drove so many liberals into the arms of the Communists. But all the evidence shows that few of the fellow travelers and traitors came from the teachers in schools and colleges.

Another price of this linking of higher education with everyday problems is alleged to have been a loss of cultural and spiritual values. During the 1930s Robert Maynard Hutchins became the leading, if at times inconsistent, spokesman for this view, joined by such men as Stringfellow Barr, Mortimer Adler and Norman Foerster. On the philosophical level this became the great issue in higher education during the years between 1930 and the Second World War. At one extreme were the followers of John Dewey with the theory of learning by doing; at the other, the Hutchins camp preaching the values of our cultural heritage as reflected in "great books." Sarah Lawrence and Bennington furnished the models for educational developments of the first type; St. Johns and Columbia College for the second. Some of the "progressives" fell into the trap of superficiality; they confused the field trip with laboratory investigation; a class junket to a county prison was "research" in criminology; one to an insane asylum was laboratory work in psychology; the designing of costumes for a play was substituted for an intensive reading of literature. On the other hand, the traditionalists, especially the "great books" enthusiasts, confused the history of science with science; they tended to define "great books" in accord with an authoritarian philosophy of the nature of man and the universe, and to overweight the selection with ancient authors. The proponents of education based on cultural heritage tend to overlook vast areas of that heritage such as the fine arts, music, technology, and folkways. By reading the canonical list of books issued by the high priests of culture a student would be unlikely to discover that Michelangelo and Leonardo da Vinci were at least as important as Dante.

In this respect the great-books enthusiasts inherit one of the greatest limitations of the old classical education: a picture of the world based on a traditional body of texts in literature, history and philosophy. In this respect the followers of John Dewey have been more adventurous: they have made the fine arts, music, modern technology, and anthropology a part of their education. But neither group has adequately explored a vast area of our cultural history: the historical influence of technology—the sort of thing discussed by writers like Sigfried Giedion, Lewis Mumford and John A. Kouwenhoven. Often the investigations in this field have been undertaken by people outside the academic world. Perhaps for that reason, such material has been neglected in college courses. The student learns about *The Federalist,* the controversy over the Bank of the United States, the building of the Erie Canal, but he hears little about the invention of the balloon frame and the steam drill, which made possible the rapid growth of towns and railroads. The well-publicized Gladsen purchase is probably far less important than the development of hybrid corn.

The point is that the defenders of cultural education have had a librarian's concept of culture. Not a modern librarian's view, of course, but one dating from before 1860. In the thirties and forties cultural education was by no means in so parlous a state as its critics alleged. Robert Maynard Hutchins wrote much more cogently against subsidized athletics than he did about the curriculum. Like many other educators of the period, he saw the centripetal forces in the curriculum, but instead of trying to organize the materials of modern knowledge into a whole, he sought the unity of an obsolete social order.

Fortunately the main body of college educators accepted neither the return-to-the-womb tendencies of Hutchins, Barr and Foerster, nor the rocket-to-the-moon programs of the Dewey-ites; they went in for neither St. Thomas Aquinas nor science fiction. Instead they tried to relate the cultural heritage to present needs, to organize the curriculum into a coherent structure, and to recognize the vocational functions of an education. The first of these is well illustrated by the widely copied work of George Pierce Baker, first at Harvard and later at Yale. Baker taught a scholarly course in the history of the drama, but he also organized the "47 Workshop" which developed the creative arts of playwriting, direction and stage design. Departments of fine arts have often combined historical scholarship with creative work. At the University of Iowa an interesting development has been a Ph.D. program which permits the substitution of creative work for the traditional thesis. The printed instructions issued to all graduate students emphasize the creative and critical elements in all scholarly writing.

A related tendency which became marked in the 1930s, although it began earlier, was the activity of professors of literature in the market place. Carl Van Doren wrote literary criticism for the *Nation*, Stuart Sherman for the *New York Herald Tribune*, and Henry Seidel Canby started the *Saturday Review of Literature*. Writing the literary history of the period, Professor Robert Spiller says of Canby: ". . . he did more than anyone else to bring the scholarly standards of the university into working relationship with the productive energies of writers, publishers, reviewers, and critics."

Unfortunately for the humanities, most professors looked down their noses on such attempts. Especially at the older universities, Ph.D. candidates still found it safer to become expert in Middle English than to flirt with modern literature. An instructor desiring promotion soon learned that a *PMLA* article on some minor seventeenth-century writer's use of an obscure Latin source was *scholarship;* whereas a critical essay on Auden or Faulkner was not. And the publication of a poem or short story damned one as a literary dilettante. As late as 1950 a Princeton professor of English defended the doctoral candidates who stopped their preparation for examination at the beginning of the nineteenth century, by arguing that if they could not cover everything, the last 150 years were the period to omit.

This failure by most professors of the humanities to relate

their work to the modern world is reflected in a study by Havemann and West, published in 1952, showing that "of all graduates the humanities and social science majors are among the most dissatisfied with their choice of college courses." This was not true of those who went into the professions, even the poorly paid ones. In other words, men and women who had gone on to take specialized training were satisfied with their background of general education; those who went directly into jobs were not. Among the generally educated graduates in business jobs, fully half wished that they had taken more specialized training. And no wonder: twenty-four per cent of the humanities graduates and thirty-one per cent of those from social science who had gone into business held rank-and-file jobs as against six per cent of such specialists as engineers. According to the Havemann and West study, "Some of them console themselves with the thought that college taught them how to enjoy living, even though they are dislocated jobwise and have less financial success than their college competitors from the specialized fields. But a great many come to the conclusion that a broad cultural background is simply not worth the price that it seems to exact in terms of workaday failure."

If, as most informed people believe, cultural education has value, its practitioners have failed lamentably to relate it to the world in which the student must live and earn a living. It is all too easy to deplore a society which fails to value culture, but it must be remembered that the much-admired cultural heritage of the past had a vital relationship to the business of living. Shakespeare's plays attracted patrons to the box office because they dealt with ideas and emotions which were vital to the audience; Locke's philosophy was studied for the light it shed on contemporary political problems; farmers and artisans and tradesmen drove miles over muddy roads to hear Emerson talk about things they were concerned with. Always, people ask of any teacher what Emerson demanded: "Give me insight into today."

10

The Wide Wide World

The issue of specialized versus cultural education came to a climax in World War II. Students in premedical courses and physics were deferred because of the essential nature of their work; majors in the humanities or business administration were drafted. Instructors in science, engineering and mathematics found it easy to get commissions in the army and navy; teachers of English and philosophy went in as privates unless they had once been in the service or the R.O.T.C. The older "experts" got good jobs in Washington; the professors of liberal subjects took on extra classes in elementary subjects to earn enough money to pay taxes and inflationary prices. Professors who had once long ago taught algebra laid aside their specialties to give courses in mathematics; housewives who had degrees in science were enticed back as instructors and laboratory assistants.

The Federal Government poured millions into research projects in science at the universities. Professor Louis A. Turner of Princeton, writing in *Reviews of Modern Physics,* summed up 100 reports which appeared in 1939 with the statement: "For the first time it seems that there is some reasonable possibility of utilizing the enormous nuclear energy of heavy atoms. . . . The practical difficulties can undoubtedly be overcome in time." Almost immediately atomic research became a cloak-and-dagger melodrama. From universities and research organizations all over the country physicists were brought into the top-secret Manhattan project. In the words of *Time:* "Its centers were full of G-men. Its couriers were Army officers, brief cases chained to their wrists. It rated the highest priorities for men and materials. From dozens of universities and industrial plants physicists, chemists and mathematicians vanished into thin air; the Manhattan District had snatched them." At the University of California, Dr. E. O. Lawrence directed experimental work in the electromagnetic method of separating U-235 from natural uranium; at Columbia, Dr. Harold C. Urey investigated the diffusion method; on a squash court under the Chicago Stadium the world's first chain-reaction pile was put in operation. On the desert near Los Alamos, New Mexico, Professor J. R. Oppenheimer, of the University of California, directed a team of physicists in the design, assembly and test of the atomic bomb. The official report on all this activity was written for the War Department by Professor H. D. Smyth. And of course back of all this lay the work of Professor Albert Einstein, since 1933 on the staff of Princeton's Institute for Advanced Study.

The development of the atomic bomb becomes a useful symbol of the academic revolution which made it possible.

All this does not prove the superior value of the technician and the weapons maker over that of the philosopher and the humanist; it simply demonstrates his greater role in modern society. There was a time when the author of *The Song of Roland* played as vital a role as the armorer, or when Milton's pamphlets could "freeze . . . the blood of monarchs." Even in our day a poet and college professor became assistant director of the Office of War Information. But Archibald MacLeish entered the academic profession not by way of the Ph.D., but through writing, journalism, and government service. So he too becomes a symbol—one suggesting that if other academic disciplines are to become as influential as science in the modern world they must, like science, be closely linked to the business of living.

During the period when the physicists were exploring nuclear energy, scholars in language and literature were devoting themselves to such topics as those in a typical issue of *PMLA,* the official journal of the Modern Language Association. Here is the table of contents for March 1943:

The "Fair Unknown" in Malory
Literary Problems in More's *Richard III*
The Braggart in Italian Renaissance Comedy

The Real Martin Marprelate
The Optics of Love: Notes on a Concept of Atomistic
Philosophy in the Theatre of Tirso de Molina
Calderon's *Silvas*
The Vogue of Decadent French Tragedies in Spain—1762-
1800
An Early Suitor of Mary Wollstonecraft
Heinrich Heine, "Blackguard" and "Apostate"
a Study of the Earliest English Attitude toward Him
Tennyson and the Reviewers, 1830-1842
Saint Antoine et les Monstres
Swinburne: *Changes of Aspect* and *Short Notes*
C. F. Meyer's *Der Heilige* in Relation to its Sources
Das Lutherbild des Jungen Nietzsche
Ammerkungen zur Dictung von Leon-Paul Fargue

In lunch-table conversation the professors of language and literature also discussed the students' deplorable lack of interest in the humanities.

The ivory tower, like the dusty rooms in Old Main, has been often heated by hot air. And the *Publications of the Modern Language Association* contain few B.T.U.s to the ton. However, despite the predilections of some scholars, the colleges were far from being ivory towers during the war. Most of the faculty could not participate in such dramatic exploits as the development of the atom bomb, but they could and did teach soldiers. Profiting by the failure of the S.A.T.C. in World War I, the armed services this time used the facilities of the colleges for specialized training programs. For instance, at Harvard there were about 3,500 men in uniform, distributed among Army and Navy R.O.T.C. units, medical students holding reserve commissions, and undergraduates in Navy V-1 and V-7 programs. More than 400 members of the faculty left for the armed services.

Professors of Oriental languages suddenly found themselves in the unusual role of indispensable men. From Michigan a seventy-seven-year-old professor emeritus, William H. Hobbs, was made an advisory member of the Office of Strategic Services. And with reason. Back in 1921 he had conducted geo-

logical expeditions to the mandated islands of the Pacific, and
between 1926 and 1931 had directed expeditions to Greenland.
A man who could tear down and rebuild a radio set, he had
kept in continuous contact, from Greenland, with the "peanut
whistle" station on the Michigan campus. His collection of
maps, some of them from Japanese scientists, were on file at
Ann Arbor. At the age of eighty-one he published *Fortress
Islands of the Pacific*. A younger colleague, Robert Hall, professor of geography, had collected a complete set of Japanese
coastal and geodetic maps, and "prefecture" maps of provinces,
towns and cities. As the Army and Navy intelligence services
had gathered no such material, Hobbs and Hall turned over
their maps to the armed services. Examples could be multiplied
from colleges and universities all over the nation. It all adds
up to the fact that the college professor as a type is neither an
unworldly Mr. Chips nor a bemused recluse. Certainly he is
not the wild-eyed radical of the caricatures in obscurantist
newspapers. In fact, to the dismay of the traditionalists in the
academic world, the professor has become a key man in the
activities of war and peace.

Nor were the alarmists right about the college student. When
the war came, he was neither too soft, too cynical, nor too radical to make a good soldier. Only rarely did he rush off to enlist
in a burst of patriotic enthusiasm; the volunteers were often as
not the boys who were bored with study or who felt the draft
board breathing down their necks. Most of them waited for
the "greetings from Uncle Sam" and kidded one another about
the notices to report for examination. Faculty members had
some difficulty in getting work out of boys who expected to
be called before the end of a semester. It was hard to sell the
idea that college credits were "money in the bank" to a generation which had been indoctrinated by the Hemingway-Dos
Passos school of writers, who pictured the soldier as inevitably
a psychological casualty. As a student told a faculty adviser, "I
hear that a man who has been in this war is in no shape to go
back to study."

But early in the war the wounded veterans began to filter

back to the colleges, and unobtrusively take their places with the youngsters, the girls, and the 4F's in the classroom. With the surrender of Japan, the colleges braced themselves for a repetition of 1919 on a larger scale. Older members of the faculty, remembering the noisy, obstreperous, alcoholic veteran of World War I, saw in the provisions of the "G.I. Bill" the prospect of chaos. As the flood of applications came in, administrators began a scramble for buildings and instructors. Conservative citizens and newspapers prophesied that the veterans would use the G.I. Bill as a kind of gravy train, a means of loafing at the expense of the taxpayer. Conservative educators argued that a large proportion of the veterans would not be "college material."

The results of the G.I. Bill surprised everyone, including the veterans. Many a returned soldier enrolled in college with his fingers crossed; he had been out of school for as much as four years; he had lost the knack of study and had forgotten most of what he had learned in school. The first few weeks in college frequently produced a state of nervous anxiety. Youngsters out of high school seemed much more at home in the classroom than men who had been in Germany or Japan. But then, to the amazement of the faculty, and of almost everybody else, the miracle began to happen. The veterans found that they could answer questions and do problems which baffled the kids.

All over the country the veterans got better scholastic grades than civilian students. In 1947, records from Columbia, Harvard, Chicago, Yale, Michigan, Denver, Stanford, Princeton, Oklahoma, Tufts and many others showed the same pattern: the veterans ahead in scholastic honors. Percentagewise, fewer G.I.s were placed on probation, fewer flunked out, fewer got into mischief. For instance, at Minnesota only thirty-five out of 6,000 flunked out in the spring of 1947—less than one half of one per cent, as compared to the usual rate of over ten per cent.

There were some squawks over dull and repetitive teaching, but also a willingness to praise good instructors. If the veteran had a complaint or a question, he was likely to bring it directly to his teacher; he had less of the characteristic polite apathy of the American student. A sociologist deploring the low wages in India might be interrupted by a man who had spent two years in Calcutta asking the question, "Have you ever tried to get a full day's work out of a Wog?" Or some ex-navy man might question the accuracy of Coleridge's descriptions of thunderstorms in the Pacific or add some firsthand information about the regions visited by Odysseus. The G.I. was good for the faculty.

Strangely enough there was little conflict between the G.I.s and the civilians: the older men did not bully the youngsters between classes; they joined the same organizations; they attended the same dances, and played on the same teams. However, they often refused to obey silly freshman regulations, such as wearing beanies, at those places where such things were still a fetish.

The American male student has always been an ingenious fellow in organizing a prank or a social event, but the veteran proved to be an expert. All he needed was permission—or the lack of prohibition—to go ahead with an activity. He was a practiced scrounger. If a dance committee planned a winter decorative theme, some G.I. managed to procure an antique sleigh; if a team needed a place to practice, someone wangled permission from the owner of a field or building; if a makeshift classroom lacked furniture, chairs appeared from somewhere. Anything from a motor truck to a beard for Santa Claus could be found; any defective device could be repaired. There was always a returned Seabee in the crowd, or someone who had run a bulldozer or a PX, or who could set up a public address system or speak over it.

One of the many things the colleges had not counted on was the married veteran. Traditionally the American college had frowned on marriage for students. Many institutions had rules which required the dropping of students so unwise as to wed or at least to do so openly. It was not uncommon, especially for girls, to keep marriages secret until graduation. But after World

War II colleges and universities often found it necessary to find or build dormitory space for married veterans. Departments of buildings and grounds were faced with a new problem—finding places for clotheslines to dry diapers. Men left word in deans' offices of their whereabouts in the event of a telephone call from a wife momentarily expecting a baby. The student passing out cigars was an ubiquitous type. A frequent academic problem was the man who tried to carry a full-time job in addition to his class work in order to supplement his allowance as a married veteran. Nevertheless, the percentage of drop-outs was surprisingly low.

Thus an educational experiment dictated by popular and political pressure proved a huge success. It also carried far-reaching implications. One of these was that Federal aid on a vast scale had not brought with it government interference or control. Of necessity there were complex problems in bookkeeping: colleges had to keep special records and follow special procedures to collect fees for tuition and supplies. After all, during the fiscal year of 1947, the Federal Government paid student fees amounting to $301,000,000—more than half of the total received that year from all students. But admission policies, methods of instruction, curriculum and academic requirements were left entirely in the hands of individual institutions. For instance, if a student's academic work was poor, the question of his continuance in college was determined entirely by the institution in which he was enrolled. If he was dropped, he was required to appear for advisement at one of the veterans' psychological testing centers before he could be certified for some other course. However, the colleges had the right to make their own decisions regarding the advisee. The Veterans' Bureau merely determined his eligibility for government aid. If college officials requested it, the advisement centers made available their excellent reports on a student's aptitudes and interests.

Another implication of the results of the experiment was that a much larger proportion of the population than had been supposed was capable of college work. This was further pointed up by the President's Commission on Higher Education appointed by Harry Truman. This commission, made up of about thirty educational and civic leaders, presented its report in 1947. Among its findings was that at least forty-nine per cent of college boys and girls were intellectually capable of completing two years of junior college, and that at least thirty-two per cent had the ability to earn a bachelor's degree. The commission suggested the need for vastly expanded facilities in higher education, particularly in tuition-free community junior colleges. Despite all the progress of making higher education available to an ever-increasing proportion of men and women, it was still true in 1947 that less than a third of those able to do college work were enrolled in institutions of higher learning. The commission reported a Minnesota study which showed that in the top ten per cent of high-school graduates, only one out of two got to college; in the top thirty per cent, only one out of three. A well-to-do dumbbell still had a much better chance of going to college than an able youth from low-income groups. Among boys with an I.Q. of 124 or better, those from the highest income groups had a four to one advantage over those in the lower groups. Furthermore, there was a great difference in opportunity in various parts of the country. Just before World War II a farm boy or girl had less chance of a college education than one from the city by a ratio of four to one. In California, with numerous state-supported institutions, a boy or girl was more likely to go to college than in Pennsylvania, and much more likely to go than one from Mississippi. Southern states with high birth rates had less money to spend on education per child than a state like California filled with elderly Iowans.

Despite the fact that the nation was spending a billion a year on higher education in 1947, this was less than one half of one per cent of the value of the goods produced in that year. The commission proposed that by 1960 there should be a budget of $2,587,000,000, or 1.19 per cent of the national production as of 1947, to provide for a minimum of 4,600,000 students in nonprofit institutions for education beyond the twelfth grade. After computing the probable income from all sources the commission came to the conclusion:

There is but one source of providing the funds needed to avoid a deficit and to balance the operating budget for higher education: the Federal Government.

Once again an agency of the national government had set goals for higher education. George Washington had done so in the proposal for a University of the United States; Congress had done so through the land grants and the Morrill Acts. It seems probable, therefore, that unless history reverses its direction, the Federal Government will eventually finance a substantial part of higher education. This suggests that the viewers-with-alarm might be well advised to channel the direction instead of trying to stem the flow. It is symbolic that the President's Commission on Higher Education was appointed by Harry Truman, who, like George Washington and Justin Morrill, was not a college graduate. The history of higher education indicates that the American people are going to insist that it meet their own needs and values.

However there are values only dimly realized by the lay public: the value of general culture—preached, though not always produced by the traditionalists—and the value of pure research, of knowledge for its own sake—sometimes pursued too single-mindedly by its proponents. The mid-1940s saw the culmination of a trend foreshadowed by the theories of Folwell, the group plan of Lowell, and the attempt by Meiklejohn to integrate fields of knowledge. The latter aim had been in part defeated by the increasing fragmentation of knowledge which crystallized in the departmental system of organization. A typical college offered about 600 courses; a university as many as 2,700. Introductory science was broken up into Biology 1, Chemistry 1, Geology 1, Physics 1, Astronomy 1, etc. Psychology deserted the mansions of philosophy to claim laboratory space, and set up its own Psychology 1. More often than not these introductory courses were introductory to nothing but increasingly specialized courses in the same field. The same phenomenon appeared in the social sciences: little or no attempt was made to link the work in economics, political science, and sociology. History severed its traditional links with literature and philosophy to set up as one of the social sciences—but not, as might have been possible, as a unifying force among them.

Because nobody else paid much attention to the odd bits of salvage from the humanities, they eddied into the English department. So, in addition to trying to teach students to read and write as well as an adult auto mechanic, and offering instruction on how to look up a word in the dictionary and get a book out of the library, English departments introduced freshmen to a smattering of Socrates, Aristotle, Plato, Bacon, Mill, Arnold, William James, Thomas Huxley, Bertrand Russell, John Dewey, T. S. Eliot and Henry Steele Commager. The typical freshman anthology was divided into essays on education, science, literature, fine arts, modern society, religion, philosophy, and psychology—the kind dealing with thought processes rather than the behavior of rats in mazes.

For the teachers of English had discovered that before students could write about these subjects, they had to get some notion of their philosophies and basic assumptions. Freshmen in Biology 1 learned how to dissect a frog, but knew Darwin only through the derogatory remarks of their pastors; premeds in Chemistry 1 were taught how to put a glass tube through a stopper without severing an artery, but not how a hypothesis is formed and tested. In laboratory experiments students learned to get, or at least report, the results defined in the laboratory manual. As Tommy Wood says in Flandrau's *Diary of a Freshman* (1900):

"My experiments in the laboratory always give beautiful results. I find out first of all from the book what Nature is expected to do; then I see that she does it."

The usual instructor in English was not well equipped by training to discuss the fine arts, the scientific method, political theory, the problems of industry and finance, or numerous other topics treated in freshman readings; he had got his Ph.D. by studying *Beowulf*, Cynewulf, Richard Rolle, *Piers Plowman*, obscure Elizabethan dramas, Jeremy Taylor, Wordsworth's turgid prose, the plays of Dion Boucicault, and by producing an "original contribution to knowledge" in the form of a dissertation on the sources of some little-known work, or on the literary reputation of somebody or other in some century or other. The literary scholar was an authority on a body of literary tripe and a master of the Indian-giver prose style which takes back in qualifying phrases everything it grants in the main clause. Nevertheless, with all the handicaps of a bad professional education he at least had the foundation of a liberal-arts course and had usually done some reading on his own; often he enjoyed music and the arts, and tended to be socially conscious. For instance, those professional men who majored in preprofessional courses, and who later engaged in seven or more civic activities, were only thirty per cent as compared with forty-two per cent for majors in the humanities and social sciences. The broader interests of humanities graduates is reflected in the anthologies they compiled.

However, the reading of a score or so of essays is not a general education. At a number of institutions faculty committees and administrators began to give thought to an interrelated program of general and specialized education. This specialization could take the form of preparation for graduate or professional study, or could lead directly to careers in business, journalism, government or management. At long last the colleges were attempting to relate their programs specifically to two basic purposes: education for living and training for making a living. The first of these included a study of the cultural heritage; of contemporary society; of the nature of the physical and biological world; and of the nature and needs of people as individuals, as citizens and in family relationships. The traditional, prescribed education had paid lip service to the cultural heritage and to social values, but had subordinated these to intellectual discipline in specific areas; the free elective system had been premised on individual differences and objectives, but it had failed to recognize the inability of the untrained student to understand and foresee his needs.

The elective system had failed even more as a means of educating the whole man; it had intensified both fragmentation and specialization. Extreme specialization was of course the vice of specifically vocational programs such as engineering, premedical training, and business. In all three of these areas there was some attempt to introduce a larger proportion of humanistic and social studies. However, the deans of medical schools more often gave attention to the humanities and social sciences in their speeches than in their admissions practices. On the whole, engineers and physicians have been among the least liberally educated products of higher education.

The importance of the movement to develop programs of general education is attested by the flood of books and articles on the subject, especially in the last ten years. Most of the plans put forth in those years owe a debt to the pioneering experiments at Sarah Lawrence, at Minnesota's General College, at Meiklejohn's Experimental College at Wisconsin, and to the reorganized College at Chicago. However, all of these except that at Minnesota were tried with relatively small groups of highly selected students and with hand-picked faculties. For instance, the College at Chicago selected its students from those who scored in the top ten per cent in aptitude tests. Because of small classes and extensive individual counseling, most of the plans were expensive to operate.

Diverse as these programs were in methods, they agreed in their effort to break down the rigid divisions between fields of study and in trying to organize education into a coherent whole. Thus in 1932 under Hutchins at Chicago, separate departments were regrouped into four divisions, each with its own dean: humanities, social sciences, physical sciences, and biological sciences. This grouping, at least in the first two years of college work, became a pattern for many of the programs in general education adopted in the mid 1940s. The two-year General College set at Minnesota in 1932 developed, under Malcolm S. MacLean, several concepts which also had wide influence: introductory courses planned to emphasize basic principles and the relationships among fields of knowledge, and to relate realistically to the problems faced by young people. These took the form of orientation courses in four areas: Individual

Orientation, Vocational Orientation, Home Life Orientation, and Social-Civic Orientation.

The theory of such plans differed from the Deweyite philosophy of Sarah Lawrence and Bennington, where student interests were the basis of individually tailored programs of study. The Wisconsin, Chicago, Minnesota plans all assumed the faculty's responsibility for organizing certain broad fields of knowledge and for prescribing at least a minimum of work in each of these. Those institutions following Dewey's ideas used the student's immediate aims and interests as a nucleus for an ever-broadening program of study and investigation.

Because of cost and the difficulty of adapting highly individualized programs to large student bodies, the theoretically democratic Deweyite theories have proved best suited to wealthy students with a background of culture and no pressing necessity to get jobs. Conducted as a rule by liberals who deplore sex segregation and discrimination, they have tended to flourish chiefly at women's colleges.

The movement toward more general education gained impetus with the publication of two major documents: the Harvard Committee's *General Education in a Free Society* (1945) and the Report of the President's Commision on Higher Education called *Higher Education for American Democracy* (1947). As the titles suggest, both reports place much emphasis on the function of education in training for citizenship—not in the limited sense of propaganda for democracy, but in the more fundamental way of developing human beings trained to understand and function in our society. By 1946 Harvard, Yale and Princeton had adopted rather similar programs of general education. Dozens of other institutions followed one or another of the basic patterns of general studies.

Among the chief difficulties of implementing such plans have been the problems of course organization and of finding qualified instructors. For instance, should literature, history and social science be organized within a framework of American Civilization or should they be concerned with the development of Western Civilization? In science, should there be an orienta-

tion course in general science, a course in the philosophy and
history of science, or a course in the scientific method as exemplified in a single field?

The problem of instruction was that most faculty members
were specialists in a single area of a single discipline. Attempts
to develop courses through the co-operative efforts of specialists,
like the humanities work at Columbia, were highly expensive—
a single course might require the services of five or six professors.
Also, co-operative ventures such as programs in American Civilization or the development of Western Civilization were difficult to integrate into a unit. The professor who taught Dante
might be a Catholic, the European historian a Marxist, and the
professor of English literature an art-for-art's-saker or a "new
critic." In the old catch-as-catch-can elective system, the student was supposed to make his own synthesis; the theory of
general education implied some synthesis on the part of the
faculty. And this involved a relatively agreed-on body of fundamental material, and a rather completely agreed-on philosophy
of education.

The extremes of the experiments have been the Mount Sinai
prescriptions of the "Great Books" enthusiasts and the super-
kindergarten methods of the student-interest-centered programs.
Stephens College, for instance, gave college credit for a course
called "Personal Appearance" in which classroom lectures are
devoted to such subjects as how to take a bath. John Dewey and
Robert Maynard Hutchins symbolize the polarities. Lesser mor-
tals not quite so sure that they had the one key to the educational
pentagon tried to strike some sort of balance between cultural
tradition and varied student aptitudes. Thus most institutions
adopting some program of general education allowed a certain
flexibility of choice within prescribed limits. A student might
be required to take a two-semester course in each of the major
fields: humanities, science, and social science. In each of these
there might be a choice of courses. The great difference from
the old "distribution" requirement was that the introductory
courses were of a broader, more philosophical nature than the

traditional Sociology 1, Survey of English Literature, or European History 1815 to 1914.

Among the many criticisms of general education have been the arguments that survey courses in large areas were superficial, that attempts to unify fields such as social science resulted in poor welding jobs, that Harvard's plan gave too little attention to the nonintellectual areas of life (e.g., recreation or family living), and that the Minnesota type of General College devoted too much attention to *ad hoc* situations (e.g., recreation and family living).

The results of the various plans or of the philosophy as a whole are still to be assessed. As Earl J. McGrath, Commissioner, U.S. Office of Education, argues in a recent symposium on general education, there is a need for experimental evaluation by means of tests before and after students have followed various programs. Professor MacLean, who between 1932 and 1940 headed the General College at Minnesota, insists on the need for research in four fields of student needs: (1) mental hygiene, self-assessment, personal understanding; (2) home and family life and interpersonal relationship; (3) vocational orientations and (4) social and civic competence. He would, for instance, study the "emotions and their place in the educative process, and in the power of feeling roused by experiences in the art laboratory, in music, in the theater, in novels and plays and movies and radio, and television as these make for better or worse students, better or worse men and women." As there are a great many different kinds of novels in the world, and as radio and TV programs are subject to change, one can see that this guinea-pig or hamster approach to students has endless possibilities.

President J. L. Morrill of Minnesota points out that general education "is no panacea for the never ending problems of education." However, it does represent a thoughtful attempt to synthesize the values and tendencies in American education since its beginning: the ideal of liberal culture, of the good life, of civic responsibility, and of vocational competence. It represents a much broader definition of general culture propounded by those who revolted against the classical tradition; it recognizes the value of research and experience in the social sciences, and of the need for a more philosophical approach to the natural sciences. In its application it uses the techniques of the psychologists in determining aptitudes, interests and achievement. It is not at war with vocational specialization but is a complement of it. The nature of general education is not fixed and final, nor is it desirable that it should be so. Not only will continued experiment be necessary to meet changing conditions, but varied types of programs are required to meet the needs of different students. Not every institution should try to be all things to all men and all women. The sophisticated boy and girl from a big city have not the same emotional problems or the same intellectual gaps as their contemporaries reared on a farm. The potential scholar can probably profit from a more intellectualized general education than can the future housewife or building contractor. Perhaps the only really dangerous type of general education is that premised on an unchanging set of values and prescribing a fixed program of study for everybody. The old classical curriculum came to grief because of a similar philosophy.

An important corollary of the developments in general education has been increased attention to the effectiveness of instruction. New programs demanded new methods. The teacher faced with the problem of integrating a whole field such as social science or the humanities could not continue to parrot the material he had studied in specialized courses as a graduate student. The chemist required to discuss the basic theories and concepts of science could not fall back on his laboratory manual. Therefore, most faculties which developed programs of general education devoted much time and thought to the problems of teaching the material.

In the language field the more efficient methods used by the armed services forced a revaluation of traditional methods. Many faculty members held out heroically against such methods on the ground that they produced superficiality, or just on the ground that they were new. But under the combined pressures of attacks on the foreign-language requirement for a degree and the evidence that more effective methods of teaching were possible, it is likely that language teaching will generally improve. In other areas the development of audio-visual aids, again accelerated by wartime experience, has had its effect. Even in a traditional subject like English literature, instructors increasingly began to use recordings of poets reading their own works and motion pictures of plays by Shakespeare or Shaw.

Even the graduate schools began to take thought of their responsibility for producing effective college teachers. As a rule they eschewed the methods courses of the teachers' colleges, but they often developed a kind of internship whereby graduate students conducted quiz sections, or gave occasional lectures under the supervision of experienced staff members. Prospective Ph.D.s sat in on staff discussions and helped to prepare examinations for undergraduates. Some graduate schools refused to recommend candidates for teaching posts unless they had demonstrated some degree of fitness other than mastery of subject matter. At Princeton, where some of these methods came into use, there was the added development of "straddles"—graduate programs combining work in two fields. This was no mere device to produce ambidextrous Ph.D.s, but a scholarly attempt to bring the fruitful techniques of one discipline to bear on the problems of some other field. It is likely that the exigencies of general education will demand further developments of this type of graduate study.

Another significant development was that two great universities, Columbia and Pennsylvania, after experiences under an ex-general and a displaced politician, chose as their presidents men from the academic world. Boards of trustees discovered, as faculties had long known, that, despite notable exceptions, the successful college administrators and money raisers tend to be persons who have made higher education their profession. In the collegiate as in the business world, the best salesmen and executives are those who know the job from the ground up.

It would be pleasant to end this account of the first 317 years of American college education with the foregoing mention of healthful symptoms. But there were dark shadows in the picture. Beginning in 1950, a new series of scandals exposed the rottenness of college athletics. The *Christian Century* attacked the failure of the National Collegiate Athletic Association to discipline seven schools for admitted violations of the "sanity code." Referring to Caesar Petrillo's ruling that college bands could no longer play at basketball doubleheaders in big city auditoriums because these were no longer amateur sporting events, the editors agreed that he was right—such spectacles were "cold-blooded money-making ventures." Just how cold-blooded college basketball had become was revealed a year later when star players at a number of universities were arrested for taking bribes from professional gamblers. Some of the clues went back five years.

But the evils went back far beyond that. In the early 1920s students at a church-related college which had one of the best teams in the East were aware that the football players who dropped out after Thanksgiving had been recruited by an alumnus who regarded the team as a racing stable, and reputedly profited accordingly. As the *Christian Century* put it in 1950, most of the presidents of sectarian colleges had delivered an inaugural address on the theme of "The Need for the Church College as a Source of Ethical Guidance to the Nation." The editors asked "where is all that moral leadership? . . . We fear that the church related college is often no better than any other when it comes to making a mockery of its moral pretensions regarding its athletic practices. Sometimes it is worse." This they said could be verified by asking almost any high-school or college student. "They know."

But administrators and alumni "quarterbacks' clubs" refused to heed. After the bribery scandals of the spring of 1951, *Time* remarked that there was no sign "that the colleges were . . . earnestly searching their souls about the commercialized nature of college sports. There was no sign that they, too, had been indicted."

Instead the stench got worse. The 1951 football season developed a succession of athletic scandals and examples of dirty play. At William and Mary both the football and basketball coaches resigned when it was revealed that the athletic department had been falsifying high-school transcripts of promising athletes. A football coach, whose moral sensibilities had been heightened by his dismissal from Indiana University, remarked: ". . . we have sold our athletic heritage for a mess of pottage. We must be willing to accept in part the blame for the inroads of professional gambling into university athletics." The William and Mary faculty issued a report stating: "We have seen this athletic program vitiate the most elementary standards of honesty and right conduct." They accepted in part the responsibility for having failed "to halt the insidious growth of these evils." Like Br'er Rabbit, most coaches and college presidents "lay low." A year later the Ivy League was engaged in a successful crusade to prevent the University of Pennsylvania from putting football games on television. The moral issue was gate receipts versus profits from TV advertising.

A hopeful sign, however, was that a number of institutions began to drop varsity football—it no longer made money. N.Y.U. wound up the season of 1952 with a deficit of $100,000.

Another shadow on the educational landscape is the financial plight of the colleges. Despite an increase of gifts from $22,000-000 in 1930 to $104,000,000 in 1950, and of Federal grants from $15,000,000 to $195,000,000, nearly fifty per cent of privately controlled institutions finished 1952 in the red. Inflation and low interest rates bore most heavily on the private institutions. But everywhere more services were required to meet modern needs. In 1950 libraries were spending five times as much as in 1930. Student services such as counseling helped to double administrative costs per student. The falling enrollments which followed the disappearance of the veterans left the colleges with increased staffs and expanded plants which could not be easily reduced. At Rollins College, for instance, thirty per cent of the faculty had to be let go; at other places the drops ranged between twenty and five per cent.

As usual in an inflationary period, the faculty took a beating. A report issued in 1951 by the Commission on Financing Higher Education showed that since 1940 the average salary for all ranks had increased only thirty-two per cent—representing a drop in real income of seventy-one per cent. A breakdown of the figures showed that for instructors the real income was about eighty-six per cent of prewar levels, but for professors only sixty-five per cent. The older men not only suffered a thirty-five-per-cent loss of purchasing power; they faced retirement on pension plans designed for the price levels of many years before. An income of from $100 to $200 a month was all that many a retiring professor could look forward to. Thus the extension of social security to faculty members was a godsend.

Tuition rates went up in many places to amounts which endangered the future of democratic education. One college, which in 1919 charged $100 to $150, had a fee of $750 in 1953. And inflationary pressures tended to force colleges to increase class size and to curtail services. Uncertainties about the number of men subject to call for military service made it difficult to plan for instructional and housing needs. By 1953 the problem of financing higher education was perhaps more acute than ever.

Once again as in the 1920s and 1930s higher education was under attack by the witch hunters. In 1950 the Regents of the University of California, despite a provision of the state constitution prohibiting such a requirement, demanded that all members of the faculty take a loyalty oath. Thirty-nine refused to do so. As a result fifty-five courses had to be canceled for the year 1952-1953. In this case the state supreme court ruled the requirement unconstitutional, but other states with no such constitutional prohibition adopted loyalty-oath bills like the Pennsylvania Pechan Act. Rural legislators became the arbiters of who should teach in colleges.

In view of the infinitesimal number of Communists on college faculties, the academic professor recognized loyalty-oath bills as an attempt to enforce orthodoxy as defined by the more conservative and ill-informed members of the community. Instructors found themselves hedging when students asked questions about controversial issues; they omitted assignments in certain writers, or carefully avoided any expression of opinion on Socrates' defense, Thoreau's "Civil Disobedience," or Veblen's *Theory of the Leisure Class*. Some student might report a garbled statement to the press. It was an atmosphere in which a boy in an English class could ask about the writer of a poem satirizing Communists, "Doesn't this show that he was interested in Communism?" The cynically irresponsible charges of Senator McCarthy led another student to write in the campus paper that it was a disgrace for a presidential candidate to have Harvard professor Archibald MacLeish on his staff of writers.

Without limiting the term to college professors, *Time* magazine began to apply the word "egg-heads" to certain intellectuals in American society. It subsequently found a more highbrow epithet: *gnostics*. *Time's* definitions are less important than the fact that it led many people to believe it was fanning suspicion of writers and college professors. As this is written, Congressional committees under Velde and McCarthy are searching for Communist teachers. Faculty groups at leading institutions and the American Association of University Professors adopted resolutions deploring the current witch hunt. For the faculty it was the days of A. Mitchell Palmer all over again.

And unless history fails to repeat itself, there will be another revolt of youth. The Communist-front American Youth for Democracy, which flourished in the mid 1940s, had hornswoggled a number of liberals but had died quickly when its real sponsorship was revealed. But a professor pilloried by the Velde or McCarthy committees became a hero in the eyes of students. Faculty members could combat Communist ideas with ease, but they found it difficult to deal with a martyr. Once again hysteria was abroad in the land.

The great error of conservatives and reactionaries is to undervalue the idealism of youth. College boys and girls rally to the support of the underdog; they reject the hypocrite and the phony. In the period following World War II, they had increasingly accepted the democratic ideal of the equality of all races and creeds. An Amherst fraternity defied its national body to elect a Negro; the Yale team of 1949 chose a Negro captain, who was subsequently tapped by three senior societies. White students on many campuses joined the National Association for the Advancement of Colored People. Students were often more ready to accept Negroes in white dormitories than timid administrators were to permit them to room there. In student papers and discussion groups there were protests against the racial and religious discrimination practiced by medical schools. At city colleges white girls walked to classes with Negro boys; Aryan men danced with Oriental coeds. In 1953 Yale dropped the cruel institution of Tap Day.

Utopia had of course not arrived. Jews and Gentiles still congregated in separate fraternities. In 1953 the *Daily Princetonian* questioned the opening of clubs to everyone. High-school graduates from the New York–New Jersey metropolitan area "did not have a social background which would fit them into the Princeton system." The paper proposed the creation of more alumni screening committees "in the metropolitan area where so many of this year's 100% problems come from." Princeton was still going in for what *Fortune* called "type casting." Even in the Ivy League colleges students got into riots. In 1951 a thousand Yale men joined in a fight between two ice-cream vendors, and five thousand Harvard students brought out the police in a fracas growing out of a mock political rally. Someone remarked that Harvard was fighting for free speech and Yale for free enterprise. Penn students continued to observe the vernal equinox with Rowbottom vandalism such as heaving garbage cans through plate-glass windows and damaging parked cars. No one has suggested any ideological implications at Pennsylvania. The academic year 1951-1952 was marked on campuses all over the country by "panty raids" in which male students, egged on by screaming coeds, invaded dormitories to make off with rayon and nylon trophies. Only the material, not the motives, had changed since Wisconsin boys conducted a similar raid fifty-three years earlier. The rites of spring in 1953 included a raid—or possibly a serenade—by seventy-five Swarthmore coeds on a boys' dormitory, where the gentlemen shoved them under showers and gave them mud baths. In Washington two representatives from the Harvard *Crimson* presented the Russian Embassy with a large bronze bird, which they described as a symbol of peace. It turned out to be the sacred ibis stolen from the top of the *Lampoon* building. It is safe to prophesy that before long some other outrageous or ingenious jape will be devised. And annually the older members of the faculty will deplore the fact that students seem even younger and more ill prepared.

Yet despite financial problems, faculty qualms, athletic scandals and Congressional committees, all signs pointed to ever-swelling enrollments. The coeds who had so perturbed journalists and deans of women had somehow contrived to bear and rear a bumper crop of youngsters. The college problem of the decade beginning 1955 seemed likely to be that of providing for the multitudinous children of the alleged "age of anxiety." Thus the colleges, mindful of generations of American youth, could say with Henley:

> And life, and all for which life lives so long
> Wanton and wondrous and forever well.

Notes

I. CLASSICISM AND CALVINISM

Page

19: Cambridge and Oxford men in America: Charles F. Thwing, *A History of Higher Education in America*, New York, 1906, p. 1

19-20: Nathaniel Eaton: Charles A. Wagner, *Harvard, Four Centuries and Freedoms*, New York, 1950, pp. 22-25

20: Dunster's curriculum: George P. Schmidt, *The Old Time College President*, New York, 1930, p. 95

22: General Assembly of Connecticut: Louis Franklin Snow, *The College Curriculum in the United States*, New York, 1907, p. 43
Professor Wigglesworth: *Ibid.*, pp. 43-44
Curriculum standardized: *Ibid.*, p. 141
Time allotted to various subjects: Schmidt, pp. 95-96

23: Benjamin Lord: Thwing, p. 76
Andrew White: *Autobiography of Andrew Dickson White*, New York, 1906, I, 27-29
Yale exports system: E. Merton Coulter, *College Life in the Old South*, Athens, Ga., 1951, pp. 15-16
Presidents from various colleges: Schmidt, p. 96
Meigs calculates fall of rebel angels: Coulter, p. 16

24: Allegheny College: Schmidt, p. 97
Yale report: *Ibid.*, p. 54 and "Summary of Report," Snow, pp. 145-154

25: White on Yale: White, I, 27-28
Wayland of Brown: Francis Wayland, *Report to the Corporation of Brown University*, Providence, 1850, p. 30
Barnard's statistics: Frederick A. P. Barnard, *The Rise of a University, the Later Days of Old Columbia College, From the Annual Reports of Frederick A. P. Barnard, President of Columbia College, 1864-1889*, ed. by William F. Russell, New York, 1937, p. 97
The Amherst faculty: Snow, p. 155

25-26: Johnson's statement: Thwing, p. 76

26: ". . . where are our classical scholars?": Wayland, pp. 17-18
"The majority of our students . . .": Barnard, p. 103

27: William Hammond: William Gardiner Hammond, *Remembrance of Amherst, An Undergraduate's Diary, 1846-1848*, ed. by George F. Whicher, New York, 1946

Eliot's estimate: Charles W. Eliot, *Harvard Memories*, Cambridge, 1923, p. 54

Dwight's students transfer: Charles E. Cunningham, *Timothy Dwight, 1752-1817*, New York, 1942, p. 143

President teachers: Schmidt, pp. 104-105

28: Dean West: Quoted, Schmidt, p. 102

28-29: Moral Philosophy: *Ibid.*, pp. 108-145

30: Eliphalet Nott: *Ibid.*, pp. 139, 204-205

31: Wayland on science: *Ibid.*, p. 196

33: Andrew White on Yale buildings: White, I, 259

Holworthy Hall: Wagner, p. 88

Privies a source of trouble: *Ibid.*, p. 86; Hammond, pp. 193-194; Cunningham, p. 187

34: Jacob Rhett Motte: *Charleston Goes to Harvard, The Diary of Jacob Rhett Motte, a Harvard Student of 1831,* ed. by Arthur H. Cole, Cambridge, 1940, p. 9

First bathtubs at Harvard: Eliot, p. 120

Bathing at Oberlin: Robert Samuel Fletcher, *A History of Oberlin College From Its Foundation Through the Civil War,* Oberlin, 1943, I, 328

Bills for damages: Wagner, p. 75; Schmidt, p. 85

Rolling cannon balls: Wagner, p. 77; White, I, 19-20; Coulter, p. 68

35: Yale in Dwight administration: Cunningham, pp. 248-251

Rutgers library: William H. S. Demarest, *A History of Rutgers College, 1766-1924,* New Brunswick, 1924, p. 326

Literary society libraries: Coulter, pp. 133, 185; Fletcher, II, 742

36: Literary society rules: Fletcher, I, 129-130

Bread and butter rebellions: Wagner, p. 75; Cunningham, p. 264

36-37: Yale dining room: Henry Boynton, *James Fenimore Cooper,* New York, 1931, pp. 30-31, and "College Words and Customs," *Yale Literary Magazine,* Vol. XXII, No. 1 (Oct. 1856)

37: Lyman Beecher: Cunningham, p. 280

Peddlers: Nathaniel Hawthorne, *Fanshaw,* and Motte, p. 58

Ice cream and soda pop: Motte, p. 84; Coulter, p. 207; Fletcher, I, 261

38: "When streams roll down . . .": *Yale Lit.,* Vol. XXII, No. 3 (Dec. 1856), p. 114

38-39: College commons: Coulter, pp. 54-55; Thwing, p. 8; Fletcher, I, 316-330

39: Pearson's diary: Wagner, p. 76

39-40: Disorders in chapel: Mary Ellen Chase, *Jonathan Fisher, Maine Parson, 1768-1847,* p. 34; Motte, pp. 45-46; Hammond, p. 184; *Diary of William Canby* (Quaker Historical Collection, Haverford College), Jan. 1, 1839

40: Students hate exercises: Coulter, p. 82; Fletcher, II, 755

Amherst faculty: Amherst College, *Faculty Minutes,* 1882-1894

President Bishop: Schmidt, p. 92

40-41: Dwight's influence: Cunningham, pp. 300-334; Schmidt, p. 188

41: "There were two very pretty girls . . .": Motte, p. 31

Princeton schedule: Charles Colcock Jones, *The Princeton and Harvard Letters of,* (Mss.), Aug. 13, 1850

42: Schedule at early colleges: Schmidt, p. 79

University of Michigan: Kent Sagendorph, *Michigan, The Story of the University,* New York, 1948, p. 67

42-43: College rules: Thwing, pp. 34 and 44; Schmidt, pp. 79-93; Coulter, p. 62; Cunningham, pp. 257-259

43-44: Violence at Southern colleges: Coulter, pp. 64-69; Schmidt, p. 86

44: Rules at Yale: Cunningham, p. 253; *Yale Lit.,* Vol. XXII, No. 1 (Oct. 1856), p. 6

Tutors protest new rules: Cunningham, pp. 254-255

44-45: Violence of disorder: *Ibid.,* pp. 253 and 264; Wagner, p. 76; Schmidt, p. 85; White, I, 79; Lafayette College, *Faculty Minutes,* May 1864

45: "There was no other outlet . . .": White, I, 22

46: Row with fire company: Amherst, *Faculty Minutes,* June 8, 1825

Haverford students: *Diary of William Canby,* Dec. 25, 1837 (Mss. in Quaker Collection, Haverford College)

II. FALSE DAWN

48: *College of Mirania:* Carl and Jessica Bridenbaugh, *Rebels and Gentlemen,* New York, 1942, pp. 57-58

Philadelphia in the mid-eighteenth century: *Ibid.,* pp. 3-4

49-50: Smith's proposed curriculum: Snow, pp. 62-65

50: "What can we figure to ourselves . . .": *Ibid.,* p. 65

51: "Concerning the foregoing plan . . .": Quoted, Snow, p. 71

52: *The American Magazine:* Bridenbaugh, p. 103

The aim of King's College: Snow, p. 155

53-54: Jefferson and William and Mary: *Jefferson Memoir,* I, 43; Snow, pp. 74-75; Schmidt, p. 154

55: Franklin on Smith: Bridenbaugh, p. 60

Smith's Tory sympathies: Ellis Paxon Oberholtzer, *The Literary History of Philadelphia,* Philadelphia, 1906, pp. 62-63

Troubles at William and Mary: Schmidt, p. 154

Decline of University of Pennsylvania: Edward Potts Cheney, *History of the University of Pennsylvania, 1740-1940,* Philadelphia, 1940, p. 186

55-56: Holley's appointment at Transylvania: Niels Henry Sonne, *Liberal Kentucky, 1780-1828,* New York, 1939, pp. 157 *ff.*

56: Holley's teaching: *Ibid.,* pp. 214-216

Controversy over religious instruction: *Ibid.,* pp. 233-234

Selection of faculty: *Ibid.,* p. 172

56-57: Meigs forced to resign: E. Merton Coulter, *College Life in the Old South,* Athens, Ga., 1951, p. 19

57: "Calvinism denied . . .": Sonne, p. 226
"The ideal of a great central state university . . .": *Ibid.*, p. 261
State universities chartered: Schmidt, p. 36 (However on p. 161
the date 1826 is given for the University of Virginia.)
Yale curriculum at Georgia: Coulter, pp. 15-16
President Cooper (1821): Schmidt, p. 220

57-58: University of Virginia: Schmidt, p. 36 and pp. 161-162

58-59: Jefferson's influence on library: Thomas Perkins Abernathy,
Historical Sketch of the University of Virginia, Richmond, 1948,
p. 10

59: Accessibility of library: Philip Alexander Bruce, *History of the
University of Virginia, 1819-1919*, New York, 1920, II, 202
Failure of student government: *Ibid.*, II, 265, and Abernathy, p. 9
Students drop out: Bruce, II, 72-73
Size of colleges: Abernathy, p. 18; Barnard, Statistical table in
Appendix

60: "The early annals of Oberlin College . . .": Fletcher, I, 3-4
"Nowhere else was the vision so clearly seen . . .": *Ibid.*, I, 208

61: Theological doctrines: *Ibid.*, I, 44
Professor Monteith's prayer: *Ibid.*, I, 40

63: Negroes at Bowdoin and Dartmouth: *Ibid.*, I, 178 n.
Negroes at Oberlin: *Ibid.*, II, 534-536

64: Stricter rules for students: *Ibid.*, I, 376-379
Female department: *Ibid.*, I, 380
Classics at Oberlin: *Ibid.*, I, 367-372

65: Revivalistic atmosphere: *Ibid.*, I, 182 n., 209-213; II, 749
Oberlin's "heresy": *Ibid.*, I, 224
Moral reform societies: *Ibid.*, I, 299-308

66: Students and faculty rescue slave: *Ibid.*, I, 394-412

67: Slaveholders send mulatto children: *Ibid.*, II, 528-529

68: Methods of travel: *Ibid.*, II, 539
First generation of faculty: *Ibid.*, II, 689
Size of colleges: Charles F. Thwing, *The American College in
American Life*, New York, 1897, p. 189
Enrollments at Oberlin: Fletcher, I, 431

69: Horace Taylor: *Ibid.*, I, 313 and 433-450

70: Plan for University of Michigan: Kent Sagendorph, *Michigan,
The Story of the University*, New York, 1948, pp. 48-52

71: Largest college in America: *Ibid.*, p. 108
"In our country . . .": Charles M. Perry, *Henry Philip Tappan,
Philosopher and University President*, Ann Arbor, 1933, p. 223
". . . to place them at everyone's door . . .": *Ibid.*, p. 227;
Tappan's faculty: *Ibid.*, p. 206; White's methods: *Autobiography
of Andrew Dickson White*, New York, 1906, I, 42 and 255-264

73: Tappan sets up art gallery: C. M. Perry, p. 234-235
Musical evenings: White, I, p. 273
Scandalized prohibitionists: C. M. Perry, p. 257

"To him more than to any other . . .": *Ibid.*, p. 230
Sectarian attack on Tappan: *Ibid.*, pp. 275-277, 281, and 296
74: Storey's attack: *Ibid.*, pp. 199-200
Mrs. Tappan: White, I, p. 299
"Tappan was the largest . . .": C. M. Perry, p. 275
Teacher training at Lafayette: William B. Owen, *Historical Sketches in Record of the Men of Lafayette*, Easton, 1879, p. 15
75: Josiah Quincy's inaugural address: Snow, p. 163
Curricular changes at Vermont: Schmidt, pp. 156-157
Francis Wayland's program: *Ibid.*, p. 158
"That such a people . . .": Francis Wayland, *Report to the Corporation of Brown University*, Providence, 1850, p. 12
76: Absurdity of crowded curriculum: *Ibid.*, pp. 14-15
Salaries and fees: *Ibid.*, pp. 44-47
77: "Seven point program": *Ibid.*, pp. 51-52
"If by placing Latin and Greek . . .": *Ibid.*, p. 74
78: Man's reasons for going to Antioch: B. A. Hinsdale, *Horace Mann and the Common School Revival in the United States*, London, 1898, p. 245
". . . a most remarkable coincidence . . .": Letter of 1852, quoted, Charles F. Thwing, *A History of Higher Education in America*, New York, 1906, p. 296
79: Mann's teaching: Hinsdale, p. 257
Letter of 1856: *Ibid.*, p. 263
"Unitarianize our sons and daughters": Ira W. Allen, *History of the Rise, Difficulties and Suspension of Antioch College*, Columbus, 1858, p. 74
". . . it is evident, we think . . .": *Ibid.*, pp. 72-73
80: *Gospel Herald* editorial: Quoted, Allen, p. 80
"Antioch now being dead to us": *Ibid.*, p. 87
". . . some souls so small . . ."; Hinsdale, p. 262

III. THE MYTH OF CLOISTERED HALLS

82: Spy Club: Wagner, p. 63
83: "Exactly two weeks later . . .": Coulter, p. 103
Delaware College: Joseph Cleaver, Jr., *The Diary of a Student at Delaware College, August, 1853 to November, 1854*, ed. by William Ditto Lewis, Baltimore, 1951, p. 79
Amherst in the 1840s: William Gardiner Hammond, *Remembrance of Amherst, An Undergraduate's Diary, 1846-1848*, ed. by George F. Whicher, New York, 1946, p. 77
84: Philological Society: Cheney, p. 197
Debates at Georgia: Coulter, pp. 123-124
Oberlin: Fletcher, II, p. 771
Debates at Virginia: Bruce, II, pp. 357-358

85: ". . . education must be completed . . .": Fletcher, I, p. 159
86: Suppression of antislavery organizations: *Ibid.,* I, pp. 163 and 184
Presidents Madison and Monroe: Bruce, II, p. 354
Honorary members at Georgia: Coulter, pp. 109-111
87: Philo Society at Pennsylvania: Cheney, p. 198
Societies lend books, etc.: Carver, p. 64
Napthali Dagget: Harris E. Starr, *D. A. B.,* V, p. 28
88: Frelinghuysen and Taylor of Rutgers: William H. S. Demarest, *A History of Rutgers College, 1766-1924,* New Brunswick, 1924, pp. 112-113
Witherspoon, Dwight, and Brown: Schmidt, p. 171
Harvard class of 1768: Thwing, *A History,* p. 171
Harvard militiamen: Charles A. Wagner, *Harvard, Four Centuries and Freedoms,* New York, 1950, p. 65
Paul Litchfield: Rev. Paul Litchfield, *Diary March 23 to July 9, 1775, Mass. Hist. Soc. Proc.,* 1st series, XIX, 1881-1882, Cambridge, 1882, pp. 377-379
89: Tories in Massachusetts: Thwing, *A History,* p. 169
President Stiles: Quoted, *Yale Literary Magazine,* X, No. 3, Jan. 1845, p. 147
Meigs, Dwight, Cooper: Schmidt, p. 172-180
"Next to the sermon . . .": *Ibid.,* p. 172
90: Harvard in mid-eighteenth century: Snow, p. 48
91: Popularity of Dwight: Charles E. Cunningham, *Timothy Dwight, 1752-1817,* New York, 1942, pp. 36-41
Virginia library: Bruce, II, pp. 188-189
Oberlin forbade Shakespeare: Fletcher, I, p. 312
92: President Waddel of Georgia: Coulter, p. 81
Reading of Oberlin students: Fletcher, II, pp. 740-741, 764, and 772
Reading of Virginia students: Bruce, II, pp. 343-345
93-94: Hammond's reading: References scattered throughout diary
94-95: Novels at Oberlin: Fletcher, I, p. 311
95: Harvard *Lyceum:* Wagner, pp. 294-295
Zelosophic Society: Cheney, p. 199
Literary magazines at Virginia: Bruce, III, pp. 106-109
Phi Beta Society at Oberlin: Fletcher, II, p. 764
97: ". . . have no tombs of their ancestors . . .": *The Zelosophic Magazine* (Pennsylvania), Vol. I, 1834, pp. 279-280
"Those seasons of refreshment . . .": *Yale Lit.,* XXII, No. 3 (Dec. 1856), p. 88
98-99: Stories in *Yale Lit.:* Vol. X, 1844
99: "I saw a youth careering . . .": *Ibid.,* XXIII, No. 11 (Nov. 1857), p. 79
100: History of *One Fishball:* Wagner, pp. 128-130
Advertisement in *Yale Lit.:* Vol. XXII, No. 3 (Dec. 1856)
Child teaches Anglo-Saxon: Wagner, p. 148

IV. STUDENT LIFE

102: A historian of the University of Virginia: Bruce, II, Chs. XXVII-XXXII

Gymnastics at Virginia: *Ibid.*, II, 337-338, and Abernathy, p. 16

103: "If swimming on the Sabbath . . .": Cleaver, p. 62

Jacob Rhett Motte: *Charleston Goes to Harvard, The Diary of a Harvard Student of 1831,* ed. by Arthur H. Cole, Cambridge, 1940, p. 72

Adventures with "wooden horse": *Ibid.*, pp. 76, 89, 95

Football "rushes" at Harvard: Wagner, p. 300

104: Andrew White at Hobart: White, I, 19

105: University of Wisconsin: Merle Curti and Vernon Carstensen, *The University of Wisconsin, 1848-1925,* Madison, 1949, I, 190 and 196

Riots in Philadelphia: Ellis Paxon Oberholtzer, *Philadelphia, A History of the City and Its People,* Philadelphia, n.d., II, 280-299

106: Haverford diarist: Diary of *James Tyson* (Quaker Collection, Haverford College), June 16, 1860

107: Girls in Delaware dormitory: Cleaver, p. 76

Standing at stile: *Ibid.*, pp. 23 and 55

Laughter at art lecture: *Ibid.*, p. 61

University of Wisconsin: Curti and Carstensen, I, 196

President Locke's resignation: Wagner, p. 63

Jonathan Fisher: Mary Ellen Chase, *Jonathan Fisher, Maine Parson,* New York, 1948, p. 14

108: Students gather at home of President Stiles: *Yale Lit.,* Vol. X, No. 3 (Jan. 1845), p. 148

Fisher's courtship and marriage: Chase, pp. 49-50

108-109: Motte meets girls: Motte, pp. 23-24, 66, and 77

109: Hammond's dates (in order referred to): Hammond, pp. 186, 109, 25, 55, and 76

110: "It was not the voluptuous kiss of love . . .": *Ibid.*, p. 100

"Miss Warner gave me . . .": *Ibid.*, p. 169

The sleigh ride: *Ibid.*, pp. 220-223

111: "I do not wish *truly* and honestly . . ." (the time is 1864): Fletcher, II, 824

"Heighho! to-morrow I must leave her . . .": *Yale Lit.,* Vol. IX, No. 9 (Aug. 1844)

Georgia University Magazine: Coulter, p. 94

Yale Lit. of the same period: April 1857

"Yale students could obtain beer . . .": Diary of Ezra Stiles, quoted, *Yale Lit.,* Vol. X, No. 3 (Jan. 1845), p. 147

112: Elijah Backus: "Yale Boys of the Last Century, The Journal of Elijah Backus Junior at Yale College, from ye first to Dec. 31,

1777" (Jan. to Dec. 1777), ed. by Ellen D. Larned, *Connecticut Quarterly*, I, 1895, pp. 358 and 360
112-113: Fines at Harvard: Schmidt, p. 81
113: Exhibitions followed by drunkenness: Chase, p. 32
University of Georgia: Coulter, p. 80
Drinking at Virginia: Bruce, II, 280-286
114: "But here as everywhere else . . .": Hammond, p. 239
Drinking at Michigan: Sagendorph, p. 90
Liquor in Delaware dormitories: Cleaver, p. 22
Sherry at Haverford: *Diary of William Canby* (Quaker Collection, Haverford College), Oct. 10, 1838
115: Hatch's lecture: Hammond, p. 120 (Junius Hatch was a student)
Georgia students break up meeting: Coulter, pp. 95-96
"nice beer and family prayers . . .": Hammond, p. 269
Dartmouth students camp out: Thwing, *A History*, p. 147
Georgia students take holidays: Coulter, pp. 84 and 222
Delaware students go to circus: Cleaver, pp. 26-27
116: "It is the anniversary . . .": Motte, pp. 31-32
Visit to auctions: *Ibid.*, p. 89
"cod-fish in commons . . .": *Ibid.*, p. 10
Hammond visits cattle show: Hammond, p. 199
Delaware student visits Philadelphia: Cleaver, p. 41
118: Dancing at Georgia: Coulter, pp. 142-143
Hammond goes to theater: Hammond, p. 101
Oberlin faculty members: Fletcher, I, 312
Sectarian colleges in Georgia: Coulter, pp. 153-161
119-120: Students' use of ponies: White, I, 18; Motte, p. 61
120: Lafayette Faculty: *Faculty Minutes*
Honor system at Virginia: Abernathy, pp. 12-13
Motte locks up room: Motte, p. 93
121: Graduate orator at Pennsylvania: Schmidt, p. 103
123: Professor Webster murders creditor: Wagner, pp. 122-123
Motte on Webster: Motte, p. 8
Harvard student of 1790: Chase, pp. 30, 38-39
124: "Brisk wielder of the birch and rule . . .": *Snow-Bound*, ll. 438-456, 466-475
125: Manual labor at Dartmouth: Thwing, *A History*, p. 145
President Kirkland gives jobs: Wagner, p. 80
126: Origin of manual-labor colleges: Fletcher, I, 42, and Schmidt, p. 88
Expenses and pay at Oberlin: Fletcher, II, 623-643
127: ". . . some lounging in the fashionable streets": Motte, p. 68
Cost of coat, $26: *Ibid.*, p. 16
Men's shirts at Oberlin: Fletcher, II, 623
127-128: Yearly expenses: Fletcher, I, 56; II, 621; Bruce, III, 182; Coulter, p. 56
128: Seventeenth-century Harvard students: Thwing, *A History*, p. 76
Party at Amherst: Hammond, p. 41

129: "... a dignified company": *Yale Lit.*, Vol. XXII, No. 3, Dec. 1856
"No office 'in the gift of the people' ": *loc. cit.*
"It matters not . . .": *Ibid.*, Vol. XXIII, No. 3, Dec. 1857

130: "... yet at this Seat of the Muses . . .": Chase, p. 21
"Nothing can equal the beauty . . .": Motte, p. 94
John Muir: Curti and Carstensen, I, 197

130-131: First commencement at William and Mary: Thwing, *A History*, p. 58

131: "It seemed as if the earth shook . . .": Cunningham, p. 172
"The college yard presents . . .": Motte, p. 104

131-132: Exhibition day at Delaware: Cleaver, pp. 64-65

V. DEATH AND TRANSFIGURATION

133: "Legree whippings": Charles M. Perry, *Henry Philip Tappan, Philosopher and University President*, Ann Arbor, 1933, p. 268
Michigan students chase antislavery speaker: Sagendorph, pp. 104-105

133-134: Moses Coit Tyler: Howard Mumford Jones and Thomas Edgar Casady, *The Life of Moses Coit Tyler*, Ann Arbor, 1933, pp. 52-53

134: Georgia students: Coulter, p. 236
Virginia students: Bruce, II, 260-261, 267-268
Military drill at Michigan: C. M. Perry, pp. 270-271
Lafayette faculty: *Faculty Minutes*, Oct. 29 and 30, 1861

134-135: Georgia in the Civil War: Coulter, pp. 239-241

135: Students at Pennsylvania: Cheney, pp. 249-251
Student petition at Lafayette: *Faculty Minutes*, Sept. 15, 1863

135-136: Pennsylvania trustees: Cheney, p. 251

136: Percentage of men in service: Thwing, *A History*, pp. 364 and 369; Abernathy, p. 23; Sagendorph, p. 99; W. B. Owen, *Historical Sketches of Lafayette College*, Easton, 1876, p. 26
Increase of students after the war: Sagendorph, p. 108; Barnard, "Appendix"; Abernathy, pp. 18 and 25; Coulter, pp. 255 and 273

137: British traveler: Sophia Jex Blake, *A Visit to Some American Schools and Colleges*, London, 1867, pp. 20-21
"... much more manly . . .": Coulter, p. 255
Cricket at Oberlin: Fletcher, II, 824; at Michigan: Sagendorph, p. 110

137-138: Baseball mania: Wagner, p. 301; Sagendorph, p. 110; Lafayette *Faculty Minutes*, Sept. and Nov. 1866; Coulter, p. 268; Fletcher, II, 825

139: Amherst faculty: *Cambridge History of American Literature*, New York, 1936, III, 413

140: "The number of students in our country . . .": Lafayette *Faculty Minutes*, Dec. 12, 1865
$300,000: Estimate based on Owens, pp. 32 ff.

141:      Lafayette curriculum: Owens, pp. 44 and 54
141-142: Classical course at Amherst: Amherst *Faculty Minutes,* May 21, 1884
142:      "An English classic . . .": Owen, p. 56
          Textbook in American Literature: Davis, Fredrick, and Mott, *American Literature,* New York, 1948, II, 368
144:      White: *Autobiography,* I, 358
145:      Attacks on elective system: *Ibid.,* I, 315
          Changed attitude at Cornell: *Ibid.,* I, 362
146:      Enrollment at Michigan: Sagendorph, p. 108
          "Throughout America . . .": *Ibid.,* p. 153
147:      "So it's back to the farm . . .": James Gray, *The University of Minnesota, 1851-1951,* Minneapolis, 1951, p. 34
          "snobs and theorists": *Ibid.,* p. 96
          "There is no spot on earth . . .": *Ibid.,* p. 35
149:      "Such a federation of schools . . .": *Ibid.,* p. 44
150:      "We purchase a telegraph . . .": *Ibid.,* p. 45
          "offer every child in Minnesota": *Ibid.,* pp. 52-53
150-151: Faculty report: *Ibid.,* p. 64
151:      "Plato to hog cholera": *Ibid.,* p. 39
          Folwell's plans laid aside: *Ibid.,* pp. 80 *ff.*
          Enrollments: Barnard, "Appendix" and *Report of the Commissioner for Education for 1870*
151-152: Barnard points to falling enrollments: Barnard, pp. 87-92
152:      Election of Eliot: Henry James, *Charles W. Eliot,* Cambridge, 1930, I, 191-201
          Eliot's background: M. A. De Wolfe Howe, *Classic Shades,* Boston, 1928, pp. 175-176
153:      Eliot's views: James, I, 167-169
153-154: Eliot's inaugural address: *Ibid.,* I, 228-231
155:      Salaries at Michigan: Mumford and Casady, p. 115
          Salaries at N.Y.U.: Theodore Francis Jones, *New York University, 1832-1932,* New York, 1933, p. 88
          Francis Child: James, I, 258-259
          Recitation method gives way: Samuel Eliot Morrison, *The Development of Harvard University Since the Inauguration of President Eliot, 1869-1929,* Cambridge, 1930, p. xliii
          Selection of Henry Adams: James, I, 256
156-157: Eliot presides over meetings: *Ibid.,* I, 243
157:      Oliver Wendell Holmes: *Ibid.,* I, 276
          "I suppose . . . this young doctor . . .": Wagner, p. 141
159:      Dismissal of Professor Fiske: *Ibid.,* p. 147
160:      "Universities are a want . . .": Barnard, p. 340
161:      "It is idle . . ." (1871): *Ibid.,* p. 94
          "If we consider . . ." (1871): *Ibid.,* p. 96
          Barnard criticizes expanded curriculums: *Ibid.,* p. 103
161-162: Barnard's proposals: Coon, pp. 79-80

162: Attacks finishing schools: Barnard, p. 255
Barnard on coeducation (1880 and 1881): *Ibid.*, pp. 268, 274-275
School of engineering, etc. (1880): *Ibid.*, p. 288
163: Opposes intercollegiate athletics: *Ibid.*, p. 205
164: ". . . when the seeker after knowledge . . .": *Ibid.*, p. 155
165: Hopkins trustee visits Michigan: John C. French, *A History of the University Founded by Johns Hopkins,* Baltimore, 1946, pp. 23-24
Election of Gillman: *Ibid.*, p. 32
166: Fields of study: *Ibid.*, pp. 65-66
167: ". . . the creation of a school of graduate studies . . .": *Ibid.*, p. 86

VI. HIGH SERIOUSNESS IN BLOOMERS

169: Employments of women: Thomas Woody, *A History of Women's Education in the United States,* New York and Lancaster, Pa., 1929, I, 164 *ff.*
170: Few pupils complete course: *Ibid.*, I, 454-455
Editors criticize women's education: Eleanor Wolf Thompson, *Education for Ladies, 1830-1860,* New York, 1947, pp. 24 *ff.*
171: Professor Silliman's views: *Ibid.*, p. 32
171-172: Tabulation of 107 schools: Woody, I, 417-418
172: Leaders of the seminary movement: *Ibid.*, I, 410
173: Seminaries utilitarian: *Ibid.*, I, 397
Financing of seminaries: *Ibid.*, I, 446-447
Catherine Beecher: Willystine Goodsell, *Pioneers of Women's Education in the United States,* New York, 1931, pp. 131-132
Emma Willard: *Ibid.*, pp. 25-27
174: Georgia Female College: Woody, II, 140, 156-157, 164-166, 198-199
175: Other women's colleges: *Ibid.*, II, 174, 184
Catherine Beecher: Goodsell, pp. 115 *ff.*; 145, 230
"absurdity of sending ladies to college": Woody, II, 147
176: Women's Educational Association: Goodsell, p. 137
176-177: Women's health: Woody, II, 101 and 105
177: "Saw some of the young ladies . . .": Hammond, p. 142
177-178: Dio Lewis: Woody, II, 103 and 116
178: Milo P. Jewett: *Ibid.*, II, 181
178-179: Matthew Vassar: Benson J. Lossing, *Vassar College and Its Founder,* New York, 1867, pp. 12-13, 26-28, 59, 81
179: ". . . It occurred to me . . .": *Ibid.*, pp. 91-93
180: "What do you think of a woman's college?": Francis A. Wood, *Earliest Years at Vassar,* Poughkeepsie, 1909, pp. 5-6
181: Buildings and faculty: Lossing, pp. 110-115
181-182: "It is my hope . . .": *Ibid.*, pp. 107-108
182: Mr. Vassar gets a letter: Wood, p. 65

182-183: Anecdotes of faculty: *Ibid.,* pp. 7, 29-30, 82
183-184: The founding of Wellesley: Alice Payne Hackett, *Wellesley, Part of the American Story,* New York, 1949, pp. 17-39
184-185: Schedule at Vassar: Wood, p. 21
185: Miss Lyman: *Ibid.,* pp. 25 and 29
185-186: The Durants supervise Wellesley: Hackett, pp. 55-64
187: Only 58 students qualify: *Ibid.,* p. 50
Girls on train: *Ibid.,* p. 55
The original faculty: *Ibid.,* pp. 37-38
Alice Freeman: George Herbert Palmer, *The Life of Alice Freeman Palmer,* Cambridge, 1908, pp. 106 and 140
188: "It does seem impossible . . .": *Ibid.,* p. 111
Alice Freeman on coeducation: *Ibid.,* p. 51
188-189: Religious views: *Ibid.,* p. 98, and Hackett, p. 88
189: Becomes president: Miss Freeman was made acting president in 1882 at the age of 25, and president a year later.
Durant's educational methods: Hackett, pp. 42 and 62
Abandonment of the word "female": Woody, II, 179; Lossing, p. 86; Hackett, pp. 30-31
190: "The object of the Institution . . .": Elizabeth Deering Hanscom and Helen French Greene, *Sophia Smith and the Beginnings of Smith College,* Northampton, 1926, p. 115
Influence of Rev. John M. Greene: *Ibid.,* p. 40
Fund raising: *Ibid.,* pp. 97 and 117
191: Requirements for admission: *Ibid.,* p. 118
Requirements at Harvard: Morrison, p. xliii
192: Statistics of 1892: Hackett, p. 107
Margaret Shinn study: Woody, II, 207
193: "If only half the college women marry . . .": *The Nation,* Apr. 24, 1890 (Quoted, Woody, II, 209-210)
Study of 1903: Woody, II, 208
194: Smith curriculum: Hanscom and Greene, pp. 57 ff.
Eliot on minds of women: Woody, II, 155
Weir Mitchell: Ernest Earnest, *S. Weir Mitchell, Novelist and Physician,* Philadelphia, 1950, p. 150
M. Carey Thomas: Woody, II, 154
G. Stanley Hall, quoted (1907): *Ibid.,* II, 272
Study of pedagogy: Fletcher, I, 345, and Sagendorph, p. 153
191-195: White visits Oberlin and Michigan: White, I, 400
195: Coeducation at Oberlin: Woody, II, 236-237, and Fletcher, II, 906
195-196: Men students object: Sagendorph, p. 112; Woody, II, 248-249
196: Wisconsin students: Curti and Carstensen, I, 370-375
Attacks on coeducation: Woody, II, 274-277
197: H. S. Tarbell: *Ibid.,* II, 263
Alice Freeman: Palmer, pp. 94-100
Statistics on coeducation: Woody, II, p. 252
198: President Eliot (1883): Quoted, Woody, II, 257
198-200: Co-ordinate colleges: *Ibid.,* II, 309-319

200: M. Carey Thomas in 1873: *Ibid.*, II, 152-153
201: President Van Hise: *Ibid.*, II, 267
Restrictions at Cornell: White, I, 402
"One might search . . .": *The Education of Henry Adams,*
"Chaos 1870"
202: Mark Twain (italics mine): Bernard De Voto, *Mark Twain in
Eruption,* New York, 1940, pp. 257-258
202-203: Katherine Coman: Hackett, p. 81
203: Vida Scudder: *Ibid.*, p. 119

VII. THE GOLDEN AGE AND THE GILDED CAGE

205: "I say our colleges . . .": Owen Johnson, *Stover at Yale,* New
York, 1912, pp. 242-243
205-206: "no kind of intellectual athletics . . .": George Wilson Pierson,
Yale College, An Educational History, 1871-1921, New Haven,
1952, p. 58
206: Poultney Bigelow: *Ibid.*, p. 592 n.
Santayana on Yale: George Santayana, "A Glimpse of Yale," *Harvard Monthly,* Dec. 1892
Perrin on Yale: Pierson, p. 93
Self-discipline of Yale athletes: *Ibid.*, p. 79
206-207: Canby on Yale: Henry Seidel Canby, *Alma Mater, The Gothic
Age of the American College,* New York, 1936, p. 58
207: Lafayette team: L. H. Baker, *Football Facts and Figures,* New
York, 1945, p. 621
Wisconsin fraternities: Curti and Carstensen, I, 659-665
Canby on materialism: Canby, p. 108
208: Canby on college life: *Ibid.*, pp. 36, 69-72
"Oh father and mother . . .": *Stover,* p. 334
Observer at Princeton: James Anderson Hawes, *Twenty Years
Among the Twenty Year Olds,* New York, 1929, p. 157
209: "He was face to face . . .": *Stover,* p. 15
Freshman halls at Harvard: Henry Aaron Yeomans, *Abbott Lawrence Lowell, 1856-1943,* Cambridge, 1948, pp. 173-174
210: "The Hutch": Pierson, p. 235
210-211: "You come from a school . . .": *Stover,* pp. 27-28
211: Number elected to senior societies: Pierson, pp. 35-36
213: Canby on Tudor Gothic: Canby, p. 232
"The youth stepped out . . .": *Ibid.*, pp. 226-227
214: Stanford Stories: Charles K. Field and Will H. Irwin, *Stanford
Stories, Tales of a Young University,* New York, 1900
215: ". . . five small clubs . . .": Charles Macomb Flandrau, *Harvard
Episodes,* Boston, 1897, pp. 261-262 and 270
Professor Fleetwood: Charles Macomb Flandrau, *Diary of a Freshman,* New York, 1912 (Published serially, 1900)

Owen Wister on Harvard: Owen Wister, *Philosophy 4*, New York, 1903, pp. 36-39 and 41

216: Percentage in select clubs: Wagner, pp. 82-84

Social organizations of other colleges: *Cf.* Hawes on New England colleges.

Lowell develops freshman dormitories: Yeomans, pp. 163 *ff.*

217: Students keep down percentage of Jews: Hawes, p. 54

217-218: "Now, take Bertie": *Diary of a Freshman*, pp. 252-253

219: Harvard requirements in the 80s: Morrison, p. xliii-xlvi

Cost of tutoring: Wister and Flandrau

Cheating at Yale: Pierson, pp. 232-246

Cheating at Wisconsin: Curti and Carstensen, I, 677

Class averages at Yale: Pierson, pp. 240-241

220: "The born leaders and managers . . .": "What Is a College For?", *Scribner's*, Vol. XLVI, No. 5 (Nov. 1909), pp. 570-577.

221: Early football: Wagner, pp. 301-302, and Coon, pp. 291-294

"Let them come on . . .": Howland, "Undergraduate Life at Yale," *Scribner's*, Vol. XXII, No. 1 (July 1897), p. 27

222: Record of Yale teams: F. G. Menke, *All Sports Record Book*, New York, 1950, p. 114, and Baker, p. 272

Football at Wisconsin: Curti and Carstensen, I, 693-702

223: Yale-trained coaches: Pierson, pp. 33-34

224: Football at Columbia: Coon, pp. 298 and 301

Football at Michigan: Sagendorph, pp. 209-225

Walter Camp: Pierson, pp. 39 and 255

225: Warner and Haughton: Wagner, pp. 308-309

Flying wedge and turtle back: Baker, pp. 564-565

Public outcry: Curti and Carstensen, I, 695-696; Coon, p. 300

44 dead in 1903: *World Almanac*, 1911

226: George Wharton Pepper: Cheney, p. 317

"Something is the matter . . .": *Outlook*, Nov. 18, 1905, pp. 668-669

227: "I believe heartily . . .": *Ibid.*, p. 666

Reform party loses at Yale: Pierson, p. 255

229: William H. Lewis: Wagner, p. 310

Phelps: William Lyon Phelps, *Autobiography with Letters*, New York, 1939, pp. 329-330

230: Panty raid at Wisconsin: Curti and Carstensen, I, 674-675

231: Yale class of 1901: Pierson, p. 232

232: "The sweet co-ed . . .": (1888): Curti and Carstensen, I, 667-668

232-233: "those paradises in pants . . .": George Fitch, *At Good Old Siwash*, Boston, 1911, pp. 223-224

"the vast army of women . . .": *Harvard Episodes*, p. 300

234: Phelps on Yale reading: Phelps, pp. 146, 209, 279 and 312

235: Latin assignment at Williams: Bliss Perry, *And Gladly Teach*, New York, 1935, p. 39

Phelps at Harvard: Phelps, p. 248

Perry at Princeton: Perry, pp. 246-256

236: "The younger generation . . .": Phelps, p. 155
"We resisted the intrusion . . .": Canby, p. 46
"You don't know the big men . . .": *Stover*, p. 330
Wilson on the faculty: "What Is a College For?"

237: Mrs. Stanford at Harvard: Coon, p. 103
Sells jewels: *Stanford Stories*, p. 207 (Quoting Associated Press)
Seth Low: Coon, pp. 88 and 108

238: Eliot builds endowment: James, II, 350
William Rainey Harper: Thomas Wakefield Goodspeed, *William Rainey Harper*, Chicago, 1928, pp. 68-101

239: Gifts of $9,000,000: *Ibid.*, p. 155
Deanship for Mrs. Palmer: Palmer, p. 267
1,000 apply: Goodspeed, p. 123
Faculty and Yerkes Observatory: Paul Shorey, *D. A. B.*, VIII, 287-292

240: President Hadley's remark: Phelps, p. 161

241: Courts regard faculty as employees: Richard H. Shyrock, "The Academic Profession in the United States," *American Association of University Professors Bulletin*, Vol. 38, No. 1 (Spring 1952), p. 38
"As to what should be taught . . .": *Ibid.*, p. 55
Dismissal of E. A. Ross: Edward Alsworth Ross, *Seventy Years of It, An Autobiography*, New York, 1936, pp. 64-86
American Economic Association appoints committee: Shyrock, p. 56

242: Ross on Wisconsin: Ross, p. 101
Thorstein Veblen: Although *The Higher Education in America* was published in 1918, Veblen states that he wrote it a dozen years earlier.

243: "President Doolittle . . .": Robert Herrick, *Chimes*, New York, 1926, p. 199
"Here in epitome . . .": *Ibid.*, p. 203

243-244: Richard A. Douglas: Pierson, p. 349

244: Canby on "growing up": Pierson, p. 349

VIII. THE AGE OF CONFLICT AND COONSKIN COATS

247: Eliot to Wilson: Charles W. Eliot, *The Road Toward Peace*, New York, 1915
Hadley on military training: Pierson, pp. 455-456
Butler changes views: Coon, pp. 125-126
F. Scott Fitzgerald's Princeton: F. Scott Fitzgerald, *This Side of Paradise*, New York, 1920, pp. 64 and 79
Hold-off night at Yale: Stephen Vincent Benét, *The Beginnings of Wisdom*, New York, 1921, p. 76

248: "None of the Victorian mothers . . .": Fitzgerald, pp. 64-65
Petting at Yale: Benét, pp. 125-126

Punch Bowl: April 1916

248-249: "The problem of evil had identified . . .": Fitzgerald, p. 302

249: Students question institutions: *Ibid.,* p. 139
"a samurai order . . .": Benét, p. 170
Wellesley bans smoking: Hackett, p. 217

249-250: "The war came . . .": Benét, p. 97

250: Phelps on war: Pierson, p. 450
Preparedness: Mark Sullivan, *Our Times,* New York, 1935, Vol. V, 207 and 258-259

251: Field Artillery Battery at Yale: Pierson, p. 458-461
SATC at Michigan: Sagendorph, p. 267

252: President Hadley writes Yale faculty: Pierson, p. 474
Dean Johnson of Minnesota: Gray, p. 252

252-253: War hysteria: Gray, 190; Sullivan, V, 474-477; Curti and Carstensen, II, 115-119

253-254: Dismissals at Columbia: Coon, pp. 122 *ff.*

254-255: "Having observed closely . . .": *New York Times,* Oct. 9, 1917, pp. 1 and 3

255: Professor William Schafer: Gray, pp. 247-249

256: "If a university censors . . .": Wagner, p. 199
Wisconsin faculty in the war: Claude Charleton Bowman, *The College Professor in America,* Philadelphia, 1938, pp. 148-149
Yale faculty: Pierson, p. 473

256-257: James B. Conant: Wagner, p. 203

257: Experts with Wilson: Sullivan, V, 534
"Down the gangplank . . .": William Allen White, *Woodrow Wilson,* Boston, 1924, p. 377

258: Coolidge's magazine articles: *Delineator,* June and July, 1921

259-260: The superpatriots: Fredrick Lewis Allen, *Only Yesterday, An Informal History of the 1920's,* New York, 1933, pp. 59-60

260: Theodore Roosevelt and Charles Evans Hughes: *Ibid.,* pp. 69-70

261: "It is too bad it is that way": "Public Opinion in the Middle West," *New Republic,* XX, 312 (Quoted, Bowman, p. 106)
"Though the children of the best families . . .": Bowman, p. 106
"shall express to such pupil . . .": Upton Sinclair, *The Goose Step, A Study of American Education,* Pasadena, 1923, p. 130

262: Faculty committee at Minnesota: Gray, pp. 255-257; Sinclair, pp. 219-221
Katherine Fullerton Gerould: "The Land of the Free," *Harper's,* Vol. 146 (Jan. 1923), pp. 137-146

263: Sinclair on Wisconsin: Sinclair, p. 230
Presidents resist pressures: Hackett, p. 222, and Wagner, pp. 99-200

263-264: Palmer red hunt: F. L. Allen, p. 56

265: Jane Addams barred from speaking: Sinclair, p. 267

269: Motorcars at Michigan: Sagendorph, pp. 291-302

273: MacCracken: John Henry MacCracken, *College and Commonwealth,* New York, 1920, pp. 18-19 and 37

273-274: Wisconsin *Octopus:* Curti and Carstensen, II, 136
274: Students carry *American Mercury:* Sullivan, VI, 413
277: Average salary in 1893: Bowman, p. 39
Arnett study: Trevor Arnett, "Teachers Salaries," 1928, General Education Board, p. 18
278: Honorary degrees: Stephen Edward Epler, *Honorary Degrees, A Survey of Their Use and Abuse,* Washington, D. C., 1943, pp. 75 and 96
278-281: Sacco-Vanzetti case: Wagner, pp. 213-216; Yeomans, pp. 483-496; *Time,* Aug. 29, 1927
281: Bishop Lawrence: William Lawrence, "The Relation of Wealth to Morals," *World's Work,* Jan. 1901, and *New Republic,* Aug. 31, 1927
Outlook on miscarriage of justice: *Outlook,* Oct. 31, 1928
282: Cattell, Thorndike, and Terman: R. L. Duffus, *Democracy Enters College,* New York, 1936, pp. 89-95
283-284: Norman Foerster: Norman Foerster, *The American State University, Its Relation to Democracy,* Chapel Hill, 1937, pp. 180, 235
284 Growth of enrollments: *Statistics of Higher Education, 1939-40 and 1941-42,* Federal Security Agency, U. S. Office of Education
285: Columbia Teachers College: Coon, pp. 221-223
Dewey denies heresies: R. Freeman Butts, *The College Charts Its Course,* New York and London, 1939, p. 317
286: Output of Ph.D.s: Epler, p. 71
286-287: *Yale Alumni Weekly:* June 14, 1918, and Pierson, p. 477
"Nevertheless . . . it becomes plain . . .": Pierson, p. 492
287-288: Meikeljohn's inaugural address: Alexander Meikeljohn, "The Theory of the Liberal College," *Freedom and the College,* New York, 1923
288: Failure to keep lawns mowed: J. M. Gaus, "The Issues at Amherst," *Nation,* 117, No. 3026 (July 4, 1923), p. 12
Favoritism to new men: Meikeljohn offered $5,000 to Stuart Sherman when the highest Amherst salary was $3,000. John Erskine, *My Life as a Teacher,* Philadelphia, 1948, pp. 50-55
288-289: "The Faculty find it exceedingly difficult . . .": "President Meikeljohn's Farewell Address," *School and Society,* XVIII, 445 (July 7, 1923), pp. 12-16
289: Criticisms of Meikeljohn: Robert Morse Lovett, "Meikeljohn at Amherst," *New Republic,* 35, 448 (July 4, 1923), pp. 146-148
290: "Under his inspiration . . .": *Ibid.*
Sarah Lawrence: Constance Warren, "The Sarah Lawrence Plan," *Nation,* 131, No. 3411 (Nov. 19, 1930), p. 549
291: Honors courses: Yeomans, p. 153; Duffus, pp. 156 *ff.;* Butts, p. 400
Rollins College: Hamilton Holt, "The Rollins Idea," *Nation,* 131, No. 3405 (Oct. 8, 1930), p. 372
Princeton plan: Charles G. Osgood, *Lights in Nassau Hall, A Book of the Bicentennial, Princeton 1746-1946,* Princeton, 1951, p. 43

Co-operative plan at Antioch: Duffus, p. 230

292-293: President Coffman's committee: Gray, pp. 351-355

IX. QUESTION PERIOD

295: Table of figures, Committee Y: Viva Boothe, "Statistical Summary of Address Given before the O.S.U. Chapter of the A.A.U.P. on the Economic Status of the Profession," Bureau of Business Research, Ohio State University.

296: Percentage decline of 5 professions: Malcom M. Wiley, *Depression, Recovery and Higher Education, A Report by Committee Y of the American Association of University Professors*, New York, 1937, p. 51
Salary cuts: *Ibid.*, p. 44
Enrollments: *Ibid.*, p. 234
Faculty shrinkage: *Ibid.*, p. 27

296-297: "the pinch of depression . . .": *Ibid.*, p. 52

297: Number in A.A.U.P.: *Ibid.*, pp. 9-10, 93, 453

298-300: Studies by A.A.U.P. and *Fortune:* The A.A.U.P. study was based on materials gathered from chapters at 125 institutions (Wiley, pp. 320-322); that of *Fortune* on questionnaires and interviews with 1,220 male and female students, faculty, etc. ("Youth in College," *Fortune*, XIII, 99-102, 153-162 [June 1936])

298: Typically undergraduate organizations: Gray, p. 367; *Fortune*, p. 161

300: Woodrow Wilson School: Osgood, pp. 49-50

301: N.Y.A.: "Financial Aid to College Students," Federal Security Agency, U. S. Office of Education *Bulletin*, 1940, No. 11, pp. 1-2

302: Federal funds for buildings: Wiley, pp. 381-382

303: Typical college girl: *Fortune*, p. 102

305: "He's the last of a strange race": George Anthony Weller, *Not to Eat, Not for Love*, New York, 1933, p. 61

306: Increasing sophistication: *Fortune*, p. 102

307: Montross stories: Lynn and Lois Montross, *Town and Gown*, New York, 1923, and *Fraternity Row*, New York, 1926
"He got up, fearful that he would say . . .": Weller, pp. 211-212

308: "When they came out . . .": *Ibid.*, 141
Study on instrumental music: Randall Thompson, *College Music*, New York, 1935, p. 107

310: Endowments, 1930: Duffus, pp. 16 and 31

310n: Growth of colleges: U. S. Office of Education *Bulletin*, 20, 1931, p. 5, and Wiley, p. 221

312: "The philosophy that underlies loyalty legislation": Wiley, p. 449

313: Robert Maynard Hutchins: *Cf.* James Gray, "Robert Hutchins . . . announced with engaging bravado that he was about to create for certain students, a good program of general education, without having any clear idea of what a good education consisted." *The University of Minnesota,* p. 429

315: Spiller on Canby: *Literary History of the United States,* New York, 1948, II, 1153-1154

316: Havenmann and West study: Ernest Havenmann and Patricia Salter West, *They Went to College, The College Graduate in America Today,* New York, 1952, pp. 151-154

X. THE WIDE WIDE WORLD

317-318: Manhattan Project: *Time,* Aug. 20, 1945

319: Harvard faculty in service: Wagner, p. 257

319-320: William H. Hobbs: *Who's Who in America,* Vol. 27, and Sagendorph, pp. 347-348

321: Doubts about G.I. Bill: Benjamin Fine, "Veterans Raise College Standards," *Educational Outlook,* 22:54-61 (Nov. 1947)
Success of veterans: *loc. cit.,* and Harold W. Stoke, "The Veterans Educate the Nation," *Association of American Universities Bulletin,* 33:467-473 (Oct. 1947)

323: Federal Government pays $301,000,000: *Report of the President's Commission on Higher Education,* Washington, 1947, V, 39

324: Percentage of boys and girls able to do college work: *Ibid.,* I, 41
4 to 1 advantage: *Ibid.,* II, 13
Needs by 1960: *Ibid.,* V, 26 and 39

325: "There is but one source . . .": *Ibid.,* V, 43
Number of courses offered: Malcolm MacLean, "Conflicting Theories of General Education," *The American College,* ed. by P. F. Valentine, New York, 1949, pp. 88-89

327: Professional men in civic activities: Havenmann and West, p. 152

328: Chicago selects top 10%: MacLean, pp. 96-97

328-329 Orientation courses: P. F. Valentine, "General Education Programs," *The American College,* p. 148

330: How to take a bath: Oliver Jensen, *The Revolt of American Women,* New York, 1952, p. 114

331: Earl J. McGrath: "The Need for Experimentation and Research," *General Education in Transition, A Look Ahead,* H. T. Morse, ed., Minneapolis, 1951, Chapter II
Professor MacLean's views: Malcolm MacLean, "The General College: Its Origin and Influence," *Ibid.,* Chapter III
J. L. Morrill: "The Present Challenge to General Education," *Ibid.,* Chapter I, p. 38

334: *Christian Century:* "Colleges in a Moral Fog," Feb. 1, 1950
"that the colleges were . . .": *Time,* Mar. 5, 1951

335: William and Mary: *Time,* Sept. 24, 1951
Coach at Indiana: *Time,* Dec. 10, 1951
"We have seen the athletic program . . .": *Time,* Oct. 1, 1951

Index

Italics indicate important entries.
Colleges are listed under their present names.

Abolition: 63, 66-68, 84-86, 133-134
Academic freedom: *see* Witch hunts
Adams, Charles Francis: 157, 201
Adams, Henry: 155, 201, 300
Addams, Jane: 203, 265
Agassiz, Louis: 144, 156
Agassiz, Mrs. Louis: 198
Allegheny College: 24
Allen, Fredrick Lewis: 263, 274
Allen, Ira W.: 79-80
American Association of University Professors: 243, 244, 295-298, 312, 337
American Historical Association: 166
American Legion: 300, 312
American literature: 72, 90
American Magazine and Monthly Chronicle: 52, 96
American Student Union: 299
American Youth for Democracy: 337
Amherst College: 10, 25, 33, 34, 40, 46, 65, 83, 91, 92, 95, 102, 113-114, 128, *139, 287-289,* 338
Andrews, E. Benjamin: 241-242
Angell, James B.: 74, 165
Antioch College: 57, *77-80,* 291
Antislavery societies: *see* Abolition
Arnold, Matthew: 29, 165, 189
Athletics *(see also* Football): 102-104, 137-138, 220-229, 334-335
Atomic bomb: *see* Manhattan Project
Automobiles: 247, 248, 269-270, 303
Aydelotte, Frank: 291

Backus, Elijah: 112
Baker, George Pierce: 155-156, 315
Bancroft, George: 71
Baptists: 56, 118
Barlow, Joel: 38

Barnard, Fredrick A. P.: 25, 26, 148, 151-152, *159-164,* 199, 217
Barr, Stringfellow: 313, 314
Bartram, John: 49
Baseball: 137-138
Bates, Katherine Lee: 192
Beard, Charles A.: *254-255*
Beecher, Catherine: 172-173, 175, 177
Beecher, Henry Ward: 133-134, 175
Beecher, Lyman: 37, 175
Benét, Stephen Vincent: 247-250
Benjamin, Simeon: 175
Bennington College: 292, 329
Bible, Study of: 45, 49, 64, 189
Birge, Edward A.: *273-274*
Bishop, Eli: 74
Bishop, Robert: 40
Booth, Lydia: 179
Bowditch, Henry P.: 156
Bowdoin College: 9, 63
"Bread and Butter Rebellion": 36
Briggs, LeBaron Russell: 199
Briscoe, Nathaniel: 19
Brown, John (Univ. of Ga.): 88
Brown University: 25, 31, 65, *75-77,* 137, 199
Bruce, Philip A.: 107
Brunnow, Francis: 72, 73
Bryn Mawr College: 197
Bulwer-Lytton, Edward: 92, 93, 95
Butler, Nicholas Murray: 237, 247, 253-255, 263
Byron, George Gordon Lord: 92, 93

Caldwell, Joseph: 43
California, University of: 336
Calkins, Mary: 263
Calvin (Calvinism): 32, 41, 57, 61, 65, 117-118

Cambridge University: 19, 20
Camp, Walter: 222, 223, 224, 227
Canby, Henry Seidel: 206-208, 213, 244, 315
Canby, William: 40, 46, 106
Carey, Isaac E.: 70
Carlisle Indians: 222, 225
Carstensen, Vernon: 263
Catholics: 56, 83
Cattell, J. McKeen: 254, 282-283, 292
Chamberlin, Jeremiah: 44
Chapel: 33, 39-42, 105
Chapman, Robert: 89
Chaucer: 21, 91
Cheating: 119-120, 161, 219
Chicago, University of: 199, 238-240, 242-243, 328-329
Child, Francis J.: 100, 155-156, 198
Church, Alonzo: 118
Cincinnati, University of: 291
Civil War: 133-137
Clap, Thomas: 43
Clarke, E. H.: 196
Classics: 22, 25-26, 51, 64, 138-139
Clay, Henry: 56
Cleaver, Joseph, Jr.: 106-107, 120
Clubs (see also Fraternities): 210-212, 214-218
Coeducation: 63-64, 163, 192, 194-198, 201
Coffman, Lotus D.: 292
College humor: 248, 273
College of Philadelphia: see Pennsylvania, University of
Columbia University: 13, 25, 27, 28, 29, 50-51, 159-164, 221, 237-238, 253-255, 285, 291, 330, 333
Commons: 36-39
Communism: 298, 299, 312-313, 336-337
Connecticut, General Assembly of: 22
Conwell, Russell: 90
Coolidge, Calvin: 10, 258, 260-261, 264, 265
Cooper, James Fenimore: 10, 37, 139
Cooper Niles: 88
Cooper, Thomas: 57, 89
Cornell, Ezra: 122, 143-145, 194
Cornell University: 143-146, 201
Coulter, Ellis Merton: 40, 57, 83
Counts, George Sylvester: 285
Cowles, John P.: 68-69
Cowman, Katherine: 202-203
Crane, Stephen: 10, 142

Cultural subjects: 12
Curriculum: 19, 20-23, 25, 28-32; Rev. Wm. Smith's, 48-55; Jefferson's, 53-54; Oberlin, 64; Wayland's, 75-77; Scientific, 138-142, 144; Cornell's, 144-145, 149-153, 161-162, 166; in female academies, 171-172; in women's colleges, 175 ff.; 286-287, 326-333
Curti, Merle: 263

Dagget, Naphthali: 87-88
Dana, Henry Wadsworth: 254
Dartmouth College: 9, 59, 63, 69, 123-125
Dating: 104, 108-112, 232-233, 304-306
Daughters of the American Revolution: 300, 312
Davidson College: 126
Davis, John H. G.: 44
Davison, Archibald T.: 308
Day, Clive: 257
Day, Jeremiah: 24, 43
Delaware College: 83, 92, 95, 107, 114, 116, 120-121, 131-132
Dewey John: 259, 285, 290, 313, 314, 329
Dickinson, Emily: 10
Disorder: 32-47, 59, 104-107, 229-230, 338-339
Dixon, Rolland B.: 257
Dormitories: 33, 71-72, 104, 181, 184, 212-213, 216
Dos Passos, John: 280
Dreiser, Theodore: 239
Drinking: 73, 105, 112-115, 270
Dunster, Henry: 20, 21, 28
Durant, Henry: 176, 183-189, 197, 202
Durant, Pauline: 183-184
Dwight, Timothy (1752-1817): 27, 31, 35, 40-41, 43, 44, 55, 61, 88, 89, 90-91, 123, 175
Dwight, Timothy (1828-1916): 212-213, 240

Eaton, Nathaniel: 19, 20
Eaton, Mrs. Nathaniel: 20, 36
Einstein, Albert: 318
Elective system: 54, 59, 77, 78, 153
Eliot, Charles W.: 27, 103, 152-159, 165, 194, 198, 224, 226, 227, 237, 242
Eliot, T. S.: 10, 24, 117, 148, 235, 274
Elmira Female University: 175, 176
Emerson, Joseph: 172

Emerson, Ralph Waldo: 10, 29, 32, 96, 117, 125, 128, 139
Emory University: 118, 136
Endowments: 237-239, 310, 335
Engineering: 72
English literature: 72-73, 90, 92, 142, 155, 192, 200, 333
Enrollments: 59, 68, 151, 284, *310*
Erskine, John: 291
Everett, Edward: 95
Exhibition Day: 87, *130-132*
Expenses: 127-128, 336

Faculty (*see also* Curriculum and Salaries): 81-82
Fairchild, James Harris: 67, 194-195
Fine Arts: 54, 192
Fines: 42-43
Finney, Charles Grandison: 41, 61-63
Fisher, Jonathan: 39, 107, 123, 125, 130
Fiske, John: 159
Fitzgerald, F. Scott: 111, 247, 249, 268, 273, 307
Flandrau, Charles M.: 207, 210, 215, 217-218, 233, 326
Fletcher, Robert S.: 60, 68
Foerster, Norman: 283-284, 313
Folwell, William Watts: 57, *146-151*, 325
Football: 102, 103-104, 207, *220-229*, 334-335
Fortune magazine: 298, 303-304, 338
Frank, Glenn: 280, 290
Frankfurter, Felix: 260, 279
Franklin, Benjamin: 10, 48-49, 122, 139
Franklin College: *see* Georgia, University of
Fraternities: 35, 128-129
Freeman, Alice: *see* Palmer, Alice Freeman
Frelinghuysen, Fredrick: 88
Freud, Sigmund: 248, 266
Frieze, Henry Simmons: 72, 73

Gale, George W.: 61, 126
General Education: 316, *325-333*
George Washington University: 278
Georgia, University of: 23, 34, 35, 38, 40, 44, 56-57, 70, 82-84, 87, 89, 111, 113, 115, 118, 134-135, 136-137, 138
Georgia Female College: 174
Gerould, Katherine Fullerton: 262, 290
Gerund grinding: 23, 26, 91

Giedion, Sigfried: 314
Gillman, Daniel Coit: 148, *164-168*
Gillman, Samuel: 95
Godfrey, Thomas, Jr.: 50
Gold Coast: 159, 212-213
Gothic, collegiate: 213
Graduate study: 72, *158*, 326, **333**
Grant, Zilpa: 170
Gray, Asa: 71, 156
Gray, James: 292
Great Books courses: 313, 330
Greek requirement (*see also* Classics and Languages): 23, 54, 64, 78, 144, 191
Greek Testament: 23, 28, 50, 64
Green, Ashbel: 88
Greene, John M.: 190
Greenfield Hill Academy: 27
Gross, Daniel: 29, 31
Gurney, Ephraim: 155-156, 198

Hadley, Arthur Twining: 224, 227, 240, 247, 251, 252
Hadley, James: 25
Hall, G. Stanley: 194, 196-197
Hall, Robert: 320
Hamilton College: 61, 86
Hammond, William Gardiner: 27, 39-40, 41; books read, 93-94, 102; dates, 108-109, 113-114, 115, 116, 118, 128, 177, 188
Hanover College: 86
Hardenbergh, Jacob: 27, 88
Harper, William Rainey: *238-240, 243*, 277
Harris, W. T.: 25
Hart, Albert Bushnell: 155
Harvard University (*see also* subjects, *e.g.* Curriculum): 10, 13, 19, 20, 21, 22, 23, 28, 33, 34, 35, 36, 37, 42, 45, 59, 68, 81, 82, 88, 90, 103, 104, 113, 120, 133, 137, 139, 151, *152-159*, 191, 198, 211-212, 215, 216, 219, 235, **238**, 315, 329, 338-339
Haskins, Charles H.: 257
Hatch, Junius: 40, 115
Haughton, Percy: 225, 227
Haverford College: 40, 46, 106, 114
Hawthorne, Nathaniel: 9, 113, *139*
Hayes, Ellen: 280
Hazing: 121-122
Hearst press: 300, 312
Hemingway, Ernest: 10

Herrick, Robert: 242-243
Hobart College: 45, 105, 148
Hobbs, William H.: 319-320
Holley, Horace: 41, 55-57
Holmes, Oliver Wendell: 95-96, 139, 157, 189
Holmes, Oliver Wendell (the Justice): 155-156
Holt, Hamilton: 291
Holyoke: see Mount Holyoke
Homer: see Classics and Curriculum
Honorary Degrees: 276
Honors courses: 162
Hopkins, Johns: 164-165
Hopkins, Mark: 156
Hopkinson, Francis: 50
Howard, Ada: 187
Howe, Joseph: 90
Howells, William Dean: 139, 142, 189
Humanities (see also Curriculum and General Education): 140, 316, 325-328, 330
Hutchins, Robert Maynard: 14, 29, 50, 141, 313-314, 328
Huxley, Thomas: 166

Indiana University: 57, 335
Intelligence tests: 282-283, 324
Iowa, University of: 105

Jackson, Andrew: 10, 56, 86
James, Henry: 139, 235
James, William: 155, 157
Jefferson, Thomas: 9, 10, 12, 23, 31, 53-54, 57-59, 80, 91, 122, 139
Jewett, Milo P.: 179
Johns Hopkins University: 164-168
Johnson, Owen: see Stover at Yale
Johnson, Rev. Samuel: 25, 27, 29, 50-51
Jordan, David Starr: 241, 247, 250, 280
Judson Female Institute: 179
Junkin, George: 74-75

Kilpatrick, William H.: 285
Kings College: see Columbia University
Kingsley, James L.: 24
Kinsey, Alfred C.: 81, 267-268
Kirkland, John T.: 33, 42, 43, 125
Kittredge, George Lyman: 142, 155-156, 199
Knox College: 126
Kouwenhoven, John A.: 314

Lafayette, Marquis de: 56
Lafayette College: 40, 45, 74-75, 120, 126, 134, 135, 137-138, 140-142, 207, 234, 273, 278
Lane, George M.: 156
Lane, Martin: 99-100
Lane Institute: 62-63, 85
Langdell, Christopher Columbus: 157
Languages, ancient: 25, 28
Languages, modern: 24, 54
Laski, Harold: 263
Latin (requirement. Cf. also Classics and Languages): 54, 64, 78, 144, 191
Lawrence, E. O.: 318
"Lay of One Fishball, The": 99-100
Lecture system: 72
Lehigh University: 140
Lewis, Dio: 177-178
Lewis, William H.: 229
Liberal arts: see Classics, Curriculum, General Education
Libraries: 35, 58-59, 92
Lincoln, Abraham: 10, 134, 143
Lipscomb, Andrew A.: 137
Litchfield, Paul: 88
Literary Societies: 35-36, 82-87, 90, 95, 131
Locke, John: 22, 29, 50, 112
Locke, Samuel: 107
Longfellow, Henry W.: 117, 139, 156, 189, 192
Lord, Benjamin: 23
Lounsbury, Thomas: 148
Low, Seth: 237-238
Lowell, A. Lawrence: 209, 216, 247, 256, 263, 279-281, 325
Lowell, James Russell: 96, 100, 139, 144, 156
Lunt, W. E.: 257
Lyman, Hannah W.: 183, 185
Lyon, Mary: 173, 177, 188

McCarthy, Joseph: 337
McCormick press: 312, 337
McCosh, James: 31-32
McCracken, John Henry: 273
McElroy, Robert McNutt: 253
McGill University: 221
McGrath, Earl J.: 331
McLean, John: 41, 43
MacLean, Malcolm S.: 328, 331
MacLeish, Archibald: 318, 337

Madison, James: 86, 139
Magazines, student: 96-99
Magdalene College: 20
Mahon, Asa: 63, 69
Manhattan Project: 317-318
Mann, Horace: 57, 77-*80*, 165
Manual-labor system: 61, 62, 69, *125-127*
March, Francis A.: 140, 142
Marietta College: 126
Marks, Percy: 268, 275, 307
Marriage: 192
Mary Sharp College: 175
Mason, Stephen D.: 70
Massachusetts Institute of Technology: 152, 158
Mathematics (*see also* Curriculum): 28, 51, 54
Mather, Cotton: 19, 23, 139
Meigs, Josiah: 23, 44, 56-57, 89
Meikeljohn, Alexander: 280, *287-289*, 328
Melville, Herman: 10, 139
Mencken, H. L.: 274
Mercer University: 44, 118, 126
Methodists: 56, 74, 118
Miami University (Ohio): 40
Michigan, University of: 13, 42, *69-74*, 91, 105, 133, 134, 135, 137, 146, 194-195, 197, 250, 269, 319-320
Military training: 250-253, 319-320
Millay, Edna St. Vincent: 275, 279, 280
Milton, John: 10, 64, 91, 99
Minnesota, University of: 74, *146-151*, 252, 255-256, 261-262, 292, 328-329
Mirania (*General Idea of the College of Mirania*): 48-50
Mitchell, Maria: 182-183
Mitchell, S. Weir: 107, 162, 194, 222, 227
Modern Language Association: 167, 318-319
Monroe, James: 56, 86
Monteith, John: 61
Montross, Lynn and Lois: 268, 307
Moral philosophy: *28-32*, 51, 54, 56
Moral Reform Societies: 65, 67, 69
Morgan, Arthur E.: 291
Morgan, John: 86
Morrill, J. L.: 331
Morrill, Justin Smith (Morrill Act): 74, 142, 146, 325
Morse, Samuel F. B.: 122

Motte, Jacob Rhett: 37, 39, 41, 92, 103, 116, 118, 120, 127, 130
Mount Holyoke College: 109-110, 170, 173, *177*, 188, 197
Muir, John: 130
Mumford, Lewis: 314
Munsterberg, Hugo: 256
Music (college): 307-309
Mussey, Henry Raymond: 263

National Youth Administration: 301-302
Nearing, Scott: 265
Nebraska, University of: 242
Necking: *see* Petting
Negroes in college: 63, 134, 338
Neilson, William Allen: 200
Newman, Cardinal John H.: 29
New York University: 112, 335
Norris, Frank: 240
North Carolina, University of: 34, 57, 70, 133
Northrup, Cyrus: 151
Norton, Charles Eliot: 155-156, 222
Notre Dame, University of: 223
Nott, Eliphalet: 30, 43

Oakland College: 44
Oberlin College: 34, 35, 36, 38-39, 40, *60-70*, 78, 82, 84, 85, 91, 92, 94-95, 104, 110-111, 118, 126-128, 137, 138, 194-195
Occupations, Women's: 63, 192
Oglethorpe University: 118
Oneida Institute: 61, 65
Oppenheimer, J. R.: 318
Oxford: 19

Packer, Asa: 140, 148
Palmer, A. Mitchell: 263-264, 278, 337
Palmer, Alice Freeman: *188-189*, 197, 199, 239
Palmer, George Herbert: 155, 188, 239
Panty raids: 230
Pardee, Ario: 140, 148
Park, Edwards A.: 190
Pearson, Eliphalet: 39
Peck, Henry E.: 67
Peck, Henry Thurston: 254
Pendleton, Ellen Fitz: 188, 276
Pennsylvania, University of: 13, 21, 28, *48-55*, 68, 87, 88, 90, 95 n., 96, 107,

121, 135-136, 196, 230, 333, 335, 338
Pepper, George Wharton: 226
Perry, Bliss: 159, 235
Petting: 66, 110-111, 248, 249, 266-267, 276
Phelps, William Lyon: 234-235
Phillips-Andover Academy: 86
Pierce, George F.: 174
Pierce, John D.: 70
Pierson, George W.: 287
Pillsbury, J. S.: 147-148
Plato (see also Curriculum): 12, 50
Pope, Alexander: 91
Porter, Noah: 206, 240
Pound, Roscoe: 159, 279
Presbyterians: 54, 56-57, 118
President's Commission on Higher Education: 323-325, 329
Princeton University: 13, 23, 28, 29, 31, 41, 44, 61, 104, 127, 211, 214, 221, 235, 247, 269, 291, 298, 300, 315, 329, 338
Privies: 33
Proposals Relating to the Education of Youth in Pennsylvania: 48
Public Works Administration: 302

Queens College: see Rutgers
Quincy, Josiah: 21, 43, 165

Radcliffe College: 162, 198-199
Randolph-Macon College: 126
Religion (see also Chapel and Revivals): 40-41, 186, 189, 274-275
Reserve Officers Training Corp: see Military training
Revivals: 41, 64-65, 79, 80
Revolution, American: 88-89, 133, 136
Rittenhouse, David: 49
Robinson, James Harvey: 258-259
Rockefeller, John D.: 238-239
Rockne, Knute: 223
Rollins College: 291, 335
Roosevelt, Franklin D.: 10, 300, 301
Roosevelt, Theodore R.: 10, 227, 228, 250, 258
Ross, Edward A.: 241-242, 263
Rowing: 137
Royce, Josiah: 10, 155
Rules for students: 32, 41-44; at Vassar and Wellesley, 184-186
Rush, Benjamin: 49
Rutgers University: 13, 27, 88, 133, 221

Sacco-Vanzetti Case: 278-282
Sagendorph, Kent: 146
Salaries, faculty: 76, 155, 239, 277, 296-297, 336
Sanders, Daniel C.: 27
Santayana, George: 155, 206
Sarah Lawrence College: 290, 291, 328-329
Schafer, William: 255-256
Schmidt, George P.: 28, 31, 41, 89
Science (see also Curriculum): 51, 54, 78, 138-141
Scudder, Vida: 200, 203, 263
Seelye, L. Clark: 194
Sex code, student: 106-108, 110-111, 248, 266-269, 304-306
Shakespeare, William: 21, 91
Sherman, Stuart: 315
Shipherd, John Jay: 61-62
Silliman, Benjamin: 31, 46, 123, 171
Sinclair, Upton: 262, 265, 279
Smith College: 189-192, 291
Smith, Delazon: 69
Smith, Samuel Stanhope: 29, 31, 45
Smith, Sophia: 190
Smith, William: 48-55, 88, 90
Smyth, H. D.: 318
Social science (see also Curriculum and Moral philosophy): 316, 331
Sophie Newcomb College: 199
Sophocles, Evangelinus A.: 156
South Carolina, University of: 57, 89
Spencer, Herbert: 165, 166
Spenser, Edmund: 21
Spiller, Robert E.: 315
Spingarn, Joel E.: 254
Stagg, Amos Alonzo: 223
Stanford, Leland: 237
Stanford, Mrs. Leland: 237, 241
Stanford University: 214, 241
Stealing: 120-121
Steffens, Lincoln: 265
Stephens College: 330
Stiles, Ezra: 22, 89, 107, 108
Storey, W. F.: 74
Stover at Yale: 205, 208-211, 236
Stowe, Harriet Beecher: 77, 95
Student Army Training Corps: see Military training
Student conduct: see Cheating, Disorder, Dating, Drinking, Petting, Rules, Sex code
Student costume: 46, 231, 303

Student government: 59
Student reading: *92-95,* 99, 264, 298-299, 306-307
Student writing (*see also* College humor): 91, *95-100,* 273
Sullivan, Mark: 246
Swarthmore College: 232, 291, 339

Tappan, Lewis: 126
Tappan, Philip: 57, *71-74,* 91, 119, 134
Taylor, Horace: 69
Taylor, John: 88
Teachers, training of: 63, 74-75, 163, 194, 285-286, 326-327, 333
Temple University: 5, 90
Terman, Lewis M.: 282
Thomas, M. Carey: 194, *200*
Thompson, Charles: 88
Thoreau, Henry: 122-123, 128, 139, 291-292
Thorndike, Edward L.: 293
Thwing, Charles F.: 20, 21, 88, 240, 310
Time magazine: 334, 337
Transylvania University: *55-57*
Trowbridge, John: 155
Truman, Harry S.: 324
Trumbull, John: 90
Tufts College: 199
Tulane University: 199
Turner, Louis A.: 317
Twain, Mark: 139, 142, 202
Tyler, Moses Coit: 72, 133-134
Tyler, W. S.: 190
Tyndall, John: 166

Underground Railway: 66
Union College: 30, 42
Urey, Harold C.: 318

Van Doren, Carl: 315
Van Hise, Charles R.: 253
Vanzetti, Bartolomeo: *see* Sacco-Vanzetti Case
Vassar, Matthew: 148, 176, *179-183*
Vassar College: *179-183,* 191, 192, 260, 265
Veblen, Thorstein: 205, 242, 298, 337
Velde, Harold H.: 337
Vergil: *see* Classics and Curriculum
Vermont, University of: 27, 57
Veterans in college: *135-137, 320-324.*

Veterans of Future Wars: 299-300
Villard, Oswald Garrison: 280
Virginia, University of: 13, 44; curriculum, 53-54; library, 56-57; 69, 80, 83, 84-85, 92, 92n., 102, 107, 113, 115, 120, 127-128, 133, 134, 135
Vrooman, Carl: 253

Waddel, Moses: 92
Wagner, Charles A.: 100
Warner, Aaron: 115
Warner, Glen: 225
Washington, George: 10, 325
Washington College (Md.): 54
Wayland, Francis: 25, 31, *75-77,* 139, 161
Webster, Daniel: 9, 84
Webster, Delia: 66
Webster, John White: 81, 123
Welch, William H.: 168
Weld, Theodore: 85, 126
Weller, George Anthony: 305
Wellesley College: 178, *183-189,* 192, 202-203, 249, 260, 275
Wendell, Barrett: 155-156
West, Andrew: 28, 246
Westerman, W. L.: 257
Western Reserve University: 65, 86
Whipple, George: 38
White, Andrew: 23, 25, 45, 72, 73, 104-105, 114, 119, *143-146,* 148, 165, 194-195, 201
White, J. William: 226-227
White, William Allen: 257
Whitefield, George: 13
Whitman, Walt: 10, 139, 142
Whittier, John Greenleaf: 123-124, 189
Wigglesworth, Edward: 22
Willard, Emma: 172, 177
William and Mary College: 9, 10, 21, 28, 53-54, 55, 57, 130-131, 335
Williams College: 46, 65, 235
Williamson, Edmund G.: 292-293
Wilson, Woodrow: 220, 236, 245-247, 250, 257
Winthrop, John: 20
Wisconsin, University of: 74, 105, 107, 146, 230, 242, 252-253, 256, 263, 265, 273-274, 328-329
Wister, Owen: 215, 258
Witch hunts: 259-264, 311-313, 336-338
Witherspoon, John: 31, 88

Woman's Educational Association: 176,
　198
Wood, Frances A.: 183
Woodbury, George Edward: 254
Woody, Thomas: 171
World War I: 250-258
World War II: 317-323

Yale Band: 60
Yale Faculty Report of 1827-28: 24,
　50, 51, 75

Yale Literary Magazine: 96-99, 102,
　104, 111, 128-129
Yale University (see also subjects, e.g.
　Football): 10, 13, 22, 23, 24, 25, 27,
　28, 33, 34, 35, 36, 37, 38, 41, 42-43,
　44, 55, 57, 59, 61, 64, 68, 72, 90-91,
　104, 111, 127, 131, 133, 134, 139,
　205-213, 219-220, 230, 233, 236, 237,
　243-244, 286-287, 299, 315, 329, 338
Yost, Fielding H.: 224